S0-ATQ-761

Thank you for
works with me.

Nancy Andrea
2000

OUR FASCINATING PAST
Charlotte Harbor: The Later Years

Lindsey Williams and U. S. Cleveland

Dedicated To Those Special Sources
Who Shared Their Recollections Of Many Topics:

Lorin A. Ainger, Fred C. Babcock, Henrietta Bartley,
Rudyard Kipling Bell, John Cerny, Beatrice Cotton,
Henry Farrington, Elmer O. Friday, Harry R. Goulding,
Claude Jones, Dr. Joe Knetsch, Esther Jordan McCullough,
Robert N. McQueen, Ron Metz, Byron Rhode,
Bernice Russell, Frank Wotitzky and Leo Wotitzky.

Charlotte Harbor Area Historical Society
Punta Gorda, Florida

Published By
Charlotte Harbor Area Historical Society

© 1996   Lindsey Williams and U. S. Cleveland
Punta Gorda, Florida

Library of Congress Catalog Card Number 96-086431

International Standard Book Number 0-9653489-1-1

ILLUSTRATIONS CREDITS
With Many Thanks

Archivo di Stato, Spain — 19
Florida State Archives — 61
Louise K. Frisbie — 147
Florida Times Union — 152
Newport News Shipbuilding Co. — 174
Yesterday's St. Petersburg — 215
Patti Middleton — 219
Frederic Remington — 229
National Museum Modern Art — 257, 261
Lemon Bay Woman's Club — 301
U.S. Army — 314, 318
American Eagle — 350, 358
Vernon Peeples — 356
Sallie Jones Elementary School — 394
Charlotte County Airport Authority — 404, 406, 409, 411, 412
Mark Renz — 421
Miami Herald — 439, 441, 444, 446
Visual Arts Center of Charlotte County — 455

COVER PHOTO

Youngsters in 1914 wait at the Punta Gorda Fish Dock on a Saturday
morning for their fisherman fathers or other kin to return from a week's
work "down the bay." They are, from left:
Verrie Coston, Joe Addison, Willie Salter and Walter Whiteaker.

WELCOME BY THE AUTHORS

Here are 105 more articles about the fascinating past of the Charlotte Harbor area — as we promised if our first book published three years ago sold out. It did, so we do. Your kind words and patronage encouraged us to expand this new book with 32 additional pages of information and illustrations. Herein we emphasize events generally later in time than our frontier days. Nonetheless, we include interesting Native-American and early-settlement history discovered since volume one.

The various chapters were written originally as a weekly series by Lin for the *Charlotte Sun-Herald* — hence the journalistic style resulting from his anecdotal approach and insistence on documentation. U.S. provided old photographs from his invaluable collection, endless facts from his library of references, personal recollections and contacts with old families.

As explained previously, we have endeavored to be both accurate and entertaining — an approach known as "public-oriented history." Our experience is that the truths of history, though difficult to dig out, are fascinating and need no embellishment.

We have credited enough of our sources as part of the running text to reassure scholars without distracting casual readers by footnotes and endnotes. Long passages of memoirs written by others are carried in italic to preserve their individual expression.

Again, we solicit comments, suggestions and corrections looking forward to reprinting.

TABLE OF CONTENTS

4

ACKNOWLEDGEMENTS

In addition to those otherwise mentioned herein, we acknowledge substantial contributions from the following:

Marian Addison
John Allen
Cindy Anderson
Frances Anderson
Faye Austin
Gus Barton
Barbara Bass
Robert Betjemann
Pete Bontsema
Bessie Bryant
Jane Cerny
Charlotte County Clerk of Court
Charlotte County Development Authority
Charlotte County Retired Teachers Assn.
Charlotte County School Board
Al Cheatham
Jim Christman
Maggie Clampitt
Dr. C. Wilburn Cockrell
Bud Cole
Betty Daniels
Bill Davis, Jr.
DeSoto County Clerk of Court
Dane Dickel
Frances Dodds
Rebecca Durig
Mike Emery
Dr. & Mrs. Charles Fambrough
Martha Ellen Fish
William Fox
Rev. Nathaniel Fredrick
Wayne Goff
Marion Gould
Rev. J. P. Graham
William Hancock
Col. Read Harding
Diana Harris
Teasie Harris
Brig. Gen. Glenn Herd
Margaret Hill
Jimmy Hoar
Joe Huckeby
Marie Hudson
Al Johns
Mabel Keys
Lois Kelly
Dr. Joe Knetsch

Maggie Krazit
Victor Larrison
Janet Leiser
Carolyn Lekon
Cathy Livimpt
Dr. George Luer
Cathy Lyden
Manatee County Historic Study Center
Dr. William H. Marquardt
Bob Matson
Margaret McQueen
Rev. Howard Melton
Walter Homer Monson
Monticello Drug Co., Jacksonville
Mike Muehling
National Museum of American History
Aubrey Nelson
Newport News Shipbuilding Co.
Pharah Pankratz
Dell Passaretti
Rob Patton
Lonnie Friday Persons
Don Platt
Punta Gorda Public Library
Randy Randall
Lew and Norma Reder
Frank and Maxine Rhode
Sylvia Willis Rivers
Charlotte Roberts
Marlon and Terry Runkle
Scale Rails of Southwest Florida
Rev. Vincent F. Scotto
Elmer Silcox
D. Frank Smoak, Jr.
Wilma Wade Spriggs
Paul Sullivan
Tampa Tribune
Gladwin Unrau
U. S. National Archives
James Van Dooren
Fred Watts
M. L. Westfall
Ann Wilson
Luke Wilson
Gladys Wilt
Carol Yoder

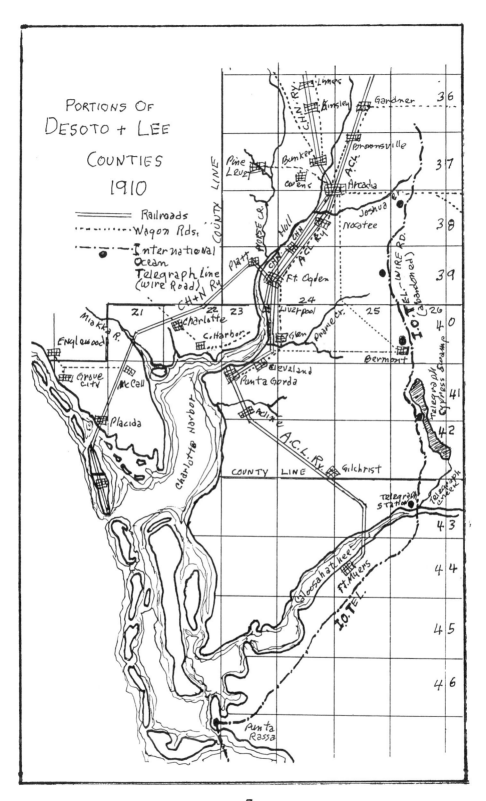

PORTIONS OF
DESOTO + LEE
COUNTIES
1910

Railroads
Wagon Rds.
International
Ocean
Telegraph Line
(wire Road)

COUNTY LINE

C.H.+N. RY.

Limes
Kinsley
Gardner
36

Pine
Level
Bunker
Broonsville
37
A.C.L.
Owens
Arcadia

MORSE CR.
Hull
Joshua
Nocatee
38
C.H.+N.
A.C.L. RY.
Platt
I.O.TEL.-WIRE RD. (abandoned)
39
Ft. Ogden

CH+N RY
24
Liverpool
25
26
40
21
22
23
Glen
Prairie cr.
Charlotte
Bermont
Miakka R.
C. Harbor
Telegraph
Cypress Swamp
Englewood
Cleveland
41
Grove
City
McCall
Punta Gorda
A.C.L.
42
Placida
Charlotte Harbor
A.C.L. RY.
COUNTY LINE
Gilchrist
Telegraph
Station
Telegraph creek
43
Caloosahatchee
Ft.Myers
44
I.O.TEL.
45
46
Punta
Rassa

7

Archaeologists (from left) Agazi Negash, Bob Coughter and Rob Patton excavate Indian mound at Charlotte Harbor Environmental Center.

Chapter 1

TEAM UNCOVERS MOUND SECRETS

New evidence indicates that a large settlement of prehistoric people lived along the shores of Alligator Creek — heretofore thought to be a no-man's land between Calusa and Timucua Indians.

A team of archaeologists from the University of Florida is mapping a two-acre site here that includes a large "platform" mound approached by a "processional way." Such construction is the mark of an important political leader. The mound is on property of the Charlotte Harbor Environmental Center off Burnt Store Road south of Punta Gorda.

A second, smaller mound along Whidden Creek also is being explored. Both mounds were noted years ago on the Florida master site file of archaeological sites. However, they had not been scientifically tested until now. The present survey has located possibly 10 other "daughter" mounds according to Rob Patton, a doctoral candidate and on-site archaeologist.

In addition to excavating test pits at the Alligator and Whidden creeks sites, Patton instructs seven university interns and an equal number of sorters recruited from throughout Charlotte County.

Digging is limited to discovering the best sites for future exploration. Nevertheless, enough man-made artifacts have been found to establish a long period of habitation.

8

The project is supervised by George Luer of Sarasota. His years of exploration in the wilds of southwest Florida have made him a leading contributor of finds to the master site file. Principal project investigator is Michael Mosley.

The Environmental Center mounds were drawn to the attention of authorities by the Calusa Heartland Steering Committee chaired by Robert "Bucky" McQueen, of Punta Gorda.

Work at the sites has been made possible by an archaeological survey grant provided by the National Park Service and administered through the Florida Bureau of Historic Preservation. It is hoped that a larger grant will be available in the future to conduct extensive excavations and learn how early people in the area organized their societies.

Both mounds are so encumbered with jungle growth, in isolated sections of the Environmental Center, they will not be available to the public until funds can be obtained for walkways through wetlands.

Why This Area Significant

Strangely, the Charlotte Harbor area has not been archaeologicly investigated. North American history began here with explorations by Ponce De Leon in 1513 and 1521, Hernando DeSoto in 1539, and Menendez D'Aviles in 1566.

The first Spaniards found the Florida peninsula inhabited by two principal cultural groups. That of the north were allied broadly as the Timucua. Tribes of south Florida were dominated by the Calusa. Timucua territory on the east coast extended from Jacksonville south to Cape Canaveral — and on the west coast from the Aucilla River south to Charlotte Harbor. Calusa hegemony included all of south Florida. Within these areas, "caciques" (big chiefs) exacted tribute from lesser chiefs.

The Calusa cacique who repulsed Ponce was variously called Stababa, Stapana, Sacaspada and Escampa by Spaniards. Rough sailors with scant education spelled the unfamiliar name phonetically as they understood it.

Timucua caciques who harassed Soto were recorded as Tocobaga (Tampa Bay), Urripacoxi (Lake Apopka) and Utina (St. Johns River).

The boundary between the Calusa and Timucua cultural groups is not precisely known. Warfare between the two undoubtedly altered their "interface" as the tides of conflict ebbed and flowed.

The late Dr. Ripley P. Bullen, noted archaeologist at the University of Florida, supervised excavation of a burial mound in 1960-62 along the north branch of Alligator Creek by Mr. and Mrs. Robert Max Jones of Punta Gorda. Their collection of several hundred pieces of pottery and shell tools is now on display at the Environmental Center.

The artifacts were largely of Safety Harbor (Tampa) origin — indicating a strong Timucua influence. A liberal scattering of Calusa pottery suggested some contact with the Calusa.

Bone fragments disclosed that the mound was used for burials at about 900 A.D. One can speculate that the north branch mound of Alligator Creek was contemporaneous with the south branch mound.

Bullen also walked several Charlotte Harbor and Pine Island sites and gathered surface material. On the basis of these inspections, Bullen concluded that the boundary between the Calusa and the Timucua tribes probably passed through the middle of Charlotte Harbor — from Boca Grande Pass eastward.

In an article for the Florida Historical Quarterly, Bullen stated: "It seems evident that the division between Timucua and Calusa territories occurred along the middle of Charlotte Harbor.

"The north shore of this body of water is very low and marshy. Probably the Calusa paid little or no attention to it. Their 'center of gravity,' if contemporary historical data are accurate, was in Estero Bay some 35 miles farther south.

"The southern limit of Timucua territory is of interest to historians since it is one of the points bearing on Hernando DeSoto's landing place.

"Reports of that expedition seem to indicate that the landing occurred in Timucua territory, and that the Indians of Ocita and of the villages of Hirrihigua and Mocozo were not very different from those encountered as the expedition moved northward."

Impossible Name

It should not surprise us that an expanse of open water would be a mutually respected dividing line between competing tribes. Another, more famous, example is that lake in Massachusetts with the impossibly long Nipmuc Indian name of "Chargoggagoggmanchauggoggchaubunagun-gamaugg" — meaning, "You fish on your side, I fish on my side, and nobody fish in the middle."

Menendez came into the San Carlos Bay-Charlotte Harbor area in 1566 and built a mission-fort which he named San Antonio. The location of that Spanish enclave has not been confirmed archaeologicaly. One of Menendez' first acts was a canoe journey with Cacique Calos to Cacique Tocobaga's town in an attempt to arrange peace between the two. Calos turned hostile when Menendez refused to use the peace talks as a ruse to kill the Timucuans.

It is known that the first 500 years of the Christian Era in southwest Florida was one of heavy, native population and intense exploitation of natural resources. A great deal of additional investigation is necessary to accurately determine the age of mounds now being surveyed here and the cultural group to which associated. There are approximately 70 significant Indian sites in Charlotte County meriting scientific excavation.

Deathbed portrait of Osceola painted by George Catlin.

Chapter 2

WHAT HAPPENED TO OSCEOLA'S SKULL

A two-line "Local Laconic" in the Dec. 1902 issue of the *Punta Gorda Herald* piqued the interest of a folks with announcement that the "skull of Osceola is in the possession of a well known gentleman of this city."

Osceola was the famous war chief of the Seminoles during the second campaign of 1837 whose head mysteriously disappeared after his death in U.S. Army custody. The well known gentleman of Punta Gorda probably was Albert W. Gilchrist, a state representative (later governor) who maintained a museum of curiosities in his local office.

The name "Seminole" has been romantically interpreted as "those of distant camp fires," "wanderers," "emigrants," or "runaways." They were latecomers to Florida, not native here when European settlers arrived.

A more accurate translation was furnished by Col. Benjamin Hawkins, an Indian commissioner appointed in 1785 to negotiate with the Creek Confederacy. He lived for many years among the Indians of southern Georgia and Alabama from which the Seminoles evolved. These Indians called themselves Mus-co-gul-gee (Muskogee). The English called them Creeks for the streams along which they lived.

After the last slave raid by British Georgians in 1702, Southern Florida was largely depopulated. Tribal wars and disease had decimated the Calusa and Timucua Indians. Into this void moved young members of the crowded Muskogee nation. According to Hawkins, their new neighbors called them Isti-se-mo-le, or "wild men," hence today's familiar name.

The newcomers were kindly received by the remaining, indigenous tribes. However, as the Seminoles increased in number, friction developed between them and other tribes. Tribal wars during the British rule of Florida 1763-1783 resulted in Seminole dominance.

Hawkins wrote that the Seminoles had several towns — some of which we can identify today with Anglicized pronunciations: Sim-e-mo-le-tal-lau-haf-see (Tallahassee). Mic-co-soo-ee (Miccosukee). Au-lot-che-wau (Alachua). Oc-le-wau-hau-thlu (Ocala). Tal-lau-gue-chahco-pop-cau (Charley Apopka). Cull-oo-saju-hatche (Caloosahatchee).

Charles H. Coe, in a 1898 book titled Red Patriot, states the Seminoles were recognized as part of the Creek Confederacy as late as 1790. In that year, the Seminole were included in a treaty between the Creeks and the new United States.

The Seminoles and other Creeks split about 1811 over allegiance to the Spanish or Americans. The disagreement degenerated to armed civil war. Pro-Spanish Seminoles harbored runaway slaves from southern U.S. plantations. The Indians kept some of the slaves by mutual consent. The rest were allowed to establish their own villages allied with the Seminoles.

First Seminole War

The first Seminole War erupted in 1818 when General Andrew Jackson invaded Florida on behalf of the U.S. to close the refuge for slaves. He advanced against a fort manned by more than 300 escaped slaves on the Apalachicola River.

The fort was destroyed when a red-hot cannon ball make a lucky hit on the powder magazine. The resulting explosion killed or wounded every black. Seminoles, under Chief Neamathla, retaliated with hit- and-run raids against Americans on the Georgia border.

Two years later, Spain ceded Florida to the United States; and Seminole attacks were directed against settlers moving in. A peace treaty was signed in 1823 at Moultrie Creek. Nevertheless, intermittent atrocities by both Seminoles and settlers continued.

A forced treaty at Payne's Landing in 1832 set aside lands in Arkansas for Seminoles and other Indians. However, the Seminoles refused to leave.

Second Seminole War

The second Seminole War began in Dec. 1835 when a party of warriors under the leadership of Osceola ambushed a detachment of 110 U.S. soldiers led by Maj. Francis Dade. Only three soldiers, badly wounded, survived. Americans retaliated in force under direction of Gen. Thomas Jesup, commander of Fort Brooke (Tampa). He pursued the Seminoles for the next two years, deporting all he could capture.

Finally, in 1837, the Seminoles had enough. They asked for a parley; and Jesup sent them a large supply of white cloth from which truce flags could be made. A place south of Fort Payton was agreed upon by both sides for the talks. On the appointed day, Oct. 27, Gen. Jesup sent Gen. Joseph Hernandez with 250 troops to surround the council. Surgeon Nathan Jarvis, a member of Hernandez' party, described the meeting:

"On our arrival at their camp, we discovered the Indians flying a white flag. They immediately gathered around us — shaking hands with all the officers. My attention was first directed to discover On-cin-ye-hola (Osceola). He was pointed out to me, but I could have designated him by his looks as the principal man among them. A continued smile played over his face, particularly when shaking hands with the officers.

"After some talk, Gen. Hernandez asked, 'Have you come to give up to me as your friend?' Cos-had-jo, a principal warrior, replied: 'No, we did not understand so. Word went from here, and we have come. We have done nothing all summer (against whites). We want to make peace.'"

With this, Hernandez signaled his troops. They moved in to take Osceola, Cos-had-jo and 12 other chiefs prisoner. From the nearby Seminole camp, Hernandez gathered in 71 warriors, six women and four Indian Negroes. Osceola and the senior chiefs were provided horses, and the whole band of captured Seminoles were marched to St. Augustine's Fort Marion. Jarvis rode the whole distance with Osceola and reported him "unwell." When the rest of the country heard about the capture of Osceola under a flag of truce, sentiment turned in favor of the famous war chief. It was unthinkable that the United States would stoop to treachery to capture him.

Seminoles Moved to Charleston

Fearing the Seminoles still at large might attack St. Augustine, the War Department in early Jan. 1838 ordered the prisoners shipped to Fort Moultrie at Charleston, S.C. Upon arrival, Osceola and several chiefs were taken to the theater to see a performance of "Honey Moon."

At Charleston, the Seminoles were treated like celebrities, and allowed visitors. Many citizens came to greet the prisoners cordially.

Osceola was joined by his two wives, two of his children, a sister, three warriors and 40 Negro retainers. Dr. Blair Weedon, the post surgeon was assigned to treat Osceola's severe throat infection, but Osceola insisted on the services of his own medicine man.

It was obvious that Osceola was nearing death. George Catlin, noted for his portraits of Indians, committed Osceola's likeness to canvas. The death of Osceola on Jan. 30, was recorded by Dr. Weedon in a letter to Catlin, as requested by Osceola.

"Although Osceola could not speak," wrote Weedon, "he signified by signs that he wished me to send for the chiefs and for the officers of the post, who I called in. He made signs to his wives to bring his full dress that he wore in time of war. Being prepared in full dress, he lay down a

13

few moments to recover strength. Then he rose up as before, and with most benign smiles, extended his hand to me and to all the officers and chiefs that were around him. He shook hands with us all in dead silence, and with his wives and little children.

"He made a signal to lower him down upon his bed, which was done. He firmly grasped his scalping knife in his right hand, laying it across the other on his breast. In a moment he smiled away his last breath."

Coe wrote that "the funeral of the Seminole Chieftain was conducted with the honors and respect due to so distinguished a foeman. A detachment of U.S. troops, followed by the medical men and many private citizens, together with all the chiefs and warriors, women and children, escorted the remains to the grave near the entrance of the fort. The coffin, with all the weapons and personal belongings of the deceased, was lowered and a military salute fired. The Indians seemed to derive a melancholy satisfaction from the honors paid to their former leader. One of the soldiers enclosed the grave with a neat paling. A Mr. Patton, a generous and sympathizing resident of Charleston, erected a marble slab at the head, on which was cut this simple but expressive inscription: OSCEOLA. PATRIOT AND WARRIOR."

Coe says that a few days after the burial, unknown persons opened the grave and decapitated the corpse, carrying off the head. Some time afterward, according to the *New York Star* of that period, the head was on exhibition at Stuyvesant Institute of New York City.

The True Story

Osceola's head was separated from his body; but in a different manner and outcome. Dr. Weedon was directed to make a plaster death mask of Osceola. Upon finishing the mask, Weedon severed the head but left it in place in the coffin — concealing the surgery with Osceola's scarf.

After the body had been viewed by several hundred people, Dr. Weedon was left alone to close the coffin. At this time, he removed Osceola's head and concealed it in his medicine satchel.

Dr. Weedon's motive was not scientific. His wife was the sister of Indian Agent Wiley Thompson who was murdered by Osceola. Dr. Weedon's great-grand-daughter is reported to have said he hung the skull of Osceola on his little sons' bedpost when they misbehaved.

Historian George Walton gives further account of Osceola's skull. Weedon's daughter married a physician, Daniel Whitehurst of New York City, and Weedon gave the skull to his new son-in-law. Whitehurst gave the skull to Dr. Valentine Mott at the New York University's college of medicine. Mott placed the skull in his Surgical Museum which caught fire. Osceola's skull was destroyed. Thus, the skull in Albert Gilchrist's little museum certainly was a local relic. Such grisly trophies looted from Indian mounds, were touted for many years as that of Osceola.

14

Portrait of Billy Bowlegs shortly
after he surrendered in 1858.

Chapter 3

BOWLEGS FOUGHT ARMY, THEN JOINED IT

Billy Bowlegs is famous as the Florida Indian Chief who fought against the U.S. Army in the Second and Third Seminole Wars to defend his homeland — and in defeat was deported to a western reservation. Not so well known is how he spent the rest of his life fighting with the U.S. Army against Confederates in the Civil War. There has been much confusion about the life and times of Billy Bowlegs because there were two chiefs by that name. Neither had deformed legs. The name is a corruption of Bolek who was war chief in the First Seminole War of 1818-23.

Armed conflict between the U.S. Army and Seminoles began when Andrew Jackson marched into Spanish Florida and destroyed an "Indian Negro" fort on the Apalachicola River. Bolek launched guerilla attacks on white settlements in Georgia and Alabama. Alexander Arbuthot, a British trader furnishing guns to the Seminoles, reported the troop strength of his customers: "Bolek 1,500; King Hatchy 1,000; Oso Hatjo 500; Himashy Miso 500 —1,000 under arms at present."

The first Seminole War ended when "King Bowlegs" (Bolek) and others signed a treaty at Moultrie Creek guaranteeing them "hunting and crop grounds south of Charlotte's River" — that is, below the confluence of Charlotte Harbor and Peas Creek (Peace River). When the land proved poor for crops, Commissioners for Indian Affairs allowed the Seminoles to move north around present Fort Meade, Bowling Green and Wauchula. Among them was Billy Bowlegs, young nephew of King Bowlegs.

Historians unfamiliar with Seminole culture, assumed that authority and chiefdom descended through the fathers, as is customary among whites. This accounts for a belief that the Bowlegs of the various Seminole wars were father and son — if not the same person with a long life span.

Kenneth W. Porter, one of the most reliable authorities on the Seminoles, points out in a Florida Historical Quarterly of 1967 that Seminole society then was matrilineal. Inheritance was by the son of a maternal sister — or a brother of the same mother — rather than by a son. Contemporary estimates of Billy Bowlegs' age, and his recorded statements, clearly establish separate identities. Thus, Billy Bowlegs was born into the "royal" Seminole family and was a chief by birthright. He and Osceola — the great war chief of the Second Seminole War — were of the same generation.

Billy Bowlegs was a young warrior overshadowed during the early years of the second war by the aggressive Osceola. The latter remained close to white settlements in order to harass them. Arpeika (Sam Jones) and Otulke-Thlocko (the Prophet) — old but influential head chiefs — counseled retreat to the farthest reaches of the reservation set aside by the Moultrie Creek treaty. Bowlegs, and other sub-chiefs, followed Arpeika south to Big Cypress Swamp. Maj. Gen. Alexander Macomb sought accommodation with the Seminoles whose numbers had decreased greatly by 1839. He authorized a trading post 15 miles up the Caloosahatchee River to provide necessities for the Big Cypress Indians.

Post Attacked

While the post was under construction, Bowlegs and two other chiefs led their bands totaling 160 warriors in a surprise attack on the soldiers. The young chiefs feared intrusion of the Army into their last refuge would bring impress gangs for removal. Eleven of the 27 Army men were killed outright. Two were burned at the stake — a rare instance of Seminole torture. A Negro interpreter named Sampson was saved from death by Bowlegs' intervention with the other chiefs.

The Army spent the next three years breaking up Indian villages in an effort to subdue the Seminoles. Finally, in 1842, the young chiefs "broke the spell of the Prophet and renounced Sam Jones" as a coward who failed to prevent destruction of the Big Cypress villages. Bowlegs was chosen head chief and given the title Holata Micco, or Chief Governor.

Shortly thereafter, Col. W.J. Worth succeeded Macomb as Army commander for Florida. He concluded it would be virtually impossible to round up the remaining 300 Seminoles. He proposed to end the Second Seminole War by leaving alone the Indians south of Peas Creek.

This was what Bowlegs wanted. He arrived at Fort Brooke (Tampa) in Aug. 1842 and signed a peace agreement to end the Second Seminole war. Bowlegs declared, "Me tired of wet feet, moving back to the hills."

Nevertheless, the government stepped up efforts to remove the Indians. Unhappily, the Third Seminole war broke out in 1849 when five renegade Indians killed a homesteader near Fort Pierce on the east coast and burned his cabin. Then the perpetrators walked across the peninsula to get whiskey at the Kennedy-Darling trading post on the Peace River. When denied, the Indians killed two of the traders and burned the store.

Bowlegs knew this would rekindle the "Winchester removal." He tried to head off another war by tracking down the renegades, killing one and delivering three to Indian Agent Capt. John Casey for "white man's justice." In turning over the guilty Indians to Casey and General David Twiggs at Fort Brooke, Bowlegs made a moving promise:

Bowlegs' Pledge

"I have brought here many young men and boys to see the terrible consequences of breaking our peace laws. I brought them here that they might see their comrades delivered up to be killed. I now pledge you my word that if you will cease this talk of leaving the country no other outrage shall ever be committed by my people; or, if ever hereafter the worst among my people shall cross the boundary and do any mischief to your people, you need not look for runners or appoint councils to talk. I will make up my pack and shoulder it. My people will do the same. We will all walk down to the seashore, and we will ask but one question — Where is the boat to carry us to Arkansas?"

To encourage Bowlegs to relocate, he and seven sub-chiefs in the summer of 1851 were taken to Washington, D.C. There they met with President Millard Fillmore and received medals. Bowlegs signed a letter saying he would emigrate, but after returning home he led his tribe back into the Everglades.

Bowlegs and Casey developed a trusting relationship enabling them to avoid open conflict. However, hostile incidents by both sides continued for another seven years. Climax of the third and last war began in December 1855 when an Army survey team destroyed Bowlegs' prize banana plants. The outraged chief went to the Army camp demanding restitution but was rudely treated. The next morning, Bowlegs and his 30 warriors attacked the surveyors. Four were killed, and four wounded.

Other Seminoles rose up also. A dozen or so on June 14, 1856, attacked the Willoughby Tillis homestead near Fort Meade. The family held out until a posse arrived. Two bloody battles in as many days resulted in five settlers and 20 Indians killed. Among the latter were the Seminole's two principal war chiefs. Casey died of tuberculosis on Christmas Day and was buried with full honors at Fort Brooke.

The Army sent search parties to capture Bowlegs, but they gave up after floundering for weeks in sawgrass and muck. Contact was finally made in early 1858 through Bowleg's niece, Polly. A delegation of 40

Seminoles and four Creeks, headed by Chief John Jumper, were brought from Arkansas to assure Bowlegs that things were not so bad out west.

Indian Commissioners sweetened the pot with a "bonus" of $6,500 for Bowlegs, $1,000 to each of four sub-chiefs, $500 to each warrior, and $100 for each woman and child who would emigrate. At last, Bowlegs agreed to go. He led his band of 125 Seminoles to Fort Myers in May 1858 to board the steamer *Grey Cloud*. The ship stopped at Tampa to pick up passengers for New Orleans. Strangely, Casey's remains were disinterred and put aboard. No documentation has been discovered for this unprecedented action, or where is his final resting place. Perhaps the gossip was true that Casey and Bowlegs' sister had been lovers.

Bowlegs in December accepted $200 to return to Florida and persuade another 75 Seminoles to join him in Indian Territory. The Army estimated there were only 60 "perfectly quiet" Seminoles left in the Everglades and so discontinued its Indian removal program.

False Report of Bowlegs' Death

Bowlegs and several warriors in 1859 went to Kansas to select a permanent home for the Seminoles. Army records compiled by Porter reveal that Bowlegs was chief of one of the Five Civilized Tribes that supported the Union in the Civil War. Creeks and Cherokees allied themselves with the Confederates. Shortly after the Civil War began, the Indian Territory tribes — which had never forgotten their own Creek Confederation civil war — split along old tribal lines in loyalty to warring American forces. Agents supplied their Indian allies with weapons.

Three pitched battles between the Indians in late 1861 resulted in heavy casualties on both sides. The Confederate tribes prevailed, but Federal forces under the command of Billy Bowlegs, recently appointed a U.S. Army Captain, arrived to challenge the southern Indians in 30 actions during the next four years.

After a skirmish at Illinois Creek, Arkansas, in December 1862, Col. Stephen Wattles of the First Indian Regiment reported that Capt. Billy Bowlegs was "deserving of highest praise." Before the war was over, it was estimated that two-thirds of the Seminoles and all their Negroes were within the Union lines. A smallpox and cholera epidemic broke out in the First Indian regiment in September 1863. Chief Bowlegs succumbed to the disease in early March 1864. Bowlegs' principal chiefs, Pascova and Long John, each wrote President Lincoln to inform him of Billy Bowlegs death.

Said Pascova: "Billy Bowlegs went into the Army to help his white Brothers and the government. He died in the service of his country. He left me here with our Agent to take care of the Women and Children." Capt. Bowlegs is buried in the National Cemetery near Fort Gibson, Oklahoma.

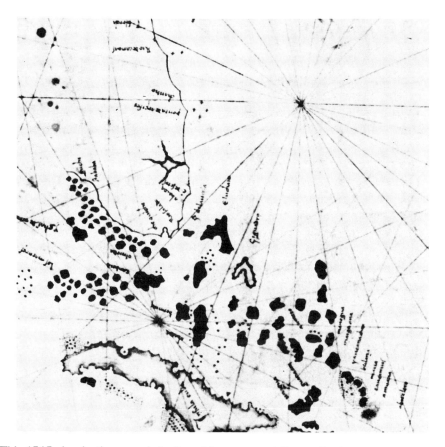

This 1515 clandestine map is believed to represent Ponce De Leon's first voyage of 1513 and is the first to use the name Florida .

Chapter 4

WHERE AMERICAN HISTORY BEGAN

The following was written by Lindsey for a study by the Charlotte Harbor Town Community Redevelopment Advisory Committee.

The history of Charlotte Harbor Town goes back at least 3,000 years when mound building by native Americans there was in full swing. Whether the builders were Calusa or Timucua aborigines is not yet known. There has been no scientific excavation of archaeological sites on the north shore of Charlotte Harbor. Efforts to fund archaeological investigation are being pursued by the Charlotte County Historic Preservation Board and the volunteer Calusa Heartland Committee.

Two important archaeological sites, determined by surface survey, are recorded in the Florida Historic Master Site File at the Secretary of State's office at Tallahassee. They are: Hickory Bluff mound with Safety Harbor

19

components (CH5), and a shipwreck tentatively identified with 16th century artifacts (CH350). A large mound at the corner of Melbourne Avenue and Northshore Drive was leveled in 1926 for a housing development. Stone and shell artifacts at the site are still being discovered by owners. Residents report that lodge pilings were discovered near Sibley-Bay Street when U.S. 41 was re-located after World War II.

Another village site occupied from 500 BC to 1500 AD at Solana on the south shore was discovered by local archaeologist B. Calvin Jones in 1976. It was excavated by the Florida Division of History and Records preparatory to construction of Interstate Route 75.

There is strong evidence from contemporary chronicles that Hernando DeSoto landed at Live Oak Point and made his base camp there — now the northern approach to the Collier-Gilchrist bridges. (See book *Boldly Onward* by Lindsey Williams, 1986.) A DeSoto Trail Committee was appointed by then Gov. Bob Graham to determine the explorer's landing site. The committee in May 1988 authorized placement of a marker at Live Oak Point stating: "Some Scholars Believe Hernando DeSoto Landed Near Here In 1539."

The Charlotte County Soil and Water Conservation Committee has obtained permission from the Florida Department of Transportation to build a passive park on unused Live Oak Point right-of-way. Leadership Charlotte has adopted the site for a public park. The DeSoto marker will have a prominent place in the little park.

Search for Canal

It is highly likely that Pedro Menendez D'Aviles thoroughly explored Charlotte Harbor in 1566-67 when he established a mission-fort named San Antonio somewhere in the harbor complex. One of Menendez's objectives was to find a reported Indian canal which enabled vessels to transverse the Florida peninsula. Consequently he ascended every major river debauching into the Gulf south of Tampa. The Myakka and Peace rivers would have been obvious streams for investigation.

The British occupied Florida from 1763 to 1783. During this period, the Crown designated as Indian reservation all of Charlotte Harbor and the area west of the Peace River.

Charlotte Harbor was an immensely fruitful source of fish and edible mollusks. Thus, we can be sure Seminoles who arrived from Georgia early in the 1700s maintained villages all along the lower Peace River and upper harbor roadstead — probably on deserted Calusa\Timucua mound sites.

An extensive fishing industry serving the Cuban market was established at Charlotte Harbor at an early date — possibly by Menendez. Bernard Romans surveyed the English possession and in 1774 visited the harbor — called San Carlos Bay by the Spaniards. He renamed it after British Queen Charlotte and noted several camps of "Spanish Indians" salting fish.

The Puente chart of 1765 indicates that a Friar Gaspar had a mission somewhere in the northern part of Charlotte Harbor — giving the latter's name (Gaspar-illa, beloved Gaspar) to a "boca" (mouth, inlet) at the northern end of Gasparilla Island.

Cuban fishing villages were still busy when the Americans gained possession of Florida in 1819. Contemporary documents record a village of 60 persons living at Cayo Pelau and a slightly smaller one at Useppa (formerly Toampa) Island. A Spanish-Indian fishing shack was in existence at Punta Gorda in 1880.

An Indian trail ran from Live Oak point up the Peace River (called Talackechopko or Blackeye Peas Creek) by the Seminoles. It is likely there was a fishing camp then at what is now Charlotte Harbor Town.

Earliest settlement by Americans was in north and central Florida. The shores of Charlotte Harbor were low and unsuited for cultivation. The "Indian Prairie" north of the swampy shore was noted on early maps as "wet and dry." Shortly before the Civil War, Cattle Baron Jacob Summerlin and Captain James McKay shipped cattle to Cuba from a dock at Burnt Store on the east shore of Charlotte Harbor opposite Boca Grande Pass. When the American Civil War broke out, Summerlin obtained a lucrative contract to furnish beef for the Confederacy. The U.S. Navy then established a blockade at Boca Grande where loading at the Burnt Store dock could be easily observed. To avoid prying eyes, Cattlemen Joel and Jesse Knight bought land in 1862 at what now is Charlotte Harbor Town and built a dock where they, Summerlin and others could load. Another Knight brother, Henry, a prominent merchant at Tampa, opened a general store at the dock to sell necessities smuggled in by Capt. McKay on his return trips from the Confederacy. Two or three cow hunters — they disdained the term cowboys — built homes convenient to the dock and store.

The old trail from Indian Prairie to Live Oak Point became a well travelled cow path — later to be identified with a prominent cattleman named Ziba King. The cowpath now is a four-lane limited-access road called King's Highway.

Return Of Damyankees

Following the Civil War, two Union soldiers at Fort Myers returned to the north shore of Charlotte Harbor and married local girls. One of the men was Nathan DeCoster who imported a sawmill, then first south of Tampa. He set up his mill at the lagoon near the intersection of Melbourne Street and Tamiami Trail (U.S. 41). The site, believed to be the location of DeSoto's camp, has a slight elevation which back then was forested with hickory trees and known as Hickory Bluff. DeCoster sold the sawmill later and bought a large tract of land a mile east which he platted as Harbor View. He became a prominent business man and citrus grower.

The other transplanted Yankee was John Bartholf who became involved in Reconstruction politics. He was appointed clerk of courts for Manatee county which then included what is Charlotte Harbor Town today. In 1869 he was appointed superintendent of public instruction. By 1873, the village that had sprung up at Live Oak Point had expanded to Hickory Bluff and Harbor View. Bartholf built a one-room school there with a palm thatch roof. When Democrats regained control of the Legislature in 1876, Bartholf lost his job as clerk of courts but was appointed postmaster at Hickory Bluff by departing Republicans.

Bartholf named the post office "Charlotte Harbor" to describe his territory which included all north shore settlements. However, the community at Hickory Bluff was still so differentiated in 1881 when he wrote a promotion booklet about the area. He said, "The settlement of Hickory Bluff comprises about one dozen families, its store, post office, church and school house. In addition there is an extensive cattle wharf from which load after load of fine beef cattle is shipped annually to Cuba."

Matthieu Giddens, an early business man, gave land in 1873 for the Trinity Methodist Church, the one-room school, and a cemetery. The church congregation, oldest in the county, has met continuously ever since but has replaced its sanctuary three times. About the same time, T.S. Morgan operated a sugar mill on property now owned by the YMCA.

Original Structures Gone

Time and hurricanes have taken all the original homes of Charlotte Harbor Town. However several "century homes" are still in place. The oldest is that built in 1895 by Mr. and Mrs. Francis Larrison on Sibley-Bay Street. He was a Union soldier in the Civil War who moved to the area from Indiana in 1884. The next oldest is that built in 1899 by John Hagan on Laura Street. *(Note: the Larrison cottage was heavily damaged by arson in 1995 and demolished the following year.*

The dock that started the settlement of Charlotte Harbor's north shore succumbed to storms and barnacles several times over the last 135 years. It has been replaced each time and serves today as a public fishing dock.

The American Forestry Association in 1993 designated the many live oak trees in Charlotte Harbor Town as the Historic DeSoto Grove. The association now offers saplings grown from DeSoto Grove acorns to people wishing trees of historic significance.

Upon recommendation of the Charlotte County Historic Preservation Board, the Board of County Commissioners in June 1993 established by ordinance Charlotte Harbor Town as a Local Historic District. An historic preservation ordinance requiring Preservation Board review of excavation, demolition and relocation of historio-archaeological sites has been recommended by the Preservation Board. The proposal currently is under departmental review prior to Commission consideration.

John Gomez,
the hermit of
Panther Key,
who made up
stories about
a pirate
named Gasparilla.

Chapter 5

THE REAL PIRATE GASPAR

New light is shed on the long time controversy about the existence and location of Gasparilla the pirate. William Gomes, Jr., of Deep Creek, asserts with believability that there really was a pirate named Jose Gaspar — though not of the fanciful stature ascribed to him by adventure writers, and not a scourge of Charlotte Harbor.

Gomes says he is a descendent relative of Panther Key John Gomez alleged variously to have been a brother-in-law of the pirate, or a cabin boy on Gaspar's ship in the early 1800s. As such, Gomez said he was 122 years old just before he drowned in his fish net July 12, 1900, according to an obituary notice in the *Fort Myers News.*

Gasparilla — a Spanish diminutive for "beloved Gaspar" — has become fixed in legend here despite lack of evidence pointed out repeatedly by historians.

We know from maps of 1765 and 1768, that Gasparilla Island and Gasparilla Pass are named after a Friar Gaspar. He probably operated a missionary nearby to "Spanish Indian" fishing camps described by Surveyor Bernard Romans in 1772. Despite detailed logs of American and British war ships during the 1820-32 joint expedition to wipe out the last pirates in the western hemisphere, there is no mention of a Jose Gaspar. It is certain there were no pirates operating off the west coast of Florida which was virtually uninhabited and devoid of shipping to plunder.

23

Gaspar the pirate shows up for the first time in a 1915 brochure promoting Gasparilla Inn. The leaflet was written by Pat LeMoyne, an employee of the Charlotte Harbor & Northern Railroad which owned the hotel. LeMoyne was said to be a publicist at the time. After the Seaboard Air Line Rail Road acquired the CH&N in 1925, LeMoyne became SAL freight agent at Fort Myers. A limited number of his leaflets was printed. These were snapped up by titillated hotel guests and since lost. However, the contents were reprinted in a 1923 book titled *The Suppression of Piracy in the West Indies*, 1820-32 by Francis B.C. Bradlee.

This book also had limited publication, but your writer has a copy. It recounts century-old pirate stories gathered largely from contemporary sources. As for Gaspar, Bradlee succumbed to LeMoyne's piratical moonbeams but did acknowledge his doubtful source:

"Through the kindness of Robert S. Bradley, Esq., of Boston, president of the Charlotte Harbor & Northern Railway Co. of Florida, a most interesting, and, it is believed, accurate account of the famous, or rather infamous, Gasparilla, is here reproduced:

"This narrative was compiled by the writer (LeMoyne) from incidents told by John Gomez, better known as Panther Key John. The latter was said to be a brother-in-law of Gasparilla and a member of his crew, who died at the age of 120 years at Panther Key, Fla., 123 miles below Marco, in the year 1900. Also from records left by John Gomez, Jr., the cabin-boy on Gasparilla's ship, who was kidnapped by Gasparilla, and who witnessed the death of this pirate and all on board his vessel. He (Gomez, Jr.) died and was buried at Palmetto, Fla., in 1875, at age 70."

Incongruities

The incongruity of Panther Key John Gomez — Gaspar's brother-in-law aboard Gaspar's vessel — helping kidnap John Gomez Jr., seems not to have bothered LeMoyne. It may have been an effort to explain away the 1870 census record which lists a John Gomez, age 42, born in Nicaragua, living on China Key in Pine Island Sound. This man would have been only 72 if it was he who drowned in 1900.

For the most part, LeMoyne's account consists of unsupported generalities — Spanish admiral, thief of royal jewels, deserter turned buccaneer, possessor of valuable treasure, gentlemanly tastes, ravisher of a personal harem on Gasparilla Island, bloodthirsty fiend.

The few specifics are disproved by historical and archaeological evidence uncovered since 1915. For example, Gaspar supposedly built 12 log houses for women prisoners on "Cayopelean." As proof, LeMoyne cites the graves there of "hundreds of human skeletons" — Gaspar's victims. There are two burial grounds on Cayo Pelau Island — one of pre-historic Indians and another of historic Cuban fishermen. Also, there are remnants of buildings, docks and a skidway for hauling out boats.

When the United States acquired Florida in 1819, former Spanish citizens were allowed to file claims for land they were occupying. According to "Spanish Land Grants in Florida" records, four people claimed portions of "Cayo Pelew: which also was described as "Cayo Puebla" (Island Village.) The claimants, and their attested years of occupation, were Antonio Pania 1812, Antonio Machaco 1813, Peruco Pompon 1815, and Julian George 1815.

Testifying were Joseph Coldace, Jose Maria Panis, Gregorio Andreas, Maximo Hernandez, Manuel Hosa, and Domingo Alvarez. The claims were not allowed because they were made in 1828, a year after the filing period. LeMoyne's yarn about the capture and murder of a "Little Spanish Princess" and her retinue of 11 Mexican maidens (hence 12 log cabins) was based on a real event in 1801. Josefa de Mayorga, daughter of the Mexican viceroy, and 11 other girls on their way to school in Spain aboard the ship *Villa Rica* were lost without trace. Big-time pirates did not kill important hostages worth big ransoms — though they did abuse them first.

FRANCISCO GOMES D'SA

A favorite device of bogus historians is to link their tales to unexplained events which no one can challenge. The author of *Suppression of Piracy* also descended to this trickery to embellish the Gaspar legend with a real event LeMoyne does not mention — robbery of the ship *Orleans* "off Cape Antonio, Cuba," in Sept. 1821.

Wrote Bradlee: "The piratical corvette mounting at least 14 guns .... was commanded by one Gasparilla, a noted desperado of the blackest dye, whose headquarters were on the Island of Boca Grande (sic, should be Gasparilla) now a fashionable winter resort."

"The pirate gave a note written in French to a U.S. Naval officer aboard saying: 'Between buccaneers, no ceremony. I take your dry goods; and, in return, I send you pimento. Therefore we are now even. (signed) Richard Coeur de Lion.'"

News of the bloodless piracy was widely circulated at the time because the pirate chief treated passengers courteously while robbing them and taking the cargo. However, Bradlee attributed it fictitiously to Gasparilla — repeating a French connection for a Spaniard. The subterfuge was exposed by a well-referenced 1929 book by Gardner W. Allen titled *Our Navy and the West Indian Pirates*.

25

Allen combed official Navy records for the period. Wrote Allen: "Commodore Daniel T. Patterson reported two acts of piracy in September. One of the vessels, the ship *Orleans,* of Philadelphia, was seized off the Island of Abaco in the Bahamas, and detained two days.

"Before leaving her, the (unidentified) pirate chief addressed a note to a United States officer, a passenger on the *Orleans.* Signing the missive Richard Coeur de Lion, he says, 'I send you pimento (etc. as above.)' From Captain's letters, 1921, IV, No. 77."

Gasparilla Inventions

LeMoyne tells of a battle off Boca Grande Pass between Gaspar and a U.S. war ship disguised as a merchantman. There were several such decoy engagements during the last war against piracy. That of Dec. 1821 involving the *U.S.S. Enterprise* — when Gaspar was alleged to have wrapped himself in anchor chain and gone down with his ship — took place off San Antonio, Cuba. In the real event, the pirate chief was unknown; and he swam ashore with his crew to escape in the bushes.

Gaspar is touted by Charlotte Harbor advocates as the "King of Pirates" who received homage from all others. Few pirates of the early 1800s — mostly cowardly scavengers — were known by name. Famous pirates were Domingo, Diableto, and Cofrecinas. Gasparilla does not appear in official records or popular literature of the period.

The most shameless exploitation of the pirate Gasparilla myth was concocted by Jack Beater of Fort Myers a few years ago. He claimed to reprint an *American Monthly* magazine article of Feb. 1824, about a pirate attack on the ship *Mary Ann* in "southern Florida" waters. The article is authentic — as your researcher confirmed at the Congressional Library — but Beater falsified it. The sole survivor, a wounded passenger, described the brutality of the French-speaking pirates who tortured all on board then killed the crew. At one place in the narrative the pirate leader was described as having "black, shaggy whiskers." Beater then inserted a fabricated sentence: "One of his men called him by name, Augustus." This cleverly connected the *Mary Ann* pirates to one "Black Augustus," another fictional pirate supposedly Gasparilla's "chief gunner."

Beater also places words in the survivor's mouth: "I next heard a pirate shout in English that Gasparilla was signaling for them to return to the pirate ship."

These and other fictions about Gaspar were pointed out by your researcher in the *Charlotte Sun-Herald* history series. These prompted William Gomes of Port Charlotte to share information about his great-great uncle Juan Gomes D'Sa, of Panther Key fame, who was Pirate Jose Gaspar's cabin boy.

Says Gomes, "Our family has always been told by my great-grandfather Francisco Gomes D'Sa — long before Gaspar was written up — that his

Uncle Juan Gomes as a lad in Portugal was kidnapped by Jose Gaspar. On the subsequent voyage to Brazil, Gaspar took a liking to Juan and thereafter reared him as his son. Of course, Juan became a pirate.

"Gaspar was a small-time pirate of opportunity — robbing becalmed, unarmed merchant ships off the shore of Cuba by rowed barges. There were scores of this type of pirates in the early 1800s. When the American and British program pretty much drove pirates off the high seas, the brigands began robbing Cuban coastal villages. Local authorities then clamped down on the renegades. Gaspar was caught and hanged in Cuba.

"Juan Gomes got away and fled to Tampa where he became a charter-boat captain carrying visitors to a Pass-A-Grille Island development near the entrance to Tampa Bay. During the Civil War he was a Union pilot at Tampa Bay. The Navy enlisting officer recorded his name as the Spanish Gomez. Thereafter, Juan answered to "Gomez" simply because it was convenient for the many Spanish-language fishermen in the area. For the same reason, our family has dropped the Portuguese name-suffix D'Sa.

Tracing Gomez

"Great-grandfather Francisco Gomes D'Sa as a young man set out to trace his Uncle Juan Gomes — going first to Brazil and then to Florida. He found Gomes on Panther Key where Gomes had retired with a wife after leaving Tampa Bay. They had no children. It is not known when his wife died. Francisco then married an American woman, Laura Young, and settled on Cayo Costa, south of Boca Grande Pass. Later they bought an island off Fort Myers Beach.

"Juan Gomes(z) was quiet spoken. Though he admitted to being a pirate in his early days, he never talked about his experiences. He was, after all, reluctant to attract official notice.

"Relatives said Juan did not know his exact birthday and boosted his age from time to time as he grew older and famous. He also answered to the English translation "John." Our best guess, from generational comparisons, is that he was 90 to 100 years old when he died in 1900."

Your researcher can accept this account about Jose Gaspar and Panther Key John Gomez. Both have common Spanish-Portuguese names. It would not be unusual that at least a couple of pirates — out of the hundreds active during the last two decades of rampant piracy — would be named Gaspar and Gomez.

Furthermore, Gaspar's locale of operation and death are said to be in Cuba where pirates swarmed. Gomez apparently did not claim linkage to every notorious piracy that could not be verified. With this approach, U.S. historians can wait until they have an opportunity to search old, court records in Cuba for the elusive Gaspar.

Spaniards fighting Indians with hand-held cannons.

Chapter 6

FIND MYSTERIOUS ARTIFACTS

Strong evidence indicates that American history began at Charlotte Harbor with the visits of Ponce DeLeon in 1513 and 1521, Hernando DeSoto in 1539, and Menendez D'Aviles in 1566-67. The British may have traded here from 1763 to 1783 when they owned Florida. However, tangible proof of these events has been lacking until recently.

Tantalizing signs of early explorers here are now coming to light. Most startling is discovery in 1994 of a small cannon ball by a public works crew digging a ditch along Burnt Store Road near the Charlotte County Environmental Center.

Your writer has long held that the DeSoto probably landed in this vicinity. According to narratives of survivors, the explorer put his army ashore to march to a pre-selected Indian village called Ocita. The army began its march somewhat south of Burnt Store Marina and spent the night at Punta Gorda before being ferried across the harbor to Ocita — now Charlotte Harbor Town. Today's Burnt Store Road would have been the direct line of march.

The curious object found by the work crew is round, ranging in diameter from 2 1/6 inches to 2 7/16 inches. It is composed largely of iron, but patches of lead adhere to the surface. It weighs 1 pound 6 ounces. Photographs were first sent to Dr. Kathleen Deagan, an expert in ancient weaponry for the Florida Museum of Natural History at Gainesville. She calculated that the ball originally was 60 mm — deformed by being fired from a small, mounted cannon. Such weapons were in use in the late 1400's and continued to be employed into the early 1800's.

Dr. Deagan and her colleague, Dr. William Marquardt, recommended that a complete archaeological reconnaissance be conducted of the environmental center. Al Cheatham, executive director of CHEC, obtained a grant for such a survey. It was carried out in the summer.

While the CHEC grant was pending, the cannon ball was examined carefully by Dave Dickel, metal expert at the conservation laboratory for the Florida Division of Archaeological Research, Tallahassee. He says the ball originally was coated with lead to provide a tight seal with the cannon's bore. Much of this covering peeled off when the ball hit water, and the iron core expanded explosively. It is difficult to date the artifact, stated Dickel, inasmuch as this size caliber was popular for several centuries. Dickel places the likely date between 1715 and 1733.

We know that the early Spaniards used "arquebusses" and "hand cannons" ranging from 50 to 90 mm. These were wildly inaccurate, but the noise and smoke frightened hostile Florida Indians far more than swords and lances.

Hand cannons were carried by gunners. In practice, they were balanced on a staff rod or the rail of a ship. One man steadied and aimed the large-caliber weapon while a second man touched off the fuse.

Had the cannon ball been fired by an early eighteenth-century British weapon, well inland at the place found, a secondary mystery would be posed. Who fired the caannon? And at whom? The Charlotte Harbor area was thinly populated in the early 1700s. The Calusa had driven off the Spaniards by 1698, and the last few Calusa by 1705 had fled to Cuba from migrating Seminoles.

A century later, Spanish-Indian fishermen came to harvest Charlotte Harbor's bountiful mullet; and runaway slaves from the United States built a fort on Pine Island. Both groups had a cannon or two for defense against the Seminoles, but neither ventured inland.

Find Mysterious Tulwar

Years ago, Dennis Price, 11, dug for fishing worms along Sibley Creek at Charlotte Harbor Town and found a strange sword hilt. That night, he and his father, Walt, cleaned off centuries of incrustation and marveled at the hilt's bright, interwoven pattern. The blade had rusted away, but the hilt ,also of iron ,was intact. Obviously the smith who had fashioned the weapon also knew how to prevent rust if he wanted to — centuries before stainless steel was invented. The hilt was small, about seven inches long, with a disk pommel. The size suggested a large dagger or a "half-sword" kept under a sleeper's pillow.

29

Old Spanish cannon ball.   Mysterious sword hilt.

Walt Price showed the artifact to your writer, thinking it might be a memento of an early Spanish explorer. The hilt was identified by Helmut Nickel, curator of arms and armor for the Metropolitan Museum of Art at New York City. Wrote Nickel: "As far as I can see from your photographs, this object is the hilt of a so-called tulwar, a saber used in India during the 1700's and 1800's. The disk-shaped pommel and the short quillons of the guard with the pair of tongue-like projections are quite characteristic for this type of sword.

"The shortness of the grip is also another characteristic. East Indians are much more slender-boned than Europeans. Therefore, their hands fit easily into these narrow grips which are far too tight for people of European ancestry. The evenly-distributed silver decoration, like a textile pattern, is also typical for 18th-19th century Indian sword furniture.

"The blade of this saber, now missing, would have been single-edged and rather strongly curved. Older blades, from the 18th and early 19th centuries, would have been likely the famous Wootz or Damascus steel. Later, when the production of this steel was prohibited by the British, in order to create a market for their own Sheffield steel, most tulwars had European-made blades. It would be next to impossible to ascertain how this object came to be buried in Florida."

With a Spanish origin for the hilt eliminated, we can speculate that it came here as British trade goods. Great Britain began its penetration of India about 1707 for trading purposes. Queen Anne's War against France and Spain was raging. In the American colonies of Great Britain, slave raiders from the Carolinas and Georgia made several forays into Florida. It is not likely, however, that British imports of India goods had yet moved beyond spices and cloth.

Upon conclusion of the Seven Years War — known as the French and Indian War on this side of the Atlantic — Spain abandoned Florida to Great Britain in 1763. For the next 20 years, the British made extensive efforts to assimilate their new colony, but then gave Florida back to Spain.

By 1763, Britain had firmly drawn India into its empire and established a large, diversified import of India manufactures.

Surveyor Thomas Jefferys was dispatched to Florida in 1768 to map the west Coast, principally the great harbor at Tampa. Bernard Romans was hired to explore the entire Florida coast — east and west. His excursion of 1773 entered Charlotte Harbor which then was considered a reach of San Carlos Bay. Romans renamed the upper harbor for the English Queen Charlotte — and so it has remained. This period of English rule was also that of Seminole expansion and trade. Swords were prime items of exchange, and tulwar blades would have been well suited to the small hands of Ameri-Indians.

Yet, if tulwars were widely traded, why haven't they been uncovered elsewhere in Florida?

Charlotte County some day will install 11 miles of sewer lines in Charlotte Harbor Town. Hopefully, ancient artifacts will be uncovered when excavation for the sewer lines begins.

New Cadiz Beads Distinctive

New Cadiz beads, widely distributed by DeSoto in trade with Indians, were discovered by Marquardt last year during his extensive excavations of Calusa sites on Pine Island.

These highly-prized ornaments were manufactured for only a few years, so they represent a distinctive time period coinciding with DeSoto's landing. New Cadiz beads often are varied color with internal, saw-tooth patterns. Many beads are of solid blue or milk white color. Some are long, and square in cross section. Soto also traded clear, crystal beads.

Private collectors have shown me New Cadiz beads and a Spanish helmet allegedly taken from Charlotte County mounds. Unfortunately, these claims can not be verified. To have scientific value, discoveries must be verified and photographed in place by qualified scholars.

Anyone living within a hundred yards of the harbor or a tributary stream should be on the lookout for armor, beads, hawk bells, mirrors, pieces of glazed olive oil pottery, and Majolica chinaware with grey background and splashy blue decoration.

Artifacts that might rewrite American history await a sharp-eyed back-hoe operator or back-yard gardener.

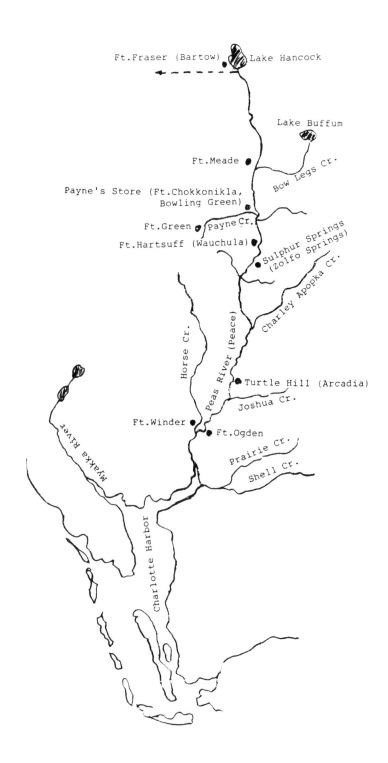

Ft.Fraser (Bartow) ● ◐ Lake Hancock

Lake Buffum

Ft.Meade ●

Payne's Store (Ft.Chokkonikla, Bowling Green) ●

Bow Legs Cr.

Ft.Green ● Payne Cr.

Ft.Hartsuff (Wauchula) ●

Sulphur Springs (Zolfo Springs)

Charley Apopka Cr.

Horse Cr.

Peas River (Peace)

Turtle Hill (Arcadia)

Joshua Cr.

Ft.Winder ●

Ft.Ogden

Prairie Cr.

Shell Cr.

Myakka River

Charlotte Harbor

Chapter 7

EXPLORE RIVER OF BLACK-EYE PEAS

The Talahkchopka Hatchee was America's last frontier, but its significance faded in history as latecomers hereabouts corrupted the translated Seminole name for the black-eye peas which grew in abundance along its banks to Peas Creek and finally to Peace River.

As the Civil War neared in 1860, slave-owning plantation owners east of Tampa Bay began looking to the Peas Creek valley as an area of expansion and refuge. However, little was known about the waterway as a possible transportation route for crops . Five white men and two black slaves set out from Fort Meade in the spring of 1860 to determine navigability of Peas Creek to its mouth at Charlotte Harbor.

They were William H. Meredith, a Hillsborough County plantation owner; Christopher Q. Crawford, a sawmill operator at Fort Meade; Rev. Oscar A. Myers, a Tampa Methodist minister; Edward A. Clarke, a Tampa merchant: Furman Chaires, son of a prominent plantation owner; "a black boy in his late teens who was taken along to do the cooking; and Lewis, another young slave, was the "porter."

The group left Fort Meade April 26 in a 10-foot skiff constructed for the purpose by Crawford and named *Nancy* after his wife. A journal kept by Meredith was published in the *Florida Peninsular,* Tampa's newspaper, shortly after the expedition's return.

The journal in its entirety, was reprinted in the Spring 1990 issue of *Tampa Bay History.* The men involved regarded the expedition to be a lark as well as a serious exploration. The following highlights of the journal show why — our explanatory comments in parentheses.

First Day

All aboard and uncabled at 7 ½ o'clock a.m., with a tender adieu to all behind. We commenced our trip with serious misgivings. The river was lower, by six to eight inches, than ever known before by Maj. Louis Lanier (prominent cattleman of Fort Meade). Obstructions by logs of all sizes, fallen and bending trees, shoals and breakers we found of great frequency. The jams and squeezes, the bumps and thumps, were most trying. Now over, now under, a log or limb or bending tree; now all on foot and looking out; now all seated; now in the water; now aboard; now astride a log.

At 6 o'clock, made camp for the night near the burnt store on the east side of the river. Here, blood and life and ashes were consecrated to the cause of early, and, perhaps indiscreet, pioneering. Of this, however, let others judge. Some of our party took a walk and found the stone that told, mournfully, yet truthfully, the sad tale of poor Whidden and Payne who had been brutally murdered and then burned at ashes by the cruel and treacherous Seminole!

(Note: Trading post manager George S. Payne, and his assistant Dempsey Whidden, were killed and their store burned by renegade Indians in 1849. The stone was a rough monument. Fort Chokonikla — now Bowling Green — was built on the site the following year).

Second Day

At 9 o'clock we came to Willoughby Whidden's ford (he another cattleman). By unanimous vote we decided there was a possibility of our larder growing short. Even our steward had woefully undersighted his own capacity, as well as ours, for stowing away this sort of goods.

Hence, our whole party with this inedible object, went to the house of Mr. W. Of course, our object was secured, for when did you call on a Floridian for something to eat and fail to get it? We secured a sack of Hayties (potatoes, then widely grown in Haiti), some eggs and sugar.

At 11 o'clock we came to an abrupt fall of nearly 2 feet. These rocks, forming a channel of about 40 feet, precipitates the water into a roaring cascade. The expedition, by common consent, called this cascade Meredith's Falls. We have no hesitancy in pronouncing this a good seat for water machinery. Had to unship bed and boarding, as well as the live-stock (men), in order to pass.

We came to David Brannon's ford (he also a cattleman). Some of our men went to the Sulphur Spring (now Zolfo Springs), a few hundred yards from the river, on the east side. They reported the water very fine. Indeed it smelt and tasted as strong as any water we have tasted in South Florida.

At 3 p.m., we struck what may be appropriately called the Great Rafts of the river, consisting of the trunks and roots of trees, gravelly shoals and deep sand-bars. These we consider the chief obstacles to the successful and profitable navigation of this valuable stream. For more than half the distance from Ft. Meade to the mouth of the river, these obstacles, more or less, lie in the way.

Being hurried by approaching night, we camped on the side of the river in a swamp of defiles and sand bars. We felt called upon to name this part of the river, and this camp place especially, All Points — having steered to every point of the compass in a distance of a mile or two. (Note: All Points was later known as Three River Shoals and Horseshoe Bend.)

Commenced raining. Bedded down for the night. The rain came down in torrents. We got the full benefit of a concentrated shower from a small hole in our otherwise good friend, the tarpaulin. Our darkies sheltered their heads only under the bowdeck of the skiff.

Third Day

Mullets are now plenty, but very hard to take with prongs. Had a heavy rain upon us, in an open river. We took a cold snack in and about the skiff at 1 o'clock, the only entirely cold dinner upon the voyage.

About this time, Messrs. M and C had a sanguinary and exciting battle with a large alligator. His gatorship had offered no insult, further than an insolent glare of his eye. This was considered provocation for the cruel onslaught. Pitch into him was the word of command. Whereupon, Mr. Myers made a fearful incision into his back. Then C made a still more dreadful stroke.

The enraged enemy attempted to pass under the skiff and heaved her bow suddenly. This tilted both his assailants into the river. Mr. M re-embarked with great adroitness. Our steward, however, supposing that the odds might be fearfully against him in single combat with this monstrous reptile, made a hasty and even ludicrous retreat to the other side of the river while his wounded foe made his escape the other way. This battle scene was much more amusing to the immediate spectators than it can be made to the reader.

We passed, this afternoon, on the east side of the river, an extensive ledge of soft or soap stone. Some of our party, after trying it upon their hands, pronounced it a clever substitute for soap. Indeed it lathered well and seemed to cleanse our hands as wall as bar soap. It would be a pleasing affair could it be substituted for soap, as it would be much cheaper. But alas! it would be appropriated to human monopoly and speculation.

Bed clothes and provisions being unpleasantly wet, we made camp at 4 p.m. on the east side of the river on an elevated bluff in an open pine.

Capt. C and others are now gone across the river being invited in this direction by that interesting domestic fowl, the cock. Their object was to seek "light," especially our present whereabouts.

Our men returned and reported that they had been to Stephen Hooker's and had seen several acquaintances. We are now about 2 to 3 miles from John Parker's and 25 to 27 miles from Ft. Meade.

(Note: Stephen Hooker was the step-son of John Parker, a prominent cattleman and later sheriff of Hillsborough County. The expedition discovered the vast deposit of phosphate which in later years, up to the present, provides fertilizer and laundry detergent to the world. It is interesting that the expedition scribe anticipated the mineral's use without recognizing its commercial value. The camp site probably was near what was later called McClelland's Ford, approximately six miles above Big Charley Apopka Creek.)

Fourth Day, Sunday

We are resting and settling apart this portion of time, at least in part, as required by the great Law Book. Capt. C, Messrs C and C, and Cook took a stroll down the east side of the river to see whatever might be interesting, but especially to see the mouth of the Charlepopka (Big Charley Apopka Creek).

Fifth Day

Mullets and trouts in abundance. Turtles hard and soft shell. Our fisherman took a fine soft-shell turtle with the gig. We found the river much improved as to capacity for navigation. Land is sorry on both sides of the river for many miles. Passed the mouth of the Charlepopka. Banks high, averaging from 10 to 20 feet.

Struck camp at the usual hour, on the east side of the river, in a palmetto rough which we called with kind remembrance, "Turtle Bluff," as we had turtle meat, with her whole cargo of eggs, for supper.

(Note: The camp site is present day Arcadia, later called "Tater Bluff," perhaps a corruption of the expedition's version.)

Sixth Day

A good and gradually deepening and widening river — from 50 To 70 yards wide generally. We find the river still crooked, though the crooks are not so abrupt and provoking as above narrated.

At 7 o'clock we came to what seemed to be a crossing place for cattle. It had the appearance of a kind of forceford — having two strings of log fences made in funnel shape, widening from the river to the pine woods. And such a fence! It was built of forks, and logs, log chains and trace chains! One of our party, being an observing man, remarked, "That looks like some of Capt. William Brinton Hooker's work. Sure enough, on our return we learned that it was one of his cattle fords. Here we found a piece of zinc-sheet, upon which the scribe recorded our names, day, and date.

Fort Ogden, on a Peace River bend.

At 9 o'clock we met three boatmen with two cypress skiffs — large and small — one laden with groceries from Ft. Augden (Ogden) for the upper settlement (Fort Hartsuff, now Wauchula, then the head of navigation). Dined on the west side of the river at a place called Haygan's Bluff, a fine body of hammock land, perhaps a little too low, but rich, with a fine place for settlement not more than a half-mile from the river.

We passed the mouth of Horse Creek about 2 or 3 o'clock. From H's bluff we found cypress abundant, and pine, on both sides of the river for many miles. From the looks of the timber, we were of opinion that there is a great deal of rich land in this neighborhood.

We arrived at Ft. Augden at 4 o'clock. This is a fine bluff on the east side of the river, indicated to the navigator by a lone black jack (oak tree) standing on the bank. This, we were told, was a noted hunting ground for the Indians. Here, too, we found, and left, a whole cargo of unprotected groceries — corn, flour, salt, etc., in an open, shutterless log cabin — without lock, bar or bolt. I guess the folks, if there be any in these parts, are honest.

Every man to his tent or bar (mosquito netting) for the night. (Note: The enterprising Fort Ogden merchant probably was Enoch Daniels who had been living in the area for a year or more. He received his supplies from Tampa via Charlotte Harbor and the Peace River).

Seventh Day

Left camp at 6 o'clock, with buoyant hopes and cheering prospects. Indeed, we began to feel that we were nearing "Old Salt" himself. We passed Ft. Winder, on the east side of the river, at 7 o'clock. We halted long enough only to have our visit recognized by the dreary silence that prevailed there. (Note: The Fort had been abandoned in 1852 after the second Seminole War. It was opposite Fort Ogden a half-mile inland.)

Being all aboard, and the Capt. at the helm, we begin to grow impatient to be at the mouth of the river. We are regaled by the sea breezes and behold seabirds. We now pass large islands with rich-looking soil and growth. We still keep to the left. Now, we pass a school of large porpoises. Know not but that they may, in their quaint evolutions, give *Nancy* (as they named the skiff) a toss. We took several unavailing shots at them with our shot guns.

At 1 o'clock we dropped anchor on the west side of the river in sight of the "tripod" raised by topographical engineers of the government (for a survey mark). Being too much fatigued to look about us, for the present, we stretched out in the shade to snooze til Rome calls us to dinner.

To the S. West, two miles or more distant, our old friend, the river, is dissembouged into Charlotte Harbor. To the S. East we behold a long stretch of pine forest rising above the broad expanse of waters, islands, marshes and sand bars — a distance of 3 or 4 miles.

The expanse of the river, at the mouth, is greatly increased by the influx of a large stream or creek called "Prairie Creek," (along with Shell Creek, now Punta Gorda's municipal water supply). which is sometimes mistaken by strangers for the river itself.

The river is high, the tide ebbing, and the sea is rough. With all hands aboard we commence our return trip. Nancy is too light and small to encounter a wide, rough sea. After struggling against wind and tide, our camp was made by 7 ½ o'clock at the same point at which we had dined.

* * *

On the return trip they visited "Jockey" Bill Whidden — well known cowhunter — at his solitary cabin on Horse Creek. A little farther on they stopped for grub at Mr. Tyre's place.

They camped again at Haygan's Bluff. There they placed their empty bread barrel upon the top of a hickory sapling to designate the head of navigation "and a signal of commerce upon the river." Meredith noted that tide marks at this point amounted to more than a foot though 25 to 39 miles (by river) from the mouth of Peas Creek.

When they passed Capt. Hooker's cow ford, they scribbled a "small scrap of rhyme" on his metal bulletin board:

"Man is a vapor and full of woes.
He cuts a caper and down he goes!"

The men took time on the return trip to examine the many fossils found in the river shallows and on its banks. They surmised the bones were from ancient manatees, but we now know they were the remains of extinct animals millions of years old associated with phosphate. The expedition members were so impressed they re-named Peas Creek "Bone River," and it was sometimes referred to as such for several years.

The party reached Fort Meade exactly two weeks after starting out. Meredith closed his journal with this observation:

"Here we give our opinion that Ft. Meade is 30 to 40 feet only above the level of salt water. From Ft. Meade to the mouth of the river it is by land 66 miles, and by water, we suppose, about 130.

"We further give it as our opinion that the judicious expenditure of $10,000 or $15,000 upon this stream would make it a good, navigable stream for six or eight months in a year for light-draft steamers.

"Besides this direct advantage to the river, the drainage of thousands of acres of the richest land in South Florida would be the indirect result. Here is an open field for enterprise and profitable outlay of labor and means."

Mule-drawn dumpsters prepare foundation for Alligator Creek bridge.

Chapter 8

PROBLEMS OF ERECTING NEW COUNTY

When DeSoto County was divided from Manatee in 1887, the area now known as Charlotte county was included. The problems of erecting a new county in the wilderness of Southwest Florida were complicated.

Highlights of those minutes provide insight to the concerns of pioneers struggling to tame the last frontier of America.

Occasional explanations by your writers appear in italics.

July 18, 1887 — Commissioners met at Pine Level in first session of DeSoto County. Members present: Marion G. Carlton elected temporary chairman, Peter Brown, T.O. Parker and S.T. Langford. Approved bond ($2,500) of F.B. Hagan as treasurer, bondmen T.S. Knight and J.M. Bourland $1,250 each.

Knight was a leading cattleman and merchant at Charlotte Harbor (town) was established in 1862.

Aug. 4, 1887 — Clerk was instructed to decline the Manatee County commissioners' request to meet them in Manatee, as Pine Level is, as we view the matter, the proper place to transact business pertaining to the two counties; and to ask them to meet with us in joint session the first Monday in September and to bring all necessary records.

Manatee County seat was moved by Reconstructionists after the Civil War to Pine Level 10 miles northwest of today's Arcadia. Thus, there were strong feelings between the two communities.

August 23, 1887 — Petition for a bridge across Alligator Creek was rejected on account of scarcity of funds.

39

Approved the bond of, and granted license, to E.B. Carlton to establish and maintain a steam ferry across the waters of Charlotte Harbor (bay) from Trabue to Hickory Bluff.

Hickory Bluff was the original name of Charlotte Harbor Town which gradually acquired the name of the post office established near the Civil War cattle dock in 1872 to serve all settlers on the bay. The name Hickory Bluff survived many years for a cluster of homes, school and church around a sawmill set up in 1866 by Nathan DeCoster on a lagoon a mile east of Charlotte Harbor post office.

Appointed recording officers: F.M. Durrance, Trabue; and Frank Knight, Hickory Bluff. Commissioners subdivided the county into voting precincts: No. 5, Charlotte Harbor at Knight's store; No. 6, Grove City at Hafer's store; No. 7, Trabue at Simmons & Carlton's store.

Sept. 5, 1887 — Entire Board met. First business was election of M.G. Carlton as permanent Chairman. The Board agreed to meet Manatee County Commissioners on the 8th inst at Manatee in joint session, as required by Acts of 1887.

Commissioners, deeming it advisable that the county should be represented in the Florida Sub-Tropical Exposition to be held at Jacksonville this winter, recommend the several communities select delegates. The communities shall form an organization and render whatever assistance they can to make a beautiful and profitable exhibit. Mr. Kelly B. Harvey was appointed organization president.

Harvey was the surveyor who laid out the town of Trabue (renamed Punta Gorda) for Col. Trabue in 1885 and became a prominent business man there. Gilchrist was the Florida Southern Railway surveyor who came to Trabue with the railroad in 1886 and resigned to become a land dealer and Governor of Florida.

On presentation to the Board of petitions, from 280 signers, more than one-fourth of the registered voters in the county, a general election was called for Nov. 3 next. The following inspectors and clerks were appointed for the several precincts: No. 4 (Pine Level) inspectors M.F. Mizell, F.B. Hagan and William Alderman; clerk Joshua Mizell.

No. 5 (Charlotte Harbor) inspectors T.S. Knight, R.R. Russell and J.B. Lastinger; clerk J.B. Thomas. No. 6 (Grove City) inspectors Robert Smallwood, T. Broadaway and J.R. Williams; clerk F.H. Hafer.

No. 7 (Trabue) F.M. Durrance, James L. Sandlin, and J.A. Daughtry; clerk K.B. Harvey.

Election was ordered on the same day to locate a seat for DeSoto county. The following precinct inspectors and clerks were appointed:

No. 4 (Pine Level) inspectors A.J. Greene, Joseph Mizell and Alfred Hagan; clerk M.T. Harwell.

No. 5 (Charlotte Harbor) inspectors Nathan H. DeCoster, R.S. Hanna and C.L. Knight; clerk J.E. Glenn.

No. 6 (Grove City) inspectors James Hamilton, R.A. Owens and McKinney; clerk McPherson.

No. 7 (Trabue) inspectors E. Fishback, W.S. Stetson and Isaac H. Trabue; clerk Albert W. Gilchrist.

Salary of C.W. Carlton as county auditor set at $25 per month.

Oct. 3, 1887 — Most of the afternoon and next day was taken up in assessing the lands of large land companies.

Granted license to John M. Pearce to establish and maintain a ferry across the Kissimmee River at Ft. Bassinger, taking his bond for $300 and fixing maximum rates as follow:

Footman 15 cents, man and horse 25 cents, horse and buggy or other single team 50 cents, double team 75 cents, one yoke of oxen and cart or wagon 40 cents, two yoke of oxen and cart or wagon 60 cents, for additional yoke 15 cents, and for each additional animal 5 cents.

Endorsed the petition of J.B. Thomas as Justice of the Peace in District No. 5 (Charlotte Harbor).

Issued an order to the treasurer of Manatee County to pay F.B Hagan, DeSoto county treasurer, the latter's share of funds as per settlement of the two Boards in joint session of Sept. 8, to wit: building fund $1,128.39; roads $555.51; schools 1,630.98 1/2; road fines $45.29 1/2 — total share $3,360.18.

Renewed the bounty of $4 per month each to paupers, $6 for man and wife, commencing last June (seven listed).

Approved bounties for scalps of wild beasts: wild cat $2.70, wolf $4.70, bear $4.70, panther $5.30. ($64.40 paid for month of September.)

Tax rates levied for next year: general revenue 4 ¼ mills, schools 4 mills, county special ½ mill, and quarantine ¼ mill.

Nov. 7, 1887 — Ordered another election be called Dec. 29 to locate a permanent county seat for DeSoto. Appointed inspectors and clerks for the several precincts:

No. 4 (Pine Level) inspectors William Alderman, F.G. Hagan, and Mr. Mizell, clerk O.T. Stanford.

No. 5 (Charlotte Harbor) inspectors M.F. Giddens, F.J. Knight, and F.J. Seward; clerk J.E. Glenn.

No. 6 (Trabue) inspectors T.R. Hector, James L. Sandlin and E.C. Jackson; clerk W.H. Simmons.

Jan. 2, 1888 — Petition granted for a public road from Charlotte Harbor to Arcadia via William Jurnigan, J.W. Daniels and J.H. Hayman's sawmill — blazing committee: William Jurnigan, J.M. Daniels and S.M. Platt. Following road commissioners appointed:

District 5, William Jurnigan, M.F. Giddens and J.B. Lastinger. District 7, James M. Lanier, Isaac L. Baer and Joseph Cushing.

March 5, 1888 — Ordered the name of the election and cattle recording districts, now known as Trabue, be changed to Punta Gorda.

Citizens of Trabue met Dec. 3, 1887, to incorporate and change the town name to Punta Gorda. Charter was recorded by the clerk of court at Pine Level on Dec. 7.

Report of blazing committee on road from Punta Gorda to Alligator Creek approved and work ordered as required by law.

County seat for DeSoto was refused as there were only 89 names on the petition.

May 7, 1888 — Hon. F.B. Hagan was appointed to represent our county in a district convention to be held at Orlando 10th inst. to devise the best means of preventing the introduction of yellow-fever in South Florida this summer, and to accept such assistance from the interior counties they will render in our common interest.

July 2, 1888 — Ordered an election Aug. 4 to decide permanent location of the county seat.

A bond was placed in the hands of the commissioners, signed by Members J.W. Whidden and L.H. Parker and Messers W.E. Daniel and J.W. Parker, for completion of a court house at Arcadia according to plans and specifications therewith. To cost not less than $3,000, provided Arcadia is elected in August as the permanent county seat. Said court house to be completed within six months from date of the election and without cost to the county.

Aug. 6, 1888 — The Charlotte Harbor road committee reported that it has laid out a public road on the most practicable route via Hayman Mill to Arcadia. Work ordered. Returns of the court house election were canvassed by commissioners. No place receiving a majority of votes, it was declared no election. Vote was Arcadia 295, Fort Ogden 186, Nocatee 110, Pine Level 59, Punta Gorda 2, Ft. Bassinger 1, Bowling Green 1, Zolfo 1.

Hayman bought his saw mill, then located near Fort Ogden, from Thomas Williams who had bought it from DeCoster.

Sept 3, 1888 — Reduced the assessment of Hotel Punta Gorda from $60,000 to $30,000.

The Board respectfully advises the people to meet in convention and nominate two places suitable for a permanent county seat. Thereupon an election will be called and the matter decided.

Oct. l, 1888 — I.H. Trabue taxes reduced for 1887 to $15,570. N.H. DeCoster taxes reduced from $66.80 to $36.

Col. Trabue at this time was the largest, private land holder in DeSoto County; but the amount of taxes indicated is hard to believe. It is true that he was "land poor" and died penniless in 1910.

Ordered that an election be called Nov. 6 to ascertain a permanent county seat. It is intention of the Board to call an election to locate the county seat in as rapid succession as the law will permit until a place is elected. Precinct officials appointed:

No. 5 (Charlotte Harbor) inspectors Ed May, R.R. Russell and T.S. Knight; clerk F.J. Knight.

No. 6 (Grove City) inspectors C.L. Leach, Lewis, William H. Cleveland; clerk William Goff.

No. 7 (Punta Gorda) Wash Guikins, D.E. Russell and T.S. Morgan; clerk E.L. Fishback.

Road from Charlotte Harbor post office to Pine Level declared a public road and ordered worked.

Nov. 12, 1888 — Entire membership of Board present. Returns of the court house election were canvassed. Arcadia having received 448 votes — of 875 cast — receiving thereby a majority of 21 votes, was declared the county seat for ten years.

On petition, the Wire Road is ordered discontinued.

Dec. 10, 1888 — Proceedings of the Board of County Commissioners of DeSoto County at their first meeting in Arcadia.

The Board appropriated $3,000 in addition to the $3,000 donated by J.W. Whidden, L.H. Parker, J.N. Parker, and others for the building of a court house. The Board and the above named men and W.E. Daniel constituted themselves a building committee and employed P.R. Read to clear the lot and build the house, paying him $1,000 in advance. Read gave bond of $4,000 with Joshua Mizell, D.D. Garner, F.M. Platt and B.F. Baldwin as sureties.

Dec. 24, 1888 — Joshua Mizell posted bond $2,500 as county Judge. Walter B. Gray gave bond of $500 as Justice of the Peace in District No. 5 (Punta Gorda), signed by M.F. Giddens and F.J. Knight. James J. Gillen bond $500 as District 5 constable, signed by T.S. Knight and C.L. Knight.

Mathieu Giddens was a prominent businessman at Charlotte Harbor Town-Hickory Bluff who donated sites for Trinity Methodist church, cemetery and school. Later was county superintendent of schools. The Knights were brothers.

Jan. 7, 1889 — District road commissioners appointed:
No. 5 (Charlotte Harbor) Marion Platt, F.J. Knight and B.J. Edwards. No. 7 (Punta Gorda) James M. Morgan, Alford Sloan and R.B. Smallwood.

Feb. 12, 1889 — Motion carried to sell the old court house and jail at Pine Level. James McBourland was highest bidder at $202, covered by a note for 12 months at eight percent interest.

Bill of July Roberts for making coffin for Joseph Chapman was rejected as Chapman was not on the pauper list.

Chapman was an African-American who accompanied DeCoster to Harbor View after the Civil War. July Roberts was an African-American who came to Harbor View prior to 1880 and owned a large farm there.

April 1, 1889 — Bond of H.E. Carlton for county superintendent of schools received with Albert Carlton and C.W. Carlton binding themselves in the sum of $1,000.

Chapter 9

CHARLOTTE HARBOR DOCKS PIVOTAL

The Long Dock at Punta Gorda.

Hearing that Florida Southern Railway was going to extend its line to Charlotte Harbor, Trabue went to Boston and persuaded the directors to build their terminal at his uninhabited town. He gave Florida Southern half of his land for a waterfront resort hotel, and right-of-way to Punta Gorda — the Spanish name for the "fat point" used by Cuban fisherman as a landmark. Hotel Punta Gorda had to have a modest wharf for the yachts of visiting dignitaries.

The railroad had to have a 4,200-foot dock for its tracks to 12 feet, mean low, of water where Morgan Line steamships could transfer passengers and freight to and from Havana. This dock they named "Punta Gorda" for the point of land at its base. When the town later became Punta Gorda, the dock was called simply "Long Dock." It was located near today's Punta Gorda Isles Yacht Club.

At the sea end there was a general store with a post office whose official cancellation was Long Dock. There also was a telegraph office and a bank of sorts where passengers could cash checks. A sweet-water well was drilled there to supply the boilers of locomotives and paddle-wheel ships. The well casing rusted away long ago, but sailors today who know where to look can spot the artesian well still flowing from the salt-water sea bed.

When Trabue's town was incorporated in 1887 as Punta Gorda, the city seal adopted at that time featured the two docks.

Trabue and Henry B. Plant, president of the Plant System railroads and a principal stockholder of Florida Southern, had an argument of some sort in 1897. Whereupon, Plant stormed aboard his private car and shouted as it pulled away, "I'll make a whistle stop of your blankety- blank town." Plant then was building a larger resort hotel at Tampa and undoubtedly wanted to eliminate competition. He took up the tracks to the Long Dock and Col. Trabue's new ice factory. The rail spur running down King Street to the hotel became the end of the line. Plant built a shorter dock reaching only to five feet of water. It served the wholesale fish houses and river steamers, but shut out Morgan steamships. The Long Dock was abandoned. Trabue's ice factory, denied railroad access, ceased operation. A new Punta Gorda Ice and Power Company started up along the King Street track. The new ice company eventually became Florida Power and Light. Its original building is on the National Register of Historic Places.

Punta Gorda's Downtown Docks

Another prominent Punta Gorda dock was that of Gus Hart about 1890. He built it and a large ship chandlery at the foot of Cross Street (Tamiami Trail south). The store burned in 1895, taking also the *Punta Gorda Herald* next door. Disheartened, the Hart's returned to their original home at Philadelphia. An oyster fisherman and packer named R.B. Smith constructed a large dock and packing house nearby at the foot of Taylor St. prior to 1895. It was commonly known as the Oyster Dock.

The old cattle dock at Charlotte Harbor Town had fallen into disrepair by 1902. A group of cattlemen then built a new dock at Punta Gorda at the foot of Maud St. The wharf was just wide enough for cattle to walk single file. Cowboys drove their herds through town to the dock, then returned to whoop it up in the saloons and bawdy houses.

Reported the *Punta Gorda Herald:* "The big cattle dock was finished last week and is now ready for business. It is 3,100 feet long and very substantial. Contractor C.L. Fries made a fine job of it. Messers King, Langford, Crawford, Hooker, Parker and Whidden — cattle owners and stockholders in the DeSoto Cattle Wharf Assn. — were here Monday to inspect and receive the dock built for them. They found it entirely satisfactory and promptly paid for it.

"Regular shipments began when Capt. James McKay's schooner took on 327 head for Cardenas (Cuba) bought from Senator J.W. Whidden, R.C. Hendry, W.W. Langford, Jerry Carlton, and T.S. and Frank Knight."

The water depth at the end of the cattle dock was not quite adequate after all, so two years later it was extended 90 feet to deeper water.

Another wharf was located at Cattle Dock Point on the Myakka River. In Feb. 1902, the *Herald* published this unusual story:

The Punta Gorda railroad dock. Fish warehouses left, Hotel Charlotte Harbor background, formerly Hotel Punta Gorda

"A STEER STORY — The steamship Fanita recently took on a cargo of cattle from the West India Dock, in the mouth of the Myakka. Amongst them was a steer belonging to Mr. T.S. Knight of Charlotte Harbor. This particular steer proved so unruly, and cut up such outrageous capers, he was turned back into the pen at the land end of the dock; and the steamer sailed off without him.

"Suddenly realizing his abandonment, and the loneliness of his position, the steer bolted out of the pen, rushed headlong to the outer end of the dock, plunged into the briny deep, and swam after the steamer. He continued to pursue the vessel until he was lost to sight.

"Some days afterward, as Capt. K.B. Harvey in his mail launch *Lorraine* was cruising about half a mile from the West India Dock, he met this identical steer coming back on the billowy surface. He had failed to catch the steamer and was very much exhausted. Veracity of the *Herald* is still in prime condition and must never be doubted. Reference: Capt. K.B. Harvey and other eminent citizens."

The King Street dock by 1906 was crowded. The constant traffic of freight trains and commercial fishing boats became a hazard for general wharf uses. City Council in April conducted a referendum on a proposal to build a "city dock." The vote was 77 in favor, six against.

46

It was three years before folks got around to building a long, city dock at the foot of Sullivan St. where a 60-foot tower had been constructed in 1903 to display storm signals. The job finally was accomplished by volunteer labor and donated materials. The pilings were cabbage palm trunks brought from the Myakka River area.

First tenant of the new City Dock was John Smith, an oyster fisherman, perhaps a son of R.B. Smith mentioned above. John applied for a permit to build a shucking shed. Council decided that "all houses on the new dock are to be built by the town and rented to occupants at an amount according to size and structure of building." The city built a 14x20 "house for oyster business" and rented it to Smith for $60 per year.

A few months later, with a half dozen automobiles in town, Council adopted an ordinance making it "unlawful to drive any vehicle or automobile walk on the public dock except for carrying goods or freight, nor to drive faster than a walk, on penalty of $10 fine."

Flies A Problem

It was the practice of oyster shuckers to dump shells on Retta Esplanade and other streets. These discards made strong roads, but the slivers of rotting oysters remaining on the shells created a stench and attracted flies in such quantity as to "obstruct vision."

Consequently Council in January 1911 adopted an ordinance to control oyster shells: "Committee appointed to find a dumping ground, also to see about disposing of the oyster shells of E.D. Willis' oyster house, and Willis instructed not to put more in same places." The committee then directed that oyster shells could be dumped only "in the bay in front of the street between Blocks 17 and 18." Today, a condo in Punta Gorda Isles sits securely on that firm foundation of historic oyster shells.

City Dock was damaged by a hurricane in 1926 and rebuilt to about half its original length. It collapsed entirely in 1930.

Largest dock in the area, though not the longest, was the phosphate loading facility on Gasparilla Island at Boca Grande Pass. It was built in 1910 by the Charlotte Harbor & Northern Railroad.

The CH&N, known locally as the Cold Hungry and Naked because of low salaries paid to employees, acquired the uninhabited plat of Boca Grande Town from Albert Gilchrist. The railroad built the exclusive Gasparilla Inn, and sold lots to northern socialites. The Inn still flourishes, but phosphate loading was discontinued in 1972. The loading chutes were removed a few years later when the Seaboard Coast Line, successor to CH&N, ceased operation there.

An important dock was built in 1916 at Lemon Bay by Peter E. Buchan, owner-operator of a large general store at Buchan Landing, Englewood. He came in 1902 to work for the Nichols Brothers store. Buchan's dock was a popular "pleasure pier" with a Royal Casino at the end for dining and moonlight dancing. After collapse of the Florida Land Boom in 1929, the casino became a fish-packing house. At Punta Gorda in 1913, the ice company built a dock at the foot of Zapata St., an alley east of King St. Before this, the company had carried ice to the railroad dock fish houses on the Atlantic Coast Line rails. ACL was successor to Florida Southern. Joint use of the rails became difficult when the dock was crowded with box cars. In October of that year, the *Herald* reported:

The Ice Dock

"Capt. C.E. Bearce has the contract for erecting a wharf, just east of the railroad pier, for the Punta Gorda Ice Co. A railroad track has been constructed from the factory to the new wharf. It is a neat piece of railroading under the direction of H.L. Blakely who has years of experience while connected with the Atlantic Coast Line."

The "ice transfer siding" was narrow gauge. Truck cars of ice were pulled by a small donkey steam engine. The tracks are said to be still there under modern paving. King Street Dock caught fire and was badly damaged in June 1915. Reported the *Herald*:

"Fire originating in the Arthur & Lewis fish house on the ACL wharf at 4 a.m. Tuesday morning destroyed five buildings, a portion of the wharf and five railroad cars. Aggregate loss has been estimated at $75,000. Cause of the fire is unknown.

"Those who share the direct loss are Chadwick Brothers, Everglades Fish Co., Arthur & Lewis, West Coast Fish Co., Punta Gorda Fish Co., ACL, Terry Packing Co., S.E. Johnson, and H.L. Blakley. It is considered remarkable that Standard Oil company's tanks near the wharf did not blow up. Dean's boat house, wharf of Punta Gorda Ice Co., J.C. Lewis fish house and one house of the Punta Gorda Fish Co. were saved."

The dock was rebuilt, but several uninsured fish houses did not reopen. The King Street dock was removed in 1928 to allow construction of the Barron Collier Bridge. A new Municipal Dock was built at the foot of Maud St. It, too, suffered a major fire in 1939 in which a resident couple and young child were trapped on a second floor perished.

The pier was leased in 1977 by Radio Commentator Earl Nightingale for today's Fishermen's Village — last reminder of the days when ships ruled the harbor.

Tintype of Boca Grande light house in 1892. Privy, right.

Chapter 10

SHINING LIGHTS SAILORS' FRIENDS

Merchant ships were crucial to the economy of the earliest settlers around Charlotte Harbor, but the vessels posed problems of navigation and health. Though the harbor is large, its useful channel is relatively narrow and hard to follow. Crews often brought in contagious diseases. Local pioneers coped with these problems in cumbersome but effective ways.

Small boats had plied the harbor ever since the Spanish came in sixteenth century. However, with the exploitation of phosphate from the bed of Peace River in 1888 it became necessary to lead ocean-going schooners and side-wheel steamers into and up the bay.

The first need was to mark the entrance through its parallel "flying bars." Congress in 1888 appropriated $35,000 "for a light or lights and other aids to guide into Charlotte Harbor." A light house and assistant keeper's house were built on the southern tip of Gasparilla Island in 1890. Its light flashed to life on the night of Dec. 31. The first keeper was William Lester who held the job for 30 years. Both houses have been restored by the Barrier Islands Park Society and are listed on the National Register of Historic Places.

The beacon was a kerosene lamp focused and magnified by a cylinder of glass prisms rotated by a counterweight. Lester's job was to keep the lamp fueled and to reset the counter-weight every two hours. Focal plane of the light was 44 feet above sea level and was visible for 10 miles on a clear night. It's white beam was varied every 20 seconds by a red flash. Once inside, large ships had to make their way to the long dock at Punta Gorda. The first obstacle was the Cape Haze shoal which still claims small boats that yield to the temptation to take a short-cut.

A smaller light house, on stilts over the a mid-harbor mud bar, was constructed sometime later. The exact time is in doubt but probably was 1900 when other navigation aids were installed. Early charts indicate the marker as "Charlotte Harbor Light," 36 feet high, visible for 11 miles, exhibiting a white flash every second.

Then earliest keeper of the Cape Haze light whom we know about was Francis Larrison, a Civil War Veteran from Indiana who came to Fort Winder on the Peace River, then Charlotte Harbor Town, in 1893. The last keeper is believed to be a man named Fine whose wife ran a men-only boarding house in Punta Gorda. The visibility of well-reflected kerosene lamps was remarkable, as attested by the Rev. George W. Gatewood about 1910. He came to Southwest Florida in 1882 from Kentucky. He was a devout Christian in a wilderness with few ordained ministers. Though lacking formal training, the Methodist General Conference licensed him to preach in frontier churches. Consequently he ranged widely and was beloved by the pioneers.

Fire Hunting a Light House

Gatewood in his late years wrote a series of reminiscences for the *Punta Gorda Herald* One of them related an incident when Senator Frank Cooper and a cracker named R.B. Singletary went "fire hunting" for deer in the Burnt Store area south of Punta Gorda.

"They decided to try a timbered tract of land bordering the bay opposite Cape Haze," said Gatewood. "In those days, there were quite a number of deer that fed in that locality. On this occasion they had only one gun between them. One would carry the fire — in a frying pan tied to a pole laid across his shoulder. The fire was made of fat lightwood (resinous pine) splinters. With it you could shine a deer's eyes as far as the ordinary gun could kill one. Pretty soon, they shined what the thought was a deer's eye. They could only see one eye, but fired. They started out to see if they had killed it, but didn't find the deer. Again, they sighted the eye and shot at it, but no deer was there. After a couple more shots of that kind, the Senator turned the gun over to Singletary who made several shots with no better results. Finally Frank Cooper says to Singletary, 'You know what we've been doing, Sing? We've been shooting at Cape Haze light.' The light was about three miles off."

The channel around this beacon gave only 8 to 10 feet of water at low tide, so it was deepened to 11 feet in 1925. The light was tended by a resident keeper at first, but was converted to continuous battery operation when the deeper channel was cut through. U.S. Cleveland, Victor Larrison, and the late Harry Goulding remember fishing with their fathers around the Charlotte Harbor light house in the late 1920s. It was functioning but unattended at that time.

Victor Larrison, grand-son of Francis Larrison, the Cape Haze light keeper, says it was a popular fishing spot. Fish would congregate under the house for shade. All three men recall that it was a square building, painted white, with the light in a turret atop the roof. A porch encircled the structure, and their fathers would boost them up so they could run around the porch to "stretch their legs."

The light house was functioning in 1939 when Cleveland and friends fished there overnight. Larrison says it was replaced shortly after World War II with the present 16-foot "Marker 6" flashing every four seconds.

Re-cycling a house

"The Punta Gorda Fish Company bought the old Cape Haze light," recalls Larrison. "They ran a barge under it at low tide, then at high tide towed both up to Tarpon Inlet just south of Fishermen's Village. A man and wife with six or seven kids lived there for a couple of years. They cleaned fish for the fish companies at the municipal dock."

There was another light house near the Punta Gorda "long dock" which was the terminal of the Florida Southern Railway in 1886. The late Maude Mauck said that at one time her grandfather, Hiram Curry, was the resident tender there. It was a red house on stilts and marked the bay's most northern two-fathom (12-foot) contour.

"Sometimes he would row to Charlotte Harbor to see his grand children and stay overnight," she said. "Yet, he would always walk down to the beach to see if the beacon was functioning properly."

Mrs. Mauck kept several brass utensils, with U.S. Light House Service markings, which she got from her grandfather when the beacon was replaced with today's Marker 2 flashing red every 4 seconds. A nine-foot channel from there to Punta Gorda's new municipal dock — now Fishermen's Village — was dredged in 1928.

A malaria epidemic in 1892 — during which local settlers tried unsuccessfully to ban ships from other parts — led to a demand for inspections of crew health. A temporary tent camp was set up in October, 1893 and the *Herald* reported: "Dr. J. F. Cronin is the genial quarantine inspector." A permanent Quarantine Station was built in 1895 by the U.S. Marine Hospital Service, consisted of a home for Dr. Cronin and two sailors who operated the pilots' boat. Dr. B.B. Blount, of Punta Gorda, succeeded Dr. Cronin in 1902.

The *Herald* in April said: "Dr. Blount, physician at Boca Grande Quarantine station, captured a 12-foot alligator and will mount the head.

He has received an elegant naphtha launch which he has named the *Gov. Jennings* in honor of our chief magistrate."

The south end of Gasparilla Island was low and swampy. Mosquitos were abundant. The environment was not suitable for health care. Consequently, the quarantine station was abandoned in 1904. The north end of La Costa Island was appropriated for the site of a new station.

Cleve Cleveland, U.S. Cleveland's father, and Cleve's brother Dell were hired to provide living quarters for Dr. Cronin and workmen building the La Costa Station. The U.S. Marine Hospital Service acquired the hull of a decrepit schooner named *Proctor*.

The Clevelands intentionally ran this aground at high side on the bay side of the island. Then, the carpenters built a barracks and an apartment for a physician over the hull. The new station house, rain water cistern, and pier to the island was built on pilings off the *Proctor's* stern. The quarantine officer at this time was Dr. Wyatt Barnes.

After the station was built, *Proctor* was abandoned and the Clevelands were allowed to salvage what they wished from the hulk. Cleve saved a porcelain-iron bath tub. He later installed it in his home at Boca Grande when he went to work for the phosphate company there. Then, he carried it with him when he moved the family to Punta Gorda in 1921. The venerable fixture is still giving good service at 509 Gill St.

The quarantine station was discontinued about 1950 when phosphate loading of foreign vessels was shifted entirely to Tampa.

LaCosta Quarantine Station was the derelict schooner *Proctor* while Cleve and Dell Cleveland built the permanent station, left, in 1904.

52

Austin and Jeannette Youmans, genealogists, record grave marker
for cattleman Joel Knight who died at Charlotte Harbor Town in 1879.

Chapter 11

GAVE FIRST SCHOOL, CHURCH, CEMETERY

The county's oldest cemetery — that at Charlotte Harbor Town —
contains the first recorded burials of local pioneers who braved a sub-
tropical wilderness and Civil War Reconstruction to build a settlement.

Their personal monuments are weathered grave stones at the Pioneer
Cemetery owned and operated by Trinity United Methodist Church. The
hallowed spot traces its beginning to 1879. A survey and directory of
burials has been compiled by Mr. and Mrs. Austin and Jeannette Youmans
of the Charlotte County Genealogical Society.

Charlotte Harbor Town, originally called Hickory Bluff, sprang up
around a dock built by Joel Knight and other ranchers during the Civil
War. From there, cattle were shipped to the Confederacy and Cuba. A

53

Bob Waterson built a home near the dock which he later sold to Thomas S. Knight, Joel's oldest son.

Henry Knight, a younger son of Joel, opened a store at the dock to serve Confederate sympathizers hemmed in by a Union blockade of the harbor. He moved to Tampa in 1884 to open a large hardware store there in partnership with Perry Wall. Tom Knight and his son Tom, Jr., operated the store thereafter.

After the war, other settlers arrived to take up homesteads — or cheap land offered by the Florida Internal Improvement Fund. As the settlement grew, so did the desire for a local church and school.

Finally, under the leadership of the Knights, a little frame building with palm-thatched roof was constructed in 1873 near Melbourne Street. The lumber was sawed on Nathan DeCoster's steam-driven mill along Mill Creek lagoon. The humble structure was used as a Methodist Episcopal Church on Sundays, and a school on week days — when preachers and teachers could be found. In that same year, Mathieu Giddens married Mary Knight, a daughter of Joel. The couple were to be instrumental in establishing the Charlotte Harbor burial ground. They located first at the settlement between Tampa and Lakeland known as Knight Station — for Sam Knight, the family patriarch and prominent cattleman.

Captured By Yankees

Mathieu, whose hard-to-spell name became Matthew in time, was a Confederate veteran from Valdosta, Georgia. He enlisted in the army at age 16 and was captured by Yankee forces in an early battle and spent much of the conflict as a prisoner of war. He was held for a year after the war because he would not sign an oath of allegiance to the victor.

The Giddens' first child, a son named Summer, was born at Knight Station. As was the custom among ranch families, Mathieu began to accumulate cattle and range land. His first purchase of land was along the Myakka River north of Osprey.

Matthieu became active in post-war politics, steadfastly opposing Republican Gov. Henry L. Mitchell. The latter was the brother of Tom Knight's wife Virginia and thus a "shirt tail in-law." Mitchell, a southerner who cooperated with the Reconstruction, was the family black sheep.

Mitchell was ousted from office in the 1876 election — the first to admit Democrats. His successor, George T. Drew, threw out the Republican "carpetbaggers" and replaced them with his own appointees. One of these was Mathieu who was named a commissioner of Manatee County, then encompassing what is now Charlotte County.

Mathieu acquired 107 acres at Hickory Bluff in 1879, probably by homestead "declaration." There is no record of his homestead claim being filed. Land surveys were lost during Reconstruction, and claims could not be substantiated. His ownership was substantiated in 1882 when he "proved" his homestead. It consisted of the southwest quarter of the southwest quarter of section 25, township 40, range 22; and a sliver of waterfront of section 36.

Joel Knight died unexpectedly Sept. 18, 1879, at age 57. The Giddens hurriedly set aside a corner of their property for a cemetery. It is likely that Joel was nursed during his final days at the home of his daughter Mary and son-in-law. In 1882 Mathieu built a two-story home on Mill Creek. The Manatee County tax roll of 1883 — on property of record the preceding year — lists Mathieu Giddens' assets as "107 acres, personal property (house) $190, one horse, 400 neat (oxen) and cattle, 15 hogs, value of animals $25,311." This was a substantial holding in those days. Note that he owned a sizeable herd of food animals that roamed the open ranges while he also worked and lived in the village of Hickory Bluff.

This value placed on Giddens' animals is an astounding amount that would place the value of each cow at approximately $60. The usual rate was $10 to $15 a head. The tax collector may have made an error in transcribing his notes, or the Giddens may have inherited a herd from Joel or Sam Knight through Mary, that had not yet been counted. Whatever the case, we find the Giddens suddenly wealthy. Mathieu began speculating in land. Records disclose scores of purchases and sales.

Census Details

In the census of 1880, three years before the wealth described above, Mathieu, 35, gave his occupation as "clerk in store for six months of past year." His wife, Mary, was 26. Their sons were Summer, 7; Larue, 4; and Marcus, 9 months. Living with them was Mathieu's brother Isbin, 22, who gave his occupation as "grocer." It is likely that the Giddens brothers were employed in Henry Knight's store.

The most important transactions were those conveying most of Charlotte Harbor east of Tom Knight's property, including the little church-school, to Mathieu. He platted the tract into town lots and filed the sub-division dedication Feb. 24, 1865. Louisa Curry died at Charlotte Harbor on Nov. 15, 1886, and was buried near Joel Knight in the Giddens cemetery. DeSoto County was split off from Manatee in 1887, and in that year Mathieu belonged to Capt. John Whidden's United Confederate Veterans' Camp 1402 at Arcadia. Mathieu was still active in politics, helping elect "regular Democrat" Albert Gilchrist of Punta Gorda, as Governor during the Democrat Party schism of 1908,

By 1890, Charlotte Harbor Town had outgrown the original church-school. In addition, the old thatch roof leaked badly. The Giddens then deeded a site at the corner of Palmetto (now Parmely) and Seneca streets where the church has remained ever since.

Two frame buildings were erected side by side, one a church, the other a 2-room school Trustees accepting the gift of land were Thomas S.

Knight, John W. Barry, Benjamin J. Edwards, Young G. Lee, and Mathieu F. Giddens. Teachers for the school usually were guests of the Giddens in their home, now gone, at the corner of Bay Shore Drive and Church St. Mrs. Esther McCullough was a teacher at Charlotte Harbor in the little 2-room school for the 1914-15 and 1915-16 seasons. She recalls with great fondness the Giddens who were so hospitable to her.

The tiny Giddens burial ground became the final resting place of six other Charlotte Harbor Town residents after Joel Knight and Louisa Curry. Then, in 1908, Mathieu and Mary transferred blocks 5 and 6 of the subdivision — which contains the early graves — to Trinity Methodist for a token $1. Receiving the gift were trustees Thomas S. Knight, T.A. Stevens, and Kelley Falkner.

The deed was conveyed "upon the express understanding that the tract of land shall be used for a cemetery; and in case the same should ever cease to be used as a cemetery, or for cemetery purposes, said tract shall immediately revert to the grantors."

The Giddens were said in the deed to be "of Hillsborough County." Apparently they were living there temporarily at the time inasmuch as they hosted teachers at Charlotte Harbor as late as 1916. Somewhat later they did locate at Tampa among their Giddens and Knight relatives. There, Mathieu and Mary died and are buried at West Lawn Cemetery.

Their most enduring monument, however, is the Charlotte Harbor Town Pioneer Cemetery shaded by beautiful live oak trees draped with Spanish moss. Wild, vine potatoes attest to former habitation.

The Pioneer Cemetery is located at Harper and Church streets east of Tamiami Trail. It is tended by Trinity Methodist and available to anyone who wishes to be buried among the hardy folks who opened Charlotte County to settlement.

JOEL KNIGHT

REV, JESSE KNIGHT

Chapter 12

KNIGHTS OPENED UP CHARLOTTE HARBOR

Earliest American settler at Charlotte Harbor was Joel Knight who with his brother Jesse established a vast herd of cattle that roamed freely on the Ninety Mile Prairie north of the bay.   Samuel Knight, son of a Revolutionary War soldier named John Knight, was born 1793 in Georgia. Samuel Knight and his wife Mary (nee Roberts) had 10 children. Among them were Jesse born 1817, and Joel born 1822.

Samuel, his son-in-law and another cattleman came to Florida in 1842 looking for grazing land offered by the Armed Occupation Act to anyone willing to move close to hostile Seminoles. The men decided on Levy County and drove their cattle there the following year. Their families, with a few slaves, followed in 1843. Two years after that, Sam Knight drove his herd on down to the Alafia range in west Hillsborough County. There he homesteaded 160 acres soon to be known as Knight Station four miles north of today's Plant City.

As was customary on the frontier, Samuel and his sons Jesse and Joel joined the militia. Joel, the family activist, became First Sergeant in Capt. Simeon L. Sparkman's company.

The U.S. Army tried to keep the Seminoles in their Peas Creek reservation (the name corrupted to Peace River many years later) and settlers out. The task was difficult because Congress enacted the Swamp and Overflowed Lands Act in 1851. Florida used this authority to establish the Internal Improvement Fund to sell wet-dry land of the Ninety Mile Prairie and Charlotte Harbor shores at $1.25 an acre. Enormous pressure was exerted by central Florida residents to "remove" Indians to new reservations on the U.S. western frontier. Joel was appointed secretary of a meeting of Alafia cattlemen to petition for removal.

The final clash between Seminoles and settlers was touched off by a Seminole attack in 1856 on the Willoughby Tillis homestead near Fort Meade. In a battle between the militia and Indians, the Seminole war chiefs were killed; and Principal Chief Billy Bowlegs agreed to go west.

After the Battle of Peace River which ended the prolonged Seminole Wars, rowdy opportunists rushed in to stake claims in the vacated Seminole refuge. In an attempt to establish law and order — where peace officers were few and far between — Joel in Alafia helped organize vigilantes known as Regulators. According to Historian Canter Brown, Jr., in *Florida's Peace River Frontier*, regulation got out of hand; and lynchings were almost a daily occurrence in Tampa.

Joel also was active in the American or "Know Nothing" political party opposing Catholics and immigrants. Its unofficial name arose from the members' replies when asked about their secret lodges.

Know Nothings Switch

The Know Nothings broke up over the slavery foment culminating in the Civil War — still stoutly termed hereabouts as the War For Southern Independence. Joel switched his allegiance back to the Democratic Party.

During the Civil War, cattle were in great demand to supply the Confederate Army. Capt. David McKay of Tampa, carried Florida beeves to Confederate and Cuban markets in his paddlewheeler *the Scottish Chief*,

McKay and Cattle Baron Jacob Summerlin at this time had a cattle dock on the east shore of Charlotte Harbor opposite Boca Grande Pass. This location was easily monitored by Federal blockade ships at Boca Grande. Consequently McKay and Summerlin — the latter a son-in-law of Samuel Knight — relocated their dock farther up the harbor to Live Oak Point in 1862. It was the highest ground there — now Charlotte Harbor Town — and hidden from blockaders.

The Knights moved their herds south to the upper Myakka River area to keep them from being confiscated by the Feds. Jesse located west of the Myakka. Joel moved east of the river. Jesse Knight forded his cattle at Myakka City then he and Joel drove their herds down the east bank of the Myakka river to a trail — today's U.S. Highway 41 — to Live Oak Point.

Summerlin and other Peace River cattlemen brought their cattle to Live Oak point over an old Indian Trail now called King's Highway after Ziba King. The latter came to Fort Ogden after the Civil War and became a prominent rancher. A holding pen and cowboy shelter was constructed at the Live Oak Point dock — now the county dock at Charlotte Harbor Town. It is believed that Joel Knight and/or his son Henry Laurens (Lawrence?) built a small warehouse at the dock to sell necessities brought back by blockade runners.

Henry had acquired sufficient experience and capital by 1884 to start Knight & Wall, the largest mercantile store in Tampa. The partners operated the Charlotte Harbor store for several years before turning it over to Thomas S. Knight, Henry's older brother.

During the Civil War, the Confederate government commissioned Florida cattlemen as officers in a Special Cavalry to guard the herds from Union raids. They were commonly called the Cow Cavalry. Joel was a Second Lieutenant, Company D, Capt. Leroy Leslie commanding. As such, Joel participated in the desultory attack on Fort Myers garrisoned by African-American U.S. Army soldiers commanded by white officers.

(For details about the Seminole Wars, Battle of Peace River, Civil War blockade and the attack on Fort Myers see Volume 1 of *Our Fascinating Past.*) After the Civil War, Joel and Jesse moved their families from Knight Station to the villages on the edge of Ninety Mile Prairie.

Joel's Family

Joel married Virginia Mitchell and had 9 children, eight of whom lived to adulthood. They were Thomas Samuel, the oldest, who became a prominent cattleman, banker and real estate developer; George W., orange grower and prominent Freemason; Mary Ellen who married Matthew Giddens, another cattleman and real estate developer at Charlotte Harbor Town; Frances Jane died at age seven; Andrew Jackson, real estate developer and financier; Henry Laurens a highly successful merchant; Charles Leffie, banker; Francis Jefferson; and Eugene Clinton. Joel took up 320 acres at Charlotte Harbor Town in January 1876. His aged father and mother, Samuel and Mary, retired from ranching and came to live with Joel. Sam died there in 1879 at age 86. Joel died the same year at age 58.

Mrs. Samuel Knight died there at age 82, and Mrs. Joel Knight died in 1902 at age 73. Sam and Mary are buried at their old homestead at Knight Station. Joel and Virginia are buried in the Trinity Methodist Pioneer Cemetery at Charlotte Harbor Town.

Jesse Knight married Caroline Varn in 1840. They had 15 children. They and the older children in 1868 homesteaded what was then called Horse and Chaise (now Nokomis, near Venice) because its silhouette from the sea resembled a horse and carriage.

Jesse kept his cattle from roaming entirely beyond recovery by running a barbed wire fence 20 miles northeast from Nokomis on the gulf of Mexico to Upper Lake Myakka. His cowboys described their range as "below the wire," meaning south of the fence.

Jesse Knight was an ordained Methodist minister. He held regular church services in his home until a large brush arbor was built in which services were held for nearly five years.

Jesse donated land for a combined church and school in 1873. Lumber was delivered by sail boat from the nearest sawmill which was on Cedar

Key 100 miles north of Tampa. The little structure served the Venice-Nokomis community for the next 20 years.

Teachers for the first six years were boarded and paid by Rev. and Mrs. Jesse Knight. There were no desks, only benches for the children.

Rev. Knight died in 1911 at age 94. He was buried in Nokomis Cemetery alongside his wife and many of his children, grand-children and great grand-children Caroline Knight died in 1901 and is buried under a marker which proclaims: "She hath done what she could."

Thomas S. Knight, oldest son of Joel, was known as the "axletree" of Charlotte Harbor Town because of his leadership. A Sarasota posse, chasing a KKK vigilante who had murdered the postmaster, stopped at Tom's home to rest after a hard day of riding. One deputy wrote: "Put up at Tom Knight's, one of the cattle kings who has a new, big, fancy house and is rich as plum pudding, otherwise just like any cracker."

(For details see Our Fascinating Past; Charlotte Harbor, The Early Years)

Eugene, Joel's youngest son, managed a family ranch in Cuba where Florida cattle were fattened for market there. Eugene and his horse were drowned there in 1911 while attempting to swim a flood-swollen river.

Mrs. Martha Ellen Fish and her brother, Walter Homer Monson, both of Punta Gorda, are descendants of Eugene Knight.

Leslie's Magazine portrayed the 1873 Yellow Jack epidemic strangling Florida and disrupting trade, to the alarm of Columbia. Note demon's foul breath.

Chapter 13

YELLOW JACK SPARES HARBOR

The Florida "yellow jack" epidemic of 1887-88 spared the Charlotte Harbor area largely because there were not enough people to sustain one — or, perhaps, quarantine measures kept the scourge at bay. Floridians liked to boast of their healthful climate but seldom mentioned tropical diseases which in those days counterbalanced curative effects of year-around sunshine. Yellow fever was common in warm, moist country. It was greatly feared because the mortality rate was high, and its method of transmission by a particular species of mosquito was not known until 1901.

Name of the disease reflects the jaundice that accompanies high fever, extreme pain and vomiting of black blood. Even today there is no specific cure. The infection has been brought under control by vaccination and by eradication of mosquito conditions.

The worst epidemic in Florida history began at Key West in the spring of 1887. Tampa was instantly alarmed. It was assisting the Cuban cigar makers at Key West to relocate following a disastrous fire which destroyed the factories there a year earlier. It was believed, probably correctly, that the infection had been brought to Tampa by Key West cigar makers. Two thousand Cubans from there had arrived already. Scores of others arrived on twice-weekly ships from Key West and Cuba, according to Eirlys Barker in the 1986 fall-winter edition of *Tampa Bay History.*

As Key West depopulated, the fever there burned itself out. Inevitably Tampa became the epidemic focal point. A quarantine station was set up hurriedly on Egmont Key where passengers from Key West and Cuba had to stay 15 days before being allowed to land at Tampa.

The quarantine was too little too late. Yellow fever was rampant. It is estimated that one thousand persons contracted yellow jack in 1887. A hundred of these died. Another 300 cases and ten deaths were recorded in the early part of 1888. Every family experienced cases of the sickness. Medical and financial aid flowed to the stricken city from throughout the nation. Tampans fled in terror, leaving their homes unguarded. Some looting occurred but remarkably this was not a serious problem.

Arsonists Burn Hotel

Small towns nearby were quickly afflicted. It was reported that yellow jack was carried from Tampa to Jacksonville in early 1888 by a "drummer" (travelling salesman) who died at the Mayflower Hotel. Arsonists burned the hotel a few days later in a futile effort to halt spread of the disease.

Nearly 5,000 cases were reported at Jacksonville that year, resulting in 427 deaths. It was thought that yellow fever was caused by microbes wafted through the air. The defense, therefore, consisted mainly of quarantine and fumigation. Yellow flags were nailed to front doors of houses sheltering patients.

Coatings of lime were applied to tree trunks, hydrants, curbs, fences and posts — a practice that survives today in the south as decoration. Street cars were fumigated daily. Streets were sprayed with a solution of bichloride of mercury. Barrels of pine tar were burned to "purify" the air. The oddest defense was discharge of cannon to "concuss" microbes. floating about. The state board of health issued printed leaflets for emergency treatment of yellow fever:

"Give a hot, mustard bath with the patient in a chair under a blanket for 15 minutes. After drying under the blanket, place the patient in bed with hot-water bottles. Give 5 grains of calomel to adults, half this amount to a child. After four hours, give a dose of castor oil or salts; also warm drinks of orange leaf tea. After the medicine acts, give ½ teaspoon of nitre in cool water every two hours, and an enema if necessary. Give 3 tablespoons of beef or chicken broth or gruel and discourage vomiting."

Doctors noted that "no red-headed people have contracted the disease and therefore appear to be immune." Authorities also observed that the number of cases declined after a frost, and was most prevalent in homes near swamps or in shade. Yet, they did not connect these phenomena with the abundant mosquitos.

Florida communities not affected mounted "yellow jack patrols" to turn away folks coming from epidemic areas. Railroad towns refused to let passengers alight. Waycross, Ga., would not even let trains from suspect areas pass through except with locked doors and at high speed.

The guard around Jacksonville numbered 433 armed men around the clock, according to Margaret Fairlie in the *Florida Historical Quarterly* of Oct. 1940. In rural areas, residents threw up road blocks to intercept and closely question travellers. The *New York Times* of Oct. 1887 reported: "Should the scourge at Tampa continue, strict quarantine will be established which will necessitate a change in the transportation of the West India mail. Some point below Tampa, probably Punta Gorda, will be selected to connect with the steamers."

This was the beginning of Punta Gorda as a deep-sea port. Col. Isaac Trabue's formerly vacant town had begun to grow with arrival of the Florida Southern Railway in July 1886 and construction of a large, resort hotel. A long dock at Punta Gorda (Fat Point) west of town enabled Morgan Line steamships to transfer railroad passengers to and from Cuba.

Refugees Intercepted

The new town of Punta Gorda, and its neighbor Charlotte Harbor Town across the bay, appreciated the prosperity that came with commerce from quarantines elsewhere. Nevertheless, they also dreaded yellow fever. Harbor patrols were vigilant in intercepting "refugees." The fishing industry there was just getting started to take advantage of the railroad and Trabue's ice factory. Strangers poured in.

Rev. George Gatewood, an early settler in what is now Charlotte County, in his old age published a memoir of those fearsome days:

"It was in 1886 that Capt. William H. Johnson — with L.T. Blocksom, John C. Lewis and J.J. McCann sailed up Charlotte Harbor in a 15-ton schooner and tied up at the Long Dock then just completed a mile west of Punta Gorda, then called Trabue. There they resumed operations in the wholesale fish business and began shipping north — over the new railroad — the catches they previously had been shipping from Tampa.

"Johnson, Blocksom and Lewis originally were from North Carolina. Upon Johnson devolved the bringing down from North Carolina the experienced men and equipment the company needed in operating on the Florida coasts. Several times when Capt. Johnson was on harbor trips — escorting company fishermen — he would be stopped by quarantine guards. However, Capt. Johnson had an effective way of meeting those situations. He knew his men had not been where yellow fever was prevalent. In each instance, it was urgent that the men reach their destination with as little delay as possible and get started on the work that was held up awaiting their arrival.

"One instance was the encounter of a guard posted in a 'shotgun' quarantine. Another was in the schooner that first brought the captain and others up the harbor to the Long Dock below Punta Gorda. The third instance was a subsequent entry of the harbor with a boat load of men whom the quarantine officer erroneously suspected of being from a place where yellow fever was known to exist.

"In polite but firm language, Johnson argued against being denied port-entry or permission to proceed to his destination. When logical argument failed, he pointed to his men — all of whom had the earmarks of rough seafarers — and urged: 'Well, look my men over and note how many there are. We've got to be going. You see no reason to prevent us from doing so, do you?'

"This always got them by. 'No' was the answer it brought each time." Capt. Johnson later became a pilot on the Boca Grande bar, dealt in real estate and was elected to the Charlotte County Board of Commissioners.

The yellow fever epidemic of 1887-88 — during which local settlers tried to ban ships from other ports — led to a demand for inspections of crew health. Punta Gorda's first newspaper, the *Beacon*, reported in July 1889: "State Physician Porter, in his report before the State Board of Health, recommended that an inspecting station and fumigating chamber be stationed at LaCosta Isle in Charlotte Harbor. He asked that a steam launch be provided that station for cruising between Punta Gorda and Punta Rassa, and also to Tampa and Manatee. The Board of Health did not accept the proposition but said it might act on his recommendation if urgently requested by the local Board of Health. Now, there is a chance for our local Board to take opportunity by the horns."

Establish Quarantine Station

It is not clear when the quarantine station was established at the south end of Gasparilla Island. In October 1893, the *Herald* reported: "Dr. J.F. Cronin is the genial quarantine officer at Boca Grande Pass."

Duties of the quarantine officer were to ride out with the Boca Grande Pass pilots to incoming ships and examine sailors for infectious diseases.

The vigilance of harbor authorities was successful. There is no evidence that the 1887-88 or subsequent yellow jack epidemics ever took a fearsome toll here.

F. French Townsend, center, and two companions are depicted at their Warm Mineral Springs camp in 1875 by the book Wild Life In Florida.

Chapter 14

MINERAL SPRING EXPEDITION RUGGED

The warm mineral springs at North Port have long been points of interest to travelers who provided much historical and archaeological information about these natural wonders.

A vivid description of Big Salt Spring, now known as Warm Mineral Spring, in its pristine state was written by F. Trench Townshend, an English adventurer. Starting in 1874, Townshend traveled in Cuba and Florida and in 1875, published an account of his journies.

He described the Myakka River as tidal, with banks about twelve feet in height. Townshend wrote: "On the surface of the river-water when boiled, there always appeared an oily scum, showing the presence of mineral oil. The river gradually widened as we descended. Hundreds of alligators watched us with startled eyes, slowly and silently sinking out of sight a few feet from our bows; water-turkeys or snake-birds uttered a shrill cry as they flew away from every overhanging tree, and kingfishers darted hither and thither, apparently bewildered by the strange sight of a canoe full of men.

"The evening sun touched with gold the rich green tops of the palms, and brightened the sombre hues of the live-oaks festooned with grey masses of Spanish moss. The bright green leaves of the wild vine and the crimson and white blossoms of the parasitic air-plant, reflected its own glowing image in the dark water. We seemed to be floating in a river of fire, I thought my mortal eyes would never look on any more gorgeous display of tropical colouring."

The party set up camp on the river bank. As they sat around the campfire that evening smoking, the guide was taken ill with a sharp attack of chills and fever. Townshend said, "So dosing him with quinine and whiskey, I made him roll himself up in a large heap of blankets inside my tent. Nest morning he appeared much better."

They were afloat before sunrise, and soon came to what the guide said was the mouth of Slough Creek, which would take them to within two miles of the salt spring.

Townshend described the creek's tortuous channel: "On either hand, swamp and rushes reached back to the pine woods some two miles distant. Banks of black mud and sand extended from the rushes into the creek swarming with alligators in incredible numbers.

"When obliged by the shallowness of the water to pass close to some of these banks, we were several times in great danger of being upset by these monsters. They would disdain to notice us until we were a few feet from them. Then a half-a-dozen would plunge into the water, right under our canoe, striking the bottom violently with their scaly backs and sending a shower of mud and water over us. Being from fifteen to twenty feet in length, they easily could have crushed our canoe with one scrunch of their powerful jaws.

Cowardly Alligators

"Were these animals not as cowardly as they are formidable in appearance, we, the first white men ever known to have ascended Slough reek in a boat, should not have lived to tell of our adventures."

As Townshend traveled up the creek and reached high prairie-land, alligators were less numerous. The stream became narrower and more shallow. Because of the sandbanks across the creek, they often had to wait until the tide rose to float over them.

Sometimes they had to unload the canoe and drag it across the bars. Townshend wrote, "Soon the obstacles became more formidable, tall cabbage-palms and water-oaks, having fallen across the creek, required to be cut through with an axe before we could advance, no light work with the thermometer at eighty-five degrees Fahrenheit in the shade, and mosquitoes nearly devouring our half-naked bodies.

"Slowly advancing thus about ten miles, we found the accumulation of fallen trees in the water so great that further ascent of the creek became impossible; landing therefore on the right bank, with knife and axe, we cut a passage through the tangled mass of jungle and forest trees, to the high prairie-land about a hundred paces distant."

They camped there, but as the creek water was too salty to drink, followed a line of bright green foliage and found "fresh but extremely black water." They returned to camp and "supping frugally on coffee, biscuit and salt pork, we crawled into our tents thoroughly worn out with our long day's labour. Soon the sound sleep of the wearied fell upon me, notwithstanding the mosquitoes and the groans of my tent companion, our guide, who was suffering much from fever and ague and from dysentery. Strange as it may seem in so hot a climate,throughout our camp life in Florida we frequently suffered much from cold in the early morning between the hours of three and six, though provided with thick coats and blankets and never undressing at night."

Anxious to find the salt spring, the party started out the next day to find a certain "bee-tree" which the guide said would guide them to the spring. Tramping through palmetto and paw-paw, they found and followed bees to a giant pine tree which stood alone. The guide then pointed out a clump of timber about three miles distant as the spot where they would find the salt spring.

Strong Sulphur Smell

Townshend's narrative continued, "Making our way across the prairie in that direction, as we approached the spring a strong smell of sulphur impregnated the air, and a light mist overhung the water. We had some difficulty in forcing our way through the dense growth of scrub-palmetto higher than our heads, acacia, oak and other trees which bordered the spring, but at last we stood on its brink.

The spring consisted of a circular basin about sixty yards in diameter; the water was clear as crystal except at the south-west edge, where it had a milky appearance, which our guide said sometimes extended over the whole basin. The bottom was covered with shells, and a brown slime which occasionally bubbled up to the surface and smelt like sulphur; the depth was from four to eight feet.

"Sinking my thermometer in the water I ascertained that the temperature at a depth of five feet was 90 degrees Fahrenheit, while that of the air was eighty-two degrees. To the taste, the water was salt and sulphurous, peculiarly nasty and offering a strong contrast to its marvel lously clear and tempting appearance.

"I was about to test the buoyancy of the water by bathing, when the scaly body of an alligator emerged from the opposite bank, and swimming rapidly towards us, made me alter my intention, and determine to remain on the safer element.

"Proceeding carefully to examine the basin, we found that two streams of most excellent fresh water flowed into it, one on the north, the other on the south-west. A considerable body of salt water flows out of the basin, within a few feet of the spot where the freshwater stream flows in on the south-west. I saw no fish in the basin, but large shoals of mullet in the salt stream flowing out. The bed and banks were very remarkable, being entirely composed of trap rock without a particle of sand or mud.

"Oleander, thorny acacia, laurel, bay paw-paw, cabbage palm, and many flowering shrubs unknown to me, formed a dense growth which marked the winding course of the two fresh streams across the prairie. The salt out-flow formed quite a small river fringed with forest trees, and a growth of palmetto almost impenetrable.

"The prairie and pine forest in the vicinity of the salt spring abounds in savannas of the sweetest grass, with circular clumps of the palmetto scattered through them. Numerous round ponds where the grass, rushes and water-lilies grow to a height of six or seven feet, have a depth of about two feet of water beneath. Nature provided the sweetest food, the thickest cover, and coolest shade. Thus, wild animals, birds, and reptiles of every description seek these tempting haunts, and afford capital sport to the hunters, both red and white, who may chance to visit the neighbourhood.

"After examining the basin of the salt spring, we scattered about in search of game which soon presented itself before me in a manner not altogether agreeable. Following the course of the salt outflow, I had struggled though the jungle which clothed the bank, forded the river, and clambering up the opposite bank had just reached the top, when I suddenly found myself within three paces of a black bear, sitting up so as to peer over the tops of the palmetto and see what was coming.

Frightened By Bear

"I confess that I was horribly frightened at the sight of the bear; but so, fortunately, was the bear at the sight of me. Before I could raise my rifle to my shoulder he had crashed into the thick palmetto and disappeared, leaving me uncertain whether I was most disappointed at not having got a shot at him, or relieved at not having been attacked in such a very awkward position."

Townshend found several herds of deer, all tame enough to get within easy shot, exotic birds, and on the muddy edges of ponds hundreds of snake tracks. He dispatched a large mocassin snake coiled in his track.

"Dysentery and fever again attacked our guide at night," wrote Townshend. "He was unable to hunt the following day, so we started across the prairie at sunrise with many misgivings as to finding our way back to camp again. When near one of the saw-grass ponds, we observed a large animal leisurely trotting towards us, which at first we supposed to be an ocelot, but as it approached, we perceived, from ts tawny grey colour, without spots or stripes, that it was a puma or Florida panther, also called the South American lion.

"Standing concealed behind a clump of palmetto it came boldly towards us without getting our wind. A rifle-bullet interrupted its course, when bounding into the long saw-grass of the pond before we could cut off its retreat, the puma disappeared with a savage growl to die a lingering death. We found it the following day stiff and stark among the tall reeds and water-lilies."

The hunters returned to camp without any palatable meat, as Townshend said the deer were almost unfit for food. He didn't explain why. According to Townshend's account, "hundreds of wild cattle roamed the area, distinguishable not only by not being branded, as all thecattle owned by settlers were, but also because of the difference in nature of the owned and ownerless animals. The former, being collected every year for numbering and branding, showed no sign of fear at the approach of man, but continued to graze quietly, or moving only a short distance, would stand and watch us as we moved about. The latter, on the contrary, would observe the greatest caution before venturing from the shelter of the forest into the open savannas, reconnoitering the ground carefully, pawing and sniffing the air before daring to feed, and on the slightest alarm dashing away like "a herd of buffalo."

The report noted that unless they were very short of food, they didn't kill any of the wild cattle.

The explorers enjoyed their camp time at Slough Creek, as they were able to enjoy the luxury of bathing every day after the morning hunt, and again in the evening. No alligators ventured so far up the shallow sandy creek. However, sand flies and mosquitoes attacked so fiercely they had to put on their clothes without drying off when they emerged from the water.

They felt no anxiety in leaving their canoe or supplies when they were hunting, as they knew there were no white men in that part of the country. A hunting party of Seminole Indians had left the area, as they learned by a "sign". The guide had pointed out some sticks stuck into the ground in a slanting direction, pointing to the downward current of the river. This was the Indian sign they were making their way back to the Everglades.

Telegraph line crew opened southwest Florida wilderness.

Chapter 15

WIRE ROAD OPENED CENTRAL FLORIDA

One of the most significant developments for Southwest Florida after the Civil War was construction of the International Ocean Telegraph Co. line to Havana via undersea cable from Punta Rassa. It facilitated a lucrative trade in cattle that had been opened up by Jacob Summerlin just before the war and continued to that country and to the Confederacy.

The idea for a Florida-Cuba telegraph cable was born in New York City — only a month or so after the end of the Civil War. — by financiers James A. Scrymser and Alfred Pell, Jr. The state of Florida was desperate for development and readily granted a 20-year franchise to build the line.

Construction began simultaneously at Gainesville and Ocala, heading south in as straight a line as possible in order to keep costs down and conserve the weak, telegraphic current. The line followed the west bank of Peace River to Fort Meade, then crossed to the east bank. Superintendent of the southern Florida route was George R. Schultz. Many years later he recalled the hardships in an interview by the *Fort Myers Press:* "I led my gang of huskies into the almost unknown wilds of central Florida," he said. "We traversed sawgrass glades, hammock land, pine barrens and

70

cypress swamps — rafting, wading waist deep and cutting a swatch through over 250 miles of almost unexplored country when alligators and rattlesnakes or moccasins menaced almost every step."

The construction crew carried huge lead-acid batteries, coils of copper wire, insulators, iron bolts and tools in mule-drawn wagons. Tents for sleeping and dining provided uncertain shelter from the frequent rains and ferocious mosquitos. Poles of "lighter" (turpentine) yellow pine trees were cut along the way — except when traversing the great Indian Prairie north and east of Arcadia. This stretch of bare land was open range for such cattle barons as Summerlin, Francis Hendry, Louis Lanier, James Whidden, Ziba King Joel Knight and the Lykes brothers.

About every 20 miles, a booster station was built. If possible, they were located near towns. Otherwise, the stations consisted of a shack for two men and shed for two horses. Station crews patrolled the line half-way between adjacent stations. A wagon track along the line was hacked out to bring in construction supplies. Thereafter it provided access to the line.

This primitive track through the wilderness was known as the Wire Road. It was hardly more than a trail, but it became the principal overland route for homesteaders to the Fort Myers area. From Fort Myers, the telegraph line ran to a recently abandoned Union Army barracks and dock at Punta Rassa. The Herculean task of stringing a line 250 miles through the jungle and swamps of southern Florida was accomplished in less than two months. For route, see map on page 7.

First Undersea Cable

In the meantime, the first undersea cable was being laid with great difficulty. A yellow fever outbreak delayed work for several months. Then the cable broke and had to be fished up and repaired. The final splice of line and cable was made at Punta Rassa on Sept. 10, 1867 — amid profuse congratulations by public authorities in both countries.

The telegraph operating and testing stations became meeting places for cattlemen who came to query brokers in Havana about prices. The cost of a 10-word message was $3.50 — a substantial sum in those days — but well worth it when thousands of dollars for a herd was involved.

First operator for the Joshua Creek station, later called Davidson, eight miles southeast of Arcadia, was William A. Johnson with his wife Mary (nee Brewer). They had taken up a homestead in 1864 at Pine Island near the Joshua Creek community. The "island" was so called because the clump of trees stood alone in the "sea" of the flat prairie.

In November, 1868, a cattleman came to the station to send a message. Johnson told the customer he would have to wait, as his wife was giving birth. The man waited patiently until a baby girl was delivered, then said, "I will give the child a starter herd of a bull and five cows for her

71

dowry if you will let me name her." Johnson agreed. The name chosen was Morning Glory, but was later corrupted to Mourning Glory.

Claude Jones of Arcadia, grandson of that baby girl, says she had her own brand. When at age 20 she married John Lee Jones, manager of Ziba King's properties at Fort Ogden, her herd had grown to 200 head. Jones later became Western Union telegraph operator at Fort Ogden and Johnson became tax collector.

In the beginning, IOTC set up a wilderness station 20 miles south of Joshua Creek and a few miles east of Fort Ogden. Then the crew encountered a vast cypress swamp where the line had to skirt the western edge. That swamp — on today's Babcock Ranch — is known as Telegraph Cypress. A booster station was located near the mid-swamp neck. From Telegraph Cypress, the line crossed the Caloosahatchee River at what is today's Olga but for many years was called Telegraph Station.

Became Western Union

Western Union Telegraph Co. bought a controlling interest in IOTC in 1873. When the Florida Southern Railway came down the Peace River valley in 1886, Western Union followed the railroad, sharing telegraph lines. IOTC stations were consolidated with Western Union offices at the nearest railroad town, and the old line was abandoned. DeSoto County Commission minutes of Nov. 12, 1888 record: "On petition, the Wire Road was discontinued."

The Western Union office at first was located at Glen (now vanished), a turpentine still near the mouth of Shell Creek where Florida Southern crossed on a trestle. The telegraph operator was Ellison A. White.

At Cleveland — platted a year earlier as a winter retreat for sportsmen — the manager of the Baxter House was John C. Hobson. His daughter, Willie, 16, married White. They moved the telegraph office to a honeymoon cottage there where the IOTC line joined the Western Union line. Willie quickly learned to operate the telegraph key.

Western Union moved its office to Punta Gorda's Dade Hotel in 1887 but apparently left an IOTC office at the White cottage. Probably Willie handled the meager overseas traffic there while her husband managed the Western Union office at Punta Gorda and opened the first telephone exchange in 1902. The *Punta Gorda Herald* noted in April 1904 that "the offices of Havana Cable moved this week from Cleveland to the Western Union here." The great inventor Thomas Edison, who once had been a telegraph operator, often stopped at the Dade (Seminole) hotel on his way to Fort Myers to watch Willie snap off a few messages.

The IOTC line to Punta Rassa was abandoned in 1942 when the undersea cable from Punta Rassa failed. Several other, more efficient, cables had been laid from Miami by then. IOTC was fully absorbed into Western Union in 1957.

A Roux Crate & Lumber Co. locomotive.

Chapter 16

ROUX CRATE HAD PRIVATE RAIL ROAD

Much has been made of the three, chartered railroads in what is now Charlotte County — Florida Southern which merged with Atlantic Coast Line, Charlotte Harbor & Northern, and Seaboard Air Line. The largest and most successful railroad, however, was privately owned and operated. It had been nearly forgotten until recognized on an old topographic map of Charlotte County showing the route of the 1867 International Ocean Telegraph Co. The maintenance road paralleling the telegraph line, though primitive, was the only overland entrance into southwest Florida. It was vacated by DeSoto County Commissioners in 1888.

We now know the Roux Crate & Lumber Railroad utilized part of the old "Wire Road" grade for a logging spur. The telegraph line and road headed straight south from Gainesville to Olga. From there, it passed through Fort Myers to Punta Rassa for connection to Havana, Cuba, over the world's first undersea cable. In its bee-line route, International skirted a vast swamp known today as Telegraph Cypress on the Babcock Ranch.

73

The Charlotte Harbor Area Historical Society collection of topographical maps show that RC&L meandered like a plate of spaghetti throughout east Charlotte County. RC&L operated in Charlotte County for only eleven years. In that short period it laid more track and made more money than any of the public railroads. While doing so, it timbered off half the county.

E.V. Babcock, an entrepreneur and mayor of Pittsburgh, came to Punta Gorda in the winter of 1911-12 to hunt and fish. He liked the area so much he commissioned timber scouts Cassius Carrier and Mr. McLean to buy thousands of acres of worked-out turpentine pines from the Perry M. McAdow Land and Turpentine Co. of Punta Gorda.

The deed of Feb. 9, 1912, does not specify the number of acres purchased — only the many parcels conveyed. We are aware that there were thousands of acres involved because the sale price was $800,000 — a huge fortune at that time. Half was tendered in cash and the remainder in 10 promissory notes of $40,000 each.

Four years later, Babcock-Carrier-McLean bought several thousand more acres from McAdow. The price recorded was "$100 and other valuable considerations." The two tracts constitute the core of what is the Babcock Crescent-B Ranch today.

Roux Crate & Lumber Company

The Roux Crate and Lumber Corporation began sometime before 1912 at Bartow by Edwin Theodore Roux and his two sons Edwin Timanius and Edwin Truman. About 1927, Roux obtained timber rights to the area around the newly constructed Seaboard Air Line Railroad dock four miles southeast of Cleveland at the intersection of State Road 74. He built a logging camp there called Saline — a play on the railroad name — and hauled timber to the SAL on his tramways. At Mulberry the cars of logs were switched to the Atlantic Coast Line for Bartow.

The Roux Crate and Lumber Co. in 1929 negotiated, but did not complete, a freight agreement with SAL. The Great Depression the following year engulfed the world, and business everywhere came to a standstill. SAL was hit hard by the economic crash. It closed its line to Fort Myers and Naples for lack of business and would have ceased altogether except for the Roux Co. freighting.

Roux survived because it had a contract with South American and South African gold mines for large, yellow pine tunnel supports. Such "lighter" timbers, naturally saturated with rosin, were strong and resistant to decay and termites.

The company purchased timber rights of the Babcock property in 1931. The terms were for "all standing and down pine timber suitable for sawmill purposes, 10 inches in diameter at the base, and the right to build (ox) team and (railroad) tram ways subject to removal in eight years." Roux then executed its old agreement with SAL which was in receivership by that time and under de-facto control by Charlotte Harbor & Northern railroad. Roux's lease with SAL was for two and a half miles of used "relaying rails, hinges, and angle bars to construct a single-track railroad in Charlotte County for use as a lumber road, connecting only with the Seaboard Air Line, for $295.30 per month."

Rails and connecting materials were to be delivered at Saline. The agreement was to terminate if freightage failed to gross at least $10,000 annually for SAL. The additional heavy-duty trackage was used to build a large wye and sidetrack four miles south of Saline to link Rouxville to the SAL. The heavy mine timbers were shipped from Tampa.

Judge Elmer O. Friday, now retired from the Punta Gorda Circuit Court, was nine years old when his father, Otto, was appointed superintendent of the Roux operation on the Babcock acreage. The senior Friday had been office manager at the Roux sawmill at Lake Garfield near Bartow. He moved his wife Mayo (Yates), Elmer, and daughter Lonnie, to Saline for eight months while the new logging camp was being built.

"We lived in a small house at Saline," recalls Judge Friday. "Occasionally I would ride out on a truck with the carpenters who were constructing the two-story commissary. I explored the woods and chased black snakes to keep out of their way."

Mr. and Mrs. Otto Friday at commissary chat with Mrs. Louis Kennedy.

"Site chosen for the headquarters was a bit of high grouind where the old Cypress Swamp telegrapah station was located. Spike Pen corral and two government, cattle dip tanks were located there later as cut-over timber land was converted to cattle pasture. When the cowboys came, they would play volley ball with me.

"We were in the depth of the Depression by then. Many cowboys were destitute. A cowman named Knox O'Neal was appointed by the Works Progress Administration (WPA) to head up a project giving them jobs dipping cattle, building pens and mending fences. They had a cabin camp near the dip tanks. When the WPA was discontinued, O'Neal went to Santo Domingo, and then to Arizona, to punch cattle. When Dad heard that O'Neal was back in the states he wrote and offered O'Neal a job as foreman at the ranch. O'Neal accepted and rode his horse all the way from Arizona. The journey took two months.

Telegraph Station

"There was a small A-frame of corrugated-tin panels at the old telegraph station under a big liveoak that still sheltered batteries and acid jugs. The apparatus was left behind when International Ocean Telegraph was bought by Western Union. Copper was salvaged, and the telegraph poles had long since rotted away. A track was laid from the Seaboard railroad to the site to transport building materials for the commissary, blacksmith shop and other auxiliary buildings. A diesel-power generator was brought in for a big refrigerator to keep meat for the loggers.

"We lived upstairs over the commissary which stocked necessities for the workers. As was common those days in isolated work camps, part of the wages of workers was issued in 'babbit' — coins of a metal alloy minted by the company. The remainder, as a worker requested, was banked by the company for future withdrawal. When a worker went to town to shop — Punta Gorda, Arcadia and Fort Myers were equidistant — he would come to the office and ask for some of his 'good money.'

"There were about an equal number of white and black sawyers, axmen, loaders and rail handlers. Only one house was built on site. It was for Tom Peters, head loader, who had a big family. The other employees lived with their families in houses and converted box cars brought from Saline on flatcars. White folks lived in one cluster of dwellings and black folks in another.

"White children were bussed to a small, frame school at Bermont about seven miles north on S.R. 31. Mr. Roux built a school at Telegraph Crossing for the black children. The Charlotte County school board hired a fine, handsome black teacher named Mrs. Cloretta Hall, and Mr. Roux reimbursed the school board for her salary. Dad always hired an old black lady — or a man too old to work but respected by the other blacks — to sort of hold things together in the 'quarters' where they lived.

76

"I still remember with great pleasure Rev. Richard "Hoss" Robinson, a sawyer and black preacher who held Sunday services at the camp. He had a magnificent, baritone voice. You could hear him coming down the road singing in the mornings before daylight. Then Tommy White, black fireman on one of the trains, would join in with his harmonius tenor voice.

"Mr. Roux kept a Punta Gorda doctor on retainer to come out to the camp twice a week to check on the health of the workers and their families. Dr. Alexander was the first. He was followed by Doctors Stebbins, Steeley and Bert Clement. We were a complete village widely known as Rouxville. The RC&L railroad operation was the most interesting activity to me. We had three wood-burning locomotives which were constantly loading logs or pushing track-laying machines around. It took two men working full time to cut firewood for the engines.

"Tramways were laid to the center of a wooded area. Loggers felled the trees, and mules dragged them to trackside. Later the mules lwere replaced with tractors operated by 'cat skinners.' A steam-operated boom lifted the logs onto 'trucks' of railroad wheels at each end of a load for transport to the Bartow mill.

When timber within convenient distance around the tramway was felled, the tracks and cross-ties were removed piecemeal for relaying elsewhere. Spikes were pulled out by a heavy pry-bar. Plates were unscrewed by two men with a long-handled wrench. In the haste to keep

School bus ferried Rouxville kids. Elmer Friday fourth from left.

production going, the steel gang would overlook some spikes and connecting plates. After a tramway was dismantled, we kids would scour the route for leftover hardware. We got a half-cent for spikes and seven cents for plates. It was hard work because the material was heavy.

"When the Babcock timber lease expired in 1939, Dad stayed on at Rouxville to superintend a transition to cattle ranching for Mr. Babcock. Mr. Roux gave up the logging and sawmilling.

"Dad was elected vice-president of the Southwest Florida Cattlemen's Association. In 1948, he was persuaded by the Association to give up the job as ranch manager and accept appointment at Deland as director of the statewide tick eradication program. O'Neal was promoted to ranch superintendent. E.V. Babcock died that same year; and his son, Fred, took over responsibility for the ranch — dividing his time between it and the Babcock lumber mills in Pennsylvania and other places up north.

"About 18 months later, California and Texas canceled their embargoes against Florida cattle so the tick program here was discontinued. We then moved to Punta Gorda, and Dad became a real estate broker. Lonnie and I attended Charlotte High School. We both went to college — Lonnie thereafter becoming a teacher at Punta Gorda, and I was elected state senator. I was appointed to the Appellate Court for workmen's compensation by Gov. Ruben Askew, and elected to the Circuit Court at Punta Gorda in 1982."

Range Rider

The late Allison Tomlison, security supervisor of the Babcock Ranch, also was a boy there in 1946 when his father, Alfred, came as a range rider and tick-infestation inspector for the state.

"Our home was a boxcar," said Tomlison. "I went to the Bermont school by bus. Our teacher was Mrs. Mildred (Goff) Knight. Bermont was the site of a settlement at the corner of state roads 74 and 31. All is gone now. The school house steps of cement are all that remain.

"My house today on the ranch is where the old telegraph station was located. The tin lean-to was still there when I was a boy. You could see traces of the old Wire Road that snaked through Telegraph Cypress Swamp and went on down to the wooden bridge at Olga — detouring now and then around ponds.

"The Roux railroad was laid down on the Wire Road for a few miles. Both have been paved over for a ranch road from our air strip. The old railroad bed west of the ranch office — the original Rouxville commissary — also is paved and the main entrance to the ranch today.

"I was born in LaBelle and grew up in the saddle. After the ticks were brought under control, my father went to work for the Lykes brothers' big timber and cattle ranch in Glades County. Now, I do here what I like to do best."

Sharpies and nets at Buchan's Landing in Englewood early 1920's.

Chapter 17

SHARPIES BEST FISHING BOAT

WARNING -- THE FOLLOWING ARTICLE CONTAINS GRAPHIC SAILING TERMS AND MAY BE CONFUSING TO LANDLUBBERS

Of all the sailing ships that plied the waters of Charlotte Harbor, none was more useful or distinctive than the "sharpie" —so called because of its long, sharp prow. Other distinctive characteristics were its flat or slightly V-bottom, shallow draft made possible by a hinged center board instead of a fixed keel, and stubby mast capable of carrying sail without need of supporting "shroud" lines.

A curious feature was the sharpie's masts which were not fixed in place. They sat in a greased socket which enabled the masts and light, firmly attached "sprits" to pivot in tandem. The sprit was a light stick thrusting the sail's outboard "leach" edge taut into the wind, held by a line to the stern. The sail was loose-footed with its inboard "luff" edge strapped to the mast. This rigging allowed the sail and sprit to be furled against the mast; and the lot taken down for rowing or low bridges.

Because of these innovations, the sharpie was ideal for lone fishermen. It was easy to build and required a minimum of rigging. One man could handle the sail of a one-masted 25-foot vessel, and he could cast nets with out interference of shrouds. Two-masted sharpies up to 40 feet long could be handled by two men but were capable of carrying a crew of four to manage mile-long "pound" nets.

The type of sails sharpie skippers used varied from area to area. A popular sail-cut in Charlotte Harbor was one that lopped off the "clew" —

or lower, outboard corner — so that several boats could work close together in managing nets. The extra corner of sail created was kept taut by a short, vertical "club" at the end of the sprit. Large sharpies requiring more sail surface avoided tall masts — which more easily tip over a ship and require shrouds — by lopping off the top corner "head" of sail instead of the clew. The extra corner created in this instance was tautened by an extra long sprit, or by a "gaff" pole hinged to the mast head.

The triangular "leg-o-mutton" sail — with its "foot" attached to a swinging, horizontal "boom" — was popularized after the turn of the century. It is the universal sail cut today for small boats.

Interestingly, the sharpie evolved from the native American dugout canoe, according to marine historian Howard Chapelle. French fur-trappers are said to have first used Indian dugouts, then two dugouts lashed together in order to carry more cargo. Finally they devised the "bateau" comprised of planks from three logs.

One log was hewed maximum width in a sort of rounded keel pointed at each end. Two other log-planks were fashioned as sides and pinned to the bottom piece. Cross braces fore and aft stiffened the craft and provided attachment for a small mast and sprit. Sidewise slippage was controlled by a "daggar board" lashed to the side.

The bateau was primitive, but it was well suited to rivers and bays. The design was translated — sharp prow and stern — into the sharpie about 1835 in New Haven, Connecticut. There still was no forc-and-aft keel. Cross planks were simply nailed to the side boards. A strong "keelson" plank was nailed inboard on the cross planks from stem to stern.

Remington in sharpie *King*.

Charlotte Harbor sharpie 1890.

This provided a "step" for the mast, and purchase for a slit-well housing a center board that could be lowered or raised as necessary.

A sharpie with squared off stern and center-post rudder — able to operate safely in rough waters — was introduced into the Carolina Sounds about 1875. The following year, a seaworthy sharpie named *Egret* was employed to carry mail from Palm Beach to Biscayne Bay. About the same time, Carolina fishermen brought the design to Cedar Key on the Florida west coast. The exact date sharpies began to appear in Charlotte Harbor is unknown. It could not have been later than 1880 because fishing was a big activity at Charlotte Harbor Town, Lemon Bay, and Gasparilla Island by then.

Four technologies came together at Punta Gorda to turn a local fishing business into a major industry. They were the Florida Southern Railroad in 1886, Western Union Telegraph the next year, the Ice Factory in 1891, and the sharpie. Fishermen in their little sharpies caught the fish. The telegraph flashed orders from big cities up north. Ice kept fish fresh while express trains rushed sea food to northern markets..

Sharpie Town

Most sharpie skippers and their families lived at Charlotte Harbor Town or up the bay near a dock at the foot of today's Cooper Street. The latter close-knit little community was known as Sharpie Town.

A mass-immigration of North Carolina fishermen in 1895 arrived under contract to the Punta Gorda Fish & Ice Co. They built two-masted sharpies with larger cargo capacity.

By 1905, even the larger sharpies could not keep up with demand. Gradually the two-masted schooner with gaff-rigged mainsails, top sails and jib became the mainstay of Charlotte Harbor fishermen. The hull was broad and therefore had a relatively shallow draft. Wind slippage was minimal because of an external keel. The great sail area was carried by only two masts and therefore was as easily handled by three or four men as with the sharpie.

With greater driving power, the fishing schooner could tow a string of skiffs to the fishing grounds, carry ice aboard, and haul heavy loads of fish back home. Charlotte Harbor schooners were shorter and narrower than their more famous New England cousins. Yet, they were cost effective for bulk freight.

Motor launches began to edge out the two-masted Charlotte Harbor schooners after the First World War. The launches were fast — a prime advantage with perishable fish. The colorful age of sail, led by the humble sharpies, was over.

Phosphate and drying sheds on the Peace River near Hull.

Chapter 18

SOAPY STONE WAS BIG BUSINESS

The state of Florida watched, with keen interest, development of its first phosphate mining operation. It wanted to share the profits.

"Soapy stone" had been discovered in the Peace River as early as 1860, but no one at the time realized its value. By 1890, however, G.W. Scott, a fertilizer manufacturer at Atlanta, Ga., quietly bought thousands of acres of land through which the river flowed and filed mining claims. Scott then sold the property to Joseph Hull and Hugh Comer who formed the Charlotte Harbor Phosphate Co. to mine phosphate pebbles from the river. Soon a half dozen other companies rushed to cash in on the bonanza. A town soon known as Hull sprang up on Lake Hale, east of Peace River, to accommodate phosphate workers. A few homes, church and cemetery are still there off Route 17.

Florida officials surmised in 1893 that the phosphate companies were mining navigable waters which, by law, the state owned. Therefore, the state filed suit against Charlotte Harbor Phosphate Co. for payment of minerals illegally taken. The company defended its claim by contending that portion of the river within its claim was not navigable "for general commerce" and therefore was private property.

Depositions from local citizens with detailed knowledge of the river were taken at Arcadia in Sept. 1893 and January 1894. A jury trial to decide the issue was held at Jacksonville Federal Court in 1896. The jury held for the company.

A copy of the depositions, in the possession of Claude Jones, retired president of the DeSoto Abstract Co., Arcadia, reveal details heretofore unknown about phosphate mining and the river. For example, we learn that the first superintendent of Charlotte Harbor Phosphate Co. was F.W. Hazlehurst. His wife was a sister of Joseph Hull and remained at Bartow. Hazlehurst went home about once a month.

He said he came to the Hull claim in August of 1890 with "five or six Negroes." They laid down a 2-mile railroad spur to the Florida Southern Railway main line. Then they built drying sheds, a dredge, flat-bottom barges and a "little steamer" to move everything around.

Test ore was taken from a sand bar by the African-Americans with picks, shovels, and wheelbarrows. Mining by dredge began in April of 1891. By the end of the year, the company had built three more dredges and three paddle-wheel tug-boats named *Maud S,, Mary Blue* and *Agnes*.

Hazlehurst used the little steamer as his command ship, going out in it every day to position the dredges. Workers' pay ranged from $1.50 to $2.25 for a 10-hour day, six days a week, and "sometimes on Sundays."

Little Environmental Damage

Contrary to popular understanding, Phosphate rarely was taken from the bed of Peace River, and little environmental damage was done. Enormous catches of fish were netted in the harbor during the river mining era and for 50 years thereafter.

Hazlehurst testified that the principal source of phosphate pebbles was the many sand bars that were exposed during the low-water months November to May. Banks without trees also were dredged. Wooded banks were by-passed to avoid toppling trees onto the dredges.

Phosphate pebbles washed from the banks naturally rolled down the river bed "like marbles" until stopped by a bar. Some mined bars would re-form within a year and were dredged a second and third time. Phosphate pebbles were sifted out by revolving screens before being routed to waiting barges.

Wet phosphate was piled into drying sheds to drain, then loaded onto to railroad cars or "lighter barges." Most of the phosphate was shipped to Punta Gorda's "long dock" by Florida Southern Railway gondolas for reloading into ocean going freighters. Approximately a third of the mineral was towed in barges to Long Dock by Capt. Albert F. Dewey who bought the *Mary Blue* and lighter barges from Charlotte Harbor Phosphate in 1892.

Fully loaded barges could navigate the lower reaches of Peace River only during the rainy season — the middle of June to middle of September. To make it worthwhile for Dewey to operate during the short barging period, the company hired him as their agent to supervise all loading at Long Dock.

Rail shipment is confirmed by bills of lading subpoenaed from E.A. Faulkner, agent for Florida Southern, who lived on the 4,200-foot long dock near today's Punta Gorda Isles Yacht Club. His records show that the first shipment of phosphate by rail occurred Aug. 21, 1891. From then until Sept. 27, 1893, 40,000 tons came via rail.

Names and nationalities of ships, given by Dewey in his deposition, provide an insight into the international make up of the phosphate trade. British sailing barks were *Muder, King Alfred,* and *Bomba.* British steamers were *Black Prince, Marima, Beta, B.T. Robinson, Cyrona, Haverton, Maria Euguena, Chittagong, Angerton,* and *Sultran.* The legal case hinged on the depth of water at various places on the Peace River, and at what times of the year. Consequently there was extensive questioning about the draft of the vessels that plied the River — every thing from skiffs drawing only three inches, to sailing vessels drawing four feet.

Floating General Store

One of the latter was brought up to Fort Ogden during the high water season by Jacob Wotitzky trying to sell merchandise from his Punta Gorda store. The venture was unsuccessful.

Largest vessel was the U.S. Government "snag boat" whose duty in 1883, before mining, was to remove sunken logs and over-hanging branches. The flat-bottom barge was 70 feet long, 20 wide, and drew only 14 inches of water. One old timer described it as "large as a court house with many rooms." It was "warped" up river by carrying 400-foot ropes ahead, tying them to sturdy trees, and hauling in the rope by windlass.

The contraption was commanded by General D. Lang. At the time of his deposition, Lang was private secretary to the Florida governor and secretary of the newly formed Phosphate Board. His mission was to open the stream to navigation six months of the year by vessels of 24-inch draft all the way to Fort Meade.

Unfortunately, 1883 was an abnormally dry year, and the snag boat got only a half-mile past Big Charley Apopka Creek before the appropriation ran out. Lang left the snag boat under the care of Dennis Driggers to await a new appropriation, but such never came. Gen. Lang returned in September 1884 with five men to drift the snag boat downstream with great difficulty and tow it to Cedar Keys.

Strangest vessel on the Peace River was the *Perpetual Motion,* built in 1882 by Harris Raulerson and Peter Messer who lived three miles upstream from Arcadia. Raulerson described it as "a flat-bottom concern of my make, about 32 feet long and 10 feet wide, drawing six inches light and 18 inches loaded." The boat was propelled by two paddle wheels, one on each side, turned by two Black men at cranks. Raulerson hauled "country produce about every three weeks to Knight's store at Hickory Bluff, also known as Charlotte Harbor. Lawrence and Tom Knight had a schooner with which they carried oranges, potatoes, hogs, chickens, and cow hides to Tampa."

On the return trip, Raulerson would carry flour, salt, coffee, grits, whiskey, tobacco and other bulk commodities to Ziba King's store at Fort Ogden. Raulerson sold the hand-driven vessel in early 1883 to Wade Altman who very soon sold it in March 1883 to George Washington Williams. The latter operated the *Perpetual Motion* until Florida Southern came down the east bank of Peace River in 1886. After that time, there was no need for general commerce on the stream.

The *Perpetual Motion* has been confused with a similar craft built by Sam Mauck and his son John to tow logs to his sawmill at Lettuce Lake. He attempted to turn the paddle wheels with small steam engines. John Cross, who founded the town of Liverpool in 1880, now disappeared, testified that he went to Mauck's mill to ride on the maiden voyage of *Mauck's Folly*.

"They never got the engines working together," said Cross. "One would stop and the other would run the boat into the bushes. I caught the paddle wheel and held it as against the engine while the engine was running. The boat was a failure for lack of proper power. Mauck broke up the two engines and sold one to Wade at his landing on the Peace River. Williams brought it up in his hand-cranked boat."

Jumped Across The River

Other witnesses testified that the Peace River would carry eight or nine feet of water in the rainy season, while they crossed it on stepping stones at several places during the winter without getting their shoes wet. Two men said they routinely jumped across the river where it narrowed to eight feet wide.

Much testimony was devoted to the Charlotte Harbor tides which were noticeable at Liverpool. The consensus was that above Liverpool, the tide was not noticeable except when north winds drove the river down, and south winds "swelled" it an inch or so.

The jury had no difficulty in deciding Peace River did not carry enough water for general commerce, and that the Charlotte Harbor Phosphate Co., therefore, was entitled to keep the money from all it had sold.

Mott Willis in naphtha-motor ferry at Charlotte Harbor Town old dock.

Chapter 19

FERRY CAPTAIN, OYSTER SHUCKER, STORE KEEPER

The town of Charlotte Harbor, oldest in the county, is undergoing a major face-lift with new zoning which will encroach on the last vestiges of its historic heritage unless steps are taken to preserve the few structures remaining from another century. Chief of these is the Mott Willis store on Bay Shore Drive near Sibley-Bay St. It last was used as a rehearsal hall for the Charlotte Players but since has been demolished.

The former general store was constructed by Mott Willis and his son Claude in 1922 to replace their older store built by the Knight family during or shortly after the Civil War.

The first village on the north shore of Charlotte Harbor was called Hickory Bluff. It sprang up around a dock built during the war to load cattle for a run through the Union blockade at Boca Grande Pass. The dock was built by cattlemen Joel Knight and Jacob Summerlin and by Capt. David McKay, owner-operator of the side-wheel steamer *Scottish Chief* out of Tampa.

Joel's oldest son was a partner in the Henry Knight-Perry Wall hardware store at Tampa Bay. Sometime between 1863 and 1870, the Knights built a two-story square-front store at the foot of the Hickory Bluff dock to distribute merchandise brought back from blockade runs.

A post office was granted to John Bartholf at Hickory Bluff in 1876. Bartholf, a former Union officer at Fort Myers, named the post office Charlotte Harbor to illustrate the entire area served — that from Gasparilla

86

Island on the west to Harbor View on the east. In time, the cluster of homes, store, Methodist church and school around the dock became known as the name of the post office. Joel Knight died in 1879, and his son Thomas Samuel was appointed executor of the estate. Earliest tax records in the DeSoto court house for 1886 indicate that Tom Knight and his brother Charles Lefley in 1886 platted the area around the cattle dock as "Knight's Addition to Charlotte Harbor."

They were listed as the tax payers for the original store on Lot 3 of Block 4 fronting Bay Shore Drive. However, Knight-Wall of Tampa was listed as the tax payer in 1888 and continued so until 1901 when the property was transferred to W.L. Thorpe. He sold the store to Artie G. Hayman in 1902.

A newspaper, *The South Florida Home* published every second Wednesday, was started at Charlotte Harbor in 1889 by Editor Young G. Lee. The issue of Feb. 19, 1890, advertised: "KNIGHT BROS. — Dealers in heavy groceries. Highest market price paid for country produce of all kinds. T.S. Knight, C.L. Knight and E.C. Knight."

Killed 11 Turkeys

The same issue noted: "Messers T.S., C.L., E.C. and Frank Knight and W.F. Nabers and Perry Wall returned Saturday on the sloop *Flossie*, Capt. Boggess, from a wild turkey hunt up the Myakka. They killed only 11 turkeys, the weather being unfavorable."

The first issue of the *Punta Gorda Herald*, published Feb. 17, 1893, provides interesting information about the Knight store: "There was a dance given at the hall over Knight's store in Charlotte Harbor last evening, and a delightful time was reported."

Lot 2, next door, was sold by T.S. and C.L. Knight to George A. Irwin in 1887. Subsequent owners were Grover Cochran, Mrs. Mourning Glory Jones of Arcadia, and Artie G. Hayman. The latter also bought the original Knight store in 1902.

Hayman sold the Knight store on Lot 3 of Block 3 for $650 — and the vacant Lot 2 for $150 — to Mott Willis in 1912. Willis was a fisherman specializing in oysters. He had a shucking shed on the beach across Bay Shore Drive from his store. When he was oystering, his wife and son Claude kept store. The family maintained living quarters above the store.

Mott Willis was a hard-working entrepreneur. In addition to his oyster business and store, he had a naphtha launch and operated a ferry service.

Esther McCullough was a school teacher the Charlotte Harbor school from 1914 to 1916. Her family and home were located at Solana so Esther took Willis's ferry across the harbor every Friday afternoon and Monday morning — spending school nights at the Matthew Giddens home.

The original Knight store had deteriorated by 1922. Then, Willis and son Claude cast concrete blocks at their oyster shucking shed and built a new, two-story store on Lot 2 next door to the original Knight store. Willis then tore down the older building.

Mrs. McCullough and Anson Gaskill recall the original Knight-Willis wood-frame store. The T.A. Stephens drug store was adjacent on lot 4. "It was a wonderful place to get cool fountain drinks," says Mrs. McCullough.

Gaskill says Willis' general store sold everything from toothpicks to saddles. It was the social center of the town. Old men sat on benches under the store balustrade and whittled as they swapped yarns. We kids played in the dirt street near by.

"Mr. Willis had a horse and wagon hitched there to deliver orders," recalls Gaskill with a chuckle. "One day I threw a cat on the horse's back and it tore up the wagon trying to throw the cat off.."

Charlotte Harbor Town about 1915. Old cattle dock at left. White building is J.H. Coram furniture store. Building at left is second Knight general store. At right is Willis' oyster-shucking shed.

Gilchrist learned surveying at West Point.

Chapter 20

MANGROVE MARSHES HARD TO SURVEY

Albert W. Gilchrist, Punta Gorda's most famous hometown hero, is best remembered as the governor of Florida 1909-13; but not so well known is his early exploits as a surveyor.

Thus, we are indebted to the research of Dr. Joe Knetsch — historian for the Florida Department of Environmental Protection, and to the master's thesis by Ric A. Kabat, Florida State University — for a view of Gilchrist's career laying out property lines in America's last frontier.

Gilchrist learned to survey at the U.S. Military Academy, West Point. However, he failed a course in higher mathematics during his third year. He had sought an Army career and did well in his other studies — including the first two years of engineering.

Gilchrist never made any excuses for his failure in one course and resigned rather than matriculate last in his class. His family said he neglected his studies during that third year in despondency over the death of his sweetheart. It is true that Gilchrist remained a bachelor all his life even though he was popular with the ladies.

One of Surveyor Gilchrist's first clients was Henry B. Plant, a railroad baron building a Georgia-North Florida system after the Civil War. Plant bought controlling interest in the Florida Southern Railway, then racing him toward Tampa. Plant directed Florida Southern to continue south to sparsely settled Charlotte Harbor. He hired Gilchrist to lay out the right-of-way to newly platted but uninhabited town of Trabue — soon renamed Punta Gorda.

Gilchrist completed the task in 1886 then resigned his position with Florida Southern to cast his lot at what was then the southernmost railroad terminal in the United States. He correctly perceived great opportunities in the untouched land certain to boom with a railroad. (For details see chapter 29, *Our Fascinating Past: Charlotte Harbor Early Years.*)

Gilchrist embarked on a career of real estate, politics and frontier surveying. New research by Dr. Knetsch indicates the future governor continued active as a surveyor longer than was thought heretofore. Dr. Knetsch was the first speaker at the newly organized Boca Grande Historical Society. Following are excerpts from his presentation:

Impossibilities Not Required.

Simple instructions can be so deceiving. How difficult could it be to determine the "mean high water" line of a beach? In the mangrove jungles of coastal southwest Florida, this could be one of the most difficult assignments given to anyone.

U.S. Deputy Surveyor Albert Gilchrist had little idea of the difficulties he was about to encounter when in June of 1897 he signed a contract to measure Sanibel and Captiva Islands.

Gilchrist had surveyed lands on Gasparilla and LaCosta islands in 1888 and discovered that much of the area had not ever been surveyed because of a ban by the commissioner of the General Land office in Washington. What surveys had been made were wildly inaccurate.

The islands of Pine, Gasparilla, LaCosta, Sanibel and Captiva were surveyed in the 1875 by Horatio Jenkins, a carpetbag politician who prospered as part of the "Ring" political machine of Duval County.

Jenkins' abilities as a politician far outstripped those he possessed for surveying. A.W. Barber, examiner of surveys, wrote in Jan. 1900: "The original survey of 1875 was grossly inaccurate and largely fraudulent. The section lines exist only on paper, by protraction."

Frustrated by lack of a "starting" on Gasparilla, Gilchrist wrote the surveyor general: "I would note that our country is rapidly settling up, owing to the advent of the rail road.

"There are numbers of islands occupied by citizens who are anxious to secure their land titles and are willing to pay for the survey. The action of the commissioner in ordering no more surveys of islands works an unjust hardship on our locality and Charlotte Bay in particular."

Gilchrist knew of the labor involved in island surveying. However, he was not prepared for the extensive criticism he was to encounter from some settlers he was attempting to assist, his superiors in Washington, and Florida Surveyor General William Bloxam.

Gilchrist in early June of 1897 drew up a plat for a town he named Boca Grande on six blocks of high ground on Gasparilla Island. Then he left his office on June 20 and headed to Sanibel by the morning steamer to begin fulfilling his surveying contract.

Upon landing, Gilchrist wrote the then surveyor general W.H. Milton, for instructions: "As to the location of the lines as regards the points and natural features as shown — especially on the harbor side — I am satisfied are irregular.

"I have checked enough of Jenkins' work on LaCosta and Gasparilla islands to know this. It would pay me to traverse the harbor side before I attempted to connect them by section lines. I have heard that this was measured by counting the strokes of the oar."

Capt. Sam Ellis, a Sanibel resident, confirmed that Jenkins' rowboat sightings for Tarpon Bay were set "by counting three feet per oar-stroke, and the map shows the land one mile too far west."

A week later, Gilchrist left for Pine Island to establish a base line which could be continued on Sanibel. On July 4 he wrote Milton that he had made two triangulations from Sanibel to Pine Island.

As if the lack of information were not enough, the rainy season began. Gilchrist wrote: "I am getting along fairly well. A storm is now raging. It has been raining for nearly three days with a howling wind.

Bucket Of Mosquitoes

"Mosquitoes are, of course, not bad during the storm. One of my men expressed the status fairly at Pine Island when he said if you swung a bucket around your head the bucket would be full of mosquitoes. The work is tedious owing to the inaccuracy of original survey. Only about one-third or one-fourth of these lines were ever run. Chances are that Jenkins crossed over in an open space and set the corners from the Gulf, avoiding the mangrove swamps.

"No posts can be set where there is mangrove growth because mean-high-water is often a mile from shore. Nor can any meander line be run at MHW along the mangroves. It would take five men a week to cut a line in red mangroves bordering the low beach."

Gilchrist reported in late August that the Sanibel survey was nearly complete. For all his work, the surveyor put in a bill for $566.83 which was more than expected. The surveyor general questioned the running of more lines than were contracted. Gilchrist again explained the necessity of re-doing Jenkins' lines: "Being far off from communication, and knowing the survey had to be finished up, I completed the work at my own risk. Instead of diminishing the amount, if there is any way of estimating the Hell of mosquitos, sand flies and mud 10 to 12 inches deep, I hope the estimate will be increased by the addition of connecting lines."

The dispute over payment dragged on for months. A new surveyor general, R.L. Scarlett, in September 1898 demanded Gilchrist come to Tallahassee to discuss the matter. However, by this time Gilchrist had volunteered in the Spanish-American War and was at Guantanamo, Cuba.

Scarlett, who thought Gilchrist was jumping ship to avoid making corrections in his survey, demanded that he abandon the Army and finish his contract. Capt. Gilchrist replied: "Under no circumstances could I leave in the face of the enemy, if we had one, or in the face of an epidemic, never. I have waited nearly a year on your department for no fault of yours or your deputy, and I trust you will wait on me, especially as I am here in the government employ." Scarlett was furious and scrawled on the face of Gilchrist's letter: "Merits no response."

Senator Intervenes

Into the fray stepped an old political acquaintance of Gilchrist's — U.S. Senator Sam Pasco of Florida. Pasco wrote Scarlett in Feb. 1899 and played down the alleged "objectionable" tone of Gilchrist's last letter. The senator reminded the surveyor general that "it is proper to grant all possible indulgence to those who have taken up arms in defense of the country during the period war." Sen. Pasco also noted that he had contacted the commissioner of the General Land Office, Scarlett's boss.

By May 1899, Gilchrist was back on the job, attempting to find non-existent lines on Captiva Island. He made necessary corrections by the end of June and filed for payment due for the original work.

Before final payment, the government sent down A.W. Barber to take pictures of the mangroves with a new camera.

Reported Barber: "In Gilchrist's original returns, he stated he had to either run outside in the water or back in dense brush almost impassable, so he went outside."

The surveyor general was disposed to think this inexcusable, and a sharp correspondence ensued over it. "I assured the deputy that the department did not require impossibilities, that the meandered shore line was not regarded as a strict boundary, and that his method would receive no further criticism. I cannot see how Deputy Gilchrist can have made any profit on this work. Certainly he has not intentionally slighted it."

Barber's report smoothed the way between Scarlett and Gilchrist. Scarlett even offered another contract, on St. Andrews Bay; but, because of other commitments, Gilchrist had to refuse.

Writing to Scarlett in March 1901, Gilchrist declared: "I have received the joyful news that I will be paid for the excess of my contract. I feel very grateful. I thank you and the others who recommended it."

Adrian Jordan (center) earned Master of Arts degree at Emery College.

Chapter 21

CRUSADING EDITOR ALSO PRANKSTER

The most colorful publisher-editor of the *Punta Gorda Herald* was Adrian Pettus Jordan who guided that pioneer newspaper from 1901 to 1919 despite harassment by his political enemies and an attempted assassination.

The *Herald* was founded in 1893 by Robert Kirby Seward, and he guided it through the early struggles. Yet, it was Jordan who made the paper into a state-wide institution through his crusade against railroad monopoly and through his wonderful "fish tales."

Adrian was born in 1850, the son of Rev. Junius and Frances (nee Pettus) Jordan, at the family plantation "Glennville" near Eufaula, Alabama. There, and at the Jordan town house in Eufaula, he was reared in the ante-bellum life of southern aristocracy. Slaves made his clothes until he was 10. Then his father, a Methodist preacher, took him to New York City for a complete wardrobe of "store bought" clothes.

The Civil War greatly reduced the affluence of his family, but at age 17 he was sent to Emory and Henry College in Virginia. Receiving a Master of Arts degree he accepted a teaching position in a school at Yalaha, Fla.

93

Jordan's early experiences in Florida were typical of the wild heartland shortly after the "War for Southern Independence." His adventures there were recounted many years later in a biographical memoir written by his son Adrian Crenshaw Jordan.

"When Adrian P. Jordan came to Florida in the 1870's, the railroads had not penetrated far down the peninsula," wrote his son. "The rivers were the important arteries of travel. From Jacksonville there was much travel by steamboat into the heart of the state. At what was then Moss Bluff on the St. Johns River, he was met by an ox-drawn conveyance on which he continued his journey. At Yalaha he remained for a year teaching school. He had board and lodging at the Phares home. Quite a number of families had settled there and were living well for frontiersmen.

"Fish, game and cattle — with farm crops and fruit they produced from the land — were ample for their needs. They had surpluses to exchange at the local store, or for cash when they trekked to distant trading points. In that new country, Mr. Jordan found much time for hunting and fishing. The Phares family kept a rowboat. Every few days he paddled out into Lake Harris and return in a little while with fish aplenty for all the household, including two other boarders.

"With a muzzle-loading shotgun, Mr. Jordan kept his landlady's table supplied much of the time with meat fresh from the forests. The woods abounded in deer and bear, but he hunted only the smaller game.

Stalked Wild Animals

"He was fond of stalking wild animals, not to kill them, but to learn their habits. He was impressed and amused by native black bears. They climbed high in trees to eat the tender buds. Bears could smell a man from afar. No matter how high they might be, when they got a whiff of a man, the bears would suddenly loose their hold and drop crashing through limbs and vines to the ground. Landing with a thud, they would grunt, jump up and scamper away so fast a person on foot could not overtake them."

After a year at Yalaha, Jordan returned to his home in Alabama and "read law" for a local attorney. He stretched his small salary by writing news for the *Columbus, Miss., Index*. Before long, Jordan qualified for the Alabama Bar. He had an active practice, and gained notice by gathering and publishing evidence that convicted the lieutenant governor of accepting a bribe from a fugitive murderer. He gave up law to become a "professor" of Latin at the University of Columbus (Miss.).

The teaching profession interested Jordan more. In 1877 he returned to Florida as a teacher at Rock Hill, Sumter County. Again he became a boarder at the homes of his pupils. One of these homes was that of Mr. and Mrs. M.C. Crenshaw, farmers and parents of Agnes, a student of Adrian's. The two fell in love and were married in Dec. 1881 — one month shy of Agnes' 15th birthday. He was 31.

Agnes' brother, George, declared that Adrian "was not grown up when he married because he liked to tell yarns and perpetrate practical jokes on folks." For example, another of Agnes' brothers, John Crenshaw, maintained "bachelor hall" — a one-room cabin behind the main house. The little structure had developed a crack in the wall. A cat had curled up in the corner, and its tail dangled through the crack. Adrian grabbed the cat's tail and gave it a yank. The ensuing shriek of fright by the cat alarmed John who could not free the animal. John ran for a crowbar with which to rescue his cat. Upon returning he found the cat streaking for the woods, and Adrian convulsed in laughter.

The newly wed Jordans took up a homestead at Lake Sara Jane, now Lake Miona, near Wildwood in Sumter County. Adrian named their home Glyktop, an ancient Greek word meaning *Sweet Place*. He was a clerk in I.E. Barwick's general store until Barwick bought a printing press and made Adrian editor of the *Orange Leaf* weekly newspaper.

Adrian quickly gained recognition as a crusading editor by attacking the Florida Railroad and Navigation Company which was acquiring land grants for non-existent track right-of-way. Through this publicity, the state Legislature passed a bill forfeiting thousands of acres of FRN grants.

Helped Elect Governor

In 1888, the Pratt brothers of Brooksville hired Adrian to edit their *Hernando County News*. Here Jordan continued his crusading. He attacked Sen. A.S. Mann and Gov. Perry, thereby helping defeat Gov. Perry for re-election and electing Sam Pasco.

Shortly after this, the Pratt brother's sold the *News* and transferred Jordan to Leesburg to manage the *Commercial* newspaper. Soon, Jordan and State Treasurer John C. Luning started the *Leesburg Times*. They waged a sensational campaign against the Florida Southern Railway for adding a surcharge of 10 cents per box on oranges. The Florida Supreme Court ruled against the surcharge.

While carrying on this fight, Jordan pushed for the first school and the first building and loan association in Leesburg — both of which were established. He personally conducted a fund drive to purchase 35 desks for the school. He was elected to one term as town clerk-treasurer, and to three terms as a school trustee.

Illustrative of the hazards of frontier journalism was the time the *Leesburg Times* was a day late because of the unexpected visit of a large black snake. The printing plant was a plain, plank building. The snake, fearsome but harmless, had found an entrance to the shop and lay stretched out on an overhead rafter. Compositors were busy setting type — by hand, one letter at a time — as the deadline neared. Suddenly the snake fell off the rafter onto one of the typesetters on a stool. The compositor was so startled he fell backwards off his stool onto the table holding that week's type. All became "pi" — the printers' term for jumbled type. It took 24 hours of frantic work to sort and reset the news.

The two Leesburg papers merged in 1893, and Jordan was named postmaster at Leesburg — serving a four-year term. With a new administration in Washington, D.C., Jordan lost his job as postmaster and so took a position as editor of a paper at Thomasville, Ga. In September 1901, Jordan heard that the *Punta Gorda Herald* was for sale. He bought it and so was publisher as well as editor. He built the two-story building at the corner of Marion and Taylor streets. The newspaper office and press occupied the second floor.

Jordan came near being wiped out by the financial panic of 1904 but held on to emerge a strong, respected civic leader. He was an active supporter of Albert Gilchrist in the latter's political races for state representative and, in 1908, for governor of Florida. Gilchrist appointed Jordan state food and drugs inspector, a post he held for six years.

Jordan pursued division of DeSoto county vigorously for 20 years, finally sharing victory with Punta Gorda and Charlotte Harbor Town residents who desperately wanted a bridge between the two communities.

Teller Of Tall Tales

During this period, Adrian gained a reputation as an influential political commentator and teller of tall tales. He reported preposterous fishing stories and regularly pulled April Fool jokes on his readers. His accounts were widely reprinted by other papers.

A well remembered fish story was that of Charlotte Harbor's "singing fish" which lured winter visitors to their death by drowning. Once he announced that President Teddy Roosevelt would stop and make a speech from a railroad car on his way to Fort Myers. The entire town turned out at the depot. When the train stopped, a confederate of Adrian's stepped out and said "April Fool!." Years later, ex-president Teddy visited Punta Gorda to catch a manta ray "devil fish."

Adrian and Agnes had five children: Adrian Crenshaw Jordan who later became editor of the *Herald,* Vernon Junius Jordan who became a dentist; Julian Weyman Jordan who also became a dentist; Lillian Undine Jordan who married Charles Kerr of Zephyrhills, Fla., and Ivan Pettus Jordan who was a pressman for the *Herald.*

Agnes died in 1907 and is buried at Punta Gorda Indian Springs cemetery. Four years later, Adrian married Sallie Agnes Green of Tampa. It was her first marriage at age 42. It also was a happy union. The family joked that, "To be adored, marry an old maid."

Adrian sold the Herald in 1919. It continued as a journalistic leader — but never again was as colorful.

He died in 1928. After a Episcopalian service he was buried at Indian Springs, to be joined in 1960 by Sallie.

First school
I taught
at Harbor view
1911

Jean Whiteaker, later Mrs. Cleve Cleveland, taught Harbor View.

Chapter 22

SCHOOLS WERE HIGH PRIORITY

Imagine that you, your spouse and several children have moved to a wilderness frontier. Four or five other families are a mile or so distant in all directions. After building a cabin for yourself, what public structure would you and your neighbors build next.?

The first settlers around Charlotte Harbor usually erected a "meeting hall" that served as a school on weekdays and an inter-denominational church on Sundays. Often, the building was a rustic cabin with a thatched roof and shuttered windows instead of glass.

The Charlotte Harbor area was reserved for Indians until the Battle of Peace River ended the Seminole wars in 1856, Thus, the first American settlers did not settle on the last frontier here until after the Civil War.

A cattle dock was constructed at Hickory Bluff — now Charlotte Harbor Town — in 1862 to run cattle for the Confederacy past the Union blockade at Boca Grande Pass. Homes were built when Nathan H. DeCoster, a former Yankee officer at Fort Myers, returned in 1866 to establish a steam-driven saw mill.

He married Emily Phillips of Key West in 1869. She had nursed him back to health after he was wounded at the battle of Fredericksburg and sent to the Union hospital at Key West to recuperate.

Another Fort Myers officer played a key role in establishing the first public schools along the Peace River and Charlotte Harbor. He was John F. Bartholf who also had been wounded at Fredericksburg and transferred to Fort Myers to command one of two companies of African-American troops there. After the war he married Mary Daniels of Fort Ogden, a Union sympathizer who had taken refuge at Fort Myers.

Bartholf became involved in Reconstruction politics and was appointed clerk of court for Manatee County at Pine Level. Pine Level, 10 miles west of Tater Hill (Arcadia), has disappeared. At that time, however, it was the center of government for the area now including Charlotte and six other counties. Bartholf was appointed superintendent of schools in 1869. Schools then were few and far between — with haphazard schedules contingent upon private donations. He built the first "free" schools in the county. Within the first year he recruited teachers and trustees for log schools at Sweet Water, Charlie Apopka Creek, Fort Hartsuff, Fort Greene, Joshua Creek, Fort Ogden and Pine Level.

Great Need Of Privy

Historian Canter Brown, Jr., says the school at Pine Level was typical of wilderness schools. Joseph Patten, the teacher, complained that "the school house is uncomfortable, inconvenient, and will need rebuilding. There is a great need of a privy." Bartholf reported the school situation to the Manatee County Board of Instruction in 1872 with a mixture of frustration and optimism:

"Owing to continued sickness in the neighborhood, attendance at Pine Level became so much reduced the teacher kindly consented to annul his contract. I am making every possible effort to put the number of schools designated in operation, but fear very much that I shall not be able to obtain teachers. What we are to do, I do not know.

"The utmost amount of funds that we can realize will scarcely enable us to establish even three months of school. Even if we had the means, I doubt very much if the attendance would be sufficient to justify the expense, as people here will not send their children to school during the cropping or cow-pen season. Due to the area being flooded with water from about the first of June until the first of October, it is extremely inconvenient for the parents to send them during that time.

"In some neighborhoods, I am happy to say this is not the case. People show a disposition to make every sacrifice, submit to any inconvenience, in order to send their children regularly to school."

The following year the Board voted to subsidize schools with an enrollment of not less than 10 pupils. The Board stipulated that the school be "conducted strictly according to law, and the teacher making monthly returns certified by a majority of the patrons as correct. The allowance was $1 per student per month for five months — the total not to exceed $25 per month. Parents were expected to match the grant. With this help, five log cabin schools were replaced with "sawed lumber" structures.

Hickory Bluff got its first school in 1873 — sharing a "small box-frame palm-thatched" with Trinity Methodist Church organized at that time. Lumber came from DeCoster's saw mill. The structure was located on the property of M/M Mathieu and Mary Giddens near the mill "beyond the cemetery."

Attendance at Manatee's nine free schools totaled "200 white pupils." Bartholf tried to obtain funds from a northern benevolence society for a couple of "colored" schools, but without success.

In his 1875 report, Bartholf proudly announced: "Free schools have been established every winter and, by my individual efforts, a liberal appropriation secured to aid in their maintenance. The people

JOHN F. BARTHOLF

are very interested in education. I believe that if some good teachers would locate here they could get schools the best part of the year."

Bartholf gave up his political appointments in 1876 and devoted his energies to selling real estate on Charlotte Harbor's north shore. In a promotion brochure titled *South Florida, the Italy of America,* published by him and Francis C.M. Boggess in 1881, he describes Hickory Bluff:

"As we approach the mouth of Peas Creek we come to the principal settlement extending about four miles immediately on the water. Hickory Bluff comprises about one dozen families, store, post office, church and school house. There are several new and handsome residences which would reflect credit upon any locality. Also there is an extensive cattle wharf from which load after load of fine beef cattle are shipped to Cuba."

Upon rumors that the Florida Southern Railway was going to extend its tracks to Charlotte Harbor, DeCoster in 1884 bought 160 acres east of Hickory Bluff. He platted it into home sites named Harbor View. The rail road veered to Punta Gorda in 1886, but by 1890 enough families had located at Harbor View to support a school.

In that year, new schools were built at Charlotte Harbor Town and Harbor View. A new Methodist church and a two-room school next door were built at Charlotte Harbor Town on land donated, again by the Giddens, the present location of Trinity. A one-room frame school was built on Rowland Drive at Harbor View.

Miss Jean Whiteaker, later Mrs. Cleve Cleveland, was a teacher at Harbor View in 1911. Years later she related that underage children were enrolled in order to meet the quota of pupils. There was no blackboard because imported slate was expensive. Students had hand-held slates.

Grunts And Squeals

Miss Esther Oswald, later Mrs. Samuel McCullough, was a teacher at Charlotte Harbor Town in 1914-16. "I had a little difficulty getting used to the grunts and squeals of hogs which made their home under the building," says Mrs. McCullough. "But I got to where I didn't notice them. Part of my duties was to sweep the floors and wash the windows."

Teacher with Mrs. McCullough in 1914 was Mrs. Betty Blanchet, daughter of an Episcopalian minister homesteading at Woodrow near the Lee County line. Sharing teaching duties in 1915-16 was Mrs. Rose Hopper. She and her husband homesteaded at Bermont near S.R. 74 and 31. He drove her and their children in a mule-drawn wagon to the dock at Punta Gorda in the dark of Monday mornings. Mother and children were rowed across to Charlotte Harbor Town where the family had rented a small house. The kids went to school with their mother. On weekends they returned to Bermont. The two daughters, Minta and Ethel, became teachers at Punta Gorda.

It was customary for board and room to be furnished teachers by families of the students. Jean Whiteaker lived close by her school, but Miss Oswald and Miss Hopper stayed with the Knights or Giddens. Seamen rowed them also across the harbor on Sundays and Fridays.

Both early schools were abandoned when the Charlotte Harbor School was built in 1917 at what is now School House Square Shopping Center. The school next door to Trinity was demolished. The Harbor View school was moved to the waterfront and converted into a home by Henry Sias.

The second public school in what is now Charlotte County met in a meeting hall built by Punta Gorda's founder, Col. Isaac Trabue in 1887. Inter-denominational church services were conducted on Sundays. The Methodists, Baptists, Presbyterians and Episcopalians trace their origins to that humble structure.

An article in the *Punta Gorda Beacon* of July 1889, indicates a free-standing school there started in the fall of the preceding year:

"The success of the Municipal School of Punta Gorda just closed, although but an experiment, has proven a wise movement on the part of the Council. All due credit should be accorded them."

Teacher at this school was a bearded North Carolinian named H.S, Lee. Mrs. Lena Corbett, daughter of the C.W. Conollys, who came to Punta Gorda in 1888, wrote: "The Methodist Church was a school house as well as a church. When it became just a church (after 1888 when the Baptists organized their congregation) it was very nicely fixed up."

The Punta Gorda school, however, was not entirely satisfactory. Several private schools were started to provide specialized education.

The Seventh Day Adventists started a school at Punta Gorda in 1895. There were 13 students in eight grades. Teachers were Mrs. C.B. Stephenson and Miss Cora Patrick. Mrs. Stephenson wrote her own textbooks by longhand. She and her husband, Claiborne pioneered evangelistic, educational and medical work here for more than 50 years.

Her son, Charles, was born in 1901 in Punta Gorda, and she only took off three weeks to deliver him. She then went back to the little school house to teach but rode her bicycle back home every few hours to nurse Charles. Shortly after this, the Stephensons moved to Brooker, Florida.

The Adventist school then was carried on here for a time by a Mrs. Honeywell. It was located across from the Good Shepherd Episcopal Church on Cross Street.

Pepper School

The most successful private school was that started in 1896 when Col. John C. Pepper, an Illinois attorney, retired to Punta Gorda with his three daughters. One of them, Norma, opened a "primary" school patronized for many years by Punta Gorda's prominent citizens.

Miss Pepper was a beloved, but strict, teacher in private and public schools at Punta Gorda for nearly a half century. It was said that "she believed in teaching her pupils to THINK. She was a definite advocate of reading, writing and arithmetic."

Her school was a one-room building on Olympia Avenue across from the Court House. The *Punta Gorda Herald* reported that "Miss Norma Pepper's primary school has a full attendance. She has all the pupils she wants and often has to refuse to take additional ones." A severe hurricane in 1910 blew the Pepper School off its foundations. Classes continued thereafter in the parlor of the Pepper home on the southeast corner of Cross Street and Retta Esplanade. The home was widely known as the "inside-out house" because the studding was exposed for many years to the elements. The inside walls of tongue-and-groove pine were weather tight so Col. Pepper never got around to putting on outside sheathing.

First public school at Punta Gorda in 1888 now part of this home.

Chapter 23

SAWMILLS SPARKED SCHOOL GROWTH

As the Charlotte Harbor frontier was settled after the Civil War, sawmill operators followed to fill the urgent need for lumber with which to build proper homes, churches, and schools. Such a mill was set up on the shore of Lemon Bay by the Heacock Brothers about 1889 to serve the growing towns of Grove City, and Englewood.

That same year, William Goff sold his home on the bay to a phosphate company and bought 120 acres at what today includes the Tringali Community Center on McCall Road. There he built a frame home and laid out a farm he called Vineland. Eventually it included a store, post office, and turpentine still. William had eight school age children at this time (20 through four marriages) all needing education. Grove City was growing and several children lived there. Consequently, Goff built the first school in the area in September 1890. This one-room frame building was located on a corner of his farm at what today is Tiffany Square shopping center. The first teacher is unknown, but Professor Edward B. Sanders, who had taught at Punta Gorda since 1896, was the second teacher in 1903.

The next school in the Lemon Bay Area was started by Carl B. Biorseth, a newspaper editor who came to the untamed wilderness with the Platt and Lampp families in 1894. They, too, had children whom they were anxious to be educated. A small structure was built for them in 1898 near the Heacock sawmill on Englewood Road, now Sarasota County, between Stewart and Harvard streets. Miss Mamie McCreary was the teacher for 10 pupils but she had to quit at Christmas because of ill health.

Biorseth finished out the semester, but no teacher could be obtained for the 1899-1900 school season. For this and other reasons, Biorseth moved four miles north to an area known as Pinedale on the north fork of the Mystik Creek (now Forked Creek). He donated an acre of land for a school, which he and neighbors built.

After its first year, the Pinedale school failed to enroll the minimum number of ten pupils required for county subsidy. By this time the Englewood school had qualified, and Pinedale children walked there. Englewood was the school center for 1902,3,4. Then it failed to qualify, and children there again walked to Pinedale for the next six years. Grace Biorseth, at age 19, was a teacher at Pinedale in 1908. In 1910, the school enrolled 17 pupils taught by Julian Roberts. Grove City got a one-room school on San Casa Drive near the present Little League field in 1900.

Mrs. Isabelle (Johansen) Hanlon wrote in a memoir how she and her sister, living on Manasota Key, were rowed across the bay by their father early Monday. Then the two girls walked to school at Pineland. They boarded with a Mrs. Kelly until school was out Friday afternoons. They walked back to Englewood where their father waited to row them home. Sometimes their teacher came with them for the weekend.

Punta Gorda's First School

The first public school at Punta Gorda was launched in the fall of 1888 when the little class in the community meeting hall moved to its own frame building believed to be that still standing at the southeast corner of Marion Avenue and Harvey Street. It is likely the structure originally was of one story. The *Punta Gorda Beacon* of July 1889 referred to it as "the Municipal School just closed .... a successful experiment."

A larger school, of one story, was built on Goldstein Street about 1896. It provided instruction in eight grades. The first teacher was a "bearded North Carolinian" named H.S. Lee. A somewhat later teacher was another man from North Carolina named Edward B. Sanders.

Rapidly expanding Punta Gorda strained the Goldstein Street school. The *Punta Gorda Herald* reported in February 1902 that the school had an enrollment of 178 pupils — "91 males and 87 females." The principal was "Professor" W.E. Bell.

Local residents, backed by the newspaper, began a drive to raise funds for a new building, longer school term, and grades nine through twelve.

The *Herald* took note of the situation in May: "Whenever anything needs to be done, get the ladies to take hold; and it will be done. Funds were needed to extend the term of the high school, and Mrs. George T. Brown went out and raised $130 by subscription.

"Then, Mrs. Perry W. McAdow chartered the steamer *H.B. Plant* and advertised an excursion in the same behalf to Boca Grande on Tuesday night. The excursion proved to be a brilliant success in every particular. Fully 200 tickets were sold; and adding the receipts from the sale of refreshments, the net sum realized was an even $100.

"The amount of enjoyment reaped by those who went on the excursion cannot be reckoned in dollars and cents. There were two bands of music, a string band and the Punta Gorda Brass Band. The ice cream, cake, sherbet, et cetera were so excellent the supply was wholly consumed. The music was fine, the refreshments perfect and the company charming. Everybody was happy. "

With such support, the DeSoto County school board — of which Punta Gorda then was a part — authorized the addition of a second story to the Goldstein Street school and instruction in the "high" subjects.

Said the *Herald* in July: "Contractor Stephenson last week began the work of raising, remodelling and adding a second story to the high school building, which will double its capacity. It would be a good idea to sell the building for a boarding house, get a four-acre lot from Col. Trabue, and put up a modern building of brick. We hope this will be done during the coming year." Within a few years, the *Herald's* suggestion became reality.

First School For African-Americans

At this time, the county's first school for African-American children was established at Punta Gorda.

Albert Gilchrist, the surveyor who laid out the track for Florida Southern Railway with the help of an all-black crew, gave up his railroad job to speculate in Punta Gorda real estate. Most of his crew also relocated there.

When Gilchrist was elected a state representative in 1903, he appointed Dan Smith to the school board. Smith was Gilchrist's former crewman, a member of the group that adopted the Punta Gorda city charter, and acknowledged leader of the African-American community.

Rep. Gilchrist sent Smith to an educators' conference at New Orleans to find a Black teacher. There, Smith met Benjamin Joshua Baker, a 31-year-old teacher at Suwanee County's "colored" school. Smith persuaded Baker to come to Punta Gorda.

Baker was born of former slave parents at Live Oak, Fla, in 1872. His mother and father could read and write — rare among African-Americans then. Education for slaves was prohibited before the Civil War because they tended to waste time reading and to want freedom.

Little Benjamin learned to read and write from his parents. However, he was 10 years old before a segregated school was established at Live

Oak. He applied himself diligently to his studies, and at age 19 passed the state examination for teachers at Lake City. He was hired for the Suwanee County school and taught there 12 years.

The Punta Gorda "colored" school was built in the Fall of 1903 on Marion Avenue "near the beach" at the foot of Cooper Street. After a few years, enrollment there outgrew the original school. A two-room building was constructed at the northeast corner of Mary and Showalter Streets, now the location of the Cooper Street Community Center. This new school was widely called Baker's Academy.

Baker, a stern but beloved educator, retired in 1940 after 49 years of teaching. He was the first teacher to receive retirement benefits under the 1939 Florida statute. He died in 1942 while a new school for African-American children was being built near his home on Charlotte Avenue. The new school was named for Baker. It continued as a segregated facility teaching grades one through seven. Senior-grade students were bussed to Dunbar High School in Fort Myers until Charlotte County schools were integrated in 1964.

First High School Commencement

The *Herald* of June 1904 devoted a front-page column to the first commencement at Goldstein Street school — offering instruction beyond the eighth grade:

"The most successful year in the history of the Punta Gorda High School closed this week with an elaborate and interesting series of exercises. This has been an exceptional year, not only in the efficiency of the teachers and the faithful work of the pupils, but also in the length of the term. The results show that our people have been fully justified in desiring and claiming a longer school year. At the beginning of year the course of study was changed to make it uniform with the State course. The closing exercises began on May 27 at the Trinka building where the public was invited to inspect a display of the work of different grades."

Teachers were Miss Ella Beesom, first grade; Miss Maggie Stetson, grades two and three; Professor J. Burdette Smith, grades four and five; Miss Cornelia Orr, grades six and seven; Miss Norma Pepper, grades seven and eight; Professor M.H. Smith, grades nine and ten.

Total enrollment was 225. Certificates of promotion were awarded at City Hall to "those finishing the grammar school courses." An admission of 10 cents was charged to help defray costs.

The first — and only — high school graduate, in 1906, was Miss Ruby Hill. Albert Gilchrist presented her diploma. There were seven students in three grades of high school. There were no eleventh- and twelfth-grade students inasmuch as the eighth-grade students had not yet worked their way through the full range of instruction.

Chief Billy Bowlegs, second from right, led delegation to Washington D.C.

Chapter 24

EARLY MINISTERS CONVERTED SEMINOLES

Contrary to popular belief, all Seminole Indians did not flee into the Everglades during a series of wars with settlers from 1816 to 1856. Historical accounts show that the Seminoles continued to live indefinitely in proximity to settlers — though Great Chief Billy Bowlegs did accept deportation with his villagers in 1858 to end the Seminole wars.

The remaining Seminoles — and other Indians who scattered throughout South Florida — were allowed to remain in their villages wherever located. Everglades Seminoles chose to stay there because hunting was good and the environment healthy. The 1880 U.S. Census of Manatee County reveals details about two Seminole villages northwest of Lake Okeechobee well removed from the Everglades.

Fish Eating Creek Settlement lists six families totaling 32 individuals by their native names. All were engaged in "agriculture and hunting." Tus-ta-nug-ge, age 80, is shown as "chief of tribe," and his brother Hos-pa-ta-ki, 78, as "medicine man." Ka-tea-la-ni, 33, appears to be a son of one of the two older men.

Largest family is that of Ak-fus-ki, 35, and his wife Tcan-hi-ka, 26. They have two daughters, ages 4 and 6, the youngest in the village. Living with them are a mother-in-law, two sisters-in-law, and a brother-in-law.

Cow Creek Settlement lists three families totaling 12 persons. They range in age from an unnamed boy, 2, to a man named Has-hi-mal-la, 48.

106

Each family has a mother and father. There is one young woman, 17, engaged in "house work" with her mother. This village has two "medicine men" — Fus-ha-tai, 27, and Ko-ma-kuts-ha-tes, 29.

Southwest Florida pioneers were intrigued with the dignified, colorfully dressed Seminoles who lived peaceably among them. The first family to settle on the south shore of the Peace River roadstead of Charlotte Harbor — now Punta Gorda — was the family of Mr. and Mrs. James and Sarah (nee Youmans) Lanier in 1879.

Their youngest child, Jesse, in later years recalled: "One of the more pleasant memories of being the only residents of Punta Gorda was of Seminole Indians coming up the bay in many canoes. They came periodically to hunt for coontie root which was processed into flour. A fleet of canoes silently gliding by the shore caused us to stop whatever we were doing to watch."

A large group of Seminoles at that time were living south of Naples. An interesting account of the relationship between Indians and pioneers is furnished in a memoir by Rev. George W. Gatewood. He came to Southwest Florida in 1882 as a young Methodist-circuit preacher:

Rev. Gatewood Preached

"When I first saw the Everglades in 1886, about 200 Seminole Indians lived in the cabbage hammocks and on the high knolls. They sustained themselves off the plentiful game. There was a white settlement at Allen's River and a store was kept there by George Storter. One also was kept at Sandfly Pass by Joe Wiggins. At these stores the Indians traded or sold their hides and furs and bought supplies. The merchants, though, had to first pay the Indians in cash for what they had to sell. Then the Indians would start to buying and pay for each article as it was wrapped up.

"While in the Everglades section, I became personally acquainted with the Indians and occasionally invited them to eat with me. Most all the men wore just a shirt, sometimes also a vest, but no pants or anything on their legs. Miami Billy, however, liked to dress like a white man when he came to the store. He kept a pair of pants hid at the head of Allen's River, whence they came in canoes. On one particular trip, another Indian got to the landing first and hid the pants. Billy had to go like the rest — in his shirt tail. He took the joke philosophically.

"Among the Indians, I well remember Squirrel Jumper, Water Turkey, Miami Billy, Tommy Osceola and Johnny Osceola. Johnny was an expert wrestler and would wrestle with the white boys who were willing to tackle him. I think he is now chief of his tribe.

"I organized a group of Methodists and built the first little church there long before the railroad came to the town of Everglades. I had the Indians for part of my congregation. When they came in they refused to sit on the benches and sat cross-legged on the floor."

107

Rev. Gatewood left the Everglade City area to take up a homestead and operate a store at Bermont, a new village east of Punta Gorda. There he preached with other ministers in a community church.

The Episcopal diocese of Southwest Florida opened a medical mission among the Big Cypress Seminoles about 1907 and assigned Rev. Dr. Irenaeus Trout, rector of the Good Shepherd Church at Punta Gorda, to assist in its development.

Rev. Trout relished his duties among the Seminoles. He proudly wore moccasins and other Indian garb on his monthly trips. Once he was bitten by a rattle snake upon dismounting from his horse. His ministrations were well received by the Indians.

The *Punta Gorda Herald* in early Sept. 1908 published a report by Rev. Trout regarding an important Seminole conversion to Christianity: "BIG CHIEF CONVERTED — I received, Aug. 27, a letter from Hotulachatsie (The May Wind), a big medicine man of the Cypress clan, written through Dr. Godden, the medical missionary of the Church in the Everglades, as follows:

Chief Wants Baptism

"'I believe that Jesus is the Son of God, and that He is both God and Man. I believe it is necessary for me to turn from wrong and live right. In this belief, I want to be baptized the first time that I see you or the Bishop.'

"This letter is fraught with the most important significance. This Indian is a big man in the council. He is an old man, and has been under our teaching for several months. According to Seminole laws, the individual Indian belongs, not to himself, but to the tribe. No matter how much an individual might want to embrace the Christian religion, if the tribe says no, why it is NO emphatically.

"That this old man of authority wrote this is evidence that tribal consent has been given — probably at the corn dance of June 14 last — and that, from now on the work of Christianity among these people will progress without hindrance. Praise God!"

Rev. Trout lost no time in gathering the new flock. He set out through the wilderness to the Seminole village on Sept. 25 and recorded his adventure in a communication to the *Herald:*

"Leaving Fort Myers on Friday morning, we began our journey eastward toward Immokalee over the worst roads I have ever travelled. The trail was in water from six inches to two feet deep two-thirds of the way. The first night we camped in the wagon bed.

"We arrived at Immokalee on Saturday afternoon about 4 o'clock, but just before reaching there, the king-bolt of the wagon broke and out we went. It was now my time to turn blacksmith, as there is no smithy in the hamlet. With the aid of Mr. Frank Brown, we improvised a pin from a tail-board rod of the wagon.

"Sunday we held two services at Christ Church which were well attended. We would have proceeded to the Everglades on Monday but for two reasons. One of our horses ran a splinter into his shoulder while in the pasture. It made an ugly wound which will take at least a month to heal. A returning ox team reported the Oklowacoochie River impassable, the water running six feet deep. These circumstances delayed our progress until Wednesday, Sept. 30 when we proceeded on our way with one horse.

"Reaching the Slough, I got down and waded, leading the horse. The water came up to my armpits. Amid such difficulties, camping over night in wet clothes, we reached Glade Cross Hospital, 65 miles southeast of Ft. Myers, on Friday, Oct. 2, at noon. Later in the day we arrived at our destination — the landing out in the Everglades.

"Indians, Indians, Indians everywhere; bucks, squaws and pickaninnies were camped on the hammock. They gladly greeted Esta Mikka (chief person), my Indian name. Che-hick-shay-et-es-chay (glad to see you) resounded on every hand. Hand-shakings were many and hearty.

"Three of the sub-chiefs, i.e. Hotulcahatsie (our first convert), Tom Billy and Little Tiger. Several leading men — Car-char-no-go-tee, Epon-kot-i-ka and others of the council whom I had not seen since the June Shot-ca-taw (corn dance) — came aside for a 'smoke-talk.' After supper of safke and (shall I say it?) venison and turkey, we sat around the camp fire and talked late into the night.

"On Sunday, Oct. 4, Conipatchie and Jack and Charlie Buster came in. After another short talk, all went away on a big hunt with farewells of 'som-mus-kar-la-ne-shaw-maw-lin (good wishes to the white man).'

Buy Alligator Hides

"I have bought for the mission, so far, over 400 alligator hides — paying nearly $400 for same. They are all good quality and mean a neat profit. Freddie, my son, 11 years old, is with me, but there is not another white man nearer than 32 miles, the nearest post office. Just how long we shall be here, I do not know. Dr. Godden, the medical missionary and trader, is in bad health and gone to Tampa for treatment. Mr. Hampton, who runs the store, has gone to the market for supplies, but we do not get lonesome because the Indians are going and coming every day.

"Last Sunday, Oct. 11, we had full morning service with sermon and organ music, singing the old hymns — Okato Chompusan (Sweet Bye and Bye), Chesus-um-pu-fek-chu (Jesus Lover of My Soul, and Chesus Hocefku- en-yek-cen (All Hail the Power of Jesus' Name).

"It was inspiring and uplifting to have the grand, majestic service of the Church, to see the white-robed priest and the cross-topped altar way out here in the wilderness. I long, however to get back home to dear old Punta Gorda and preach once more to my faithful people there."

St. Mark Progressive Baptist original church.

Chapter 25

ST. MARK BAPTISTS SPLIT THREE WAYS

Uncle Dan Smith, acknowledged leader of the African-American community at Punta Gorda, built the first house of worship there in 1886 — a rustic "brush arbor" attended by blacks and whites of all denominations. Smith and Rev. Robert Meacham, travelling missionary for the African Methodist Episcopal Church, also built Bethel A.M.E. three years later. Those of Baptist background organized their own congregation as St. Mark Progressive Baptist Church in 1893 and licensed G.W. Jones to preach. Baptisms were conducted in the harbor. The first place of Baptist worship is not known. Most likely it was in Rev. Jones' home.

The first documentation of St. Mark is a news story published by the The *Punta Gorda Herald* on October 27, 1893, under the headline AMONG THE COLORED PEOPLE:

"N.J. Morris of Tampa, A. Laska of Bartow, and G.W. McClemons of Homeland, all Baptist ministers of their respective homes, came down Saturday and took part in ordination ceremonies at St. Marks (sic).

"G.W. Jones, who has been only a licensed preacher for the colored Baptist church here, was duly ordained; and H.C. Simmons was ordained as deacon. There was one conversion, Welcome Barker, who will be baptized on the first Sunday in November.

"G.W. McClemons delivered a creditable sermon at the morning service, while Rev. N.J. Morris conducted the ordination services in the afternoon in a manner very appropriate to the occasion. A pleasant surprise party was tendered Rev. Jones at his home in the evening, which was heartily appreciated by the pastor."

Note that this article indicates Rev. Jones was preaching locally for some time prior to his formal ordination.

The St. Mark congregation still did not have a sanctuary, so Bethel invited the Baptists in 1894 to share the little Methodist building on the south side of Helen Avenue between Milus and Mary. The Baptists soon began building their own sanctuary. In December, 1895 *The Herald* carried the following notice signed by Rev. T.W. Sanders (Saunders) and headlined AID A NOBLE CAUSE:

"There will be services at the colored Baptist Church next Sunday, and everybody are cordially invited to come out. At the services last Sunday, we raised a collection of $20.29 for the completion of the new church. We intend to complete, in and outside, before we stop and especially appeal to white citizens to meet and assist us in the noble work. Mr. J.L. Sandlin gave us $5, and I believe he will give more when asked. I respectfully ask that every gentleman who can will do the same. Nothing is troublesome that we do willingly. Come and bring an offering for the completion of the Lord's House.

"Respectfully, T.W. Sanders, pastor."

White Folks Help

James L. Sandlin was a prominent, white businessman who came to Punta Gorda in 1886 within a week or two of Dan Smith. The first St. Mark sanctuary is believed to have been on the corner of Ida and Mary Streets along the railroad track where an old map shows an unnamed church building.

The sequence of ministers during this early period is confusing. Recollections of early St. Mark Baptist members have Rev. Jones serving from 1893 until 1901 when Rev. W.M. Smith was called into service. The 1900 Census lists Rev. G.W. Jones, 39; wife Hannah, 25, as the Baptist minister. Yet, it is clear that Rev. Sanders spoke as pastor of St. Mark during the period of Rev. Jones' tenure. Rev. Sanders does not appear in the 1900 census, but he does in the 1910 census as "black, Methodist minister, 48; wife Silvia, 50."

It is possible that Rev. Sanders was an evangelical minister with a short-term mission to build churches for African-Americans. His limited pastorate also would explain why he is not personally remembered, nor why he may have undertaken similar service for the Methodists at a later date — if the 1910 census is correct. As we noted, black Methodists and Baptists shared fellowship easily.

No documentation has been discovered for Rev. W.M. Smith, but he is credited by St. Mark historians with adding "Missionary" to the church name to emphasize responsibility of members to recruit others. Dan Smith is said to have left Bethel A.M.E. in 1893 to help organize St. Mark and name it. Accompanying him were other pioneer African-Americans — Sam Kenedy, Columbus Reese, Alex Stephens, Peter Andrews and A.C. Dorsey who became the second deacon. Smith's change of denomination is said to have been at the urging of his sweetheart, Louisa, a Baptist. They were married in 1897. He was ordained a deacon for St. Mark but declined a call to pastor — also at the insistence of his wife.

From 1904, the history of St. Mark is more easily followed. Three stories in the *Herald* in May 1904, provide a view of the activities of St. Mark and its role in the lives of African-Americans:

Brass Band Picnic

"The colored Baptist Sunday school had a May picnic on Alligator Creek Monday. They went out of town with banners waving and a brass band discoursing stirring music. The day was a happy one for them from beginning to end."

Notable Wedding

"A notable wedding in colored social circles occurred on April 26, at the home of the bride's mother in this city. The contracting parties were A.C. Dorsey and Miss Maida Saunders. The ceremony was performed by Rev. Williams, pastor of the colored Baptist church."

Celebrate Thanksgiving

"Bayview Lodge No. 3995, and Trabue Household of Ruth No. 1175, G.W.O. of O.F., will celebrate thanksgiving at St. Marks (sic) Baptist church at 3 p.m. on Sunday, 8th inst. The societies will march in procession from Odd Fellows Hall, when an entertaining program, with music, will be rendered. The sermon will be preached by Rev. C.H. Smith, P.N.F. Memorial service will be led by S.P. Andrews, P.N.F., assisted by P.W. Miller, P.N.F. Marshal for the day is Jerry Harris, P.N.F., and master of ceremonies is C.B. Simon, P.G.M. The public is invited."

There is no further documentation of Pastor Williams. Rev. C.H. Smith (no known relation of Dan) is enumerated in the 1910 census as single, age 44, Methodist.

The little church on Ida Street was inadequate by this time. So, the four St. Mark trustees dug into their own pockets Feb. 1, 1905, for $75 to buy Lot 15 of Block 66 from F.I. Brown. The latter was receiver for the bankrupt Florida Commercial Real Estate Company. The site was the southeast corner of Virginia and Dupont streets. Trustees were Dan C. Smith, Lem Jackson, N.H. Haines and D.A. Williamson.

A recollection that Albert Gilchrist "donated" the lot, though contrary to the deed, may indicate however that the future governor of Florida gave money. This certainly was typical of Gilchrist who came to Punta Gorda with a colored survey crew, promoted the first county African-American school at Punta Gorda, and was a life-long friend of Dan Smith.

Rev. W.B. Marshall was called to St. Mark in 1906 and served until 1909. He was a firm believer in keeping abreast of the latest things and travelled a great deal to meetings in larger cities.

The Baptist presence was further enlarged in 1909 with formation of the St. Mary Primitive Baptist Church. In that year, the new congregation purchased a lot on the southwest corner of Mary and Helen Streets from S.F.J. Trabue, nephew of Col. Trabue, for $15. Trustees were Rev. M. Austin, Benjamin Anderson and John McGehee.

The 1910 census shows Rev. J.L. Livingston, 45, was a Baptist Minister living in the home of Louis Zanders, 31, an unmarried "drayman" (wagon driver). Rev. M.L. Cherry, Sr., was called into service after Rev. Marshall and served one year. In 1911, he became the travelling representative of the Florida Baptist College at Jacksonville. He was succeeded by his son, the Rev. M.L. Cherry, Jr., who served until 1923.

Under the inspirational leadership of Rev. Cherry, Jr., St. Mark membership grew to more than 100 — thereby requiring a larger sanctuary. Jesse R. Sandlin, a white Baptist merchant and brother of deceased James L. Sandlin, sold St. Mark the adjoining Lot 16 for $65 on May 21, 1912. The existing church was salvaged for a larger church that stood on this spot until 1976. (See photo).

Rev. Cherry was especially patriotic. In October of 1918, he sponsored a large, three-column advertisement in the *Herald* urging all citizens to buy Liberty Bonds in support of the European War — now known as the First World War. Under the leadership of Rev. Cherry, a number of church auxiliaries were instituted, and one deacon, Mac Scott was ordained.

Rev. J.L. Lyon was called into service for St. Mark from 1923 to 1927. The 1927 Punta Gorda City Directory lists Rev. Andrew J. Warren as pastor of St. Mark and Rev. Levi Miller as pastor of St. Mary. Bethel A.M.E. is listed, but no pastor is named.

Preached To Prisoners

Rev. Warren was noted by the *Herald* in October 1930 for his ministry to county stockade prisoners as well as to his law-abiding flock. At that time, work-gang prisoners were housed in a concrete enclosure and dormitory at Carmelita and Florida streets — today the county softball fields. Area ministers, white and black, took turns preaching to and baptizing inmates Sunday afternoons under the auspices of the King's Daughters and Sons prison ministry.

Other African-Americans participating were Rev. T.M. White, pastor of Bethel A.M.E., and a Rev. Brown, Baptist, whose first name and church are unknown. Rev. Warren resigned from St. Mark in 1932 to become the third pastor of Macedonia Baptist. He was succeeded at St. Mark by Rev. Steward Eldridge Siplen who served only one year. He so angered the St. Mark congregation they locked him out of the sanctuary one Sunday. In an ensuing melee in which deacons attempted to force Rev. Siplen to sign a letter of resignation, he stuffed the paper into his mouth and nearly choked. Police were called to restore order.

The congregation then called into service the Rev. R.L. Cason who served until 1947. He ordained one deacon, Marion McCloud. The *Herald* of May 1934 reported that Rev. Cason delivered the baccalaureate sermon at the 21st annual commencement of Baker Academy, local colored public school.

Rev. Cason is said to have "turned out" a dozen or so members in October 1933 for reasons not now remembered. These un-churched members elected S. Caldwell their moderator. They met on the second and fourth Sundays in the Centenary M.E. sanctuary.

Break-Away

Going with Caldwell were Mr. and Mrs. Dan Smith, Mr. and Mrs. Cornelius Harris, Martha Andrews, Anna Roberts, Lennie Hill, Mary Robinson, Louis Birden, David Pollock, John Kennedy, Lillie Ward and Jerry Young Howard. The break-away Baptists called Rev. I.W. Washington from Arcadia, Fla., and formerly Savannah, Ga., as pastor of a new church they named Macedonia Missionary. Harris was licensed as a preacher at this time and later ordained a minister by Rev. Washington, as was Caldwell and Richard Robinson as assistant pastors.

Rev. C.W. Dawson was called by St. Mark in 1947. He began St. Mark's affiliation with the Progressive Association, the Sunday School Convention, the District Congress and other Baptist organizations. The number of deacons grew to six, including Birden, Anderson, Washington, Wiley, Williams, and McCloud. In the latter part of 1954, Rev. Hill was called. He was succeeded the following year by Rev. C.J. Jones until 1960. It was during the latter's tenure that Hurricane Donna partially destroyed the sanctuary. Upon the completion of repairs, Rev. J.L. Harris was called and served until 1962.

After a short period without a pastor, Rev. Ted McNeil was called. Deacons Geroy Neal, James Felder, Robert Jones and Gus Barton were ordained. The increase in membership led to construction of the present St. Mark sanctuary in 1976. Rev. McNeil served until 1979. His tenure of 17 years is the longest to date. Since then, St. Mark has been served by the Reverends W.P. McCoy, Eddie Nails, and Nathaniel Fredrick.

A five-mast schooner loads phosphate at Boca Grande in 1920 while a steamship waits its turn. Tank cars contain fresh water.

Chapter 26

FROM SAIL TO STEAM

A 6-foot panorama photograph of the South Boca Grande phosphate shipping station in 1920 provides a striking view of the transition from sail to steam at Charlotte Harbor.

The rare photograph is a treasured memento of the pioneer Cleveland family. U.S. Cleveland is president of the Charlotte Harbor Area Historical Society at Punta Gorda. He was born in 1919 at the station where his father, Cleve Henry Cleveland, was an electrician keeping a power station and hundreds of motors purring.

The 180-degree sweep of the southern tip of Gasparilla Island was made by a Tampa photographer using a revolving camera geared to an unwinding roll of film. It shows four steam freighters waiting to load after a majestic 5-masted schooner. A steam dredge puffs smoke as it works to keep the dock channel open to deep-draft ships.

The schooner is of particular interest. With five masts, it had reached the practical limit of sailing vessels for carrying bulk cargo. A 7-masted schooner had been built in 1902 but was too cumbersome and slow when loaded. The unknown ship at South Boca Grande probably was 400 feet in length and carried phosphate across the Atlantic.

The commercial value of phosphate pebbles in the Peace River was recognized in 1890 by Joseph Hull and Hugh Commer, fertilizer

115

manufacturers at Savannah, Ga. Their primitive operation here was purchased in December 1894 by the Peace River Phosphate Mining Co.

Phosphate at first was hauled by rail to a long dock at Punta Gorda. Later, the rock was transported by barge to large ships waiting in deeper water near Boca Grande Pass. (For details of the Peace River phosphate operation see Chapter 45 of Vol. I.) As Peace River phosphate played out, the mining company bought richer acreage inland farther north and formed the American Agricultural Chemical Company. The firm built the 40-mile Charlotte Harbor & Northern Railroad in 1907 to carry ore from Mulberry to South Boca Grande.

The only inhabitants on Gasparilla Island at that time were a few fishermen at the north end, and a lighthouse keeper on the south tip. Albert W. Gilchrist of Punta Gorda, a railroad surveyor and later governor of Florida, had bought and platted six U.S. government blocks on the highest part of the island for town lots in 1897; but none were sold. American Agricultural bought Gilchrist's property and constructed the stately Gasparilla Inn for winter visitors.

Exclusive Getaway

The company and Gilchrist formed the Boca Grande Land company — with Gilchrist as president — to sell beach-front lots to wealthy families from the north who liked a quiet, exclusive getaway.

Phosphate was transferred from rail gondolas on the dock to ships while AACC built an integrated loading facility. Storage bins and conveyor belts to load ore directly onto ships were inaugurated in 1911.

Railroad tanker cars supplied steamers with boiler water brought from Horse Creek at Platt. There was no palatable water on the island, except from rain cisterns. Workers at the station lived in company houses. The company also operated a general store and post office for its personnel.

Cleve Cleveland moved his family to Punta Gorda in 1921 so his eldest son Gerald, could go to school. Cleveland managed the city-owned electric power plant and lines, later sold to the Florida Power and Light Company. His wife, Jean, taught school for a year then went to work in the city clerk's office. Eventually she became city clerk for many years and lived to be 100 years old.

U.S. Cleveland today bears a constant reminder of the family relocation. Personal belongings were carried by rowboat to a barge to be towed to Punta Gorda. As the family boarded, little U.S. held onto the edge of the rowboat. It bumped against the barge and pinched off the tip of the middle finger of his right hand.

Last shipment of phosphate from the station was in 1972. A few years later, the giant wooden structures were demolished as a safety precaution. These were replaced with steel storage tanks of bunker oil which is barged as needed to the Florida Power and Light plant at East Fort Myers.

Chapter 27

ALL STREETS NAMED FOR TRABUES

What's in a name?
That which we call a rose,
By any other name would smell as sweet.

From *"Romeo and Juliet"*
by William Shakespeare.

As if Punta Gorda doesn't have enough controversies to stir up the populace, another arose over what street might be renamed appropriately in honor of Rev. Martin Luther King, Jr.

The choice was difficult because every street in the old, central district has overtones harking back 110 years when the city was laid out by Col. Isaac H. Trabue and his wife Virginia S. (nee) Taylor.

Real Kentucky Colonel

Isaac was a real Kentucky colonel who served in the Federal Army during the Civil War. His father, Chastain, and grandfather Stephen Francis James Trabue, operated coal mines that served northern railroads with fuel necessary to prosecute the war.

After the war, Isaac became a lawyer involved in the family business. However, his health was poor so he noted with interest in 1883 a newspaper advertisement describing the climate and unspoiled beauty of Charlotte Harbor. The advertiser was John Cross, a recent British immigrant engaged in real estate, citrus, and ox-team freight hauling at Liverpool, Fla., on the Peace River south of Fort Ogden. Cross founded the Liverpool in 1880 and was an enthusiastic promoter of Southwest Florida. His ventures prospered when phosphate was mined in the Peace River but collapsed when the mineral played out and Cross ran away from his debts and family.

Responding to Cross' ad, Trabue purchased 30 acres on the south shore of Charlotte Harbor sight unseen from James Madison Lanier. Then Trabue purchased an additional 300 acres from the Florida Internal Improvement Fund at $1.25 an acre.

Isaac leased a large portion of the acreage the following year to John Trabue, his cousin, who planted a citrus nursery. The colonel directed John to hire a surveyor to lay out the property in town lots, reserving a strip along the shore for public parks. John engaged Kelly B. Harvey who was surveying the area at that time for Hamilton Disston. The latter was a Philadelphia saw manufacturer. He had bought four million acres of "swamp and overflowed lands" around Charlotte Harbor and Lake Okeechobee from the Internal Improvement Fund for 25 cents per acre. .

Harvey completed his assignment in December 1884 and sent his sketch to the colonel at Louisville, Ky., for approval. Isaac named the town "Trabue" and the streets after family members, for the most part. He did include Cross, Harvey, and several other friends. Before returning the plat to Harvey, Isaac recorded it at Jefferson County, Ky., on Jan. 6, 1885. Harvey had it filed Feb. 24 in Manatee County — then encompassing Charlotte Harbor.

With plat in hand, Col. Trabue persuaded the Florida Southern Railway, to extend its line from Bartow, Fla., to his uninhabited plat. However, he had to give half his original holding to Florida Southern as an inducement to build a $100,000 resort hotel. The railroad chose the eastern half of the town of Trabue. Col. Trabue and a friend, William F. Wood, bought adjacent land for development. At one time, Trabue was the town's largest land holder, but he died broke in 1907.

The first train arrived in July 1886. The hotel was opened to visitors in time for the 1886-87 winter season. The town itself — the southernmost railroad terminal in the United States — boomed.

New arrivals, led by Harvey, drew up a city charter in the winter of 1887 in order to tax themselves for streets and ditches. While they were at it, the organizers changed the town's name to Punta Gorda which the hotel had adopted for the geographical "Fat Point" so called by early Spanish-Indian fishermen.

Streets Memorialize Family

Though the town name was changed, the streets were left alone. Thus, the community remains the only one known in the United States whose streets memorialize a family. Following are the original streets and the people for whom named — starting at the east side:

WILLET — for Willet Chastine Trabue, a nephew.

RETTA ESPLANADE — for Henrietta Trabue, an elderly aunt who came to the town of Trabue in 1886 and died shortly thereafter. Her nickname was Retta; as was Isaac's sister, Henrietta Jane, who married Dr. **Milus Cooper Nesbitt.** Esplanade was simply a French name for a beautiful walkway. Each of the doctor's names were used for street names.

MARION — a brother, sometimes misspelled Marian, the feminine form, on later maps.

MILOT — believed to be a spelling error for Milus which appeared on all subsequent maps. See Retta Esplanade, above.

OLYMPIA — for Olympia Dupuy, Isaac's cousin through his Uncle James Trabue.

118

COCHRAN — maiden name of sister-in-law Caroline Cochran, wife of Isaac's brother Edmund. Now named Martin Luther King, Jr. Blvd.

VIRGINIA — Isaac's wife, Virginia S. (nee) **Taylor.**

CHARLOTTE — Virginia's mother, Charlotte **Taylor**. She was America's first woman entomologist (insect scientist) whose beautiful drawings in color are on display at the Punta Gorda Public Library.

HELLEN — sister, Judith Hellen, who married Dr. Thomas A. **MacGregor.**

STEPHEN — for Stephen Francis James Trabue, Isaac's grandfather, brother and nephew. The latter, a lawyer, moved to Punta Gorda and became city attorney, mayor and county judge.

ROBERT — for Robert Berry Trabue, Isaac's nephew who married Maude (nee) Barr.

WILLIAM — for Isaac's brother, uncle, and nephew.

WOOD — for William F. Wood, a business associate who developed the first two subdivisions of Trabue-Punta Gorda.

NESBIT — Misspelling for Dr. Milus Cooper Nesbitt. See Retta Esplanade, above.

KING — May be for Archibald King, a friend of the Trabue family in Kentucky who owned the famed Weehawken Plantation. The Trabue-Punta street also might be for Ziba King, a prominent Fort Ogden rancher and merchant whose cattle path to Charlotte Harbor Town became King's Highway. It is not likely that Isaac knew him in 1884, but he might have been suggested by Cross and/or Harvey as a good business move. Ziba King later was a partner with James Sandlin in a general store on King Street across from the Hotel Punta Gorda.

TAYLOR — maiden name of Isaac's wife. See Virginia and Charlotte.

CR0SS — for John Cross, real estate agent who brokered Isaac's initial purchase of 30 acres from James Madison Lanier.

HARVEY — Kelly B. Harvey, surveyor who laid out the plat for Trabue town. He remained to become a prominent businessman but also ran away later from his wife and debts.

GILL — for Charles W. Gill, husband of Isaac's sister, Ann Elizabeth.

McGREGOR — mis-spelling of Isaac's brother-in-law, Dr. Thomas MacGregor. See Hellen.

CHASTEEN — also spelled Chastain and Chastine. Isaac's father, brother and nephew. See Willet, above.

BARRY — mis-spelling for Isaac's nephew Robert Berry who married **Maude** (nee) Barr. Also, Alice Elizabeth Berry, Isaac's niece through his brother Stephen. Correct spelling is used on later maps.

SHREVE — origin unknown.

PITMAN — origin unknown.

ALICE — for niece Alice Elizabeth through his brother, Stephen F.J. Trabue. She never married.

MAUDE — for wife of Isaac's nephew, Robert Berry. See Robert. above.

COSBY — for Isaac's Aunt Lucinda Dupuy (nee) Cosby, wife of his uncle, James Trabue. See Olympia.

BROWN — This street, originally west of Fishermen's Village, is no longer in existence there. The present Brown Street was cut through in recent years. The first is believed to be for F.Q. Brown, agent for the Florida Commercial Co., real estate division of the Florida Southern Railway. If this is correct, then both men were business acquaintances before the railroad decided on its route south of Bartow. Inclusion of Brown's name on the 1884-85 town plat suggests Trabue may have had inside information from his friend about Florida Southern's plans, or Brown obtained his position upon the recommendation of Isaac after the railroad arrived. The original street was not named for George Brown, the noted mulatto ship builder, who did not arrive in the area until 1890. Origin of today's short street is unknown and possibly was intended to honor George Brown.

ELIZABETH — Isaac's mother. Also the middle name of his sister Ann Elizabeth who married Dr. Charles Gill. See Alice and Gill.

WILSON — origin unknown. The name is included in William F. Wood's first addition to the town of Trabue and may have been appended by Wood.

INVILLE — origin unknown. Obliterated in 1984 when a high-rise condo was built on Marion Ave. in Punta Gorda Isles.

TRABUE — originally a short street west of Fishermen's village but obliterated when Punta Gorda Isles was developed. The name has been applied more recently to a two-block-long street in the city's west side.

HENRY — Isaac's brother, Dr. Henry Trabue.

JOHN — for an uncle and cousin. Renamed Tamiami Trail.

Wood's first addition west of the original plat also included street names recalling other Trabue family members — Dupuy, Lucinda, and Fisher. The latter represent Mary (Taylor) Fisher, sister of Isaac's wife, Virginia (Taylor). Both ladies are buried at Indian Springs Cemetery southeast of Punta Gorda. At Isaac's request before death, his body is buried at Louisville.

Wood's Second Addition, east of town, included Trabue family names of Mary, Boots and Adrienne. Boots was extended along a section line to become Cooper St., after Dr. Milus Cooper Nesbitt.

As for renaming these old streets for modern heroes, there is no legal reason why this cannot be done. Once streets and parks are dedicated to a municipality for public use, their names can be changed at will — and often are to avoid post office confusion. City Council chose Cochran Street to rename Dr. Martin Luther King and devoted funds to improve it.

Punta Gorda First Baptist Church 1903. First full-grade school on Goldstein St. at left background. Note kerosene street lamp.

Chapter 28

FIRST BAPTIST OLDEST SANCTUARY

The oldest church building in Charlotte County is the sanctuary built by Punta Gorda First Baptist between Jan. 1890 and Nov. 1892 now occupied as a lodge by the Rebekas, women's auxiliary to the International Order of Odd Fellows. The Peace River Baptist Association reported in 1888 that a new church had been organized at Punta Gorda. Prior to that time, Baptists participated in ecumenical services at a community meeting hall on the southwest corner of Marion and Gill streets. The town's founder, Col. Isaac Trabue contributed the building in late 1886 or early 1887 for a school and inter-denominational church.

Desiring emphasis on their doctrine, the Baptists left the community center to meet in rented quarters. According to church lore, the first sanctuary was a roller skating rink over a livery stable. Baptisms were conducted in the harbor near Sullivan Street.

First Baptist records state the original congregation consisted of nine members. Among them were M/M James L. and Mary L. (nee Seward)

Sandlin, M/M James M. and Martha (nee Sandlin) Morgan, and Mrs. Nancy Linquish. Others are not known.

Sandlin and Morgan were close friends, business partners, and perhaps relatives. They purchased land for citrus groves along Alligator Creek in 1884. When the Florida Southern Railway arrived at Punta Gorda in 1886, the two men moved into town and engaged in real estate, mercantile and shipping enterprises.

Contemporary public records about the church sanctuary are scarce. Being exempt from taxes, there is no listing on the tax roll. In addition, there is no record of deed transfer — not unusual in those days when a person's word was his bond, particularly for church transactions.

We know that Block 31 on the original survey of Trabue (Punta Gorda) was bounded by Olympia, Harvey, Marion, and Cross (Tamiami Trail south) streets. Albert W. Gilchrist, a land speculator and later governor of Florida, bought Block 31 on Jan. 1, 1890. He revided it into 40 town lots, with Goldstein street running down the middle.

Descendents state that Sandlin and Morgan at this time bought, and donated to the congregation, lots 9 and 10 on the northwest corner of Cross and Olympia streets. It is thought that lumber was supplied by Morgan who operated a saw mill on Taylor Road near Alligator Creek.

First Charter Member

When Mrs. Sandlin died Nov. 23, 1934, the *Punta Gorda Herald* reported:

"Mrs. Sandlin was perhaps the first charter member of the local Baptist church which was organized here 45 years ago. She and her husband, (who died in 1903) gave the property on which the church is built. It may be stated as a fact that through the years, her first thought was always of her church, in which she was very active to the end of her life. Funeral services were conducted by the Rev. Sutley, pastor, on Sunday afternoon. Not all who came were able to get into the church."

The first, official record discovered discloses that "James L. Sandlin, trustee for the Punta Gorda Baptist Church," on Nov. 13, 1892, transferred 10 feet off the north side of Lot 9 to Bart K. Watts for $45. Watts was president of city council. He did not obtain title to the adjoining Lot 8, from L.T. Blocksom, until four months later.

It was customary for churches to have at least three trustees, but no record of others have been found. Certainly the church was constructed prior to selling part of the site. The first issue of the *Punta Gorda Herald* on Feb. 17, 1893, noted:

"Two handsome structures, a Methodist and Baptist church, white, together with a parsonage for Methodist ministers, two colored churches, and a large school house are among the public buildings erected by the citizens for the benefit of this community."

First pastor of First Baptist was Rev. Thomas J. Sparkman, who was appointed superintendent of schools in 1887 when DeSoto County was formed, and was chairman of the DeSoto County Temperance Association in 1895. This likely is the same man who in 1885 bought a proved-out homestead of 160 acres north of Charlotte Harbor Town along Ziba King's cow path from Pine Level. The latter village was the Manatee County seat 10 miles northwest of today's Arcadia and included what is now Charlotte and DeSoto counties.

Rev. Sparkman pastored baptists at Punta Gorda and Fort Myers simultaneously for at least seven years. The *Herald* reported in its Church Directory of Oct. 20, 1893, that "Rev. T.J. Sparkman, pastor, conducts regular services every first and third Sundays, at 11 a.m. Sunday School every Sunday, T.J. Wellhouse, superintendent."

In June 1895, the Herald reported that Rev. M.S. Stevens of the Punta Gorda Baptist Church officiated at the marriage of Robert L. Earnest and Miss Gertrude Ebney at the residence of her mother, Mrs. E.T. Ebney.

The worship schedule changed in June 1910 when the *Herald* announced that Rev. Martin A. Wood, Baptist pastor, would conduct services every second and fourth Sundays at 11 a.m. and 7:30 p.m.

Adopt Tithing

Also in 1910, the congregation adopted tithing, formed the Women's Missionary Society, and constructed a concrete baptismal pool. A pastorium costing $3,500 was built behind the church in 1922, and Sunday school rooms were added in 1927 and 1929.

A building on a large lot was acquired on Retta Esplanade in the early 1940s for a new sanctuary. A construction program began, and Sunday school classes were held at both the Cross Street and Retta Esplanade facilities. Worship services were held at the Cross Street sanctuary.

The rapidly growing congregation outgrew the Retta Esplanade site before a new sanctuary could be built. Consequently the present site of First Baptist on Gill Street was acquired in 1959. The Crosland Chapel and Sunday school were dedicated Jan. 28, 1962. The old pastorium was moved to the present site, but later torn down. With completion of the Crosland Chapel, the Cross Street and Retta Esplanade properties were sold to the Golden Rule Rebekah Lodge 60.

The church began its greatest out-reach effort in the late 1950's with establishment of the Port Charlotte Mission. The first Mission service was held in the Port Charlotte Community Center on Mother's Day, May 8, 1960. Dr. John H. Witt preached the sermon. Dedication services for the Mission were held Jan. 1, 1961; and the first building dedicated July 16, 1961. The Mission became First Baptist Church of Port Charlotte.

Punta Gorda First Baptist voted in January 1975 to undertake a $1 million three-phase building program. First was an addition to the

Crosland Chapel. The educational building was completed in January 1976. Phase three consisted of paving, drainage and landscaping.

During this busy period, the church sponsored the South Punta Gorda Baptist Mission. Rev. Jack Edgeman was the first pastor there. The Mission became Trinity Baptist Church.

Punta Gorda First Baptist has 700 members guided by the Rev. Charles Mack Hutson — and is still growing.

Today, the first sanctuary awaits a new mission. The spire roof was taken off in the early 30s (prior to 1935) when the wood shingles needed replacing and no one could be found to undertake the dangerous job. The belfrey was removed by the Rebekahs in the late 60s (after 1962) when the flat cap replacing the spire began to leak. The bell was given to the Palmdale Methodist church in Glades County.

PASTORAL ROSTER

Records of early pastors are missing, but those remembered by long-time parishoners or discovered in the *Herald* are:

Rev. Thomas J. Sparkman, 1889-93
Rev. _____ Graham, June 1904
Rev. W.P. Head, April 1908
Rev. M.S. Stevens, 1895-6
Rev. Thomas R. Woodson, 1914-15
Rev. Dr. Martin A. Wood, 1910
Rev. R.A. Sublette, 1/16/19
Rev. W.R. Poindexter, 4/17/19
Rev. Harry Grady Kenney, 1919
Rev. _____ Swain
Rev. E.L. Andrews
Rev. Dr. A.J. Holt, 1924-26
Rev. Dr. James S. Day, Jr.
Rev. James H. Sutley, 1934.
    Conducted 50th Anniversary service on Oct. 5, 1939.
Rev. Arvil Miller, Early 1940's
Rev. John F. Price, 1945   His 1945 welcome in the church included a large
    delegation of visiting Methodists.
Rev. George Wehrman, 1956-64.
    Conducted last service in original sanctuary on Jan. 25, 1962.
Rev. Dr. Reaves Dean
Rev. Ray Bateman, 1968-75
Rev. Dr. Harold Brown, 1976-81.
Rev. Milford Howell, 1981-82.
Rev. Dr. Charles Haywood Day, 1982-85.
    No relation to James Day.
Rev. Randy Randall, 1985-86
Rev. Charles Mack Hutson, 1986-present.
    Conducted Nov. 5, 1989, Centennial Service.

(NOTE: Roster includes some interim ministers.)

First Good Shepherd Church at Punta Gorda. Rectory next door.

Chapter 29

SIX-SHOOTER FUNDED EPISCOPAL CHURCH

The merry party aboard Caldwell Hart Colt's yacht *Oriole* — anchored off Hotel Punta Gorda in early 1894 — fell silent with shock.

"Man overboard!"

Everyone rushed on deck where crewmen with boat hooks tried to grapple a body floating face down in the water below. My God! It's Caldwell" Obviously he had drowned, unnoticed.

Caldwell, 34, was the only son and principal beneficiary of Samuel Colt's fabulous fortune amassed by invention and manufacture of the "six-shooter" revolver that "won the West." He and his mother, the elderly widow Elizabeth, wintered regularly at Punta Gorda, then a mecca for wealthy sportsmen.

In grief, Mrs. Colt commissioned Louis Tiffany, the famous artist, to create a stained-glass window in memory of her son. It was to illustrate the good shepherd theme of Christ for the Episcopal church under construction at Punta Gorda.

Episcopalians at Punta Gorda were few in number when the town's founder, Col. Isaac Trabue, built a town hall in 1887 for a "unity" church

125

and school. Baptists formed their own congregation in 1889 and left the community hall to meet in rented store quarters. This was inspiration for Presbyterians and Episcopalians to do likewise. The Methodists bought the hall and added a bell tower and chancel. The small Episcopalian congregation met at Magnolia Hall. It was the second floor of a lumber warehouse on the site of Punta Gorda's present post office, according to a memoir by Mrs. Willie A White and Mrs. J.F. Corbett. Mrs. White, the town's first telegraph operator, and Mrs. Corbett were long-time members.

Mrs. Virginia Trabue, wife of Isaac, was acknowledged leader of the Episcopalians. She began writing letters to Episcopal Bishop William C. Gray at Orlando asking for a mission church at Punta Gorda. Bishop Gray came in December 1892 to investigate the possibility. He was hosted by William Huckeby at Cleveland. Mr. and Mrs. William H. Cleveland, homesteaders at what is now Harbour Heights, rowed across Peace River to have their 12-year-old son Cleve baptized by Bishop Gray. The ceremony was held in the lobby of the Baxter House hotel.

Later that month, Cleveland School Teacher Sarah Morton decorated the first Christmas tree in the area for her pupils. Bishop Gray blessed the parents and children who came.

Bishop Gray concluded the potential congregation was large enough, and their faith strong enough, to support a mission church. He and Rev. William Bradley, Caldwell Colt's close friend and tutor, came to Punta Gorda several times to counsel the little flock.

Gilchrist Donates Site

Albert Gilchrist, a land speculator who one day would be elected governor of Florida, donated a church site on the northeast corner of Cross St. (Tamiami Trail, south) and Virginia Avenue in January 1893.

The *Herald* in February reported: "The Saint James Episcopal Church is soon to be erected in Punta Gorda according to Right Rev. W.C. Gray, bishop of the new church. This will make six churches in Punta Gorda, including colored." Mrs. Colt, daughter of an Episcopalian minister, offered to donate $1,000 — enough for the lumber — if the new sanctuary was named Church of the Good Shepherd. This was the name of her family church at Hartford, Conn. The offer was gratefully accepted.

Additional funds accumulated slowly. It was not until the winter of 1894-95 that a second contribution of money by Elizabeth Colt, and her memorial gift of the window, enabled construction to begin. Her sister, Caldwell Colt's aunt, Hettie Hart Beach, donated a baptismal font. Lumber came from Huckeby's sawmill at Cleveland.

The *Herald* reported in May 1895 that "Work on the new Episcopal Church is progressing." Rev. Samuel D. Hodgman was appointed the first minister. The church, with an impressive bell tower and steeple, was completed late that year.

126

Bishop Gray came and consecrated the church on Jan. 25, 1896. On that same day he conducted the first Episcopalian baptism there — of a baby boy, Elnece Nelson Ribaner. Sadly the infant died later that year and so became also the first burial from the new church.

Rev. Hodgman served only until Nov. 1896 and was succeeded by Rev. James D. Warren who served until 1897. Rev. Dr. A. Kinney Hall, who was married to William Huckeby's niece, tended the congregation from 1898 until 1899. With his going, the church closed for a year. Reverends W.H. Bates and B.M. Brodin came intermittently, as was customary for mission churches, until January 1902. Then, Rev. Thomas J. Purdue served Jan. 1902 to April 1904.

During this period of short terms for pastors, the church women continued active on behalf of congregational concerns. The *Herald* of January 1902 noted: "Mrs. Trabue went to Tampa to attend the annual meeting of the Women's Auxiliaries of the Episcopal Church."

The pulpit was empty once more after Rev. Purdue left until Rev. William P. Browne took charge Dec. 1905 - Apr. 1907.

Colorful Pastor

One of Good Shepherd's most colorful pastors was Rev. Irenaeus Trout who served 1908-1909. To make him welcome, the Women's Auxiliary members assessed themselves 10 cents a month each to purchase a rug, mattress, comforter and curtains for the rectory.

Rev. Trout re-organized the Sunday school for children and ministered to the Seminole Indians at Immokalee. He was particularly proud of having begun the conversion of the Seminoles to Christianity. (For details of his Indian missionary work see Chapter 24.)

By this time, music had become an important part of worship. Said the *Herald* in Sept. 1908: "Mrs. P.W. McAdow has been appointed musical director for the Episcopal Church." Mr. and Mrs. McAdow were prominent citizens of Punta Gorda who moved there from Montana in 1896 after making a fortune in gold mining.

Rev. Dr. Robert Campbell became rector in 1910, preaching three Sundays of the month. First Sundays were spent at other nearby mission churches. Rev. Clement T. Blanchet served 1911-25 — the longest term up to that time.

The tenure of Rev. Henry E. Payne Dec. 26, 1925, to 1938 was marked by two of the most destructive hurricane in Florida's history. Church of the Good Shepherd was heavily damaged in the 1926 storm.

His rectorship started pleasantly. The *Herald* of Jan. l, 1926 reported: "Dr. and Mrs. Henry E. Payne and their little daughter arrived here from Brooklyn, N.Y., on Wednesday and were located in the rectory of the Episcopal Church. They were met by a committee of ladies of the church who inducted them into their new residence which had been specially prepared for them. The ladies served a simple repast to the trio. The Doctor has been engaged for the permanent service of the local church."

The Great Hurricane of 1926 came ashore at Miami on the night of Sept. 17. Much damage was done, but the loss of life was small. An eerie calm followed. People rushed into the streets and began clearing wreckage unaware that the eye of the hurricane was passing. Then the main force of wind hit. Scores were killed while digging out of the wreckage. Wind instruments clocked speeds of 125 miles per hour before being blown down. The deadly hurricane roared westward, knocking down everything in its path.

Lake Okeechobee was blown out of its basin, sending a seven-foot wall of water crashing through Moore Haven. All buildings were destroyed, 386 people were killed.

When the hurricane reached the west coast Sept. 21, wind had dissipated some. Still, the damage at Punta Gorda was the heaviest in its history. Many buildings were destroyed. Miraculously, no one was killed.

Church of the Good Shepherd was lifted off its foundation, and its beautiful bell tower toppled into the street. Rev. Payne declared in the *Herald:* "The church building is destroyed, but the church still lives! Services will be held in the Rectory next Sunday morning. Every Christian in Punta Gorda ought to be in their respective places of worship to pray that God will comfort our bereaved and suffering neighbors, and to thank Him for the deliverance of our city. Thank God for his mercy!"

The church was not totally destroyed, however. Rev. Payne appealed for contributions to repair the sanctuary and re-position the bell tower. He asked that donations be given to him, Mrs. Sadie Farrington, Mrs. Willie White, Charles Steele, or W.W. Sinclair.

Repair Damage

In November, the *Herald* reported: "The rather formidable task of straightening out the wreckage of the Episcopal church, and preparing to raise it upon new foundations, is about completed.

"The plan is to raise the building just where it fell, build a concrete foundation and then repair the damage to the wood-work. The base of the tower will be placed back and a belfry erected."

Charles Cerny stretched steel rods across the sanctuary and pulled the sagging walls back into plumb. The lattice work of the original belfry was beyond repair. A small second-floor room of the tower was converted to a belfry by removing windows and replacing them with louvers.

Repairs were accomplished just in time to weather the next hurricane in November of 1928. This storm took a more northerly course and did less damage in Charlotte County, but devastated the Lake Okeechobee region. In Moore Haven, Belle Glade and Clewiston and other towns south and west of the lake, 2,700 persons lost their lives.

Rev. Payne died in 1938, and the church was closed during the unsettling years of the Great Depression and World War II. It was reopened in 1945 intermittently with "supply priests." Rev. J. Hill Johnson and Rev. A. Bruce Laurenborg. The Rev. John E. Massie became vicar of Good Shepherd in April, 1948 with charge also of the mission churches St. Andrews of Boca Grande, and St. Edmund Martyr in Arcadia where he resided. Good Shepherd at that time had just 15 members.

The eight members of the Women's Auxiliary in 1951 painted the rectory, long vacant, in preparation for Rev. W. Jusserand deForest who arrived in November. Rev. A. Leonard Manley, from London, Ontario, was supply priest from 1952 until mid-1957. Rev. Massie took up duties again at Good Shepherd until the last Sunday of 1957.

The Rev. J. Saxton Wolfe in Feb. 1958 became the first, resident priest at Good Shepherd in 20 years. He was followed by Rev. James Hubbs 1959-66, Rev. Benton Ellis 1967, Rev. Dr. Charles E. White 1968- 69, Rev. John B. Chapter 1970, Rev. Robert M. Caldwell 1971-85, and Rev. Vincent F. Scotto Jan. 1986 to the present.

Rapid Growth

During the rapid growth of Southwest Florida in the 1950's and 60's, Good Shepherd sponsored formation of two mission congregations — St. James at Port Charlotte, Rev. Peter A. Madson; and St. Nathaniels at North Port, Rev. Raymond Allington. Sponsorship of mission churches by a mission church is unusual. Brotherhood of St. Anthony was started in 1961, Daughters of the King in 1962, and the Parish Day School in 1963. The church became a full-fledged parish in May of 1963.

Good Shepherd membership soared to 315 families in the 1970's — outstripping the little pioneer church at Cross Street and Virginia Avenue. The present church site of 4.5 acres at Shreve and Henry streets was purchased in 1978, and construction of a new sanctuary began the following summer. The new church was dedicated on May 23, 1980.

The congregation had hoped to move the old sanctuary to the new site and enlarge it. However, cost of temporary take-downs of utility wires proved prohibitive. Instead, the style was duplicated as nearly as possible — thus preserving the old Florida appearance of the exterior, and the beautiful Gothic beams in the sanctuary. The parish bought an adjoining five acres in 1991 and plans a major expansion in the next two years — a testimony to the faith and perseverance of a dozen pioneers true to the Episcopal faith, and to a grieving mother.

Construction crew of 1890 at Punta Gorda grades a new street.

Chapter 30

HORSES ON HOTEL VERANDA A NO-NO

Discovery of a journal of ordinances at Punta Gorda city hall sheds new light on the reason(s) why citizens of the new town of Trabue in 1887 rebelled, incorporated and changed their community name to that of the landmark called "Fat Point" by Spanish-Indian fishermen.

Col. Isaac Trabue bought — sight unseen — 30 acres of swampy land on the south shore of Charlotte Harbor in 1884. Several investors of Louisville, Kentucky, at that time speculated in Florida land being opened to settlement by railroads.

Surveyor Kelly B. Harvey, then investigating a route for Florida Southern Railway, was hired by Trabue to plat his tract in 1885. The two men quarreled over payment — a dispute resolved when Harvey accepted four lots on a street he named for himself. Trabue persuaded the railroad company to choose his uninhabited town site for its southernmost terminal and resort hotel. With arrival of the first train in July of 1886, the town of Trabue literally sprang up over night.

That train brought 200 carpenters, lumber and gondolas of marl fill. Workmen, white and black, lived in tents while they built the huge Hotel Punta Gorda. A few business men came to supply necessities. Some entrepreneurs set up establishments to furnish whiskey and friendly women with no morals to speak of. Fighting was the principal sport on Saturday nights. There were five murders that first year. The Manatee County sheriff sent a deputy to lock up the worst brawlers in a boxcar.

Wives of respectable business men, and wealthy patrons of the hotel, demanded pleasant surroundings. An advertisement in the town's first newspaper, The *Punta Gorda Beacon,* on Oct. 28, 1887, invited citizens to a meeting in Thomas Hector's pool hall on the evening of Dec. 3 to incorporate Thirty-four registered voters, including four African-Americans, voted that night to incorporate as Punta Gorda and elected a city council. Trabue and two others objected, but the reformers would not be denied. A number of men immediately rowed across the harbor and walked 30 miles to register the vote at the county seat of Pine Level.

In relating this event 36 years later, Harvey wrote: "At that time, there were no streets, sidewalks or ditches. High saw grass, palmetto and pine woods were everywhere. Mosquitos were fierce. When it rained we waded, and the few lady pioneers stayed home. The largest owner of property, Mr. Trabue, could not be induced to contribute to, or make, any drainage or public improvements. Therefore, I started a movement to incorporate a town to tax for improvements and government."

Trabue challenged the incorporation and name change in the courts for 10 years without avail. His only comment in later years was laconic: "The people of the town got mad with me, and to vent their spleen they changed the name of the town and post office."

First City Council

The first city Council was comprised of Mayor William H. Simmons, Clerk Thomas Hector, Marshal John Stanfield and councilmen William Burland, Neil Dahl, James L. Sandlin, Joseph O. Swisher, and Harvey.

These men were charged with the task of building a city government from scratch. Their first working session was held Dec. 10, 1887, in Sandlin's office. Minutes of that and subsequent early meetings have been lost. However, the newly found Ordinance Journal gives us an insightful glimpse of their labors. It was compiled shortly after April 1896 when the original statutes were codified and "repassed" by council. The first council meeting adopted seven ordinances. It is interesting to note what was most pressing on the councilmen's minds — and, by the amount of the fines, what transgressions were thought most grievous.

1. All ordinances shall take effect after having been published for three days by posting upon three conspicuous places.

2. Any person found guilty of carrying a concealed weapon shall be fined not more than $15.

3. Any person found guilty of indecent exposure of person, or of profane or obscene language, shall be fined not more than $25.

4. Any person who disturbs any public gathering, assembled for a lawful purpose, shall be fined not more than $300.

5. Any person found drunk and disorderly, or incapable of taking care of himself, shall be taken into custody by the Marshal and brought before the Mayor; and upon conviction be fined not more than $50.

6. Persons obstructing the public streets, sidewalks, or ditches without special permission from the Mayor shall be fined not more than $25.

7. Any persons violating any of the ordinances of the town who fail or refuse to pay their fines shall, at the discretion of the Mayor, be kept in custody or required to work out their fines on any public work designated by the Council at the rate of $1 per day.

More Laws Two Days Later

This first meeting on ordinances must have ended unfinished. Councilmen met two days later to continue. They adopted nine more ordinances, but numbers 10, 11 and 12 were repealed by the time of codification.

8. Persons committing a breach of the peace shall be fined not more than $250.

9. Persons found guilty of gambling shall be fined not more than $100.

13. Hog pens will not be allowed within 600 yards of any dwelling within the corporate limits of the town without special permission from the Council. Fine not more than $100.

14. All slaughter houses, meat and fish markets, and fruit and vegetable stands shall be kept in a clean condition, and all offal shall be removed daily to a place designated by the Council. This includes sawdust, sweepings and shells. Fine not more than $50. The Marshal shall inspect the slaughter houses, markets and stands daily.

15. Any person offering or espousing for sale diseased or spoiled meat, game, fish, fruits, vegetables, or any other kind of food unfit for use shall be fined not more than $100.

16. Sawdust shall under no condition be used for filling up holes, or for surfacing streets, alleys, or sidewalks. Fine not less than $100.

Another Day Another Ordinances

The next day, Council labored on with five more ordinances:

17. No slaughter house or slaughter pens shall be permitted within the corporate limits of town without special permission from the Council. Fine not more than $100. (A note in the margin of this ordinance suggested "consolidate 15 and 17.")

18. Any person throwing or dumping refuse of any description into the waters of Charlotte Harbor within the corporate limits of the town shall be fined not more than $50.

19. All sidewalks of the streets shall be of the uniform width of ten feet, and all porches or verandas built over the sidewalks shall be of the full

width of the sidewalk — the columns standing in the curb and the floor to be level as the sidewalks. Fine not more than $50.

20. Any hog found running at large shall be impounded by the Marshal. After having been advertised for three days at the Council room, the hog(s) will be sold to pay expenses unless the owner appears and pays the costs of impounding — which cost shall be 25 cents for each hog per day.

21. Any person keeping or frequenting a house of ill fame within the corporate limit of the town shall be fined not more than $100.

Least Offensive Deportment

The least offensive illegality was carrying a concealed weapon ($15). The worst ones were disturbing a public assembly ($300) and disturbing the peace ($250). Frontiersmen routinely carried firearms. Local cowhunters (please, not cowboys) drove their cattle to ships at the cattle dock west of town. Then they returned to raise a ruckus in the bars or ride their horses up the hotel steps to scatter guests sitting on the wide veranda.

It was not until March 26, 1888, that Council adopted ordinance 26 ordering: "All property, real and personal, shall be subject to taxation and a Town Assessor appointed."

Ordinance 27, passed April 3, 1888, set forth the duties of Council. Perhaps the enthusiasm of starting a new town was waning. Section 5 warned: "Any member not appearing within half an hour of the time of meeting shall be fined 50 cents; and any member absenting himself entirely shall be fined $1." Harvey unfairly blamed Trabue for town problems. It was Trabue who went to the Boston headquarters of Florida Southern and bargained to bring the tracks to his bare swamp instead of to Charlotte Harbor Town then a well-settled village. Trabue had to give half his acreage to the railroad as inducement. He also built a community hall which served as the town's school and ecumenical church for several years.

Benefitting most from the growth of Trabue/Punta Gorda were land speculators such as Harvey, Sandlin and Albert Gilchrist whose nomination for mayor was rejected. Gilchrist was a surveyor and engineer for Florida Southern who quit to make a fortune at Punta Gorda and later become governor of Florida.

Trabue at one time was the largest property owner in the county as he, too, capitalized on opportunities. However, he was "land poor" — that is, he bought more than he could sell easily. He died in 1907, and his body was shipped to Kentucky for burial. Virginia, his widow, was unable to pay the taxes on their property. She died in poverty, having deeded the modest Trabue home on Cross Street to the city in return for abatement of taxes during her life. Mrs. Trabue, a founder of the Good Shepherd Episcopal Church, died in 1924 and is buried near her sister, Mary, at Indian Springs Cemetery near Punta Gorda.

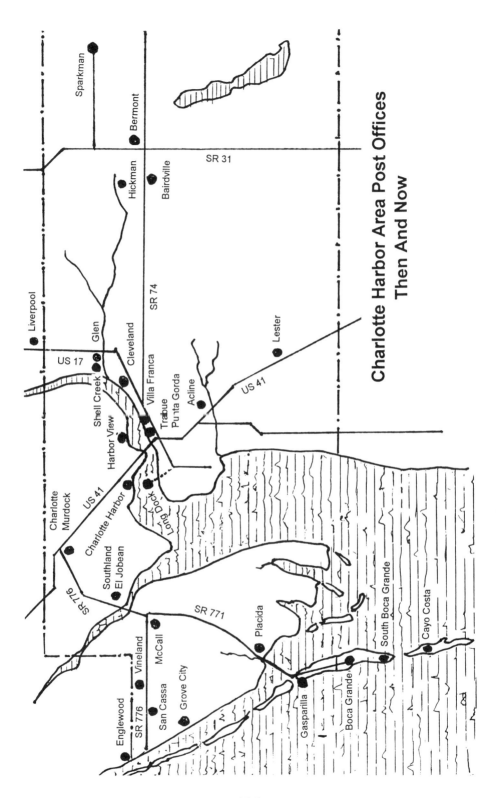

Charlotte Harbor Area Post Offices
Then And Now

Chapter 31

SETTLERS CRAVED POST OFFICES

As folks moved into southwest Florida to settle America's last frontier, they coveted a post office. That was proof the wilderness had been conquered and communication established with the rest of the nation.

Thus, I am indebted to the National Archives at Washington, D.C., for microfilm documentation of the first post offices in Manatee, DeSoto and Charlotte counties. These authenticate post offices in the area now known as Charlotte County.

Charlotte Harbor

A post office was established at Charlotte Harbor on Mar. 1, 1872 and closed Jan. 10, 1874, but we have found no record of its postmaster or exact location. It likely was Thomas Knight, proprietor of a general store.

The office was re-established Dec. 6, 1876 with John F. Bartholf as postmaster, operating from his home on Bay Shore Drive. Bartholf was a Union officer at Fort Myers during the Civil War, and returned to Florida to participated in the Reconstruction. He was appointed clerk of courts at Pine Level, the Manatee County seat. Later as superintendent of public instruction he built nine log cabin schools, including one at Hickory Bluff.

Bartholf resigned as clerk of courts in 1876 in order to avoid recognizing Democrat ballots in the disputed Hayes-Tilden presidential election. As compensation, Republican bosses made Bartholf postmaster for the villages of Hickory Bluff, Harbor View and settlers around the harbor. Though in the community of Hickory Bluff, he called the post office Charlotte Harbor to delineate his jurisdiction. The post office name in time replaced the community name of Hickory Bluff by common usage.

Hickory Bluff was the principal village where cattlemen in 1862 built a dock from which to ship cattle past the Union blockade at Boca Grande Pass Harbor View was platted shortly after the war by another Yankee soldier from Fort Myers, Nathan DeCoster.

Bartholf ran for the state legislature as a Republican in 1885 and lost. With this he changed his political registration to Democratic and moved his family to Bradenton where he became postmaster. He moved again to Jacksonville when the Sara Sota Vigilance Committee, a vicious anti-Reconstruction clan, got after him.

Harbor View

Harbor View grew and got its own post office on Aug. 14, 1890, with DeCoster as postmaster. His application for an office was certified by Robert Meacham, a prominent African- American, who was the third postmaster at Punta Gorda. The Harbor View post office was discontinued in 1932 and its operations transferred to Charlotte Harbor town.

Cleveland post office 1910.

Cleveland

As the Florida Southern Railway pushed its tracks to the Punta Gorda cape, towns along the route quickly acquired post offices. One of these was Cleveland -- named for the recently elected U.S. president.

Cleveland was platted in 1884 by Dr. A.T. Holleyman who built a hunting lodge called Baxter House. He applied for a post office the instant the railroad reached his property. The office was established March 6, 1886, at Baxter House. Postmaster was Alice A. Holleyman whose relation to the doctor is unknown, other than it was not his wife. The office became a Rural Station of Punta Gorda in 1955.

Trabue-Punta Gorda

In anticipation of the arrival of the railroad to his town plat, Col. Isaac Trabue prepared a post office application on Feb. 5, 1886, with his Aunt Lucy Dupuy Trabue recommended as postmaster. Name of the post office, was to be Trabue. However, Col. Trabue was vague about its proposed location. He stated only that it was to be "on Peace River on the south bank called Charlotte." He also stated the office would be located at the terminus of the railroad. No doubt he meant the town of Trabue rather than the end of the tracks on the long dock west of town.

The application form requested the number of inhabitants in the village. Trabue wrote, "This is a new town at end of the railroad to be completed by 4th of March." Certifying the application was Thomas S. Knight, the postmaster replacing Bartholf at Charlotte Harbor town. The application was denied, and there is no record of a subsequent application.

Nonetheless, a Post Office Department list of new offices notes the Trabue office was established Aug. 12, 1886, at "the depot" with Nannie Scott postmaster. The first railroad depot was located in the turning wye (triangle of railroad tracks) on King Street (U.S. 41 north). It now is a vacant field on the east side of Tamiami Trail south of Charlotte Avenue. The main line continued west to the Punta Gorda Long Dock.

Col. Trabue had not waited for formal, post office approval. He arranged with Albert Gilchrist, the railroad surveyor, to send one of the African-American workers up the track each day for five months to the Cleveland post office and bring back mail.

There weren't many letters because there were only a half-dozen residents and a couple hundred itinerant carpenters. The latter were building the railroad's big hotel at the foot of King Street. What mail did arrive was held and distributed by Trabue at his little land office in his front yard at the corner of Retta Esplanade and Cross Street.

That little structure, 110 years old at this writing, has been restored and moved next door to the present post office by Old Punta Gorda, Inc. It is the oldest building in Charlotte County.

Nothing is known about Nannie Scott. Tending a post office in those days generally was a public-service sideline by some shop keeper. There was little profit in stamps. Nannie's motive certainly was not to make a living as a postmaster. She may have located the post office at the railroad depot because the hotel was still under construction and there were not yet any commercial buildings.

Name of the Trabue post office was changed to Punta Gorda on Jan. 14, 1888, a month after citizens voted to incorporate and change the town's name. Nannie Scott was succeeded as postmaster by George McLane on Jan. 29, 1889.

Long Dock

The Florida Southern Railway was interested in establishing a freight and passenger connection to the Morgan Steamship Line from New Orleans to Havana. It constructed a 4,200-foot dock near today's Isles Yacht Club. Enoch A. Faulkner operated a general store there to accommodate passengers. On April 17, 1893, he was granted a special post office to be supplied from the Punta Gorda office at the railroad depot. Faulkner abandoned the Long Dock post office after a year or so. It was re-established early in 1895 — prompting the U.S. post office topographer on Feb. 4, 1895, to request verification of the location.

The reply appears to be in Col. Trabue's distinctive penmanship, but was signed by Postmaster Iva (or Ira) W. Bright whose identity is otherwise unknown. The office was discontinued Feb. 3, 1898, shortly after Henry B. Plant, principal stockholder of Florida Southern, took up the rails from Punta Gorda to the dock following a quarrel with Trabue.

Villa Franca

Cuban cigar makers came to Punta Gorda in early 1890 and bought homes to the east in an area soon known as Spanish Town. The street Rio Villa is a reminder of the settlement. A post office named Villa Franca (generous village) was established there Oct. 27, 1890, but the postmaster is not known. The office was discontinued May 25, 1891, and its operations transferred to the Punta Gorda office.

Acline

The Atlantic Coast Line Railroad, successor to Florida Southern Railway, extended its line from Punta Gorda to Fort Myers in 1904. The first whistle-stop south of Punta Gorda was at a turpentine still, sawmill camp and store. The railroad called the place Acline — acronym for ACL.

A post office was established at the store May 9, 1910. The post office was discontinued Feb. 17, 1927. Thereafter, store owners, Mr. and Mrs. George A. McGraw, relied on the sale of bootleg whiskey. Their place became notorious as the "Bloody Bucket" because of the frequent brawls there. McGraw and a robber killed each other in 1931.

Lester

A lumber camp and railroad whistle-stop next south of Acline, now the Tucker's Grade highway. Post office established there Oct. 9, 1912, and discontinued Nov. 15, 1913. Services were transferred to Acline.

Shell Creek

Shell Creek, a village of 50 inhabitants, was 1 mile east of the Peace River and ¼ mile north of Shell Creek. It received a post office June 22, 1888, with William F. Smallwood postmaster. The application was certified by Alice T. Holleyman, acting postmaster at Cleveland. Office discontinued Feb. 6, 1895, and services transferred to the Cleveland office.

Glen

A turpentine still north of Shell Creek and a stop on the Florida Southern Railway. Established May 15, 1901. Discontinued Apr. 8, 1902 — probably because it was given up by the postmaster unknown. Its operations were transferred to Cleveland. Re-established May 16, 1903, and discontinued July 31, 1916. Glen appeared as a rail stop on maps for many years after all traces of the still had disappeared.

Hickman-Bairdville

Hickman was located on the north shore of Shell Creek, nine miles upstream from Peace River. A post office was established June 7, 1901. Relocated Feb 7, 1912, to Baird's Ranch two miles due south. Renamed Bairdville with Luther C. Baird postmaster. Discontinued March 31, 1914, and operations transferred to Cleveland.

Bermont

When the land now the eastern part of Charlotte County was opened to homesteading in 1905, the area was quickly populated. The social and commercial center called Bermont consisted of two stores, a "goodwill hall" that served as school and church, and a dozen houses at the intersection of S.R. 74 and S.R. 31.

Reason for the name is unknown, as is the name of the first postmaster of May 19, 1908. Possibly they were the same. Well known postmasters in later years were storekeepers Rev. George W. Gatewood and Walter Lee Rhode. Mail was delivered twice a week. The office was discontinued Nov. 15, 1928, and mail delivered by star route from Cleveland.

Sparkman

A village two miles northeast of Bermont. Named for State Senator Sparkman who was instrumental in opening the land to homesteaders. Post office was established Oct. 23, 1914, and discontinued Oct. 31, 1942, with mail distributed by Cleveland. Sparkman, Bairdville and Bermont disappeared without trace as automobiles became commonplace.

Cayo Costa-Boca Grande

An on-again-off-again post office on Cayo Costa was established at the Boca Grande Pass quarantine station May 18, 1887. It served a half-dozen fishing families, the medical officer, harbor pilot, customs agent and occasional freight ships. However this first post office — named Boca Grande for the pass — was discontinued just 35 days later. The meager mail was routed to the Punta Gorda post office. A second office at the station was established April 29, 1892, and discontinued Jan. 17, 1894.

A third post office, this one named Cayo Costa, was established May 3, 1890, and continued until Dec. 31, 1925. At this time, the Cayo Costa facilities were moved to the South Boca Grande post office on the south end of Gasparilla Island.

Boca Grande (On Gasparilla Island)

Albert Gilchrist in 1888 surveyed the military reservation on the southern half of Gasparilla Island. He was told not to measure the northern portion lying in newly erected Desoto County. John Peacon and his brothers, of Key West, had maintained a fishing camp there since 1877.

Gilchrist bought up land on the island and was anxious to promote its development. He requested a permanent post office there in late 1893. Corroborating information was requested by the postmaster general. Gilchrist prepared a handwritten reply on Dec. 28. He wished an office within 100 to 150 yards of Boca Grande Pass and named Gasparilla. The application was signed by the proposed postmaster, Willie Henry Johnson. It was certified by Enoch Faulkner, postmaster at Long Dock.

The reply and an accompanying map by Gilchrist gives us a contemporary account of development on Gasparilla Island. Declared Gilchrist: "There is no village (at the proposed site) but there is a pilot and quarantine station, light house, fishery, about 250 (people) plus the visiting seamen." In the margins of the map, Gilchrist wrote: "Fish ranch at D (Peacon's camp) employing 15 to 20 men for about 8 months. Fish ranch at C (north end of Cayo Costa) employing 4 to 5 men for about 8 months. Fish ranch at E (slightly south of Peacon's cove, later known as Lock Joint where dock pilings were clad with grooved shells of concrete) employing 12 to 15 men for the entire year.

"In addition to these fish ranches, there are at least 50 to 75 fishermen fishing for 8 months within a radius of 10 miles of Boca Grande. In addition to the foregoing, there are often 3 or 4 vessels of 1200 to 3000 tons of phosphate being loaded by barges and lying within 5 to 8 miles of Boca Grande. During the year, fully 1500 seamen would be accommodated. Moreover, 25 to 50 men who work on the barges in loading the vessels would be accommodated."

It is likely that Gilchrist inflated the figures. Even so, Boca Grande Pass and the islands north and south sustained a lively commerce. Gilchrist's request was approved Jan. 13, 1894, but discontinued five months later — probably on the basis the island was adequately served by boat from Punta Gorda. By 1897 Gilchrist had purchased six government blocks and platted them for a proposed town to be called Boca Grande. A permanent post office named Boca Grande was established at today's location May 3, 1899, but the National Archives furnishes no details.

South Boca Grande

The Charlotte Harbor & Northern Railroad built track to a large, phosphate loading facility on the south end of Gasparilla Island in 1907 and petitioned for a post office to serve its employees. The office was granted Nov. 16, 1908, and named South Boca Grande. It was discontinued May 4, 1945, and operations transferred to Boca Grande.

San Cassa

An ambitious development west of Vineland at Englewood South. A Post office established March 9, 1927, and discontinued Nov. 14, 1931. Postal operations transferred to El Jobean.

Second El Jobean post office built 1923, closed 1970.

Southland-El Jobean

Southland, on the east bank of the Myakka River where S.R. 776 crosses, began as a camp for sport fishermen in 1887. When the Charlotte Harbor & Northern Railroad came by in 1907 it built a small station there. Soon there was a turpentine still and a fish house.

Mrs. Margaret "Madge" Kinney, a young divorcee, came to Southland in 1919 where she made a living as a dressmaker and mail carrier. She rowed across the river every day and walked to McCall to pick up mail for residents of Southland.

There she met Postmaster John Densten's son, Roy, whom she married a few years later. Mrs. Kinney succeeded in obtaining a post office for Southland on Oct. 6, 1921. She described it as "about the size of an outhouse." Mail was snatched or dropped by passing trains.

A consortium of Massachusetts and Florida developers led by Joel Bean of Boston, bought Southland n 1923. It was re-platted and named El Jo-be-an — an anagram for Joel Bean. The post office name was changed to El Jobean Oct. 1, 1924.

Bean also built a combination store, post office and home for Madge if she would remain. She ran the little facility that still stands, but in disrepair, until she retired as postmaster. Thereafter, she operated it under contract as a rural station of Punta Gorda for some additional years. It was moved to another store in El Jobean, then to South Gulf Cove.

Englewood

The Nichols brothers of Englewood, Ill. — Herbert, Howard and Ira — bought 1,091 acres of land off Lemon Bay in 1894 from John Cross and platted them into lemon groves and town lots. They opened a resort inn the following year and was granted a post office there July 5, 1895.

Vineland

Vineland was a large farm owned by William Goff on Oyster Creek and a trail, now S.R. 776, where the Tringali Community Center is located. He came into the area in 1878 and established a home, citrus grove, sawmill, turpentine still, and school. A post office was established there Sept. 30, 1897, with Joseph Huber postmaster. The application was certified by Richard Talbot. The office was closed July 31, 1902.

Grove City

Grove City, on Lemon Bay between Englewood and Placida, was platted by John Cross of Liverpool (now vanished) on the Peace River south of Fort Ogden. He succeeded in obtaining a post office March 16, 1887. The initial postmaster was Frank H. Hafer, an associate of Cross, but he was replaced within three months by Richard Talbot. The office was discontinued June 18, 1910.

Placida

The CH&N also in 1907 built a bunk house for trackworkers at the mouth of Coral Creek. Luther O'Bannion kept a wholesale fish house and store for fishermen there and at Peacon Cove. The railroad named the place Placida and petitioned for a special post office to encourage development of the fishing industry as a shipping customer.

The Placida post office was established Oct. 4, 1907, in O'Bannion's store with him as postmaster. The office was discontinued Oct. 31, 1917, and its operations transferred to Gasparilla. The facility was re-established in 1953 when the Gasparilla office was moved back to the mainland and renamed Placida.

Gasparilla

To further stimulate the fishing industry, the railroad built two wholesale fish houses along its track at the north end of the island in 1914. Two years later the CH&N built 16 small homes for renting to Peacon Cove fishermen. The little settlement was called Gasparilla, and included enough children that it had its own school.

The railroad also obtained a post office for Gasparilla Dec. 10, 1910, and appointed Arthur P. Osteen postmaster at the Charlotte Harbor Oyster and Fish Co. He was succeeded by William McElya, Oren Vickers and then Frances Vickers. By 1924, a hard-working fisherman named Gus Cole had bought both the Gasparilla fish houses and assumed the postmastership there July 17. He served until the office was moved to Placida in 1953.

McCall

McCall, at the intersection of S.R. 776 and S.R. 771, began as a store built by John Densten in 1909 shortly after the CH&N completed its line from Arcadia to Gasparilla Island. Densten was appointed postmaster March 15, 1909.

The railroad there swerved south across the trail from Englewood to Cattle Dock Point on the shore of Myakka River. Consequently, the Densten store was the nearest point for west county shippers. McCall was platted in 1911 as a railroad town.

Densten remained postmaster until the office was discontinued March 15, 1927. Its operations were transferred to the post office at El Jobean where Postmaster Margaret Kinney Densten had since become his daughter-in-law.

Charlotte-Murdock

The Charlotte Harbor & Northern Railroad, built in 1907- 8, placed a section workers' bunkhouse and loading dock for a nearby turpentine still at its intersection with a sand trail between Charlotte Harbor Town and Englewood. J.M. Moody built a store at the intersection and was awarded a post office April 15, 1908, named Charlotte.

John M. Murdock, a Chicago promoter, acquired acreage around the depot and bought Moody's store in 1911. The postmaster general gave permission to change the post office name to Murdock on Aug. 22. Murdock platted his property into five- and ten-acre plots for a farm colony. He built a two-story hotel to accommodate prospective buyers.

A.C. Frizzell, a young telegraph operator at the CH&N depot, bought Murdock's property and buildings at bargain prices when Murdock went bankrupt and abandoned his family. Frizzell went on to make a fortune raising cattle, distilling turpentine and cutting lumber. The Murdock post office continues today as a substation of the Punta Gorda office.

Liverpool

Town, now vanished, founded in 1880 by John Cross on Peace River. It served as a "port" for Fort Ogden and the early phosphate industry due to the difficulty in navigating the shallow, winding Peace River above that point. Post office established Feb. 13, 1883; discontinued Apr. 18, 1895. Services transferred to nearby Fort Ogden.

NOTE: For early stories about Cross, Grove City, Englewood, Liverpool and Acline, see *Our Fascinating Past: The Early years*.

Capt. Dewey's first paddle-wheel steamer was the *Mary Blue*.

Chapter 32

PADDLE WHEELER DIED BY FIRE AND WATER

Paddle wheel steam ships were instrumental in opening Charlotte Harbor to settlement and commerce — starting with the *Colonel Clay* during the Seminole war of 1849. Yet, none are as fondly remembered as the little *Mary Blue* owned and operated by Capt. Albert F. Dewey from 1890 until it burned and sank in 1902.

The *Clay* ferried Indian Agent John Casey from Fort Brooke (Tampa) to a peace pow-wow with Seminole Chief Billy Bowlegs. The place was Burnt Store near today's marina of that name south of Punta Gorda. A temporary peace was arranged, but it was the beginning of the end for Seminole dominance of Charlotte Harbor.

Capt. James McKay, owner-operator of the stern wheel *Salvor,* and his partner, Cattle Baron Jacob Summerlin, built a dock at Burnt Store in 1862. From there they shipped beeves to Cuba and to the American Confederacy. This trade was interrupted two years later when the U.S. Navy captured and confiscated the *Salvor* off Key West. The Navy then blockaded Charlotte Harbor at Boca Grande Pass from where Burnt Store dock could be observed.

Undaunted, McKay had a larger and faster stern wheeler built which he named *Scottish Chief*. Cattlemen Jesse and Joel Knight then built a new dock in 1862 on the north shore of Charlotte Harbor.

A village that came to be called Hickory Bluff — today's Charlotte Harbor Town — quickly sprang up around the new dock. It was the harbor's first, permanent, American settlement.

The new location was out of sight of the sailing bark *U.S.S. Gem Of The Sea* patrolling Boca Grande Pass. With the advantage of secrecy, speed independent of wind, and knowledge of the harbor's many other inlets, McKay easily evaded the *Gem*. Capt. McKay made six blockade runs from Charlotte Harbor and Tampa until October 1863. The *Scottish Chief* was surprised at its Tampa mooring by a Federal raiding party and burned to the water line.

Sailing schooners and sharpies ruled the harbor until 1886. At that time, the narrow-gauge Florida Southern Railway pushed its tracks to Punta Gorda. Its purpose was to connect with the "splendid side-wheeler" *Morgan* needing a refueling stop on its New Orleans-Havana run.

Mining of phosphate pebbles from the bed of Peace River began in 1890 south of Arcadia. A miners' town called Hull sprang up around drying sheds and a railroad spur. Albert F. Dewey of Savannah, Georgia, came with the Peace River Phosphate Mining Company to tow barges of ore to sea-going freighters at Punta Gorda's long dock.

Dewey and the company carpenter — an African-American named George Brown — built a small fleet of 60-foot "lighters" (barges) for the ore; and a flat-bottom, stern-wheel tug boat which Dewey named *Mary Blue* after his wife.

Two years later, Dewey bought the *Mary Blue* and barges and contracted to haul ore — but with the freedom to transport general cargo for other customers around the harbor.

Thus, for 12 years, the *Mary Blue* was a familiar sight to the early settlers. It was the ship that citrus growers hired to haul their products to the rail head at Punta Gorda.

Spectacular Demise

Mary Blue met a spectacular demise during the dark hours of morning July 29, 1902 — oddly through a combination of fire and water. The event was reported by the *Punta Gorda Herald*:

"About 1 o'clock Tuesday morning, the tow boat *Mary Blue,* which was owned by Mr. Albert F. Dewey, took fire and was burned to the water's edge.

"At the time, she was lying at the Long Dock with a lighter loaded with coal between her and the dock. Engineer John Rogers and Fireman Jim Moye were asleep and did not awake until the boat was completely enveloped in flames. They escaped with only their night clothes on.

145

"Their presence of mind, however, enabled them to prevent a greater disaster than the loss of their boat; for, on running out on the lighter of coal, they cast off the hawsers by which the Blue was moored to the lighter and dock. This saved the warehouse and the other vessels and lighters lying at anchor hard by. The tide was at ebb and carried the burning boat away from the dock. She drifted around to the old pilings on the shore side. After being almost completely consumed, the remains of her hull sank in shallow water.

"The *Mary Blue* was built at Hull, 15 miles above here, about ten years ago, and has plied these waters ever since — engaged chiefly in towing phosphate lighters. She was a flat-bottomed stern-wheeler valued at $10,000. A few of our citizens saw the fire of the burning boat and thought it was the Long Dock. They woke up Mr. Dewey and called his attention to it. Upon a careful scrutiny with the aid of glasses, it was seen that it was the *Mary Blue*.

"Origin of the fire is inexplicable. The loss is quite a heavy one to Mr. Dewey, but with his usual pluck and determination he began Tuesday looking around to buy another boat."

Capt. Dewey bought a replacement for the *Blue* at a Fort Myers bankruptcy sale. She was the *Bassinger*, two years old, 60 tons burden, an drew only two feet of water — ideal for Charlotte Harbor duty. Somewhat later he added another little stern wheeler named *Phoenix*.

Until the railroad was extended to Fort Myers in 1904, a trio of large, comfortably appointed stern wheelers vied for passengers and mail on the eight-hour run to Punta Gorda. They were the *Thomas A. Edison, St. Lucie,* and *H.B. Plant.*

Paddle Wheelers Golden Age

This was the golden age of paddle wheelers at Charlotte Harbor. In addition to the important, commercial tasks — the big steamers were popular among harbor residents for dances, picnic excursions and moon light cruises.

Capt. Dewey's *Bassinger* burned about 1911 while anchored and unoccupied in the Peace River off Cleveland. The *Phoenix* was the last of the paddle wheelers. It fell on hard times when the phosphate company built the Charlotte Harbor & Northern Railroad to the deep-water dock at Boca Grande Pass. The Phoenix sank under "suspicious circumstances" while on its way up the Peace River to Cleveland where it was to undergo repairs at George Brown's ship yard. It was strange that the steamer sank in the only deep, river-bed hole in the Peace River after the crew had removed all food and portable objects.

The *Edison* burned at Fort Myers in 1914. The *St. Lucie* and *H.B. Plant* took up service as excursion boats at Tampa.

It was the end of the romantic paddle wheelers at Charlotte Harbor.

James Mitchell "Acrefoot" Johnson holds alligator on his lap.

Chapter 33

ACREFOOT A MIGHTY WALKER

James "Acrefoot" Johnson and his son, "Rattlesnake," became legends in their own times for feats hard to believe but confirmed by many faithful witnesses.   James Mitchell Johnson came from Lake City to Fort Ogden with his widowed mother, two brothers and four sisters in 1869 when he was 17. Mrs. Margaret Johnson was 55. All but her youngest son, John Gibson, age 12, quickly landed jobs as board-and-room hired hands. The 1870 census shows only "Gib" living in his mother's home.

At that time, Charlotte and DeSoto counties were part of Manatee County. Fort Ogden, a former Seminole War stronghold, was the largest community south of Fort Meade on the Peace River.

The Johnson family settled on a tract near Ziba King, a dry goods merchant, postmaster and prominent cattleman. Neighbors pitched in to build the family a cabin during a one-day "log rolling." King loaned Mrs. Johnson several wild cows so her son could have milk.

It took a half-dozen "piney woods" longhorn cows to provide enough milk. A scrub cow yielded hardly more than a tea cup of "bluejohn" milk — so called because of its blueish white color resulting from very little cream. Nevertheless, the milk provided essential calcium.

The cows were valuable also for another reason. Early Florida pioneers pastured some cows away from their calves held in a large pen. This compelled "mammy" cows to return to the pen at evening time. Manure that fell in the pen enriched the sandy soil. Every few weeks, depending upon the size of the herd, the pen was moved so the fertilizing process could be repeated. Sweet potatoes were planted in the vacated spots summer and fall. The fall crop, called "stand overs," were dug up as needed in winter. Thus, the settlers had nutritious vegetable all year long.

Jim Johnson grew up to be a giant of a man — 6 feet 7 inches tall, 250 pounds, and strong. In 1877, he married a local girl named Margaret Chester. The 1880 Census lists him as age 28, Margaret 18, and a son Elias age 2. He gave his occupation as "farmer." As can be seen, James was 25 when he married and Miss Chester not yet 16.

With a wife and son to care for, Jim took a sub-contract to carry mail over the Peace River route between Fort Ogden and Fort Meade — a distance of 49 miles by modern highway — somewhat more by early trail. It is likely that the government contract was assigned to Postmaster King. Johnson's name was never recorded by the Postal Service. His pay was $26 per month.

Horse Too Slow

Jim rode his horse at first, but the 100 miles or so round trip of trails and roads was so difficult the animal had to be rested frequently. Anxious to get the job done so he could return to his farm and cattle, Johnson began walking the route. Once a week — twice later — he started out at daybreak and reached Ft. Meade before dark. Dropping off his pouch of letters, Johnson would walk another 10 miles to Bartow where he spent the night with his sister. This enabled him to avoid the 25-cent charge for a bed at the Fort Meade Hotel. The total distance walked one-way, in one day, was about 60 miles! He repeated the route in reverse the next day.

At cock-crow, Johnson's sister would prepare a hearty breakfast consisting of a dozen eggs, a gallon of coffee, a big pan of buttermilk biscuits and a large bowl of grits lathered with syrup. He stuffed biscuits in his pockets for munching along the way. These he supplemented with raw palm hearts gathered en route.

Some of the route was along the Wire Road constructed by the International Ocean Telegraph Co. to service its line to Punta Rassa and cable to Cuba. Much of Acrefoot's route, however, veered off to pick up and deliver mail to the settlements of Joshua Creek, Long Point, Gum Heads, Dark Cow Pens, Crewsville, and Bereah.

The ease with which Johnson performed his official duty on foot earned him the nickname for which he became famous. It is not clear whether "Acrefoot" was inspired by the size of his brogans, reputed to be size 14, or by the alleged length of his stride.

One day be emerged onto the Pine Level-Bunker road from a foot-path he had laid out through a swamp. Johnson overtook Dr. Hayden who was driving a horse and buggy. "Hop in," said the doctor. "Well, thanky," replied Acrefoot. "I will rest a minute."

Acrefoot planted one giant foot in the buggy and hoisted himself aboard. After a couple of minutes conversation about the weather and such, Johnson announced, "Much obliged, Doc. I'll be going now. I'm in sort of a hurry." He hopped out and strode ahead. Within minutes he was out of sight.

According to Acrefoot's Grandson Gib, years later, the mailman came home from Fort Mead one afternoon barefooted, having discarded his worn out shoes along the way. "Grandma reminded him of a big square dance that night at Fort Ogden. There was nothing Grandpa liked better than dancing, but he had no shoes.

"That was of no concern to Grandpa. He walked 30 miles to Fort Myers, down the Wire Road (three miles east of today's State Route 31). He swam the Caloosahatchee River at Telegraph Station (now Olga) pushing a lard can with his clothes inside to keep them dry. After rousting up a merchant and buying a pair of shoes, Grandpa swam back and got home in time to spend the rest of the night dosey-doh-ing."

Turned Down Marathon

Ziba King, Francis Boggess and two other prominent cattlemen once offered to finance a trip to New York City for Acrefoot so he could participate in an international walking marathon. Johnson thanked them kindly, but declined, "Boys, I'm too busy for that sort of thing. The mail must go through. Can any of you take my place?"

When Johnson's son Elias was half-grown, the boy developed a high fever that could not be brought down with cold compresses. Acrefoot strapped a chair to his back and carried Elias in it to a doctor in Fort Myers. This incident spawned the fable that Acrefoot gave up the mail contract because the postal service wouldn't let him carry passengers as well as mail on his jaunts.

Acrefoot lost the mail contract to the Florida Southern Railway when the latter's line was extended from Bartow to Punta Gorda in 1886. He didn't mind giving up his mail job because he moved to Nocatee where he landed a more lucrative contract to furnish the railroad with cross-ties and with cordwood to burn in the locomotives.

Should a train come by while he was around, Acrefoot would run alongside — to the delight of passengers. In a final burst of speed he would pull ahead of the train and duck into the woods when out of sight. Bets were made as to whether the fleet-footed giant would be waiting at the next station to greet them.

Johnson was strong and energetic. He could cut and split more wood than any two men. To win a bet, he once cleared a palmetto field faster than two men could stack the roots he grubbed out. He flung the roots alternately right and left to the stackers as he moved through the palmettos. After several hours in the hot sun, the stackers cried uncle and Acrefoot won the bet.

Acrefoot usually carried a rifle while on his mail runs or cutting wood. Not for protection from desperados who infested the wild forests, but to dispatch panthers, wolves, bears and rattlesnakes.

Acrefoot and Margaret had eight children — three sons and five daughters. His son Guy augmented the family coffers by catching rattlesnakes and selling them to medical colleges and zoos. A grandson named Brogden was recognized as the tallest man in Florida — standing 6 feet 10 ½ inches in his stocking feet.

A monument to Acrefoot has been erected in Arcadia. During the 1970's, an Acrefoot Johnson Race was held annually in Punta Gorda from Ponce DeLeon Park to Memorial Auditorium as an event in a History Festival. Postmaster Hugh MacGibbon organized the event which usually was won by a Charlotte High School trackman. The trophy was awarded by the post office in honor of its most famous mailman.

Acrefoot Johnson's son, Guy, made a lot of money selling rattlesnakes. He started out catching the poisonous reptiles with a 12-foot pole and snare. After a few year's experience, he used a 3-foot stick and a pocket handkerchief to throw over the head of the snake so it couldn't see.

During the bust of the Florida Land Boom in the late early 1930's, a stranded northern journalist named George End asked Guy if he knew where work could be found inasmuch as End's family was starving. Guy said he would buy all the rattlesnakes the tenderfoot could catch. That afternoon, End's two boys brought in a 6-foot rattler, but they had killed it. End sought to gain something by skinning the snake and selling the hide. He noticed that the snake's meat was white, like turtle meat. End had heard that Texas cowboys ate rattlesnakes; so, being desperate from hunger, he fried some of the snake meat. His whole family found it delicious. Mrs. End canned the rest. End learned to catch live snakes and made a comfortable living selling them to Guy. Nevertheless, he felt he had stumbled on a potential new business canning rattlesnake meat.

The American Legion held a convention in Tampa about this time. End knew the value of publicity, and being a veteran, took some canned rattlesnake to the convention. He persuaded the commander to serve snake as an unannounced side-dish. The diners enjoyed the surprise delicacy but there were mixed feelings when the nature of the dish was disclosed. The stunt gained wide publicity. Newspapers published stories about End and Johnson — penning the name "Rattlesnake" for Johnson.

Rattlesnake Steaks

Orders for rattlesnake steaks poured in. End opened a large canning plant at Tampa. Now, he bought all the rattlesnakes Guy Johnson could catch. Next door to his plant he opened a store, a snake-pit tourist attraction, and his own post office named Rattlesnake, Florida. One day, End was showing off an old rattler that always had been docile. This time, however, the snake bit End on the hand. He refused to go to the hospital, electing to treat the wound with a remedy he devised. The cure didn't work, and End died in a few hours.

Guy continued hunting rattlesnakes for his science customers. One day he delivered a shipment of 150 rattlers to a medical school in Georgia. He was stopped at the state border for a tick inspection. Guy threw back the tarpaulin over his caged snakes, and the reptiles set up a racket. Bug-eyed inspectors declared the snakes tick free.

During his career as a snake hunter, Guy guided many famous herpetologists and naturalists. Among the latter was Marjorie Kinnan Rawlings who wrote *Cross Creek* and *The Yearling*. Guy estimated he caught more than 5,000 rattlers — all within a 50-mile radius of Nocatee. The largest rattlesnake was captured on Hope Island in the Peace River Swamp near Fort Ogden and measured 8 feet 7 ½ inches in length.

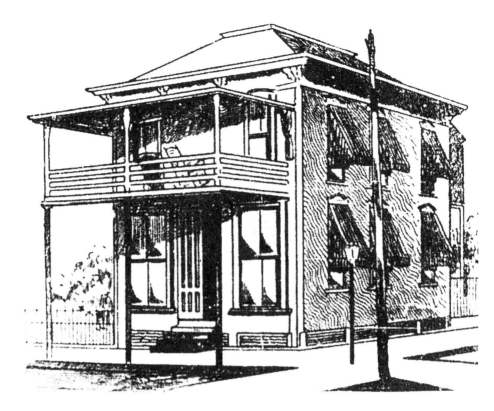

Punta Gorda Bank organized by Ziba King in 1893.

Chapter 34

SUITCASE OF CASH SAVES BANK

Banks rank with city halls, churches, schools, railroads and post offices as institutions essential to establishing communities in the Florida frontier — not less so than at Punta Gorda. It should not be surprising, therefore, that early bankers here were a colorful lot.

The first banker, for example, was a jack-of-all trades named Stephen P. Hinckley. He was a coastal shipper and wholesale marchant who came to Punta Gorda from Mobile, Alabama, in 1888. The scope of his business interests is revealed by an advertisement Feb. 19, 1890,in the *South Florida News* published at Charlotte Harbor Town:

"S.P. HINCKLEY — Wholesale dealer in grain, hay, salt, heavy groceries. Also manager of the Polk County Bank branch and El Palmetto Cigar Factory. Warehouse on wharf in bay convenient to all steamers and boats. Office on Marion Ave. back of Hotel Punta Gorda. My new schooner *Lizzie M. Eels* now makes regular trips between Punta Gorda and Mobile to merchants only."

The narrow-gauge Florida Southern Railroad had reached the largely uninhabited south shore of Charlotte Bay — the estuary of Charlotte Harbor — four years earlier. The Polk County Bank at Bartow, 73 miles north of Punta Gorda on the railroad line, was the nearest banking facility.

Willard Emerson, the bank president, and Warren Tyler a financier, established a cigar factory at Punta Gorda some time prior to the newspaper ad above to compete with unionized Cuban cigar makers at Tampa. Hinckley had $3,000 worth of stock in the venture — a large sum in those days.

Cubans were accustomed to banking their wages, and borrowing small amounts. Therefore, a "working man's" bank was important to success of any enterprise involving them. Until this time, the local economy thrived on cattle sold to Cuba and paid for in gold doubloons. Enormous amounts of gold were stashed under the beds of cattle barons who distrusted under-funded frontier banks with flimsy safes. Besides, cattlemen were widely respected for their skill with firearms and readiness to use them.

The Polk County Bank apparently intended to construct a permanent bank building. By a deed dated 10 days earlier than Hinckley's ad, the bank purchased lots on the corner of Olympia Avenue and Taylor Street — today's location of the county courthouse — from real estate developers Whitledge & Tatum for $300.

Cattleman Starts Bank

The bank was not satisfied with its Punta Gorda prospects. It sold part of its local property Oct. 10, 1893, to Ziba King for $100. He was a prominent cattleman who owned the adjacent southeast corner of Taylor Street and Marion Avenue. Remainder of the bank's Punta Gorda property was sold to Lucy (Laura?) A. Davis for $250.

King built a two-story frame bank building on his Marion Avenue lot then leased it for $20 a month to the newly organized Punta Gorda Bank with himself as president and John Farrington as cashier. The banking room was on the ground floor. Farrington and his family lived on the second floor. The building was destroyed in the great fire of 1905, years after the bank had moved to a new location. A deed of April 13, 1896, transferring a small lot on Marion Avenue, describes the Punta Gorda Bank as "a branch of the Fort Meade State Bank."

Perry M. McAdow, a wealthy, 59-year-old mine owner from Montana, confined to a wheelchair, came to Punta Gorda with his 28-year-old bride, Marian, for the winter season 1896-97. He liked the area so much they never returned to Montana.

With a great deal of money to be protected and invested, McAdow bought a controlling interest in the Punta Gorda Bank. According to the tax-roll for 1897, McAdow also bought a large lot on the northwest corner of Marion Avenue and Cross Street and built a larger banking office.

153

Punta Gorda Bank re-organized and relocated in 1897.

From this base, McAdow introduced kerosene street lamps for the town then electric lights, the first telephones and a botanical garden now the site of Holiday Inn. He owned orange groves, pineapple farms, a turpentine camp and vast acres of pine forest. McAdow was a large investor in the Punta Gorda Ice and Power Company and then president. He appointed Farrington general manager. Eventually the company was absorbed by Florida Power and Light Corp.

Punta Gorda Bank was granted a state charter 1899. It noted that McAdow was president, Farrington vice-president, and C.L. Huddleston cashier. Its capital was only $15,000.

A rival Merchants Bank was started April 12, 1912, in a handsome building still standing, but occupied as a private residence, on the south side of Marion Avenue between Taylor and King streets. Two years later it was granted a federal charter and renamed First National Bank of Punta Gorda. President was Edwin W. Smith, a wholesale fish dealer. Vice-president was John T. Swinney. Cashier was C. Edward Smith and Assistant Cashier was Charles F. Curry.

Saddlebag Of Gold

As McAdow grew old and ill, his bank was recapitalized as the Punta Gorda State Bank. W. Luther Koon, a prominent cattleman, provided the additional capital with a saddle bag of $20 gold coins — a cattleman's customary, private horde.

In a complex transfer of deeds April 28, 1917, the inventory of bank-owned properties were turned over to the new entity for $10. Koon was president of Punta Gorda State Bank. Vice-president was Albert F. Dewey, owner of the Charlotte Harbor Lighterage Company.

154

Initially, the bank leased a one-story concrete block building on the northeast corner of Olympin Avenue and Nesbit street "to be used as banking rooms." The building formerly embraced J.S. Goff Hardware and C.A. Carver Jewelry. A new Punta Gorda State Bank office was built in 1921 on the southwest corner of Marion Avenue and King Street.

Another reorganization occurred in 1925 when the advertising tycoon Barron G. Collier bought a large interest in the bank and ownership of the old Hotel Punta Gorda. Capital of the bank was doubled to $50,000 and Collier named chairman of the board. Koon continued as president. W.R. Deloach became cashier and Grace Laubach assistant cashier. Directors were Mrs. McAdow who ably managed her late husband's many ventures; Thomas C. Crosland, a large fish dealer; Clay and Steve Chadwick, brothers in real estate, groves and wholesale fish; W.W. Wilson, real estate; C.M. Carrier real estate and groves; and R.K. Seward merchant.

Koon was a careful banker, requiring strong collateral for loans — and prompt repayments. Deloach once complained to Esther McCullough, then executive director of the Chamber of Commerce, that Koon would lend money only "to someone who had a cow."

The Charlotte Bay Hotel, a modern three-story structure, was built in 1925 on the southwest corner of Marion Avenue and Taylor Street. The hotel's prime, corner space was occupied by the Fidelity Trust Company headed by Smith and Swinney of First National Bank of Punta Gorda. Another vice-president was J.N. Sikes. W.R. Sparks was cashier.

Panic Runs On Banks

The stock market crashed in 1929 heralding the Great Depression. Panic-stricken bank customers throughout the country rushed to withdraw their money from banks whose mortgages backing up deposits suddenly became worthless. Punta Gorda's three banks — Punta Gorda State Bank, First National Bank of Punta Gorda, and Fidelity Trust Co. — were not spared these crushing "runs." First National and Fidelity Trust collapsed.

Only Punta Gorda State Bank survived. Punta Gorda historian Byron Rhode says it was saved when Collier arrived at the height of a run with a suitcase of cash to meet all demands. Large depositors were persuaded to accept partial withdrawals over a period of time. Many customers — encouraged by the banks ability to pay off, and fearful of holding large amounts of cash in their homes — returned next day to re-open their accounts. Collier, Koon and the other stock holders suffered heavy losses when hundreds of mortgages defaulted.

Punta Gorda State Bank stayed in business and reorganized in 1960 as First National Bank of Punta Gorda. It built a one-story bank and office building on the northwest corner of Olympia Avenue and Nesbit Street, later putting on a four-story addition. The bank was reorganized as First Florida Bank in 1990, and bought by the Barnett bank system in 1993.

Mr. and Mrs. Peter Buchan, left, on porch of their Englewood general store at Englewood. Note beach in front.

Chapter 35

BUCHAN MADE ENGLEWOOD GROW

The Nichols brothers of Englewood, Ill., founded the community now straddling the Charlotte-Sarasota county line in 1896 and named it after their hometown — but Peter E. Buchan (pronounced Buck-an) provided the spark to make it grow.

The area known as Englewood has a history much older. Hamilton Disston, a wealthy saw manufacturer from Philadelphia, in 1881 bought four million acres of "swamp and overflowed land" from the Florida Internal Improvement Fund for 25-cents per acre. Included was "Mangrove Bay" and most of the lands around Charlotte Harbor. His plan was to drain the Everglades for a vast sugar plantation. Disston sold his west coast property to finance his Everglades venture. Disston's agent at Liverpool — now gone, near Fort Ogden — was John Cross, a former coffee plantation operator from Bombay, India. He bought and optioned large tracts on Mangrove Bay from Disston in 1886. Though Disston went broke, Cross turned a nice profit on his investment. He platted part of his land around Mangrove Bay for small lemon groves which he called "Grove City On The Gulf." He also affixed the name "Lemon" to the bay.

Cross promoted Grove City at the Chicago Exposition of 1893. Herbert, Howard and Ira Nichols were so impressed they bought 1,091 acres of property north of Grove City from Cross and started their own town. A few people built houses at Englewood, and James A. MacKenzie of Chicago built a saw mill at the end of Yale St. However, lot sales were disappointing. Without construction there was no market for lumber. There was no highway to the development. Access was by boat. To attract settlers and sportsmen, the Nichols built the Englewood Inn in 1898 and leased MacKenzie's mill building for a general store and post office.

Out on Manasota Key, Charles Dishong operated a fishing camp. Charles Johnson had a little store to supply the men there. Steve Chadwick, a North Carolina fisherman working from Cortez Island, visited the Dishong camp. Impressed with the wealth of fish available in Lemon Bay, he brought his brothers, Hubbard and Clay, to Manasota Key in 1898. They began shipping fish to packing houses in Sarasota and Tampa. By 1901, the Chadwicks started their own wholesale fish company. Steve ran the fishing camp at Stump Pass, while Hubbard and Clay managed the packing house at the Punta Gorda railroad terminal. This was Englewood when Peter Buchan and his wife Florence arrived in 1902.

With this background, we pick up the history as related by Jack Tate who married the Buchan's only child, Margaret. Now retired from the grocery business, Tate is an Englewood pioneer in his own right.

Appointed Convict Captain

"My father, O.A. Tate was deputy sheriff for Sarasota County. He was appointed convict captain at Englewood in charge of prisoners assigned to road construction. We arrived in 1926 on a Saturday. I was 13 years old. On Monday I applied for a job at the big Woodmere Lumber Camp.

"They put me in charge of the commissary Ne-Hi soda pop dispenser. It was a large chest with tubes running through chopped ice. Each tube was filled with bottles of a particular flavor. You pushed a warm bottle into its proper tube and a cold bottle came out the other end. You got a lot of pop for a nickel. It was a simple job, but it gave me an opportunity to learn the grocery business.

"Pete Buchan was from Dahlonega, Ga., where his father was a jeweler. Pete married Miss Florence Jerome. They located at Orlando. He fell under a train he was trying to board and lost his left leg. Thereafter, he wore a wooden leg, but it never slowed him down.

"Somewhere Pete knew the Chadwick brothers. A year after they started their fish company he accepted their offer of a job as bookkeeper. The Buchans lived for the first few months with one of the Chadwick boys in Punta Gorda — then they located at the Englewood main office.

"Pete struck out on his own in 1908 as manager of the Nichols' general store, but gave it up after two years. The Englewood Inn burned the

PETER E. BUCHAN   MRS. FLORENCE BUCHAN

following year, and there just wasn't enough business. The Buchan's left the area — I never heard to where. He returned in 1912 for a visit. As soon as Pete walked in the store H.K. Nichols exclaimed, 'Hi. Have you come back to buy the store?'

"That was not Pete's intention, but the price was so attractive he finally agreed. He was to get the inventory for $315 and take up the building lease with MacKenzie for $10 per month.

"Things were tough at first. With the store, Pete became the postmaster of Englewood, but a big day consisted of selling six stamps. To increase the volume of mail necessary to keep the post office in operation, Pete made little boxes for single grapefruits and mailed them to friends.

"To attract more people, Pete organized a work group of other settlers to open up Blind Pass. They believed a second inlet would be convenient for fishermen and increase the fish population. They rounded up some mules and drag-scoops and began work. They got water flowing through a passage about a foot deep at low tide. However, the channel filled back up after the first storm. More people were moving into the area, and business was better. Therefore, the following year Pete bought all of Block 8 at the bay-side corner of Dearborn and Olive streets from Mrs. Winifred E. Watson for $100. Also in 1913, Pete was elected to the board of trustees for the Englewood School District. His and Florence's only child, Margaret, was born the following year.

158

"Pete did not save up enough money for a new store — with living quarters above — until 1916. That building now is a handsome home still in my family. He also built a 250-foot dock where supplies could be delivered by schooner from Tampa.

"The year 1921 was a momentous one for the Buchans. Little Margaret, age seven, was sent to live with friends in Sebring during the school year in order to be properly educated. The hurricane of 1921 flooded all the Englewood coast with chest-deep water. Pete and Florence had seen lesser storms drive water up to the store's walk so were not alarmed at first. This time, however, the fierce wind blew the store-home off its blocks and split the lower floor. The outside stairs were torn loose.

"Pete decided the time had come to abandon the damaged building. He tied bed sheets together and lowered Florence to the raging water below. Then he followed, carrying his watch in his mouth to keep it dry. The Buchans took refuge in the home of Prof. Edward Somermeier who was retired from Ohio State University. His place was on higher ground and pilings four feet above grade level. The house is better known today as the Jergen Mansion or Rinkard's Guest Home.

"When Buchan's store split open, most of the groceries spilled into the flood. Bulk foods such as sugar, flour, grits and coffee beans were spoiled. Canned goods were washed ashore. Of course, the labels all soaked off.

Canned Food A Bargain.

"Nevertheless, folks picked up the cans and returned them to the store. They also helped Pete push his building back on its blocks. Thereafter, Pete offered the cans, with their unknown contents, for 10 cents each. No one knew whether they were going to get spinach, beans, corn or what. They bought anyway because it was a bargain — and maybe it would be peaches. Later that year, Sarasota County was divided from Manasota County. A slate of officers — with Pete recommended for the first commissioner representing Englewood — was sent to Gov. Hardee. He approved it. As commissioner, Pete worked tirelessly to get a good road into the area from Sarasota. In late 1923, Mr. and Mrs. Harry Chapin — grocers in Arcadia — visited Englewood and were entranced with its bay-oriented life style. While talking shop with fellow grocer Pete, it was agreed that Chapin would lease the store; and the Buchans would move to Tampa where little Margaret could be educated.

"During Chapin's operation of the store, he joined with a man named Royal to build a casino at the end of Buchan dock. Remember, this was in the 'Roaring Twenties.' The casino was complete with bootleg whiskey, slot machines, dance band and good food. It was the most popular spot in the Lemon Bay area — especially with the winter crowd at Boca Grande.

"Chapin ran the store and casino for four years then gave up his lease. The casino closed. It and the store remained empty for two years while

159

Englewood expanded rapidly during the Florida Land Boom. My father and two brothers bought the casino building and took it apart piece by piece. With the material they built a nice two-bedroom home still occupied on Dearborn St.

"The bubble burst in 1929 and was followed by the Great Depression. I met Margaret that year when the Buchan's visited their old hometown. She was 15 and I was 16. I asked her to go to the picture show with me, but she refused unless some one else went along. I suggested my sister, and Margaret said OK. Thereafter, I kept up a correspondence and went to Tampa whenever I could to see her. I drove a school bus during my last year at Nokomis High School. With the money I made, I bought a second-hand Ford. Then I began courting Margaret in earnest.

Bartered Fish

"No one had any money during the Depression. Stuart Anderson organized the Lemon Bay fishermen into a sort of cooperative. They iced their fish then hauled it north in their car, bartering for what ever they could until the fish were gone. They would come home with peaches, syrup, chickens or whatever they obtained. The operation grew, so Anderson rented the Buchan store and lived upstairs with his wife. Later he started the Lemon Bay Fisheries and used the store building for an office and warehouse.

"Margaret and I were married in 1932. Mr. and Mrs. Buchan gave us a little house on Olive St. The following year, the Buchans moved back to Englewood where they could be near their daughter and supervise their properties. Anderson at that time moved out the old Buchan building to start his fishery. It took us many months to dispose of old furniture that he left behind. The building was stacked floor to ceiling with stuff that would sell today for high prices as antiques.

"When the place was renovated into a large home, the Buchans moved back in. They also backed me in building a new grocery next door. They always treated me more as a natural son than as a son-in-law.

"Pete ran for commissioner and was easily elected. He served from 1933 to 1951 — finally retiring at age 80. Among his accomplishments was construction of the Englewood Road, acquisition and filling of Blind Pass for a park, building of Orange Park and a county airstrip still bearing his name. He managed his investments and dabbled in real estate until his death in 1968 just a couple of weeks before his 97th birthday. Mrs. Buchan died in 1971 at age 91."

Atlantic Coast Line Depot was showpiece in 1929.

Chapter 36

NEW LIFE FOR OLD DEPOTS

Charlotte County's last railroad depot — on the National Register of Historic Places but in disrepair and arson-scorched — was reborn in the summer of 1996 when ownership was transferred to Old Punta Gorda, Inc.

The latter, a non-profit organization which saved and operates Col. Isaac Trabue's land sales office and first post office of 1886, is converting the old depot into a community meeting center.

Babcock Ranch folks bought the empty structure several years ago with intention of turning it into an upscale restaurant. They put on a new tile roof at great expense. Then a spate of new restaurants nearby changed the market mix sufficiently to make the venture less attractive. For several years, the Audubon Society stored donated furniture and other articles there for periodic auctions.

Gulf-Seminole Railroad of Fort Myers — successor to two other railroad companies that first built tracks to Punta Gorda — repaved the passenger boarding walk in 1993. During the winter season, Seminole's excursion train stops to pick up customers for a leisurely trip back through time to old depots at Fort Ogden and Arcadia.

Following the Civil War, three railroads pushed into Florida to take advantage of generous land grants. The state offered 10,000 acres along the right-of-way for every mile of track laid. The incentive was real estate. Passengers and freight were secondary.

Coming down the center of the peninsula was the narrow gauge Florida Southern Railway. Henry B. Plant headed a consortium of investors pushing down the west coast. Henry M. Flagler developed the east coast.

When Florida Southern approached Bartow in 1883 — heading for Charlotte Harbor Town — Plant became worried that the railroad might throw a spur west to Tampa where he was planning a major development. Consequently he bought a majority interest in Florida Southern in order to freeze out competition.

Col. Isaac Trabue, of Louisville, Ky., at this time bought 30 acres, sight unseen, from James M. Lanier on the bay opposite Charlotte Harbor Town. He visited his purchase in 1885 and discovered what eager Yankees often did. Much of his land was underwater during the rain season or at high tide.

To recoup his investment, Trabue platted his parcel into town lots and rushed to Florida Southern headquarters at Boston, Mass. He offered half his land if the railroad would come down the east side of Peace River and build its terminal at "Trabue." Florida Southern directors agreed, and the tracks reached Trabue in July 1886. However, the rails didn't end at Colonel Trabue's tract but continued on west another two miles to Punta Gorda (Fat Point) a centuries old landmark for Cuban fishermen.

The railroad constructed a 4,200-foot long dock and depot near today's Isles Yacht Club. It reached a 14-foot deep channel in the middle of the Bay and enabled Morgan Line steamships to tie up and take on transfer passengers for Key West or Havana, Cuba.

First Depot at "Wye"

A triangular shaped rail "wye" was constructed at the south edge of Trabue's would-be town and a spur extended down the middle of King Street (now Tamiami Trail, north). Trains backed around the wye to head north for the return trip. The first train carried marl fill, lumber and the vanguard of 200 workmen who built a 150-room hotel in six months.

A small, frame depot was built inside the turning wye — now an empty lot east of Tamiami Trail and Taylor Street. Passengers were picked up and returned by carriage. Business tycoons with private Pullman cars were routed down the King Street spur to park alongside Hotel Punta Gorda.

By 1897, Henry B. Plant had added Florida Southern Railroad to his Plant System. He saw Punta Gorda as competition for his development at Port Tampa. To remove that thorn in his side, Plant took up the rails to the long dock and Trabue's ice factory. Then he built a shorter dock in shallow water at the foot of King Street where gondolas of coal could be pushed to steam driven yachts owned by hotel guests. He also built a large, frame depot on the east side of King Street opposite the hotel to accommodate passengers. Without rail connection at Punta Gorda, Morgan Line was forced to change to Tampa dockage — fitting nicely into

Plant's plans. Plant died in 1899, and his vast rail system was bought in 1902 by the Atlantic Coast Line.

The little 1886 depot sat empty until 1904 when the ACL extended its tracks to Fort Myers. Increased traffic brought a brief resurrection for a new purpose. Reported the *Punta Gorda Herald* in April: "The old Coast Line depot at the wye has been fitted up as a packing house." Part-time workers now filled boxes with oranges and winter vegetables where rich and famous visitors originally came to enjoy unparalleled fishing, hunting and boating.

During the First World War, young soldiers kissed their sweethearts goodby at the King Street depot one last time before marching off to "make the world safe for democracy."

The downtown depot proved to be more of a nuisance than a convenience. Fishing companies set up packing houses on the railroad dock where boxcars banged back and forth at all hours. The smell of fish dampened the appetites of hotel guests. Winter visitors stopped coming.

Town residents also disliked the trains that took up one of its main business streets. Sparks from the wood and coal burning locomotives set roofs afire. New-fangled "horseless carriages" generally lost encounters with trains backing down to the depot.

Depot and Dock Relocated

Barron Collier, a wealthy advertising executive, offered to renovate the old hotel if the town would remove the depot and dock. Local folks readily obliged. The municipal dock was relocated to Maud St., now Fishermens Village. Atlantic Coast Line was glad to return to the railroad wye — site of the first depot — where packing houses, lumber yards and oil tanks provided valuable freight business. The *Herald* in Dec. 1928 headlined plans by ACL for a new depot:

"Contracts were let by the Atlantic Coast Line Railroad company this week for construction of a new passenger and freight depot. The work was awarded to the R.W. Burrows Construction Company of Bartow.

"It will be located on the main line of the railroad with one end of the passenger walk reaching nearly to Taylor street, and extending southwest from the street near the tracks to William Street. The new depot will be one-half mile from the business center of the city. However, any inconvenience that may be incurred because of this walk or haul is considered by the fact that the railroad will remove the tracks from King Street and open up this important business area more convenient to auto traffic.

"The new bridge is to enter this city on this street — now occupied by railroad trains. Freight hauls to and from the fish dock will go to the Maud Street pier where new fish houses are nearing completion."

The new depot's "unusually attractive design" was neo-Spanish, then popular in Florida, Texas and California which have strong roots in early

Spanish occupation. Atlantic Coast Line built several of its Florida Land Boom era depots from the same blueprint. Only those at Punta Gorda and Bradenton still exist. The twin depots have two waiting rooms — one for "whites" and one for "colored." Very few examples of this segregation arrangement remain to testify about historic civil rights problems.

Because of the sturdy construction with masonry materials, the two ACL depots are in remarkably good condition.

Lesser depots were built by railroad companies in Charlotte County. The first one was at Cleveland in 1885 where the Florida Southern halted for several months while the last leg of track was being extended to Punta Gorda. During the era when pineapples were cultivated extensively at Solana, a small depot was maintained there for shipping the fruit. It was called "Pineapple Center." (See chapter 59, *Our Fascinating Past* Vol I)

A depot for shipment of turpentine, lumber and winter vegetables was Acline south of Punta Gorda. The name — pronounced Ack'-line — was a contraction of Atlantic Coast Line. The name survives as a road where the depot once stood on highway U.S. 41

The Charlotte Harbor & Northern Railroad, built in 1905-1908 from Gasparilla Island to Mulberry, mostly carried phosphate ore to deep-water ships waiting at South Boca Grande. The CH&N built fine depots at Murdock and Boca Grande. Smaller ones were at Placida, McCall and El Jobean, none at South Boca Grande.

The Boca Grande depot, in the Lee County portion of Gasparilla Island, is another beautiful example of land-boom neo-Spanish architecture. Stunningly restored, the two-story depot today is home to smart shops and professional offices — as is the old ACL depot at Arcadia in DeSoto County. The ACL depot at Fort Myers has been converted to a busy historical museum.

With renovation of the old Hotel Punta Gorda — renamed Hotel Charlotte Harbor by Collier — prominent visitors swarmed through the beautiful Taylor Street depot for a few years. Then came collapse of the Great Florida Land Boom, and the slide into the Great Depression. Once again, young men kissed their sweethearts at the train station and went off to World War II. Sadly fewer came back on the train than started off.

The ACL depot at Punta Gorda closed its doors to passengers in 1971 and to freight a few years later. Diesel locomotives could not compete with airlines, Interstate highways, 18-wheel trucks and go-anywhere automobiles.

Nevertheless, the outstanding demonstrations of new life for old depots in Lee and DeSoto counties surely prove there is a future also for Charlotte County's last one.

Punta Gorda First Presbyterian Church was at the edge of town.

Chapter 37

PUNTA GORDA PRESBYTERIAN COUNTY'S OLDEST

As First Presbyterian Church of Punta Gorda — oldest of the denomination in the county — observes its 100th birthday it recalls the difficulties of gathering a flock in a new, frontier village.

The town's founder, Col. Isaac Trabue, built a one-room frame community hall in 1887 where the early Methodists, Baptists, Presbyterians and Episcopalians shared services. As the village grew, each denomination organized congregations and met in available halls.

Eleven Presbyterians in September 1895 decided also to form a congregation and build their own sanctuary. One of these, R.E. Coffelt, was appointed to write The Rev. Henry Keigwin, Synod missionary at Orlando, and request advice on how to proceed "decently and in order."

The *Punta Gorda Herald,* then a 2-year-old newspaper, reported the outcome on October 25:

"A new church has been established during the week — the First Presbyterian. As a result of correspondence with friends in Punta Gorda, Rev. George Case visited the place on the 25th day of Sept. (1895). He preached on the following Sunday, and on every night of the succeeding week (except Saturday) and obtained the names of 16 persons on a petition for organization of a church.

"This petition was sent to the Presbytery of South Florida (in session at Dunnellon) on Oct. 1. That body appointed Rev. Henry Keigwin and Rev. Case as a committee to organize a church if the way was found clear. The committee met the petitioners on Sunday, Oct. 13, in the Methodist Church and effected an organization.

"Mr. R.E. Coffelt, lately of Chicago, and Mr. J.B. Noyes, lately of Mayesville, Ky., were installed in the office of Ruling Elders. The former held that position in St. Joseph, Mo.

"Prof. M.L. Williams and Mr. J.A. McHargue compose the Board of Deacons though they are not members. Rev. Keigwin preached the sermon, and Rev. Case delivered the charge to the Elders and the church.

"This makes four churches in Punta Gorda — Methodist, Baptist, Episcopal, and Presbyterian. The Lutherans and Catholics have services occasionally.

"Union evangelistic services are being conducted in the Baptist Church every night by Revs. Keigwin and Case, with the assistance of Rev. M.S. Stevens, resident Baptist pastor. The merchants of the city have kindly consented to close their places of business from 7:00 to 8:15 p.m. during these services."

Church Duly Organized

Rev. Keigwin proclaimed the church "duly organized under the care of the Presbytery of South Florida, of the Presbyterian Church in the United States of America." This affiliation is of particular significance. As the Civil War drew near in 1857, Presbyterian churches split over the issue of slavery. Southern congregations became the "Presbyterian Church in the Confederate States of America." Those of the north were the "Presbyterian Church in the United States of America." After the war, the southern churches reorganized as the "Presbyterian Church in the United States."

The postwar period was a time of mission zeal by northern PC-USA into Florida. Friendly relations with the southern PC-US resumed in 1882 but tensions continued until 1983 when the two largest Presbyterian churches reunited under the PC-USA banner.

A PC-USA northern church in Punta Gorda — deep in the heart of former Confederate territory — was unusual for that time. However, the little town in 1895 was the southernmost terminal of the nation's railroad system — then the principal mode of travel. It should be noted also that the town's founder and most prominent citizen, Col Isaac Trabue of Kentucky, had been a Union officer during the Civil War. He was instrumental in obtaining the 1890-92 Punta Gorda postmastership for an African-American named Robert Meacham.

Thus, Punta Gorda was a fertile field for PC-USA missionary activity. The two principal organizers of First Presbyterian USA church at Punta Gorda, Coffelt and Noyes, were pointedly noted as newcomers by the *Herald*. There are no local, public records of them so they did not stay around very long after the church was organized. Rev. Case was appointed "missionary in charge" of the new church at Punta Gorda until it could support a full-time minister.

The original eleven petitioners adopted a constitution and signed the charter. They were Coffelt, Noyes, Mrs. Olive Coffelt, James W. Carter, James Irwin, Mrs. Nellie Swift, Mrs. Mattie Aull, Mrs. P.J. Barry, Mrs. E.J. Soule, Miss Juleien E. Soule and Charles Soule.

Coffelt, one of the first deacons, was the teacher at Punta Gorda's new one-room school — now part of the residence at the southeast corner of Marion Ave. and Harvey St. His home, though was at Arcadia. It is probable that he and Deacon J.A. McHargue were members of the Presbyterian church there but living at the time of the census in Punta Gorda. Williams shortly thereafter became a lawyer at Bartow but after a short stint returned to teaching at Fort Myers.

McHargue became a member of First Presbyterian Punta Gorda and signed the church Articles of Incorporation 18 months later. He was dismissed by letter of transfer to the Presbyterian Church at Moultrie, Ga., in 1900.

Mrs. Mattie Aull was the wife of Eugene Patrick Aull, manager of the National Hotel at Cleveland, Fla. Mrs. Barry was a widow living at Charlotte Harbor Town. Other signers of the charter left no records of property and are missing from the 1900 census of Punta Gorda, Cleveland and Charlotte Harbor.

Meet Over Bakery

In the *Herald* church notices of January 1896, Presbyterians are noted as meeting Sundays at Jack's Hall — the second floor over a bakery on Marion Ave. — now site of the City Hall parking lot.

At a congregational meeting in Jack's Hall on Jan. 29, trustees were elected with authority to acquire and hold property. They were R.E. Coffelt, J.B. Noyes, Dr.J.M. Samuel M.D., Miss Juleien Soule and Mrs. J. Mizell the wife of Postmaster Joshua Mizell.

Minutes of the meeting recorded that "it was agreed and understood that Mrs. Mizell should hold office as a trustee on condition she become an enrolled member of the church in Punta Gorda," which she did.

Coffelt and Noyes disappear from church records thereafter. Their memberships at First Presbyterian had been validated by letters of transfer from churches at their previous locations.

The fledgling church took its first steps toward obtaining a sanctuary and a resident pastor a year later. At a meeting in January 1897, it was decided to make an effort to have services twice a month. Rev. C.E. Jones was elected "stated supply minister" to preach on that basis. The congregation pledged to raise $150 per year for the minister and asked the Board of Missions to provide another $250. The arrangements were approved. Rev. Jones came twice a month to preach, pray and administer sacraments.

During an evening service at the Baptist Church a month later, Dr. Samuel, a 55-year-old widower, formerly of Tennessee, was elected an Elder. Three days later Col. John C. Pepper, a retired lawyer from Chicago, was elected a Trustee.

The church was incorporated in accordance with the laws of Florida in May 1897. Finally, in July 1898, The Rev. Clearance H. Ferran was called to become the first full-time pastor. Trustee Pepper was elected Elder, and both he and previously-elected Elder Samuel were ordained by Rev. Ferran. Rev. Ferran set about building a sanctuary. At a congregational meeting held after prayer services in June 1900, five trustees were elected. They were Col. Pepper, Dr. Samuel, James R. Elliott, Charles E. Midget a carpenter, and Bruce Wade a druggist. These, with the addition of Belton Bassett, were appointed a building committee.

During that summer and fall, an "every-member-canvas" was conducted. Contributions were received also from friends in Arcadia, Eustis, Orlando, Illinois and Indiana. The Presbytery Board of Church Construction gave $975.

Lot Purchased

With these funds, the lot upon which the church now stands was purchased for $250 from Mrs. Isaac (Virginia) Trabue. A few years later she donated an adjoining lot for a pastors' residence though she was a charter member of the Good Shepherd Episcopal Church.

Construction of the frame church building began in Dec. 1900. It was completed four months later amidst a field of palmettos and dedicated April 14, 1901. Rev. Keigwin delivered the dedicatory sermon from Psalms 87:3 — "Glorious things are spoken of Thee, O city of God." Dedicatory prayer was offered by Pastor C.H. Ferran. Elder Pepper reported the church was completed at a cost of $5,000 — and, in good Scot tradition, free of debt.

Rev. Ferran continued to push for church improvements, as reported in August the following year by the *Herald*: "A fine organ for the Presbyterian Sunday School was received this week. Pastor C.H. Ferran bought the instrument while he was passing through Jacksonville. The money was donated by J.M. Cameron, consulting engineer for the Consolidated Ice Company."

Rev. Ferran served until Sept. 1903 when he accepted a call by the Presbyterian Church of Lake City, Fla.

The first sanctuary and steeple, withstood many storms until Hurricane Donna hit Sept. 10, 1960. This time, the steeple gave way. Rev. Reese Y. Henderson and Trustee President James Taylor discovered another misfortune which they disclosed in a letter published by the *Herald*:

"Dear Friends: Hurricane Donna hit First Presbyterian a crippling blow. The steeple has blown over, and the roof uncovered in a number of places. Water damage was considerable, and the front doors blown in.

"The present board of trustees thought we had coverage for this type of disaster. However, upon investigation we find that we are not covered. In fact, in all its 60-year history, the church has never carried windstorm insurance — a mistake which is apparent to all now.

"However, that is not our immediate problem. We are desperately in need of major repairs and with no money with which to make them. Therefore, we are asking that members and friends make a sacrificial gift to the church so we may put our building back into operation. In the meantime, services will be held in the Community Hall at the Trailer Park on Nesbit St."

Fire Destroys

Enough money was scraped together to cap the bell tower and repair the roof. The church bell was given to the Presbyterian Conference Center at Lake Placid, Fla. Complete repairs were estimated to cost $19,000. The congregation elected to try and raise money for a completely new sanctuary. he drive started in March 1961. Fire started by spontaneous combustion of painting rags in the old Sunday School wing hastened building plans. This time, the damage was covered by insurance. The new church, in modern A-frame style, was dedicated March 4, 1962.

Over the years, First Presbyterian has been blessed with the services of 29 other pastors after Rev. Ferran. Most stayed only for brief periods in the early, struggling years. However, The Rev. Dr. J.H. Albert served from Oct. 1912 through 1917; The Rev. Dr. Larimore C. Denise served 1948-1952 inclusive; and Rev. Alexander Linn was pastor 1952-56.

A notable pastorate was that of The Rev. Dr. Fred H. Buchholtz, father of Mrs. Vernon (Edna Jane) Peeples, of Punta Gorda. Rev. Buchholtz served from Dec. 1945 through June 1947.

Rev. Reese Y. Henderson holds the record for service — 25 years 9 months — from March 1959 until his retirement Dec. 31, 1984.

Rev. James Nelson Latta, the present pastor, has served since April 1986 — the second longest tenure and is well known for the radio broadcasts of Sunday services. Under his leadership, the congregation has grown a steady 10 percent and raised funds for the addition of bell tower, steeple, stained glass window of Jesus calming the troubled waters, and other improvements. With this demonstration of faith, the congregation is poised for another century of "ministry and mission" at Punta Gorda.

Tucker's Grade still passable in Babcock-Webb Wildlife Management Area.

Chapter 38

TUCKER'S GRADE ROUTE TO NOWHERE

Travelers on Interstate 75 at exit 27 south east of Punta Gorda often wonder about the man whose name survives on road-side signs marking Tucker's Grade. His saga begins at a cattle corral known as Willow Pens halfway between Tamiami Trail (U.S. 41) and State Road 31. The area was opened to homesteaders in 1908. About a dozen settlers took up acreage along a cattle trail through the vast pine forest.

Moving cattle in Florida was much different than on the plains of Texas. Dense forests of Florida prevented gathering cattle in herds that would stay together at night. Cows could too easily wander off into the thickets. Consequently, holding pens were constructed along a cow path — about a day's journey apart — to keep cattle during the night. Willow Pens consisted of several holding areas on the route to the deep-water dock at Punta Rassa south of Fort Myers.

A story in the *Punta Gorda Herald* of May 1913 gives us an insight into the homesteading process:

"The homesteaders of Willow Pens and Bermont are beginning to prove up their claims. Several have already done so. Christian J. Schultz

170

and George C. Hartman are among those gentlemen undertaking to prove up more recently. Mr. Shultz makes the commutation proof, while Mr. Hartman makes 5-year proof."

Homesteaders could obtain title to their land upon proving they had built a home with a door and window, cultivated three acres, and lived on the property three months of three consecutive years within five years following issuance of a "patent." These requirements could be "commuted" (reduced) by payment of some money, or by performance of some public service such as building a road or bridge.

Farther west — at the intersection today of Tamiami Trail and Green Gulf Blvd. — another village of homesteaders was taking root along the Atlantic Coast Line Railroad. The *Herald* reported in June 1913:

"TUCKER'S WOODS — This section is thriving. C.P. Stanton has his house completed and enclosed with a fence and will soon move into it. Charles Richmond has moved into his house and is clearing ground for crops. Charles McWilliams has the timber for a house now on the ground and is getting things in shape to move out and take up his residence. G. Johnson has set up his tent on his claim and is ditching, grubbing and making ready to build. Mrs. W.T. Morgan and Miss Ruth Nelson have taken up their residence on the Morgan claim. John Boyle has been out from Punta Gorda clearing a building site on his father's claim."

Tucker Takes Homestead Patent

Among the homesteaders was a Punta Gorda businessman named Capt. Allen B. Tucker. He also was an officer in the Florida Militia. It was common practice for town people to file homestead claims inasmuch as the three-month residence was not onerous and was generally overlooked anyway. The state was anxious to get marginal land on the tax rolls. In addition to a homestead claim, Tucker bought other large tracts along the Willow Pens path.

With so much growth, the old cattle trail was woefully inadequate. Tucker undertook to fix this problem, along with other DeSoto County roads south of Charlotte Harbor. Charlotte County was not to be split off from DeSoto until 1921. Tucker and other civic leaders prevailed upon the county commission to issue bonds for road construction in the Punta Gorda area — as noted by the *Herald* in Feb. 1915:

"Secretary A.B. Tucker, of the trustees of the Punta Gorda special road and bridge district, visited Arcadia in an official capacity on Saturday. He reports that purchasers of the bonds have called for the balance of the issue amounting to $117,000. This is the last call, taking up the entire issue of $200,000. Draft has been made for this amount, and it is expected to have the funds in hand in due time."

Shortly after this, work began on a "grade" (a road right-of-way raised by scraping dirt from ditches on both sides to the middle, but with no improved surface) along the east-west boundary line between townships 41 and 42. Because of Tucker's close association with the effort, his name became attached to the road through common usage.

Though it was never paved, the road was more important than just a convenient route to Punta Gorda's market and shipping facilities. Tucker intended that it continue eastward across Telegraph Swamp and through what is now Babcock Ranch. Destination was to be the road from Palmdale to the bridge at LaBelle and thence to Fort Myers.

Before the grade was completed, a bridge over the Caloosahatchee was built at Olga, and a road surveyed between it and Arcadia. Florida's first automobile road map printed in 1915 shows the route. However, the impending First World War led the state to postpone construction. State Road 2 (now 31) between Arcadia and Olga was completed in 1922. The Tamiami Trail bridge over the Caloosahatchee opened in 1924.

Because of the prospect of a shorter route to Fort Myers, Tucker's Grade was never finished. It ended abruptly in the wilderness. Nevertheless, travelers going to Fort Myers from the Charlotte Harbor and Peace River communities from 1915 to 1924 often took the Tucker's Grade

Allen Tucker, seated third from left, with Rotary Club charter members of 1926. Others are from left, standing, Gray Holmes, George Dewey, Kirby Seward, John Skipper, Chester Blount, John Jack, Charles Johnson, Potter Lucas, Vernon Jordan, Baynard Malone, James Sikes, Farmer Bowen. Sitting: W.H. Johnson, James McClelland, Tucker, Wallace Mobley. Center: President W.S. Whitfield. Trophy was for 100 percent attendance at Cleveland, Ohio, convention.

shortcut — striking out from there through the countryside of palmettos, pines and cypress swamps for the 1903 bridge at Alva or the 1922 bridge at Olga. Both were closer to Fort Myers than the LaBelle bridge.

Tucker's Grade is in use today as an access road between Interstate 75 and U.S. 41, and as service roads on the Babcock Ranch and the Babcock-Webb Wildlife Management Area.

With access north and south, settlers along Tucker's Grade prospered — as disclosed in a Jan. 1920 issue of the *Herald*: "Farmers of Willow Pens Township met Saturday evening and organized a farmers' institute. The meeting was held at the home of Mrs. Agnes Hertzke, a large number of farmers being present, and the gathering was an enthusiastic one.

"C. Overholser and Mrs. Hertzke both made interesting talks, after which the following officers were elected: George Yobst, president; C. Overholser, secretary; and Tony Rudin treasurer. Godfrey Belor and Mr. Madden were elected reporting committee.

"A well known farmer of the Willow Pens section, Yobst says that if truckers fail to make money in Florida, it is the fault of the man and not the country. He has had a successful Fall season raising peppers, beans, cucumbers and sweet potatoes. He is now preparing for a spring crop of beans and cucumbers. Yobst has been farming in Florida for seven years. He is considering buying a truck to haul his stuff to the (railroad) station. Yobst homesteaded, but as he had never received his naturalization papers he has not received the patent for his land."

Peddled By Ox Cart

Mrs. Hertzke was an industrious truck farmer who raised a variety of vegetables. Esther McCullough, who came to Punta Gorda with her parents in 1914, remembers Mrs. Hertzke peddling her produce on Saturdays from an ox-drawn cart. "She told me she started out from her farm at midnight to be at Punta Gorda by noon when the fishermen returned from their week's work down the bay and collected their pay," says Mrs. McCullough. "Mrs. Hertzke's had a green thumb. Her vegetables were the best around; and fresh from the field."

The Seaboard Air Line Railway had a loading dock called Tucker's Woods on Tucker's Grade. The Atlantic Coast Line Railroad also had a dock at the western end of Tucker's grade near a village variously called Broadbent, Lester or Rogers. The intersection of Tucker's Grade and S.R. 31 was known as Tucker's Corner. John T. Rose kept a general store there. The grade at this point is now closed by a fence opposite the present entrance to Babcock Wilderness Tours. In the mid-1920's, the grade was extended east to Glades County through the Babcock Ranch.

Visitors tour the ranch on part of the old Tucker's Grade through Telegraph Cypress Swamp — the latter so named because it once was skirted by the International Ocean Telegraph line.

The *Albert F. Dewey* at sea trial near Newport News.

Chapter 39

SHIP 13 RAN OUT OF LUCK

The Coast Guard board of inquiry at New Orleans in the summer of 1941 wanted to know why the crew of the *Albert F. Dewey* abandoned their ship in Cuba.

Testified fireman-oiler Louis Cherney: "There were 13 of us in the crew, we sailed 13 days after signing on, the captain's birthday came on the 13th of July, the boat's hull had the number 13 on it, and the letter "M" on the funnel is the 13th letter in the alphabet."

Another crewman added, "And the chief engineer's name — William Carter — has 13 letters in it!".

Subject of the hearing was the steel-hulled tugboat that began her long career in 1895 pushing barges of phosphate ore at Punta Gorda, Fla. She had been ordered by her namesake, Albert F. Dewey.

Dewey came from Savannah, Ga., in 1890 to hauling ore from the Peace River Phosphate Mining, Co., at Hull (now disappeared) to waiting ships off Punta Gorda's 4,200-foot Long Dock.

Dewey realized he could haul ore more economically if he pushed a string of barges to ocean going freighters at Boca Grande Pass. Consequently he commissioned a propeller-driven coal-fueled tug from Newport News Ship Building Co.

Details of specifications were recorded by William A. Fox, editor of the ship company magazine *Masthead*. The tug's hull was 98 feet stem to stern, 19 feet abeam, and a draft amidship of 11 feet 6 inches — just enough to let him navigate the 12-foot upper harbor channel. The cost was $40,000 — a huge sum in those days.

The *Albert F. Dewey* was launched and christened Jan. 31, 1895, by Miss Louise Parker, daughter of Newport News banker H.E. Parker. The new tug, only the 13th vessel built by the shipyard, underwent trials on the following April 13 and was delivered to Capt. Dewey two days later.

The sturdy boat was typical of her time, but her flamboyant owner ordered a gilded stag bolted to the roof of her pilot house instead of the usual eagle. Perhaps Capt. Dewey was emulating Sir Francis Drake who sailed around the world in 1578 on a ship named *Golden Hind* having a gilded stag figurehead.

The *Albert F. Dewey* also was provided with varnished woodwork, polished brass and awning rails in anticipation of her employment in the hot Florida sun. She looked more like a yacht than a work boat.

The *Dewey* sailed for Punta Gorda under the command of Capt. Collin Hyers who was to be her master for all her Florida days. Capt. Dewey's fleet hauled up to a thousand tons of phosphate a day, and his new flagship worked hard.

According to Punta Gorda historian Vernon Peeples, the *Dewey* was chartered by the New York Herald in 1898 for service as a newspaper dispatch boat from Cuba during the Spanish-American War.

Things began to go awry in 1902 — starting with destruction by fire of the phosphate drying sheds and other structures at Hull. The loss amounted to $200,000, of which only $50,000 was covered by insurance. The easily mined pebble phosphate dredged from the bed of Peace River was about played out anyway.

The company sold its mining rights to the Agricultural Chemical Company, which moved upriver and began building the Charlotte Harbor & Northern Railroad to haul ore to Boca Grande.

A Sea Rescue

A sea rescue by the *Dewey* was praised by the *Herald* in August: "The cattle schooner *B. Frank Neally* returning from Cuba two weeks ago became becalmed and drifted north of Miami 200 miles off course. Capt. Dewey's tug boat found the ship and towed it to the West India Dock at the mouth of Myakka River. There it was loaded with 325 cattle by T.S. Knight and towed again to Key West."

Many cattle died on the return trip, and Capt. Dewey was blamed. It was usual for some cattle to die on the trips to Cuba. However, Knight believed more than necessary perished and demanded compensation. Dewey refused and harsh words were exchanged.

He sold his tug boat to the U.S. Army Corps of Engineers in 1906. The *Dewey* was renamed the *C. Donovan,* converted to oil fuel and assigned to the New Orleans District, later to Galveston. While in this service she eased countless Europe-bound cargo ships to sea during the first World War. She was sold to Jahncke Service, Inc., of New Orleans in January 1937. Jahncke gave the ship her original name *Albert F. Dewey.* He used her for coastal towing until June 1941. At the advanced age of 46, the tug was sold to Minder Construction Corp. of New York, and her strange adventures began.

Strange Adventures

World War II had begun, but the United States had not yet been drawn in. Nevertheless, the U.S. in 1940 had 99-year rights to build bases in a number of British possessions in return for 50 "over-age destroyers."

The Minder company sold Dewey back to the Corps of Engineer in July 1941 to be used in construction of air bases for the Caribbean Defense Command. Among these were a new seaplane base, an air base and harbor facilities on St. Lucia, British West Indies.

The old boat left New Orleans and chugged across Lake Pontchartrain. She started taking on water in her engine room and had to stop for repairs. She left again, but 80 miles out of Gulfport, enroute to Key West, she almost overturned in a storm. She put in at Panama City, Fla, then proceeded to Tampa and Key West.

After refueling at Key West, Dewey proceeded along the northern coast of Cuba where she ran into more heavy weather. She stopped at Puerto Padre, and then made it to Antilla on Cuba's northeast coast.

Upon arriving at Antilla, Captain F. E. Yarech and his 12-man crew presented a petition to the U.S. consul, charging the boat was unseaworthy. An inspection board upheld this opinion. Without a doubt, the old tug was in poor shape and nearing the end of her days. Yet, she had one job left to do. Coast Guard records show that the tug left Antilla under the command of Capt. John S. Fulcher on Sept. 1, 1941. Capt. Emil O. Nass took command of her at Port Castries, St. Lucia, on Sept. 25.

After this, nothing is known about her fate. In all probability, says marine historian William A. Fox, she was employed in dredging and construction at the seaplane base and harbor at Port Castaries.

When the threat of war passed by the area late in 1943, the bases were decommissioned. The old tug may have worked on other construction projects during the war. Considering her condition, however, she probably was scrapped in the Caribbean before the end of hostilities.

The *Albert F. Dewey* was not Newport News Shipbuilding's luckiest ship, but she had a long career and served in three wars.

Today, she is remembered by an old half-model displayed in the lobby of the Newport News Shipbuilding general office building.

Albert Gilchrist at his desk in Punta Gorda in 1903 when he was a state representative. He shows a *Jacksonville Metropolitan* newspaper endorsing him for governor five years before he was elected. Note map of the Long Dock then the terminus of Florida Southern Railway — also the romantic valentine under neath, treasured by bachelor Gilchrist.

Chapter 40

CITY MOURNED GOV. GILCHRIST DEATH

Albert Waller Gilchrist was, without question, Punta Gorda's most distinguished citizen. He became governor of Florida in 1909 after serving four terms in the legislature as a state representative, the last as speaker of the House. His death at 5 a.m., May 16, 1926, at age 68, merited an unprecedented Sunday "extra" edition by the *Punta Gorda Herald*. A banner headline proclaimed: CITY MOURNS AT DEATH OF GILCHRIST. A front-page editorial, edged in black border, expressed the sentiments of his home-town:

"Gov. Gilchrist was not a man of brilliant attainments. He was not the polished scholar type, not sensational or flamboyant. Rather, he possessed those fundamental traits of human character which have been admired throughout the ages — rugged honesty, generosity, devotion, love, sympathy. His motto was: 'See no evil, hear no evil, speak no evil' which he took from a temple in Japan where he saw a statuette of three monkeys illustrating that motto.

"He made the Three Monkeys his slogan in his campaign for governor. His closest friends never heard him speak evil of anyone. He believed that mankind is inherently good and to be trusted. He adhered steadfastly to a purpose to live a useful life, be of service to his fellows and do what he could for the advancement of Florida — to whose interests he was unselfishly devoted."

"Gov. Gilchrist's death was directly traceable to a tumor in the left thigh, which led to an operation last June in Columbia, S.C., where he was attended by his half-brother, Dr. Robert W. Gibbes.

"The tumor returned; and last November, while in New York for medical treatment, Gov. Gilchrist disappeared. He was lost to all his friends — both in the great city and to friends here with whom he corresponded. Finally, a search made upon the request of the Florida state Senate revealed him sick and alone in New York City Hospital.

"Ironically, the Florida Legislature was at the time naming one of its two new counties 'Gilchrist' in honor of the former governor who was suffering, alone, in a hospital on East 42nd St. The story of his suffering and faith is best told by an excerpt from a recent letter to A.P. Jordan (good friend, and publisher-editor of the *Herald*):

Gilchrist's Last Letter

"The latter part of June 1925, a major surgical operation was performed at Columbia, S.C., on my left leg. The operation was satisfactory to the surgeon; but 'the cat came back.' It has developed that another operation is necessary. I arrived at this hospital Nov. 11, having been treated in Columbia, S.C., Oct. 9. Here, generally on alternate days, a serum is injected in the left leg, usually causing a chill and a fever lasting eight or nine hours. The greater the chill, it is claimed, the greater the benefit. I expect to be here until some time in February. Before leaving, there will likely be another operation.

"Outside of this medical treatment, I am in good general health; no sore, no pain except a little sometimes from radium treatment. It is difficult to get a stenographer, and I am not in position to do much writing. Dr. William Coley attends me. He says he will cure me. I believe he will."

The *Herald* story gives an interesting account of his life:

"The former governor was a descendant of an early Virginia family of colonists, from which house George Washington and James Madison also trace their lineage. He was the son of General William E. Gilchrist of Quincy, Florida. Albert was born Jan. 15, 1858, in Columbia, S.C., while his mother was visiting her parents. (The family name actually was Kilrase. After the general's death, his widow changed it to Gilchrist in the belief the original spelling would hinder her son's advancement.)

"Albert was raised at Quincy, and there commenced working at an early age, as he said, 'on a promise' of $15 a month. When 20 years old,

Gilchrist won an appointment to the West Point Academy. As a cadet, sergeant and lieutenant he studied army tactics for three years.

"He returned to Florida and later, during the administration of Gov. Perry, was appointed inspector-general of the state militia. He retained this office under the succeeding administration and continued under Gov. Mitchell who advanced him to the rank of brigadier general.

"In 1896, he was appointed to the board of review for West Point. Two years later, when the U.S.S. Maine was blown up in Havana harbor, the echo rang in Gilchrist's ears. He sought an opportunity to make his military training of use to the government. He resigned as a militia brigadier general and was among the first volunteers. He entered the infantry as a private at a salary of $15.60 per month.

"During the ensuing war with Spain, he served in Cuba, won the rank of captain and was mustered out at the close of hostilities as acting major.

"Five years before the war, when only 35 years of age, he made a successful race as representative from DeSoto, the largest county in the United States, and was re-elected to the following legislature — having made his reputation for competency. He was as stalwart in rugged honesty, say local admirers, as in stature and physical strength. Gilchrist was tall, heavy set and muscular.

Railroad Engineer

"Before the war with Spain — when the Florida Southern Railway built southward from Pemberton Ferry to Charlotte Harbor — Gilchrist preceded this development with the road's engineering and surveying forces. He was responsible for all cross-tie purchases, and made the acquaintance of one of his later partners in politics, Herbert J. Drane. The latter is now state congressman but at that time was a cross-tie contractor making sales subject to Gilchrist's approval.

"The incoming railroad came with its rough and ready workmen. The fishing industry sprang up as soon as shipments could be made by rail. The original Punta Gorda boom brought big payrolls and new wealth.

"His old friends tell of numerous exciting incidents. One of these, arising from trouble between two rival saloons, tested his ability to cope with wooly boys of the bar rooms.

"Word was received that a certain desperado had made an oath to kill Gilchrist as soon as he entered town. The young politician, upon receipt of the news, greased his pistols and sent back a written message naming a place in the woods, advising that he would have two guns with both triggers cocked. Gilchrist was the only man to attend the convention beneath the pines.

"When the rails were laid, Gilchrist settled here, determined to grow up with the new town; but it has been said that the town instead grew up with him until finally it was left behind.

"He became state representative two more times from DeSoto County which then included Punta Gorda, was speaker of the House in 1907 and in 1909 was inaugurated governor of Florida. His business during and following this time was real estate development and investment — in which he was considered unusually successful.

"The question of establishing a hospital for indigent, crippled children was given an adverse report by the Senate committee. However, the need that hundreds of Florida children had for such an institution touched the heart of the governor too deeply. He hammered after the measure until it passed both houses with enough money appropriated to admit these children and treat them free of charge at St. Luke's Hospital, Jacksonville.

"Gilchrist never married. Possible love affairs have not come to light. Nonetheless, his kindly love for fellow men, his tenderness toward children and the effort he put forth in fostering and establishing two perpetual welfare institutions (St. Luke's and Masonic Home and Orphanage at St. Petersburg) leads one to believe that such expressions of love could only come from the heart of a man disappointed, ever striving to find solace in bringing joy to others."

Proclaim Funeral Holiday

Mayor John Jack proclaimed the day of Gilchrist's funeral, Tuesday, May 18 a half-holiday so the town could attend. Services were held at Good Shepherd Episcopal Church for which he had donated its site. Burial was at Indian Springs Cemetery, south of town.

An American Legion honor squad fired a salute with shotguns during the playing of taps. The discharges tore into nearby pine trees, showering bystanders with needles and cones.

Gilchrist left his fortune to various charities, but the will was contested by the Gibbes heirs who were awarded $60,000. Largest bequest was $500,000 to the Masonic Home and Orphanage — he had been Master of Punta Gorda Lodge and Grand Master of Florida.

Other donations were $10,000 to the University of Florida, $10,000 to the Florida State College for Women (now Florida State University), $5,000 to the Florida School for the Deaf and Dumb, $5,000 to the State Hospital for Indigent Children, $7,500 to beautify the grounds of the Punta Gorda school, $2,500 to the "school for colored children" for like purpose, $5,000 for beautifying the approach to the Charlotte Harbor Bridge, and $1,000 to the Martha Reid Chapter of the United Daughters of the Confederacy. His collection of curios and relics was left to the Baptist Children's Home for orphans at Arcadia. The home was moved to Lakeland in 1950. Fate of the curios is unknown.

A bequest still being administered was a $5,000 trust to the Punta Gorda Masonic Lodge to purchase ice-cream for boys and girls on Halloween. The bequest is still observed faithfully.

An oranges packing house in 1903 at the Punta Gorda railroad switch.

Chapter 41

QUEEN OF VEGETABLE PACKERS

Early communities south of the Peace River roadstead — Punta Gorda, Cleveland, Solana, Acline — are justly remembered as production centers for cattle, fish, citrus and pineapple. Not so well known is the cultivation of winter vegetables and the "packing houses" serving growers.

Packing houses operated for only a few weeks at a time — timed to the various harvests of tomatoes, bell peppers, cabbages, squash, cucumbers, eggplant, string beans, water melons and cantaloupes.

We are fortunate in having the recollections of Byron L. Rhode who a decade ago shared his memories of the packing business in a letter to his good friend Mrs. Sam McCullough (Esther Oswald Jordan).

Rhode was born in 1904 at Williston, Fla., but came to Punta Gorda with his parents two years later. His earliest memories, therefore, are of events in and near Punta Gorda. In his senior years he began setting down his reminiscences in a notebook to preserve for history.

When the notebook came to the attention of U.S. Cleveland, president of the Charlotte Harbor Area Historical Society, he prevailed upon Byron to allow publication of the notes in a book *Punta Gorda Remembered*. The book is now out of print but is available in Charlotte County libraries for reference. Now retired, and living in Charlotte Harbor Town, the

following text is extracted from Rhode's heretofore unpublished correspondence to Cleveland and Mrs. Esther McCullough.

Rhode Memories

*I knew Belle and Fred Quednau for many years. She was a beautiful
woman, and Capt. Fred was her only boy friend. Back during the First
World War, there was a girl named Florence Acuff who lived down in
Estero. She was writing letters to Capt. Fred. He used to run boats to
places all up and down the coast. He also was a fine looking man.*

*At that time I was working in the post office. One day, Belle said to
me: "Baron" — for some reason she, Fred and their daughter Tosie
always called me that instead of Byron — "I know that old Acuff girl is
writing letters to Fred. I can't prove it, but I want to know. Is she?"*

*I said, "Belle, it's against the rules for me to tell you that, but you
know his post office box number. If a letter from her comes, I will lay it
on top of his mail where you can look in through the glass and see it."*

*Back then there was a large packing house on the tracks between the
old depot and Frank Rigell's Lumber Yard (later the West Coast Lumber
Co.). That lumber yard was first started up by John Hurton whose father
built a nice home on Cross Street for his crippled daughter, Nellie.*

*The packing house was built and owned by Old Man C.C. Carlton.
(Others packers from time to time along the tracks there were the Punta
Gorda Citrus Growers Exchange, Chadwick Brothers Packing House, and
Skipper Brothers & Holderby Packing House. At Solana there was the
J.W. Byrd Packing House for pineapples.) There was a lot of truck
farming plus citrus growing hereabout.*

Belle A Fast Packer

*Belle worked at the packing houses. Fruit and tomatoes were washed,
sized, wrapped in colored tissue paper and packed in crates for shipment
by train. She was really a fast packer and had quite a reputation for it.*

*The fruit had to be top quality. All inferior fruit was hauled out in the
woods and thrown away. Today, almost all fruit goes to the juice plants
regardless of quality — or it is bagged up in 5-pound bags. Even the
rinds are processed into dairy feed.*

*Folks were glad when the packing houses opened and put a lot of
people to work. First, the pickers of both fruit and vegetables. Next, the
people who hauled it to the packing houses in 2-bushel field crates. These
were unloaded and stacked in, or on one side of, the packing houses.*

*Then, men would pull a stack of field crates onto hand trucks and
wheel them over to men who dumped the contents onto a long conveyor
belt. The conveyor carried the fruit through a washer and a dryer. As the
belt moved along, people on each side picked out the culls. The rest of the
fruit was wrapped and packed one-by-one into shipping crates.*

182

I knew two young men who came every year and had the contract to make up the crates and nail on the lids after filling. The crates were made up in the loft and came down a conveyor to the packing floor. These boys were very fast. They put a bunch of nails in their mouths and took them one at a time to drive them with shingle hatchets. As the filled crates moved down the conveyor they quickly nailed the lids on. Finally, men with hand trucks rolled the crates into iced boxcars. Today this is all a bygone era. Punta Gorda doesn't even have an ice plant any more.

As a young woman, Belle (McBean) was a dressmaker. She made shirts for people like T.C. Crosland and Harry Dreggors. After she married, Fred wanted her to quit, but she didn't. Not too long ago, Belle made for Blanche (Rhode's wife) a bonnet like women used to wear.

The first railroad depot was over behind the concrete-block high school on Taylor Street and in the "wye" across the tracks from the Carlton Packing House.

This depot was used until 1897 when a new one was constructed on King Street near the Hotel Punta Gorda and the fish houses on the adjacent railroad dock.

According to a squib in an April 1914 Punta Gorda Herald: "The old Atlantic Coast Line depot has been fitted up as a packing house." (The site is now a vacant lot between Taylor and Nesbit streets. The 2-story school built in 1909 was on the southeast corner of Taylor and Charlotte.)

How A Wye Works

As a passenger train came down the main line from Arcadia and approached the switching "wye" (a triangular configuration of tracks) south of town, the engineer slowed down. The brakeman jumped off and ran ahead to throw the switch onto a spur curving down King Street to the (second) depot. When passengers had alighted, the train backed out onto the main line again for the run to Fort Myers.

Freight trains were switched through the wye to drop off empty refrigerator cars for the packing houses. Then, the train was routed backwards by a second switch down King Street to the fish houses to drop off refrigerator cars for them.

On the return trip from Fort Myers, all trains ran past the wye and waited for the switches to be thrown. Then, the trains backed down the two wye spurs to board passengers at the depot, or to hook on cars loaded with fish or produce. Upon pulling back to the mainline, the train slowed down to let the brakeman get off and restore the through-switch for the next oncoming train. The brakeman ran to catch the end of the train.

This went on for years. Northbound trains would roar up King Street past Marion Avenue without a signal or flag man. One day, Dave Hobbs was going down Marion Avenue in his automobile — approaching King Street — while a train was backing in.

183

The engineer was blowing his whistle, but the engine was a couple of blocks behind the lead box-cars shielded from view by buildings. Hobbs casually assumed the train was headed in and that it was still a block or so away. He pulled across the tracks, and the train hit him.

The crash knocked Hobbs and his car clear up on a vacant lot next to the Traveler's Hotel, It did not kill him, but it crippled him up. That's when he got the money to open his plumbing business. After that accident, the train slowed up in both directions; and a flag man ran ahead to stop traffic.

That switching wye is gone today, but it accounts for the several triangular lots around today's old Atlantic Coast Line Depot, the third depot at Punta Gorda.

Solana had a railroad loading platform known as Pineapple Center along the railroad. Acline and Cleveland had loading docks for taking on melons and cantaloupes which do not require refrigeration.

Truckers — vegetable farmers, not drivers of 18-wheel vehicles — were prospering in March of 1915 as noted by the *Herald:*

"George McLane has an impressive looking field of beans. The long lines follow the sweep of the canal and, stretching at right angles from the road, looks like some of the advertising pictures sent out of the state.

"Shipping began last week, and all the pepper men are getting crates out now. Rountree has been shipping peppers from his patch near town for two weeks. Capt. Smith is shipping with satisfactory results.

"Chadwick says he is going to put in a field of oats soon where part of the potato planting was. Some fine lettuce was shipped from his packing house last week, and the city has had a good supply of celery from here.

"A.C. Caldwell and his father have put in two acres of tomatoes, seven of watermelons, and two of beans.

"It is said that certain parties are guilty of buying up all the lots in Punta Gorda that can be had in anticipation of a sudden rise in the prices of real estate. It is believed that outside capital is interesting itself here.

"Since the soil in the vicinity has been found to be so well adapted to trucking, and large numbers of truckers are expected this fall, it is asserted that our city will experience the same increase in population that Wauchula experienced, and that property here will double as quickly as it did there.

"From an outside source, it is learned that certain interests are going to take hold and develop Punta Gorda at a rapid rate. Owners who have held their property so long, and paid the taxes, should not be too much in a hurry to sell. Surely the boom is coming!"

Punta Gorda drillers 1908 bring in an artesian well.

Chapter 42

FOUNTAIN OF YOUTH

The legend of a "fountain of youth" in Florida persists to this day in Punta Gorda. It is true that the many mineral springs and warm weather — helped along by a heavy dose of faith — does make people feel better.

Early settlers in the Charlotte Harbor area were enthusiastic boosters of the legend. When the *Punta Gorda Herald* was short on news, the editor would spice up his columns with stories on the wonderful properties of local artesian wells. The *Herald* issue of Sept 10, 1908, for example, published a front-page story headlined   A LOST MAGICAL SPRING:

Far be it from our wish to snatch any laurels from the goddess of Fame which may not belong by right to fair Punta Gorda. But, if our city has been more favored than many other spots in sunny Florida, they are the gifts of an all-wise Judge. Thus, we are entitled to that which He has seen fit to bestow upon us. Gratitude only, not pride, fills our hearts when we pause to consider His beneficence.

In the matter of attractions, not least of those that we do not boast of, is a spring of magical mineral waters that restore the hirsute covering to the unfortunates who have been compelled to part with their crowning glory — and which gives the luxuriant tresses of happy maids an additional luster to enhance their charms.

This spring is located a short distance from our town. It was discovered by a Northerner seeking health in our environs. He had pitched his tent beside the convenient supply of pure drinking water.

In taking his daily ablutions, he noticed that his shiny pate was taking on an unaccustomed fuzz. This brought great joy to his heart and peace to his soul. For three months he kept away from the haunts of men to nurse his great secret and watch its development.

On the day that he returned to civilization, it was his unique privilege to walk among his fellows as a stranger, unknown to one and all alike by his friends and acquaintances. Not only was his shiny head-piece covered with a luxuriant mat of tumbled tresses, his face was almost lost to the world behind an impenetrable thicket of whiskers that spread in waving locks from a slightly cleared place below his eyes.

Having a business-like turn of mind, he did not divulge his secret and spread it broadcast as he might have done; but, going to his old friend, the late lamented Col. Trabue, he told his story. A plan was formulated for putting the magical waters on the market.

Before this great boon to mankind was put within their reach, the discoverer of the spring was stricken with heart-failure; and he never revealed the location of the priceless spring.

He had said it was not more than five miles from Punta Gorda. Its peculiar properties seemed to be well known to the beasts and birds of the forest. During the molting season, the place was fairly alive with deer, raccoons, opossums and numberless birds that came to bathe in the limpid waters to renew their coats.

Hunters acquainted with this story have kept up a still-hunt for this great prize for the last ten years. When it is re-discovered, it certainly will enrich its discoverer beyond his wildest dreams.

The hair-restoring spring topped Editor Jordan's earlier one about "OUR MUSICAL WELLS." In this imaginative yarn, he wrote that in the previous six years, a number of artesian wells had been driven for various commercial purposes — an 8-inch well at the present ice factory, four 8-inch wells at the defunct ice factory, an 8-inch city well and several lesser ones scattered about town.

* * *

As a matter of course," wrote Jordan, "no two of these wells have exactly the same pressure, nor do they discharge the same quantity of water. Consequently, the roar of each well is in a different key.

Some musical soul called attention to the similarity these roars bear to a chime of bells. As well after well added its own distinctive note to the scale, the range and variety of the chime became almost infinite in its combination of harmonies.

On quiet evenings, when the air is heavy and sounds are carried long distances, the combined rhythm of our many wells, ranging from deep base to rippling trebles, throb and swell through our little burg. They thrill all true devotees of music with the rapture that Nature Only can impart when conditions are right and Man meets her half way.

The *Herald* continued to promote the wonderful effects of well-water that tasted and smelled of rotten eggs. In an issue of Feb. 1915 — at the height of the winter season when the population of northern visitors was largest — the *Herald* devoted half its front page to serious testimonials under a banner headline

"PUNTA GORDA CLIMATE AND ARTESIAN WATER."

They are of historical interest in that they reveal ailments affecting a *Who's Who* of prominent settlers:

"That Punta Gorda's artesian water has curative properties is testified to by many people who have been benefitted by drinking it. Ex Gov. A.W. Gilchrist considers it a remarkable and valuable asset to this locality. He thinks that people suffering from those ailments which it will benefit should know of it. Of a number of testimonials he has collected, several follow — others will be published later.

Edward Wotitzky —"Years ago I went to New York to consult a specialist in regard to indigestion. No good was accomplished. Returning to Punta Gorda (1905), I found the artesian city well just completed. I tried its water. In a week's time I was much improved. In a month's time I was cured. I have suffered with kidney trouble bordering on Bright's disease. I was attended by a doctor. In three months after using this water, I was discharged. I am now free from both such troubles. I was born in New York City."

Gus Hart — "About eight years ago I came to Punta Gorda, stopping here from November until May. I had been under a doctor's care for seven or eight years for gout and kidney trouble. In a very short time, the Punta Gorda artesian water relieved me from all pain. I have not since had a doctor for such a disease. My home was Philadelphia."

George S. Stone, M.D. — "I came to Punta Gorda in May 1910 from York, Pa. I was a physical wreck, suffering from nervousness, indigestion, kidney and bronchial troubles. I could scarcely walk as far as 100 yards. I am now in perfect health. I ascribe the renewal of my health to artesian water, so far as curing the indigestion and kidney trouble. The cure of bronchial trouble I ascribe to the climate. The water here possesses great therapeutic value in all kidney, rheumatic, gouty and stomach troubles. I am a practicing physician. I was born in Williamston, S.C."

Josh Mizell —" Several years since I was turned down for life insurance on account of Bright's disease. The doctor said I would not live six months. The New York doctor at headquarters also turned me down. I commenced drinking the Punta Gorda artesian water and became cured. I have since taken out life insurance. I have not suffered since from kidney trouble. I am now in good health. I was born in Hernando County, Fla."

Harry L. Decker — "I came to Punta Gorda in Sept. 1908. I have lived here ever since. I came from New York City, having been born in New Jersey. When I cam here I was suffering from rheumatism. I have thoroughly recovered from such. I ascribe my cure to the artesian water and to the climate."

D.L. McSwain, M.D. — "I have been practicing medicine in this county for 16 years. I came from DeFuniak, Fla. I am satisfied that the artesian water of Punta Gorda is good for kidney and bladder diseases. It is a very light water. I am satisfied it is good for the stomach."

David N. McQueen, M.D. —" The artesian water here is light and pleasant to the taste. There is no feeling of weight after drinking large quantities, as there is in drinking rain or distilled water. I have known much benefit to be derived from drinking the water among my patients. It is beneficial to disorders of the kidneys, bladder and stomach. I have resided in Punta Gorda for the past 12 years, coming here from Fayetteville, N.C."

E.K. Whidden, M.D. — I have found that the artesian water of Punta Gorda will relieve many skin diseases if baths are taken frequently. In fact, there are few diseases with which I have to contend that cannot be almost or totally relieved by the persistent use of this water, for drinking, bathing, etc. I use it in many ways. With frequent use, as good results can be obtained as with the waters of Hot Springs, Ark. I have lived in Punta Gorda for about 12 years, having been born in this county."

* * *

The city artesian well described was located in the center of the intersection of W. Marion and Cross St. It was capped in 1927 when Cross Street was paved with brick and concrete curbs laid.

A second artesian well of mineral water on the northeast corner of Marion Avenue and Taylor Street in downtown Punta Gorda survives. Its tile fountain was erected in 1931 when Marion was widened. It had a spigot for filling jugs, a bubbler drinking fountain and steps at one side for children. The steps were removed in 1971 when Taylor was widened.

A few years later, when Florida Department of Transportation expressed concern over the water's radium content, the City removed the bubbler drinking fountain. By popular request, the spigot was permitted to stay. Devotees of the water rich in radium can still fill their jugs. Most of them leave the cap off the jug for 24 hours to allow the rotten-egg smell and taste to dissipate.

With tongue in cheek, members of the Charlotte Harbor Area Historical Society say this well is the real Fountain of Youth, and they guarantee you will reach your 100th birthday if you drink a glass of water from this fountain every day. The catch is that you have to do it every day for whatever number of days it takes you to reach 100 or all bets are off.

Babcock-Webb manager Larry Campbell inspects one of many bomb craters.

Chapter 43

CIA HAD SECRET CAMP AT BABCOCK-WEBB

With construction of the Seaboard Air Line Railway from Sarasota to Naples in 1925-26 — near the Tucker's Grade settlements south of Punta Gorda — it became feasible to exploit the virgin pine forests.

Perry McAdow of Punta Gorda, and others, leased convicts to bleed pines for sap. As this killed the trees, lumber companies took over the leases to fell timber. Among firms in the Tucker Grade area in 1929-31 were those of the Russ Lumber Co., Keyesville Lumber Co., and Roux Crate Co. Spurs, or "tramways," from the Seaboard main line meandered through the forests to logging camps and sawmills. When a section had been cut, the rails were picked up and re-laid to a new area.

Following the lumber men was A.C. Frizzell of Murdock. He had come to what is now Charlotte County in 1918 as a telegraph operator for the Charlotte Harbor & Northern Railroad. He made a fortune salvaging pine stumps, then parlayed this into cattle, lumber and automobile dealerships. Oldtimers say Frizzell hired blacks to push out pine stumps with an old automobile converted to a tractor. A wide depression was dug into the ground, lined with sheet metal, and the stumps piled in.

After setting the wood afire, workers covered the smoldering mass with sand taken from the depression. Workers tended the kiln for three days and nights. A pipe in the depression carried off pine tar sweated from the stumps to an old bathtub. As the tub filled, the thick pine tar was ladled into barrels. These were shipped to the Hercules Powder Company at Jacksonville. There the tar was incorporated into 117 products ranging from gunpowder to flavoring for lime sherbet.

Cecil Webb Built Lodge

Well known to settlers along Tucker's Grade was Cecil M. Webb, a prominent miller at Tampa who maintained a hunting lodge at Willow Pens. He is remembered by Byron Rhode, and formerly manager at Punta Gorda for the B&B supermarket.

"I knew Cecil Webb very well. I used to buy meal, grits, beans etcetera from him. He drove a truck for the Eelbeck Milling Co. He saved his money, borrowed some more, bought a couple of trucks and went into business for himself. He called his company the Dixie Lily Co. He became very successful — and rich. I was told that as a young man he walked away from his home up in North Carolina wearing a pair of overalls — just like A.C. Frizzel did from Alabama.

"Webb was involved in politics. At one time he was chairman of the State Road Department and also the Fresh Water Fish and Wildlife Game Commission. He maintained a hunting preserve at Willow Pens. He brought out politicians and the bosses of big grocery chains to hunt. His place was stocked with quail, turkeys, ducks, pheasants etcetera. He wined and dined them and had guides to take them out to hunt.

"Webb died a fairly young man. His son and widow sold out to a large milling company — the Martha White Brand."

Wildlife Preserve Created

Congress adopted the Pittman-Robertson act in 1937 which provided federal funds for creation of wildlife preserves open to hunting on a managed basis. To be eligible for the funds, the state Legislature in 1939 earmarked monies from the sale of hunting and fishing licenses. However, the governor vetoed it. Spessard Holland became Governor in 1941, elected in part by his promise to create a large wildlife preserve. He paid a surprise visit to the Game and Fresh Water Fish Commission in July 1941 to urge support for the wildlife reserve bill. The governor stated he was not pushing a particular tract but strongly favored land acquisition. "The cattle industry is increasing so rapidly that the time is not far distant when there will be no open territory where the man in ordinary circumstances will feel free to hunt," he said.

Leo Wotitzky, of Punta Gorda, was elected state representative at this time. He and the late Attorney Earl Farr went to Tallahassee to lobby for a preserve in Charlotte County. "I was especially interested in the Bairdville-Willow Pens-Tucker's Woods area," says Wotitzky, "because I and Tucker's son, Paul, used to go on field trips there with the Boy Scouts." The commission investigated several sites and decided on Charlotte County. The price was low and a large area was available.

Fred Babcock Contributions

First purchase was for 19,130 acres in 1941. It was assembled by Fred C. Babcock, president of Babcock Florida Co. and owner of the huge Crescent-B ranch nearby. Another 9,621 acres was donated by Babcock the following year. Additional lands were bought from various individuals to expand the preserve to 63,335 acres. The tract was deeded to the Game Commission and dedicated originally to Cecil M. Webb, chairman. Then in May 1995 the Commission re-named the tract the Fred C. Babcock-Cecil M. Webb Wildlife Management Area in recognition of the contributions Babcock had made quietly over the years to the unique project.

The area had a colorful history prior to being set aside as a game preserve. It has been the location of even more exotic events since then, according to Larry Campbell, manager-biologist for the reserve:

"During World War II, 16,000 acres of the management area were set aside as a bombing and strafing range by the Air Force, then a part of the U.S.A. Army. Airfields for training pilots were located near Punta Gorda in Charlotte County and Buckingham in Lee County. The target was a 4x8 panel of plywood on posts. Bomb craters, parts of 500-pound bombs and shell casings from 50-caliber machine guns are still in evidence. Just a couple of years ago — during a long, dry spell we found the tail of an airplane sticking up in a pond. We pulled it out and discovered it was a World War II P-47 trainer from Punta Gorda Army Air Base. There was no trace of the pilot, so apparently he got out all right.

"The Charlotte County Air Port is now a first-class, civilian airfield. Buckingham Air Field was dismantled after the war and the runways broken up. The pieces were given to us to make rip-rap dams.

"The area was officially closed in 1943 and designated as the Charlotte County Refuge. Eight years later, game animals had increased in number sufficiently to allow the area to be classified as a wildlife management area, and hunting was permitted for the first time.

"The Game Commission in 1957 entered into a 25-year contract with the Hercules Powder Co. for removal of pine stumps from Webb. Most of the wood was removed by 1976, and the lease has now expired.

"My predecessor, Scott Krug, was involved in a strange adventure involving Webb that we can only wonder about. One day in 1960, some well-dressed men in two long, black cars drove up to the manager's office and showed Central Intelligence Agency badges. They asked Scott to meet them the next day at the County Air Port. Of course he agreed.

"At the airport, the CIA agents took Scott aboard a big transport plane waiting on the runway. They explained they wished to talk without the possibility of being 'bugged.' While flying around in a big circle, the CIA asked permission to send a group of 'rangers' from a secret camp in Lee County onto the management area at night. The mission was to practice explosion techniques on old stumps.

"For many nights thereafter, the mysterious rangers blew up all the stumps in the reserve. When these were uprooted, the rangers blew up the old tramway bridges that we used to get around on.

"To this day we don't know for sure who the night-raiders were or what they were up to. They slept during the day at an off limit camp on Useppa Island. It is interesting to note that the last explosions at Babcock-Webb occurred about April 15, 1961 — and the aborted Bay of Pigs invasion by Cuban exiles took place two days later.

"The Webb hunting dog field-trial grounds were set up in conjunction with various kennel clubs. The clubs donated materials and supplies to build the clubhouse, stables, kennels and picnic area. Since 1969, the grounds have been open for limited quail hunting.

Boy Scouts Have Camp

"Boy Scouts of America has been granted 1,280 acres in the northeast corner of the field-trial grounds for a camp. The Scouts have invested $400,000 in camp facilities.

"Since Commission purchase, cattle grazing leases have been let in the area on a continuous grazing basis — one cow per 10 acres. At first, lessees were required to convert ten acres per square-mile section of land into strips of bahia pasture grass. This has been replaced with a 3-pasture rotational grazing system. In 1971, the Game Commission entered into an agreement with the Florida Department of Transportation (DOT) for fill dirt for the embankment of Interstate I-75. Approximately 3.5 million cubic yards of material were excavated to create a 395-acre fishing lake. DOT also built an asphalt access road to the lake along the shore line and landscaped it with native cypress, oak and cabbage palms. Another lease was granted the City of Punta Gorda for a waste-water spray field on 884 acres of improved pasture in the northwest corner of the Webb area.

"A managed wildlife area provides benefits to people as well as to animals, birds and plants. Our control dams, for example, hold back storm water from flooding North Fort Myers and puts the excess back into the underground aquifer. It is a pleasure to see the public enjoying a wild area. Folks come from all over the world to glimpse our red-cockaded woodpeckers. National Geographic photographed them for a story, and the *Wild Kingdom* television show came several times."

Irene Gatewood models uniform of the Punta Gorda High School basketball team. Varsity games were played on the hotel lawn.

Chapter 44

PIONEER TEACHERS RESPECTED, POORLY PAID

Few pioneer teachers made a full living from the profession — cash being a scarce asset in early southwest Florida. Teaching salaries were supplemented with farming or trade skills.

Motivation for most teachers was the feeling of personal satisfaction derived from providing a community service. Consequently They were accorded great respect. If young and single, teachers were given board and room amongst leading families. Men with administrative authority, such as principal or superintendent, were commonly addressed as "professor." Few women on the frontier held administrative duties — partly because unmarried women teachers were too young, and when married they gave first priority to their families.

Nevertheless, young women generally were the first teachers in backwoods communities. It was not unusual for women teachers in charge of lower grades to be 15 or 16 years of age. Few teachers had "normal school" (college) training. Those that did not have a teaching degree had to attend six-week training courses at Arcadia, Wauchula or Bartow in the summer every three years to qualify for a teaching certificate.

Boys in their teens rarely went beyond the sixth grade. Their labor was needed for the strenuous work of helping support the family. They tended cattle, pruned citrus trees, farmed vegetables, fished, trapped coons for pelts, hunted alligators for hides, or apprenticed for trades. Those boys who did go on to eighth grade tended to be boisterous and unruly. Young women teachers near their own age had difficulty controlling them. Teachers of all grades administered corporal punishment freely with switches for youngest children, hefty paddles for older boys.

The practice was approved by parents. A common admonition was, "If you get a licking in school, you will get another when you get home!"

Professor U.S. Whiteaker was typical of his era. He left LaBelle, Missouri, with his bride, Nora (nee Chapman), in 1888 to teach at Brooksville, Fla. Whiteaker supplemented his meager teaching pay over the years as a farmer, grocer, carpenter, and cigar manufacturer.

At Brooksville, Nora bore a daughter, Jean, who grew up to become at teacher at Harbor View on the north shore of Charlotte Harbor and the mother of U.S. Cleveland. Unfortunately, Nora became seriously ill and was given only six months to live. Whereupon, the Whiteakers returned to Missouri so Nora could spend her last days among her kin folks. Despite the prognostication, Nora regained her health after a couple of years; and they came to Punta Gorda in 1906 to open a grocery.

Attendance Nears 200

The *Punta Gorda Herald* reported in September 1907: "Punta Gorda Grammar and High School opened with an enrollment of 150 and bright prospects for a most successful year. The morning was spent in classifying (entrance exams), grading, assigning, and passing out books. Attendance is increasing day by day and will soon reach 200. The small boys inhabiting our streets of late now will be in school for the next eight months."

The faculty listed was G.B. Davis, principal; Mrs. Mary Butler, first assistant (with Davis teaching grades 7-12; Miss Hattie Huested, grades 5-6); Miss Parnelle Chevis, grades 4 and part of 3; Miss Viola Anderson, grades 2 and part of 3; and Miss Blanche Wilcox, primary.

By 1908, the combined school was overcrowded, and only Miss Anderson and Miss Wilcox returned. Five new faculty members were hired for the 1908-9 school year. They were Prof. C.A. Keith, principal; Prof. U.S. Whiteaker, assistant principal who continued to operate his grocery with the help of Nora; Mrs. Celia Richard; Miss Anna Price; and Miss Agnes King. Their grades taught were not mentioned.

Whiteaker drew up plans for a new, larger school of concrete blocks. A site was purchased on the southeast corner of Taylor Street and Charlotte Avenue. Work began in the summer of 1910 when it was noted that the enrollment at the Goldstein Street school had reached 225 pupils, taught by six teachers.

The *Herald* noted at the start of the school year in September: "Professor C.A. Keith's third year. He regrets that the new school house could not be completed. The local school board is Capt. F.M. Cooper and Messers F.R. Blount and H. R. Dreggors."

Whiteaker taught only two years at the school he designed, then left to try his hand at cigar manufacturing. This industry soon moved to Tampa and left him isolated. He then accepted teaching jobs at various towns where carpentry work also was available. Among his assignments were those at Okeechobee, Gasparilla, and Boca Grande. Eventually he returned to Punta Gorda and spent his last years as a farmer and carpenter.

Goldstein Street school was first in county for senior grades 9-12.

Classes at Goldstein Street school marched to their new building on Taylor Street in the spring of 1911. Though all 12 grades were taught, the senior class seldom topped a dozen students. The play ground was divided for boys and girls, with large privies for each sex. A couple of years later, wings on each side of the building were added for indoor rest rooms.

High school boys had teams for football, baseball and basketball. Girls had a basketball team, and a Glee Club for singing.

The old school building was sold to Dr. Eugene J. Whidden who converted it to a "Sanitorium" (sic). He sold it in the early 1920's to Clay Chadwick, who turned the building into hotel rooms which he named The Inn. The structure was remodeled a few years ago, listed on the National Register of Historic Places, and divided into apartments.

Mrs. R.G. Walls opened a "finishing school" for girls in 1913. It taught "general business practices, secretarial skills, and the arts."

195

With opening of the Punta Gorda High School on Taylor Street, Miss Pepper closed her little private school in her front parlor and returned to the public school. She devoted the rest of her active life teaching the primary grades. The oldest residents of Punta Gorda today recall with fondness their first years at Miss Pepper's school.

The late Nathaniel "Doc" McQueen recalled Miss Pepper for an interview by Historian Angie Larkin. "When I went to school, Miss Pepper was my first teacher. She was a little grey-haired lady — tiny and sort of stooped, and she carried a big palmetto switch. She'd hit the blackboard a real whack to get your attention. She never used the switch. She didn't have to. She was a forceful lady, and could stare a hole in you.

Lesson In Capitalization

"I still remember her lesson about capitalization. She would say, 'When you go to the circus, little children sit in the front row. Back of them are the big folks, the capital letters. Little children a,b,c,d — big folks A,B,C,D.' After 70 years, I've never forgotten that. It's what made Miss Pepper the fine teacher that she was."

Miss Pepper's enthusiasm for teaching inspired some of her pupils to follow in her footsteps. One of these was Minta (nee Hopper) Harper. M/M Calvin and Rose Hopper brought their family from Texas to Punta Gorda in 1913. Rose supplemented the family income as a teacher at Cleveland, Charlotte Harbor Town, Punta Gorda and Acline. Minta's teacher here in the third grade was Miss Pepper.

Minta completed her public school education in Charlotte County, and was the first girl to receive a state scholarship for teaching. Upon receiving her teaching certificate, Minta taught a year at Lake Butler then returned to Punta Gorda to teach mathematics. She married Willie Harper and continued teaching for 38 years.

Another of Miss Pepper's prominent pupils was Leo Wotitzky, grandson of a merchant who came to Punta Gorda in 1886 just as it started to develop. Leo was fortunate in having Miss Pepper as a teacher all the way through school. Leo started college during the depression, but had to drop out for lack of funds. He took a teaching job first at Crescent City, then at Punta Gorda High School where he taught mathematics and edited the *Herald.*. He married Miss Zena Cox, a home economics teacher. He was elected to the state legislature, but returned to college and earned a law degree to become one of the county's leading attorneys.

About this time a Punta Gorda drug store held a Miss Popularity contest in which customers voted when making purchases. The winner was Miss Sallie Jones, a Pepper pupil who was destined to become an outstanding teacher and administrative educator in the county.

Coca-Cola truck, with "bathing beauties" in July 4, 1931 parade.

Chapter 45

GENUINE COCA-COLA COSTS NO MORE

When one searches for objects to be "as American as" — apple pie and baseball come easily to mind. More appropriate, perhaps, is Coca-Cola.

Duly chronicled by your writers have been the local arrivals of railroads, post offices, steamships, newspapers, ice factories, electricity, telephones, automobiles, airplanes and many other harbingers of moderation.

However, folks knew the task of settling the last frontier was complete when a Coca-Cola bottling plant was built. In Charlotte County, the date was March 25, 1915.

Cool drinks always were greatly appreciated in south Florida where summer never ends. Nevertheless, the most essential ingredient, ice, did not become available in the Charlotte Harbor area until 1891.

That was the year Col. Isaac Trabue, founder of Punta Gorda six years earlier, built a little ice factory on Berry Street. Stimulus for the venture was the need by commercial fishermen; but ice-cold lemonade, tea and hand-churned ice cream also provided a valuable market.

Punta Gorda Druggist W.A. Roberts developed a clientele for refreshments by advertising in the May 1895 *Punta Gorda Herald:* "COOL DRINKS A SPECIALTY, Next door to Sandlin's."

It is likely that Coca-Cola was available at Roberts' drug store because the drink was originally developed and sold as a headache remedy. Emphasis was on fountain drinks. Pre-mixed and bottled "Coke" was not introduced until 1899,

197

Coca-Cola was invented in 1885 by John Styth Pemberton, an Atlanta druggist. He called his concoction "French Wine Cola — Ideal Nerve and Tonic Stimulant." It consisted of wine, kola nut flavoring, and mild cocaine-tea brewed from coca leaves stirred in an iron kettle in back of his shop. The following year, Pemberton substituted sugar syrup for wine, renamed the drink Coca-Cola and sold the extract in reclaimed beer bottles to other druggists. Pemberton died in 1888. His estate sold the formula to Asa Candler who formed a corporation to aggressively sell Coca-Cola.

The drink was widely popular in Atlanta as a hang-over remedy and afternoon pick-me-up. No wonder. It was based on weak cocaine — then hailed by the medical profession as a "wonder drug" and legally sold without prescription.

When cocaine was discovered to be addictive, and had afflicted thousands of Americans, Coca-Cola Corporation removed cocaine-tea from its formula and substituted "secret ingredient 7X." It is alleged that only two Coca-Cola executives know the secret ingredient and personally add it to the mixture. Less romantic competitors assert the ingredient is ordinary caffeine. Even this is removed in some lines of Coke for health-conscious customers.

Whatever the winning combination, Coca-Cola syrup was a hit. Thus, we can be confident it was offered here in carbonated water shortly after ice became available.

Dr. Best Concocted Extracts

The success of coca and kola extract perhaps influenced Dr. J.W. Best of Punta Gorda to develop flavorings. The *Herald* of April, 1902, reported: "Mr. Perry McAdow bought from Col. Trabue the business lot on Marian Avenue adjoining McLane and Oliver stores to erect a building for a laboratory of the Fruit Extract Manufacturing Company. He and Dr. Best are the principal stockholders. Dr. Best's extracts took highest awards at the Atlanta Exposition several years ago." Unfortunately Dr. Best died five months later, and the extract operation was abandoned.

Interest in soft-drink extracts was revived at Punta Gorda in May 1913 when the first "soda fountain" was installed in Cochran's Drug Store. This mixed carbonic gas with water and dispensed it in a thin stream under pressure.

Demand for nose-tickling bubbles and fruit syrups led Clay L. Porter, a well-driller and manufacturer of concrete blocks from Kentucky, to take on another sideline. He built a "soda pop" plant behind today's Farr legal firm on Olympia Avenue.

Porter advertised: "Manufacturer of and dealer in SODA WATER, EXTRACTS, and Concrete Building Blocks in Latest Designs."

It is believed he handled Koke, one of the many imitations of Coca-Cola. Porter was a fun-loving bachelor. Men enjoyed telling "spicy" stories about his conquests. He left the area and is said to have gone to Mexico where he "met a bad end."

Coca-Cola, "The Genuine Thing," was brought to Punta Gorda in March 1915 by H.H. Hawkins. He had obtained a franchise for Fort Myers two years earlier from Tampa Coca-Cola Associates. His machinery at Punta Gorda was housed in a sheet-iron building built for him by Mrs. S.J. Hewitt. It was located behind the Hewitt Brothers garage and hardware store just west of today's post office.

An advertisement in the Herald proclaimed: "DRINK COCA-COLA ... Bottled In Punta Gorda. Ask For the Genuine. It Costs No More. We Cater To The Trade In Bottled Coca-Cola and High Grade Soda Water... Coca-Cola Bottling Company, H.H. Hawkins, Mgr., Punta Gorda, Fla."

It is interesting to note that the now familiar "hobby-skirt" bottle shape was not introduced until late that year in order to distinguish Coca-Cola from its many competitors.

Hawkins joined the Army in September 1917 and sold the Punta Gorda franchise to Adam Silcox, agent for the Standard Oil Company, for $2,500. Silcox operated the bottling works until September 1921 when he moved his family to Miami for a couple of years.

Edgar Rountree, freight agent for the Atlantic Coast Line Railroad (successor to Florida Southern Railway), had three sons — Erwin, Edwin ("Ebby") and Elvin. The two oldest boys often played "hookey" from Charlotte High School to go swimming.

Caught Them Frolicking

Their father caught them frolicking in the harbor one day and declared, "You're not going to do that any more. You're going to work." Rountree bought the Coca-Cola franchise on mortgage for $3,500 and launched his oldest sons on their life-time careers. Edgar built a new plant at the corner of Elizabeth and Allen streets. Erwin ran the machinery. Ebby handled the distribution and customer contacts.

Rountree's territory was that between the Peace and Caloosahatchee rivers plus Sanibel and Captiva islands. For island deliveries, Ebby traveled through Hawkins' territory to cross on a ferry boat.

Ebby was a dedicated past-president of the Punta Gorda Rotary Club. As such, he scrupulously observed the Rotary requirement of regular attendance. He not only achieved a perfect record of 42 years at Punta Gorda, he also recorded 25 years of perfect attendance at Fort Myers Rotary where he stopped for lunch when making Sanibel deliveries. Ebby married Bernice Blacklock, a home economics teacher at Charlotte High. Her father was state director of the agriculture extension service at Gainesville. Nathaniel "Doc" McQueen was extension agent at Punta Gorda and often went to Gainesville on official business. While there one day, McQueen mentioned that Charlotte High School needed teachers.

Bernice was recently graduated and looking for a teaching position. She took the train to Punta Gorda and was quickly hired by Superintendent Sallie Jones.

"With my home-ec background, I just naturally got involved with the Rountree family business of syrup mixtures," says Bernice (pronounced Bern-iss).

"During World War II we couldn't get help, but the Army Air Field (now the Charlotte County Airport) requested more Coca-Cola. Therefore, I went to Avon Park, Florida, and bought a second set of bottling machinery. This doubled production but made it necessary that I go to work in the plant as an inspector. Ebby made parts for the machinery when there were breakdowns. New parts for non-military purposes were not available.

"People from Fort Myers drove up to Punta Gorda to buy cases of Coca-Cola from us because we bottled with high-pressure. This better preserved the bubbles which consumers preferred."

In time, Edgar, Erwin and Elvin died. Ebby and Bernice retired and sold the franchise in 1970 for a reputed $100,000 to Coca-Cola Associates of Daytona Beach. It closed down the Punta Gorda bottling works and transferred operations to a warehouse and distribution center at the southern end of Cooper Street. This, also has since been closed and consolidated with a larger plant.

TODAY IS OUR
OPENING DAY
We have our Punta Gorda plant all ready for business and are prepared to take care of all local and out-of-town orders for bottled
Coca-Cola and High Grade Soda Water
Wolesale Orders Solicited
Coca-Cola
Bottling Co.
H. H. Hawkins, Mgr.

Now, Coke is sold in disposable pop-top 12-pack cans. A move to "improve" Coca-Cola taste several years ago was met by such an uproar the company had to return to the old, "classic" formula. Another clamor for the hobby-skirt bottle is gaining ground.

There are some American icons you just don't mess with.

Charlie Cerny clowns with rattler just killed.

Chapter 46

THE CELEBRATED SNAKE FIGHT

Next to fish stories, Charlotte Harbor area folks liked snake yarns. There were plenty of encounters to talk about in the old days when the countryside was still wild and sparsely settled. Consequently it is understandable why interest ran high in a snake fight being arranged by Dr. George Stone in Jan. 1914.

The *Punta Gorda Herald* reported details: "A scientific exhibition of an unique and very unusual character is to be given here at an early date. It is being arranged by Dr. Stone who wishes to try out the truth of the contention that a black-snake can whip a rattlesnake.

"He has procured a huge and savage rattler from Sarasota that our former townsman Thomas Hartigan captured and sent over — there being a scarcity of venomous reptiles in these parts. It is expected that a black-snake of desirable size will soon be secured. Then the date and other details of the exhibition will be given out.

"It is now intended to construct a safe enclosure some 40 feet square — in plain view from the grandstand at the ball park — and turn the snakes into this where they can be seen by all who may wish.

"Dr. Stone thinks this will out-class the famous Spanish bull fights. It is thought that moving pictures will be made of this fight and exhibited all over the country. The doctor has other investigations and experiments to conduct with the rattlesnake after the exhibition. He may secure results of value to the medical profession in treating snake bites."

The statement about a scarcity of snakes in the vicinity of Punta Gorda was a large measure of "poetic license" to reassure winter visitors. In truth, snakes were plentiful — too much so in the eyes of most residents who killed anything that crawled on its belly. As predicted, the proposed snake fight did arouse widespread interest. A month later the paper noted: "Punta Gorda's coming snake fight is causing a large amount of excitement. The *Philadelphia North American,* the *New York Herald,* and the *New York American* have written their correspondent for a detailed story of the fight — with all the photos that can be procured."

An advertisement ballyhooed a "GRAND SNAKE FIGHT, Feb. 14, baseball grounds. Diamondback rattlers, King snakes and Black snakes. 25 cents. PROCEEDS GO TO LADIES CIVIC ASSOCIATION."

Apparently a suitable black snake was hard to come by. It was not until October that the event was staged. The *Herald* was brief, for obvious reason: "The mortal combat between a rattlesnake and a king snake — promoted by Dr. George Stone and A.J. Kinsel at the local baseball park — turned out to be a 'dud.' The two snakes, released together amid much talk and betting, ignored each other completely."

The paper did not say whether ticket refunds were made — nor if the Ladies Civic Association, led by Mrs. George Stone, received any funds for their project of building a second floor on the little "city hall."

Plugged His Own Leg

Alexander J. Kinsel undoubtedly had a stake in the fight. He was a shoemaker and tanner with a two-story tin-clad factory on King Street (Tamiami Trail north) opposite Herald Court. He and his wife lived on the second floor and rented rooms. Byron Rhode, a Punta Gorda oldtimer, says the smell of soaking hides kept the rooms from being very popular.

Kinsel tanned alligator and rattlesnake hides and made them into shoes, wallets, purses and belts. Alligator shoes cost $5 to $10, rattlesnake belts $3, and wallets of either skin somewhere in between. He also bought furs and animal hides for re-sale to big companies up north. Many local men trapped and hunted for him.

One of Kinsel's suppliers was Paul Rasch. His friends, which was nearly everybody, called him "Paulie." He spent some time cutting hair in the Pioneer Barber Shop of his father, John, but liked hunting best. While out guiding a hunting party, Rasch was struck on the leg by a rattlesnake. He promptly unsheathed his skinning knife and "plugged" the fang wound on the calf of his leg like you would a watermelon. He bled profusely but put on a tourniquet and hobbled back to the hunters' car.

They took Paulie to the little Punta Gorda hospital where anti-venom serum was administered. However, he had done such a good job ridding himself of the poison, he nearly died from the serum. He had a hole in his leg for the rest of his life.

Mass Snake Fright

John Rasch and Joseph Ralph were cited by the *Herald* in August 1908 as "good and upstanding" verifiers for a "mass" snake fright:

"Ralph, a Punta Gorda taxidermist, was a devout Catholic. In 1893 there was a cigar factory here which employed numerous Cubans who were also of the Catholic faith. Hearing that the group were without religious services, a priest from Tampa came down and arranged to celebrate Mass in Ralph's shop which was filled with numerous, eerie-looking stuffed birds, beasts and reptiles. The only living creatures in the place were several rattlesnakes in a box, and three small dogs."

Sparkman hunters show off 6-foot rattlesnake killed on rabbit shoot.

"In the midst of the services, as all were kneeling in prayer, the dogs became excited and dashed across the leg of one of the Cuban women. At the same instant, the snakes began to shake their rattles ominously. Thinking she had been bitten, the woman arose with a shriek and dashed off down the street, followed by other members of the congregation — all equally excited. A period of some hours was said to have elapsed before the entire citizenry could be quieted."

Shy Creatures

Rattlesnakes are shy creatures and will avoid humans and large animals if not disturbed. Nevertheless, they do command respect. Mrs. Esther McCullough, a long-time resident of Charlotte County, recalls a typical encounter with a rattlesnake when she lived in Cleveland.

"I had the front door open but the screen door latched. I heard Fred, our hunting dog, barking terribly on the porch. I went to see what was provoking him. Fortunately I looked down as I was about to unlatch the screen door. There was a big rattler shedding its skin. Fred looked like he would attack the snake any minute. I knew I would lose my husband if anything happened to his hunting dog, so I raced to the back door and called in Fred. When I returned, the rattler was gone. We feared it had gone under our house, but a careful inspection did not reveal it.

"A week later, the bait shop up the street killed a rattlesnake about the size of that which commandeered our front porch. Nevertheless, we watched where we walked ever after.

"There was a snake patch between Cleveland and Punta Gorda consisting of palmettos and swamp. We often saw rattlers and water moccasins crossing the road. When we could, we ran over them."

Straddled A Rattler

Though snake bites were not common, all were potentially fatal. Consequently folks were wary of rattlers and moccasins.

Back in the 1920's, Chester Roberts was a boy at Charlotte Harbor Town. The family home was exactly in the middle of what is now Tamiami Trail where it intersects with Harper Ave. The Trail then looped into the village as Bay Shore Drive.

"Kids went barefoot most of the time, and we were well aware of the necessity of keeping our eyes open for snakes," recalls Chester. "One day I had been playing in the fields and started home for supper. As I climbed over the fence around our property I noticed a big rattler stretched out on the other side where I was about to step. I eased over slowly then dashed home for a rake. I went back and killed the snake. As I did so, I noticed a bulge in its belly. I pushed against the bulge with my rake and forced out a cottontail rabbit the snake had just swallowed. Undoubtedly that was why the rattler did not move or strike as I eased over it.

"Another time I was down near the pier and Wes Vickers' store. As I stepped off the store's walk into the grass I heard a rattler blow — that is, hiss. I froze. I was straddling a big one. Then I heard a second rattler blow. I didn't waste any more time. I leaped an Olympic distance and yelled. Old man Vickers — later a county commissioner — came out and killed both snakes. He always went around barefoot with his pant legs rolled up. It was lucky he didn't get bitten.

"There was a type of small rattler we called ground rattlers. People today call them pygmies. Their bite won't kill you, but it will make you awfully sick. We used to just step on their heads."

Rector Survives Bite

People were aware that prompt attention to snake bites was essential. A vivid description of the procedure is furnished by an article in the April 1908 Herald:

"Last Friday night, Dr. Irenaeus Trout, rector of our Episcopal church, when out about 17 miles from Fort Myers on his way to the Indian mission in the Everglades, was bitten by a rattlesnake. This forced him to abandon his journey and come home.

"He was on horseback accompanied by a companion, a Mr. Balcom. Night coming on, they stopped to camp. Upon dismounting, Dr. Trout stepped too near the snake which in the darkness he could not see. "He was bitten on top of his right foot. He was wearing soft buckskin moccasins, a present from a Seminole friend. They were easily penetrated by the reptile's fangs.

"The doctor at once put a tight ligature around his leg just above the ankle and scarified the wound with his pocket knife. His companion sucked the wound to extract the poison.

"They killed the snake which was about three feet long. Then, they returned to Fort Myers where Dr. Trout received the best medical attention. This enabled him to come home Sunday morning.

"Immediately after being bitten, Dr. Trout suffered great pain. It extended from his foot up to his shoulder and continued through all of Saturday. His foot and leg became greatly swollen, and from Saturday until Sunday noon he suffered from nausea.

"Most of these symptoms passed away by Sunday night. By Tuesday, Dr. Trout was almost completely relieved.

"To the fact that the snake was young and small, and that its bite was promptly and correctly treated, may be attributed the fact Dr. Trout escaped with his life. His experience rather discourages him from attempting any more trips into the Everglades."

Carver-Anger homestead in 1919. Lorin Anger, center, sits with his third wife Ora Etta, left, and her daughter Mary Etta Sanders. Children are those of Lorin and Ora — Julia, left, and L.A. Ainger, Jr.

Chapter 47

ANGER TO AINGER

First marriages on the Florida frontier usually stemmed from love — as nature intends — but partners frequently became widows or widowers at an early age as the Grim Reaper took its toll far from medical help. Subsequent marriages were a matter of survival in a wilderness where mutual cooperation by husband, wife and many children meant the difference between life and death for whole families.

Consider, for example, the vicissitudes of Lorin Alexander Anger who came to Grove City Bay in 1898. He had three sets of families of his own and readily merged them with two others — with the consent of each wife, of course. Lorin Alexander Ainger, Jr., of Englewood, more popularly known simply as L.A., explains five family origins.

"Jot and Hannah Carver came from Springfield, Ill., in 1886 to take up a homestead on Rocky Creek, now called Ainger Creek," relates L.A. "They built a little cabin and were putting in orange trees, banana plants and a garden when Jot took sick and died. Hannah buried Jot in the 10-acre 'burying ground' donated by Dr. Hill."

"The white-picketed cemetery in Englewood was the final resting place also of 16-year-old Mrs. Howard (Nancy Jane) Bowman. Jane was the daughter of William Goff who had come to Lemon Bay with his wife Mary

206

and three daughters in 1878. Jane died giving birth to a daughter that her husband named Minnie. Baby Minnie was taken by Goff's second wife, Rebecca — Mary having died of an unknown disease. Rebecca, who had been Mary's best friend and classmate, weaned her own baby Ellie early in order to nurse the newborn.

"Jane Bowman was the first burial in the area, and Jot's was second. Though the record of burial is clear, we are not sure of the plot. Some folks think that perhaps both repose under Indiana Ave. (S.R. 775) which was widened a few years ago to include the edge of the cemetery.

"Hannah Carver, unable to work her 40-acre homestead alone, returned to Springfield, Ill., to live with her parents. People in those days wrote lots of letters. One of Hannah's close correspondents was Lottie May — perhaps an aunt — who had moved to Calif., to marry Lorin Anger, son of a former Springfield resident.

"The Anger family had set out for California by wagon train during the Gold Rush of 1849. Lorin was just six month's old. His father died on the trail, and his mother continued on alone to rear Lorin and her older children by farming. When Lorin grew up he married Lottie May, and they had six children. One day Hannah received a letter from California, but it was from Lorin Anger, not his wife. Lottie had died. Lorin, now a widower, proposed that widow Hannah marry him and help raise his children. With no other prospect, Hannah accepted.

"Lorin had been a potato farmer, but at this time he had a yoke of eight mules with which he hauled supplies to the Inyo County borax mines. Soon Hannah bore him a son.

"Life at the edge of the desert depressed Hannah. She described to Lorin the cool waters of Lemon Bay and the lush, tropical vegetation there. Lorin suffered from recurring malaria, and the large amount of quinine he took for relief nearly destroyed his hearing. At age 50, when the hard life of a 'mule skinner' began to pale, Lorin allowed as how life in Florida on Hannah's homestead might be preferable. Accordingly the combined family, including seven children, took the train from California to Tampa, Fla., in March 1898," L.A. recounts.

A Letter From Hannah

A letter from Hannah to her parents in Springfield tells of the journey and problems of getting started in an untamed wilderness. The letter was postmarked March 14 at Grove City.

"We arrived here safe, and all are enjoying good health," wrote Hannah. "We came through very quickly, arriving at Tampa on Friday eve about 6 o'clock after we started from California on Wednesday. We had lunch enough to last to Tampa and some pickles and (hard boiled) eggs.

"We stayed at the Crescent Hotel until the following Tuesday evening. Mr. Chapman (of Lemon Bay) came after us. He had bad weather and could not get there any sooner. We were five days coming down from there. On the boat we furnished our board (food) and it only cost us $9 boat fare from Tampa.

"As it was rough on Old Tampa Bay, we went into harbor and stayed one day and two nights. Then we came to Big Sarasota Pass and had a head wind. We anchored there until we had a good wind. When we started, the Gulf was as smooth as the bay. We came from Sarasota to here (Lemon Bay) Sunday night and into Grove City last Monday morning.

"We rented a house here and went right to housekeeping. We went out to the (homestead) place Tuesday and decided on a spot for a building. Lorin has put in the order for lumber at the saw mill and will put up a house as soon as possible.

"While they are sawing the lumber, he and the boys are fixing a place for garden. I put out the rhubarb that Mr. Carver gave me. It has commenced to sprout, so I think it will do well.

"The fire and frost (of 1894) has killed most of the orange trees. Some one was kind enough to themselves to take all the barb wire from the fence and all the young banana plants. They took an ax and cut in deep enough to get all the staples. However, they left the land; and we can soon have a good garden.

"They have started a town close to the place — about a mile — and call it Vineland. It is the distributing P.O. for Grove City and Englewood. Mail comes to all places once a day, so it is much better than it used to be. Direct to Vineland, DeSota (sic) County, Florida.

Baby Fat As A Pig

"Lester says to tell Grandpa he can eat clams and fish all right. The baby is fat as a pig and weighs 16 lbs. and cries often for Aunt Amanda to come. Tell Aunt we often think of her and all send her love.

"We are going to have a school at Vineland. There are 10 scholars — just enough to get a school for next winter. Ask Maggie if she doesn't want to come down and 'teach the young idea how to shoot.' She will only have a mile to go from our house if they build where they are talking of. The children have gathered some shells for you. I will send them when I have time to pack them.

"Lorin and Ed and Bert have gone to the place today. If Lorin is not too tired this evening, perhaps he will write some too. With love to you all I remain, your daughter: H.M. Anger."

L.A. says, "My father put in a large vegetable plot and sold produce. His principal customers were the Tarpon Inn at Grove City and the Englewood Inn which catered to winter visitors. The Tarpon Inn was destroyed by fire in 1904, and the Englewood Inn five years later.

"Hannah bore another child, increasing the family to 10 members. Apparently the difficulty of cooking, cleaning and caring for so many was too much for Hannah She took her two children to Springfield and divorced Lorin.

"A year or so before Lorin Anger arrived, Professor Edward B. Sanders and his wife Ora Etta (nee Riggs) came to Charlotte Harbor from North Carolina. He taught at Punta Gorda's full-grades school. They had two daughters — Lillian, born in North Carolina; and Mary Etta born at Charlotte Harbor. The first school in west county was built at Vineland by William Goff in 1900. When the first teacher left in 1903 Prof. Sanders took the job — relocating near the school.

"Sanders was responsible for changing the spelling of the Anger family name to 'Ainger.' He explained to Lorin that while the old English pronunciation was long-A, Americans pronounced it with a short-A, as in 'angry.' Lorin replied that he certainly didn't want his children to be associated with a negative meaning and so consented to have them registered at school as 'Ainger.' However, he and the older children continued to use the original spelling," says L.A. Ainger.

Ora Sanders recalled those early days in west county during a 1958 interview with the *Englewood Herald.* "There were no paved roads when Ed and I came to the area. Travel was by horse and wagon. Vineland was a small place out on McCall Road.

Four Miles To Get Mail

"We used to walk about four miles into town to get our mail. That was in Grove City. It was a pretty little town with a lot of small, white frame houses and a lovely hotel. When the hotel burned down, people just didn't come back any more. The houses weren't cared for, and they seemed to tumble down.

"Englewood only had one store near the water and no school. When my husband taught school in Vineland, he had all eight grades in the one-room school house. People over in Englewood wanted a school so badly they started one with only six children.

"During the early days, Lorin Anger was a trustee on the school board. He and my husband became good friends. We visited back and forth. When Friday afternoons rolled around, Ed would hitch up the horse and wagon and drive over to the Anger farm for vegetables and eggs. I often remarked how nice it would be if we had a farm.

"One time, Ed teased me and said, 'My love, when I get rich I'll buy Mr. Anger's place and hire a man to run it the way you wish!' Little did I know that not too long in the future I was to take an active part in the running of that farm."

Teachers had to qualify every three years. While taking an examination at Arcadia, the county seat, Prof. Sanders collapsed and died. His widow, Ora, without a means of earning a living, returned with her daughters to her parent's home in North Carolina.

Friends Ora and Edith — and their children — kept in touch by mail. After Lorin's second wife left him, he occasionally addressed a letter to Ora; but she never answered.

Ora described the situation many years later, at age 90, in the 1958 newspaper interview:

"The children used to say, 'Mama, why don't you write to Mr. Anger? Why don't you answer his letters? When are we going back?'

"My answer was, 'Never,' but so many things can change in 2½ years. I went back to visit Edith and was warmly received by my old friends. Lorin came over and asked me to stay and marry him, so I did.

"We raised a little bit of everything on the farm except money. Our produce was taken to the railroad stop (Charlotte Harbor & Northern), then called McCall, and shipped to Pennsylvania and New York.

"The children used to play in the creek that ran back of the old barn. They painted signs and posted them along the creek and roads, calling it Ainger's Creek. It is called that today. They played hard and worked hard on the farm, but we were a very happy family. I never regretted coming back to Englewood.

"Later, we sold the farm and built the two-story house I am now in on McCall Road. We named the place Hill Crest. At first we had a little store in the front room of the house. Then we built a wooden frame store next door. It burned down and Ainger's Superex Market took its place (today, True Value Hardware). I reckon I now have about 40 grand-children. The last time I counted there were 22 grand, and 17 great-grand. I love them all," she said.

The store, gas station and Anger-Ainger home on McCall Road in 1931.

Chapter 48

AINGER SCHOOL NAMED FOR PIONEER

Lorin Alexander Anger, who came to Grove City on Lemon Bay in 1898 had three wives — one at a time — and thereby accumulated a large number of children. To spare them ridicule he changed the family name spelling to Ainger. Most of Lorin's children, blood-born and adopted, had grown up and left the farm when he and the widow Ora Sanders of North Carolina, former friends, were married. Ora was accompanied to Grove City by her youngest daughter, Mary Etta. Ora bore two children by Lorin — Julia and Lorin Alexander Ainger, Jr. Lorin senior was 67 when Lorin junior was born in 1915. Lorin junior grew up as the baby of the family.

"I guess I was kind of wild," he admits today. The family let me get away with a lot. Julia was only 18 months older than me but was a little mother who looked after me.

"I never did destructive stuff, just things like taking watermelons for a beach party out near the Hermitage on Manasota Key. The sea turtles came ashore there in May and June to lay their eggs. People came from miles around to take the eggs, but they always left a few so there would be young turtles left to replenish the stock.

"Panthers and coons got most of the eggs. There were a lot of panthers around in those days. They screamed like a crying woman. It was not so long ago that panthers roamed here. When my oldest daughter, Esther (Horton) was in high school we gave her a used convertible car to get back and forth.

"One night, I took her car to attend a school board meeting at Punta Gorda. On the way home — where U.S. 41 crosses the Myakka River —

211

a panther leaped out of the woods right over the car and into the woods on the other side. I still shudder to think what would have happened if that great cat had landed in the car with me!

"Folks also would 'turn' turtles after the eggs were laid. This means turning the turtles on their backs, rendering them helpless. Then you could stick them through the head opening into the heart and kill them. Turtle meat is tender and delicious, like veal.

"One night, a bunch of us boys turned 11 turtles just for sport. We killed one for the meat but let the others go.

"As a teenager, I got a job as a fisherman with Bill Anger, my nephew older than me; and with Clay Chadwick who married my sister Julia. When Dad was 78, in 1926, and no longer able to farm, he built our big house-store on McCall Road. He went to the big Woodmere saw-mill camp on Englewood road about a mile south of the intersection with U.S. 41. It was said to be the biggest mill east of the Mississippi.

"Woodmere had its own store, school and fire department; and even a theater for its employees. Timber was cut for miles around and hauled to the mill. They sawed lumber and milled fancy trim. The sawdust made a huge hill on which kids liked to play.

Wanted No-termite Lumber

"Dad told the foreman, 'I want to build a house, but not with any boxed pine. I'll wait until you saw up some trees that haven't been bled.' Virgin pine is full of rosin, and termites won't eat it. Boxed pine were trees that were slashed so sap would run into little boxes to be scraped out, boiled and distilled into turpentine. This was a big industry back then. When the trees died after being bled for a few years, they were sawed up.

"Julia and I helped in the front-room store, later our parlor. We bagged bulk commodities like grits, beans, sugar, and cornmeal. Food wasn't put up in convenient boxes back then. We weighed out quantities in paper sacks, tied them with string, and marked prices on the sacks.

"I also pumped gas and oil when we built the separate store next door. In those days you literally 'pumped' gas. A pump operated by hand drew gasoline from an underground tank up into a 5-gallon glass globe marked off in one-gallon increments. You pumped the number of gallons requested into the globe, then drained the gasoline by gravity through a hose into the customer's automobile. Valve for the hose was at the bottom of the globe, not the end of the hose. You always lifted the hose and gave it an extra minute to drain so customers were sure they got every drop.

"If the customer needed oil, that also was pumped by hand into a one-quart tin pitcher with a flexible spout which enabled you to pour the oil without spilling. There weren't different grades of gas and oil at first — gas was gas, for 20 cents a gallon; and oil was oil, for 15 cents a quart. Years later, Texaco brought out a premium gas and three grades of oil.

"I was lucky enough to get Miss Muriel McRae to marry me in 1937. At that time, Dad turned operation of the store over to me, and I enlarged it. Dad died Dec. 13, 1944, just seven days after his 95th birthday. He is buried in Englewood

"Hill Crest was damaged in a hurricane so I moved our home to a back street. When my mother died in 1965 at age 97, I moved the house to New Point Comfort. Later I sold it to Jesse Mitchell, an African-American who worked for me in the store. He moved it to Playland where it was burned later for volunteer firemen practice.

"The original store was destroyed by fire in 1949. Englewood had no fire department at the time. I was devastated at first, but many wonderful people — even my competitors — came forward to help me get started again.

"There was a bright side to the fire, however. Englewood did not have a fire department, and the fire demonstrated the need for one. A drive started for a volunteer department, and we soon got our first fire truck.

"My father was very interested in politics. He would have liked to run for office, but his poor hearing was too much of a handicap. He read the Tampa Tribune thoroughly every day to keep up with political events. I caught the public-service itch from him.

LORIN A. and MURIEL AINGER

"I was elected to the county school board for 24 years, two terms as chairman. My proudest moment was when the folks in Englewood named the new junior high school after me ten years ago upon my retirement from the board. I also served many years on the Englewood Chamber of Commerce, the Cemetery Board, Englewood Rotary Club, and the Affiliated Florida Supermarkets board at Tampa.

"My 30 years on the Englewood Bank and Trust Co. board of directors, now Barnett Bank, were particularly satisfying. As late as 1958 there was no local bank. Every Friday afternoon, store owners or their wives had to drive to Venice to get cash for all the pay checks tendered on Saturday, the biggest shopping day of the week.

"Four of us merchants got together and decided it was time to get a bank for Englewood. We went to Attorney John Hathaway and he put us in touch with William H. Hart, a retired superintendent of banking for the

213

state of Ohio. He told us the first step was to raise money for capital and apply for a certificate of need from the state of Florida.

"Mr. Hart was reluctant to get involved again, but relented on two conditions — first, that there would be no lawyers on the board; and second, that the directors would not take any dividend until all other stockholders had been paid. We readily agreed.

"Our first application for a certificate was refused on the grounds we were 'under capitalized.' We were discouraged and about to give up when Mr. Hart said, 'Shame on you. You are too pessimistic. What the bank board is telling you is that there is more business here than you realize.'

Started First Bank

"We went out and sold enough extra stock to double our original capital. This time the certificate of need came back approved. We opened a bank where the funeral parlor is now located. It consisted of one room, a fold-up table, a couple of chairs and two employees. It was an immediate success. Before long we were able to add trust services. I went off the bank board in 1988 when I reached the mandatory retirement age of 73," L.A. states.

Mrs. Ainger also has historic family roots. Her grandfather Charley Addison and grandmother Annie (nee Lancaster) homesteaded at Fort Winder. They furnished cattle, hogs and citrus for the U.S. Army during the First World War. Some where in her lineage, says Mrs. Ainger, there was a Choctaw Indian "guide and forager" for Maj.Gen. Andrew Jackson when he invaded Spanish-owned Florida in 1818. Jackson came to destroy a fort of runaway slaves on the Apalachicola River. As a result of the diplomatic negotiations that followed, the United States acquired Florida. Jackson became the first governor of Florida in 1821 and seventh president of the U.S. in 1829.

"Jackson granted prize lands to his five Choctaw guides and put the properties in trust for them at 5 percent interest until claimed," relates Mrs. Ainger. The Indians never got the land or money. My ancestor was named 'Rideout' whose grant was discovered by a priest, Father Dork. The late Senator Claude Pepper tried to obtain recompense for the many heirs, but without success."

Today L.A. and Muriel continue active from their home on Linden Drive. In addition to their daughter Mrs. Esther Horton mentioned earlier, they have two other daughters: Mrs. Susan Covart, a teacher at Valdosta, Ga., and Mrs. Ann Anderson, a long-time Publix employee at Venice, Fla.

Pilot Tony Jannus, right, flew his plane to Punta Gorda in 1914.
With him in this earlier flight was bridge engineer George Gandy.

Chapter 49

FIRST AIRPLANE HERE WAS A BOAT

As the first airplane to visit the Charlotte Harbor area swooped low over the water — its eight-cylinder engine and propeller roaring with a never-before-heard sound — a crowd of 1,000 people waiting at Punta Gorda's Sullivan Street dock broke into cheers.

The event was doubly momentous. Not only was the plane the first seen hereabouts, it was a flying boat! The splash-down seconds later startled the crowd which feared the aircraft had foundered.

Historian Byron Rhode, now age 91, was a boy here at the time, but remembers the event well. "The pilot had called ahead by telephone to make sure there was fuel available for a return flight, so word got around fast. Half the town showed up to see the modern miracle. Gulf Oil had a tank at the dock where the Memorial Auditorium is now located. The agent was Jim Cooper. He waved in the plane taxiing across the water to the dock while the crowd applauded."

Another boy then was Henry Farrington, now retired at Rabun Gap, Ga. He recalls how awe-struck he was. "The two pilots got out and asked Morris Strahn, the liveryman, to watch the plane while they walked up to town on business. Mr. Strahn climbed into the cockpit to keep an eye on things. How I wished I could sit in so wondrous a machine. The plane had two wings of canvas, sticks and wire. The body of the plane was actually a small boat. It was a great curiosity to all the fishermen who were used to boats that floated but could not fly."

The plane had received local notice earlier in the *Punta Gorda Herald* of Jan. 8, 1914:

AEROPLANE SERVICE FIRST BETWEEN TWO CITIES IN THE SOUTH — The first daily aeroplane passenger and express service between two cities in the South, possibly in the country, was opened with a successful flight of a hydro-plane from St. Petersburg, Fla., across the bay to Tampa, an air line distance of 18 miles.

A.C. Pheil, former mayor of St. Petersburg, was the passenger. The flight was made in 23 minutes, at an average height of 80 feet above the water. A fare of $5 each way is charged. A small amount of baggage also is carried at a specified pound rate. The only limit fixed in the case of a passenger is that he or she must not weigh over 200 pounds; or if weighing more than that, an extra charge of five cents a pound is made.

According to the excellent history *Yesterday's St. Petersburg* by Hampton Dunn, the pilot was Tony Jannus. His plane was a Benoist air boat. Before coming to St. Petersburg, Jannus had set a world's record by flying 2,000 miles in continuous, but not sustained, flight from Omaha to New Orleans.

$400 Ticket

Pheil won the privilege of being the first passenger by bidding $400 at auction. A *Tampa Times* reporter noted that "upon landing, the passenger scampered to a telephone to call home and let the folks know he made the journey safely."

The St. Petersburg-Tampa Airboat Line continued on regular schedule. The first parcel flown contained photos from the *St. Petersburg Times* to the Tri-Color Engraving Co. in Tampa. They were due to be flown back the next day, but Jannus' plane capsized in the bay. The engravings were shipped by train. First express package sent was a Swift & Co. premium ham. The firm took out a full page ad in *Colliers,* then a popular national magazine, to boast about a "first."

Jannus won the honor of being first commercial airline by just two weeks. The *Herald* reported somewhat erroneously on Jan. 20:

"The first regular daily mail and passenger service by aeroplane in the world was successfully inaugurated between Pablo Beach and Atlantic Beach by Aviator George A. Gray.

"The mail pouch was dropped from an elevation of about 100 feet directly in front of the main entrance of the Atlantic Beach Hotel by the aviator, who then circled about, landing his passenger at the entrance from the lawn. The aviator, Gray, has made more than 1,000 successful flights without a serious accident, and is considered one of the best man birds now operating aeroplanes."

Dunn records that by March 17, 1914, Jannus at St. Petersburg had carried 1,200 passengers without an accident. However, after three months, everyone there had experienced the thrill of flying, and business dropped off.

It is believed that Jannus and his unnamed passenger came to Punta Gorda during the last eight months of 1914 to drum up new business. We cannot be sure of the exact date because issues of the *Herald* for that period are missing. There is no mention of him in subsequent issues. As boys, Rhode and Farrington did not fix a precise date or purpose in their minds. Apparently the mission to Punta Gorda was not successful. Jannus suspended his airboat business and later flew for the Russian Aero Service. He was killed there in 1916 when his plane crashed.

There was no more airplane activity in the Charlotte Harbor area until the United States entered World War I in 1917. Two air training fields were hastily constructed on the treeless plains around Arcadia by January of 1918. Carlstrom Field was seven miles southeast of Arcadia, and Dorr Field was 11 miles east. (See Chapt. 70, 71)

Esther McCullough, a young woman at the time, remembers the "dashing aviators" who came to the big Hotel Punta Gorda for Saturday night dances. "Then we often saw their Army planes flying around."

Jannus Airboat Company, first commercial airline, inaugurated flights across Tampa Bay Jan. l, 1914, above, and to nearby towns later.

Farrington says the first, wheeled plane to land at Punta Gorda was one from Carlstrom Field. "The plane's engine stopped, and the pilot glided to a landing on a dirt road paralleling the railroad tracks opposite today's Walmart on U.S. 4l. The Army sent a truck to haul the plane back."

Dorr Field was closed after the war, but Carlstrom Field continued in operation until 1923. Following the First World War, surplus war planes were snapped up by civilian enthusiasts. One of these was Arnold "Slim" Keys a Punta Gorda mechanic who had his garage downtown on Taylor Street near Marion Avenue. His widow, Mabel, says Slim learned to fly from a flying school at Fort Myers. He bought a damaged, two-seat American Eagle plane and put new wings on it and rented space for a hangar in the old Punta Gorda Steam Laundry building on what is now Dundee Road east of Cooper Street. He grubbed out palmettos for a landing strip behind the building. Family milk cows in the neighborhood discovered the grass on the field and became a hazard at times.

Hit By Propeller

Henry Farrington also was fascinated by planes and often went out to Keys' field to help maintain it and start engines by spinning the propellers. In return, Farrington got to ride with Slim in the plane.

"One time I was spinning the prop when the engine back-fired. The blade kicked back and struck me on the arm. I was lucky I didn't lose the arm," says Farrington. "My arm swelled up, and I thought it was broken at first. My mother didn't like me flying so I had to wear long-sleeved shirts for quite awhile so she wouldn't see the awful bruise."

Keys also bought an airboat which he tied up at the municipal dock, now Fishermans Village. Esther McCullough says Slim gave her a window fan made from an old airboat propeller.

Other flying buffs in the 1920's were the Raymond brothers Wesley and Willis, developers and contractors. At first they used the recently-filled Gilchrist Park for a landing field, taking care to dodge the McAdow home and Banyan tree. One day they ran out of gas and just barely made it back to the landing site over the McAdow house. As it was, the plane skidded against the seawall and flipped over.

After this, the Raymonds built a two-runway field south of town, now Burnt Store Isles. Runways were at right angles to each other so planes could always take off and land into the wind. The runways were marked at the corners by orange pyramids. There was no hangar and no permanent ground anchors. Eventually the city bought the property, improved it and operated it as a municipal airport. During World War II, the Army Air Force built a training field east of town where hundreds of pilots learned gunnery skills. After the war, the field was turned over to Charlotte County which has since greatly expanded it — a fitting tribute to the intrepid aviators who took the first steps of aviation here.

1886 Church Service held in palmetto thatched arbor by African-Americans

Chapter 50

ARBOR FIRST AFRICAN-AMERICAN CHURCH

Charlotte County's two oldest African-American churches owe a great deal to the piety of Daniel C. Smith — a member of the survey crew that laid out the right-of-way to Punta Gorda for the Florida Southern Railway in 1886. Albert Gilchrist of Georgia, later Governor of Florida, was the engineer of the all-black survey crew. He and his men gave up their railroad jobs to participate in expected growth of the new town.

Shortly after the first passenger train arrived in August, Dan Smith erected a "brush arbor" for the first religious service. It was not until the following year that Col. Isaac Trabue constructed a community hall for inter-denominational church services by white folks.

In addition to Dan Smith, six other members of Gilchrist's crew stayed on at Punta Gorda. We know the names of four: Sam Kenedy, Graham, Fuller and Ransom. The names of two others are unknown but probably were among other African-Americans living in the little settlement in 1886: Isaac Howard and wife, Columbus and A.G. Reese, S.P. Andrews, Lynn and Rhoda Jackson, and Henry Simmons.

That first service consisted of a prayer meeting by the Howard, Reese and Jackson families, and bachelors Smith and Simmons. Several whites attended. We do not know their names for sure, but they undoubtedly include settlers known to be friendly with the "colored" population. Gilchrist, Col./Mrs. Trabue, Mr./Mrs. Jacob Wotitzky, Mr./Mrs. Ephraim Goldstein, and Mr./Mrs. James L. Sandlin. The black community

219

continued to meet informally in the rustic arbor until the arrival of a remarkable African-American minister, Robert Meacham in early 1888.

Meacham was born before the Civil War to a slave mother and her white master, State Senator Banks Meacham. The Gadsden County plantation owner readily acknowledged his mulatto son and saw that he was educated. After the War Between the States, Robert became active in the African Methodist Episcopal Church and was ordained in 1866. When Congress in 1877 enfranchised black males 21 years of age, he easily won a Florida Senate seat from Jefferson County.

He was an influential Reconstructionist until Democrats regained control of the re-districting machinery. Meacham in 1879 tried unsuccessfully to overcome gerrymandering by running for Congress.

At the same time, Meacham was deprived of his pastorship on trumped up charges of insobriety. He was reduced to carrying messages for an old, political friend until 1887. At that time the A.M.E. conference hired him to organize churches at Key West, Punta Gorda and Fort Myers.

The Key West mission was successful, and Meacham arrived at Punta Gorda in early 1888. There he made friends with Dan Smith and Col. Isaac Trabue, a staunch Republican from Louisville, Ky., who had served with the Union Army during the Civil War.

Col. Trabue Gives Site

According to a March 1889 deed, Col. and Mrs. Trabue gave a 40 x 85- foot lot on the south side of Helen Avenue, 80 feet east of Milot (now Milus) Street, to the newly organized A.M.E. church. Trabue accepted $1 as a legally binding sale price, but specified: "Said lot is to be used for church purposes. If ever sold, it is to revert to this donor." Witnesses were "M.T.B. Thomas," the first pastor; and James Sandlin. Trustee for the church was Dan Smith. Lumber was procured from Nocatee and was paid for by Jacob Wotitzky. Smith and other members built the sanctuary.

The *Fort Myers Press* reported in December 1889: "Rev. Meacham, formerly of Punta Gorda, is the colored minister of the A.M.E. Church here. He has started a project for the erection of a church for his people." The effort there was temporary because on January 24, 1890, Meacham was appointed postmaster at Punta Gorda upon a recommendation by Col. Trabue. Six months later, the *News* said Meacham had "quit the church."

White Punta Gordans protested Meacham's appointment at an "indignation meeting" in February of that year, but Meacham overcame opposition with tact and dignity. He certainly attended Bethel Church during this period. Meacham resigned his postmastership in March 1892.

It is interesting to note that also in 1892, "the A.M.E. church at Cleveland" bought a lot there. Trustees were George Brown, a prominent ship builder; H.R. Samuel and William S. Thompson. However, no African-American church was ever built there.

Rev. Thomas, the first minister of Bethel, is believed to have been transferred to Mt. Olive A.M.E. at Fort Myers about 1895. Because of the Methodist policy of frequent rotation of ministers, a complete roster of Bethel pastors thereafter is not known.

Bethel gave up its Helen Avenue property in June 1897 and bought from S.P. Andrews by mortgage Lot 8 of Block 35 on the northwest corner of Olympia and Wood streets, its present location. The lien was secured by a mortgage of $340 and paid in April of 1900.

The pastor in 1900, according to the Census, was Rev. James Johnson, age 34, and wife Maria, "living in the parsonage."

He was succeeded by Rev. G.W. Vaughns who died Nov. 9, 1902. Said the *Punta Gorda Herald:* "A great concourse of colored people attended the funeral services. The dead preacher leaves a wife, but no children. He came here from the upper part of the state, and was regarded as a man of genuine piety, an exemplary teacher of his race by whom his demise is sincerely deplored"

Other Ministers

The 1910 Census lists four "black" Methodist ministers. Two widowers were Rev. R.A. Jordan, 55; and J.L. Livingston of Bethel, he living with the Louis Zander family. Charles H. Smith, 44, is listed as "mulatto" living with his brother-in-law I.I. Pesche. Revs. Jordan and Smith perhaps were retired ministers.

Rev. T.W. Saunders (Sanders) is listed as "minister, Methodist, 48, wife Silvia, 50." They stated that theirs was each their second marriage of 12 years. His name is misspelled, and his denomination — formerly St. Mark Baptist — is in error, or he switched denominations when he married Widow Emmy. It is certain he was pastor of St. Mark in 1895. (see following chapter). *The Herald* reported in March 1918: "The conference of Central Florida A.M.E., sitting at Apopka this week, assigned W.W. Hamilton to the church at Punta Gorda." Rev. Hamilton in May of the following year permitted a little breakaway black congregation called the Centenary M.E. Church, Rev. J.S. Miller, pastor, to hold a special service at Bethel. Rev. Miller's wife, Marie, was the sister of Ship Builder George Brown. Centenary, commonly called "Mrs. Mary Gile's Church," was located at the corner of Charlotte and Milus streets.

Bethel purchased Lot 7 of Block 35 from the estate of James L. Sandlin for $100 for a parsonage in December 1921. The frame sanctuary next door was severely damaged by Hurricane Donna in 1960, and the present sanctuary was built in 1962 to replace it. The building drive occurred during the administration of The Rev. J.A. Proctor and was spearheaded by Sister Louise St. Clair.

The pastor in 1992 was The Rev. Joe L. Ivey. At this writing, the pastor of Bethel is The Rev. Ronald Fortune.

Sparks' manufactured sea monster.

Chapter 51

FISHERMEN LASSO SEA SERPENT

Fabulous fish fables were staple topics of gossip at Punta Gorda when the village was inhabited mostly by men who made their living netting denizens of the deep. Adrian P. Jordan, publisher-editor of the *Punta Gorda Herald*, spiced his news columns with improbable fish stories widely quoted by other state newspapers. Yet, a real catch in March of 1915 was stranger than fiction. The *Herald* tells the story best:

* * *

A big noise was made over a huge fish at Miami a year or so ago, and reports said that it was the most wonderful catch ever made. Remarkable as it was, it is rivaled by the sea serpent brought in here the other day.

This enormous snake of a fish fell into the hands of Hugh Ingram, T.B. Ingram and Sam Cottrell. They had gone out with the intention of getting back by noon. However, it was about 1:20 p.m. as they rounded Punta Gorda Point coming up from down the coast. It was 6 o'clock before they reached town. Running in as close as possible without getting aground on the shoals off the point, they came upon this inhabitant of the deep as it glided slowly along the bottom, apparently moving with the tide.

222

Hugh Ingram was first to see it as he glanced over into the water to ascertain if there was a sufficient depth for the boat, the speed of which had been reduced on nearing the shoals. The boat, too, was running with the tide. "Keep off from that log," he called to the elder Mr. Ingram who was steering the boat. "It's no log," he added after a second glance. "Look at it move."

Cottrell, who was running the engine, looked over. "What is that doggone thing?" he asked. "Looks like a whale of an eel. Gee, fellows, let's find out what it is."

The engine was stopped, and the boat allowed to drift. The object of their interest seemed unconcerned, even when they came near it. The boat drifted close to its head as it moved slowly along with but a slight motion to that portion of its body that could be seen. The water was not clear enough for it to be seen in its entirety. It was not until it had been landed that an accurate idea was gained as to its full proportions.

In the absence of a harpoon, Cottrell quickly devised a lasso of a water-soaked rope that lay on the bow of the boat. He attached a sinker to it and with dexterity becoming a cowboy, threw it so that it fell directly over the head of the reptile-like creature as it moved along. "I couldn't do it again, if I tried a hundred times," Sam afterwards asserted.

As the noose drew taut, the big serpent became vigorously active. The sudden lurch he gave caused the rope to draw close to its body so that it could not slip as may be thought it would have done. It is really unexplainable how the rope did hold, for ordinarily any one of the fish family could slip through it. But suffice to say that it held, and held tight.

Boat Pulled Aground

A hitch was taken with the rope around a cleat on the gunwale of the boat. As the reptile made off in a direction to escape from his would-be captors, he went farther in on the shoals. The boat was carried along and went aground. Overboard went the three men, holding to the line and following up their prey. The serpent was soon stranded in the shallow water, which for three-quarters of an hour he churned into turbulent sea.

After so long a time, seeming to give up the fight, he was dragged up on the beach. With assistance afterwards procured, he was placed aboard the boat and brought to town.

It was an exciting and thrilling experience the men had, lasting the entire afternoon. The trophy they brought in was such as has never before been seen here. It is not known that another such object was ever taken from the sea. It created much consternation when brought ashore.

It is 43 feet long with a continuous fin running down the center of the back the full length, 18 inches from back to belly and 12 inches from side to side midway its length. It has a fish-like head and gills, with anterior rays rising from its head and tipped with red. The skin resembles that of a catfish, silver-streaked with dark. It is considered to be a sea-serpent.

Dr. George S. Stone bought the reptile-like thing with a view to having it preserved for scientific and exhibition purposes. Messers Ingram and Cottrell hardly know how they caught the creature. They are congratulating themselves on having escaped from the encounter unharmed, rather than on having brought in such a catch.

* * *

According to Dr. Ernie Estevez, ecologist for the Mote Marine Laboratory at Sarasota, the "sea serpent" was an extraordinarily large oar fish. "They are a deep water fish that sometimes come into shallow water when they are sick or dying," says Dr. Estevez, "which explains why the specimen described was so easily caught."

The Mote scientist says the laboratory has several preserved specimens of smaller size. "We have seen only a half-dozen or so oar fish in the past 10 years," declares Dr. Estevez.

The big fish at Miami mentioned in the *Herald* article was a whale shark caught in 1912. It was 45 feet long and weighed 15 tons.

The fascination of local folks with sea monsters was illustrated in 1937 when Bill Sparks created one for a hoax. He was proprietor of Sparks Tackle Store on downtown Marion Avenue and so had access to most of the materials needed. A quick trip to Luther Koon's Butcher Pen with its many discarded cow heads provided the rest.

One of his customers caught a 500-pound Jewfish and gave it to Bill. He carted it back to his store on his car's front bumper with intention of photographing it for a testimonial to his wares.

As often seems to be common with fishermen, Bill couldn't resist embellishing the catch. He attached cow horns to the upper and lower jaws to give the appearance of giant, protruding fangs. He even affixed an extra large horn to the top of the fish's head. Then he painted big spots on the fish's skin to make it look like a new species of sea life.

The subsequent photograph was so sensational, Bill had it made into post cards and made a good bit of money selling them to tourists for a nickel each. In 1980, when Sambo's built a restaurant in Port Charlotte, they decorated it with a collection of local historical pictures, including an enlargement of this photo. The restaurant has since been closed and the pictures disposed of.

Punta Gorda's reservoir dammed up by Seaboard Air Line railroad bed.

Chapter 52

RESERVOIR AN ORANGE BLOSSOM SPECIAL

Of all the epochs of Charlotte County history, the most significant began with coming of the railroads — starting with the Florida Southern Railway in 1885 and ending with the Atlantic Coast Line in 1967. In between was the hustling Seaboard Air Line whose name was a boast that it consisted of the most direct routes. Commercial flying was still a vision.

Florida Southern opened up the west coast, as the Florida East Coast Railroad did for the Atlantic side. Challenging both was E. Davies Warfield, president of Seaboard.

The Seaboard was cobbled together at the turn of the century by John Shelton Williams of Richmond, Va., from a score of bankrupt, short lines. The system extended from New York City to Coleman, Fla., where the tracks diverged to Tampa and to Miami — competing with the original railroad barons. The SAL was fondly referred to as "She's Always Late." However, its Orange Blossom Special trains were immortalized by a wonderful fiddle tune. Warfield succeeded to the SAL presidency in the early 1920's. World War I and the subsequent Florida Land Boom provided profitable business for all.

225

By 1925, smart investors began cashing in their speculations — though collapse of the national economy was not to occur until the 1929 stock market crash and subsequent Great Depression.

Nevertheless, Warfield believed the anticipated "correction" would be short. He proposed to position himself for the rebound by extending his line to Punta Rassa (southwest of Fort Myers) and build a seaport there to rival Tampa. In addition he would take the line on to Naples which was growing rapidly but had no railroad.

He began selling stock in the venture and buying right-of-way. His first act was lease-purchase of Charlotte Harbor & Northern Railroad in Dec. 1925. The latter, built in 1907-10, transported Peace River phosphate at Fort Ogden to Tampa via Bradley Junction, and to Boca Grande via Murdock. This moved Seaboard 80 miles on existing track toward its goal, leaving only 30 miles of new track to build to Fort Myers, and 35 more to Naples.

A Punta Gorda booster leaflet called *Weekly Doin's* took note of Warfield's promotion in its Christmas 1925 edition: "The recently published folder by the Seaboard Air Line Railway shows the proposed new line to Fort Myers. This line passes within but a short distance of Punta Gorda. Why doesn't the Civic Association take steps to try and induce the Seaboard to come through this city?"

True to its policy of shortest possible routes, Seaboard headed from Fort Ogden straight to Fort Myers — bypassing Punta Gorda seven miles east over Shell Creek. It did, however, open markets to the wilderness settlements along Tuckers Grade.

Charlotte County Right Of Way

Agent at Punta Gorda for purchase of Charlotte County right-of-way for Seaboard was Dr. Alfred G. Grunwell, formerly health officer for the Panama Canal. In retirement he was president of the S.E. Investment Co. His son, William, became a prominent marine engineer at Punta Gorda.

In April 1926, Dr. Grunwell transferred the first strips of Charlotte County right-of-way to Seaboard All Florida Railway Corp. — holding company for Seaboard Air Line. In September he transferred a second tract. Warfield put 500 men to work to push the line to Naples as soon as possible. The tracks crossed the Atlantic Coast Line at Gilchrist Station on the Charlotte-Lee county line and reached Fort Myers Nov. 24, 1926.

In the meantime, the Atlantic Coast Line became concerned about the aggressive expansion of its rival. ACL had bought out Florida Southern in 1902 and extended its line from Punta Gorda to Fort Myers in 1904. Now, it raced to keep up by extending its line to Sarasota and Venice, and to Naples.

For the purpose of stock sales, Atlantic set up a Tampa Southern Railroad subsidiary. It built a "Fort Ogden extension" from Sarasota to the

ACL mainline east of Peace River. This "short cut" reduced travel time by half an hour between Tampa, Punta Gorda, Fort Myers and Naples.

The Fort Myers Southern Railroad subsidiary was established by ACL to build the Naples extension through Bonita Springs.

Seaboard did not pause at Fort Myers because Atlantic was already half way to Naples. Warfield was determined to have the honor of being first to Naples and ordered his huge crew to work around the clock. The effort paid off. Seaboard reached Naples on Dec. 22, 1926. Atlantic arrived 11 days later.

The first Seaboard passenger train pulled into Fort Myers on Jan. 7, 1927 — with Warfield, Florida Gov. John Martin and 600 distinguished guests aboard. The town closed all stores to celebrate. A month later, SAL laid tracks from Fort Myers to LaBelle and a month after that to Punta Rassa.

Seaboard's remarkable construction feat proved a Phyrric victory. The railroad's financial resources were exhausted. The Roaring Twenties came to a jarring end before it could recover. Seaboard went into receivership in 1931, as did many railroads throughout the nation. With this protection from creditors, the railroad managed to make expenses by hauling lumber from south and east Charlotte County, and phosphate from newly dis-covered open-pit mines north of Arcadia.

Zemel's Railroad

Nothing was ever done to develop Port Punta Rassa. Passenger service to Fort Myers and Naples was discontinued in 1932. All trackage between Fort Ogden and Naples was abandoned about 1939. The right-of-way reverted to adjacent property owners. Charles Zemel thus acquired the largest portion. The old, unused grade became known as "Zemel's Railroad." Seaboard presence south of Fort Ogden after this consisted of its ownership of CH&N. SAL exercised its lease-purchase agreement with CH&N in Dec. 1946 by voting the stock it held. The merger agreement gives us a list of the communities affected;

"Whereas Seaboard Air Line owns all 35,000 shares of the Charlotte Harbor and Northern capital stock, and 5,000 shares of preferred stock at $100 each, the following lines are transferred to Seaboard — those extending southwesterly from a point of connection with the Plant City-Alooma line of the Seaboard line at Ridgewood, Polk County; viz Ochan, Bradley Junction, Fort Green Springs, Ona, Kinsey, Arcadia, Hull Junction, Platt, Murdock, McCall in Sarasota, Charlotte and Lee Counties to the end of the line at South Boca Grande 97.66 miles; also South Mulberry 1.27 miles in Polk County; five locomotives, 174 cars and all associated right-of-way and track."

The Atlantic Coast Line extension between Sarasota and Fort Ogden was discontinued in 1949, and the tracks taken up.

The Charlotte County section of the Seaboard continued to operate profitably carrying phosphate and passengers to Boca Grande. It was a lifeline for Charlotte County folks north of the harbor.

T.E. Koon recalled: "If you didn't have any money, you could ride the train and pay next trip. A lot of fishermen carried their fish on the train to market, sold their catch, then paid the conductor on the return trip.

"The train had no schedule. Oh, they posted one all right, but the train could be either late or early, depending on the mood of the engineer on that particular day. It didn't really matter. If the engineer saw a covey of quail, he might stop the train and go hunting for an hour or so.

"Greedy Leffers, in the old days, used to hobo from Placida. He'd hook a ride in a gondola car to Murdock where he would roll off in a pile of sand. One dark night he jumped at the usual pile of white sand he saw there, but it turned out to be a pile of rocks they'd just unloaded. It like to have killed him. Bruised him all up."

The Seaboard in 1949 began selling off state-bonus property the CH&N had acquired when its tracks were built in 1907-10. One of the largest tracts was 3,250 acres in Charlotte Harbor town — "except 20 acres off the south edge of government lots 1 and 2, for the dock known formerly as Knight's Cattle Dock in Section 11."

The Charlotte County right-of-way abandoned by Seaboard in 1939 across Shell Creek and its shallow valley was taken by the City of Punta Gorda in Oct. 1962 through the power of eminent domain from Zemel, Sam Houston Huffman, Leland W. Tolliver, and Albert Kerstein.

Create Reservoir

The public purpose was to incorporate the old grade with a dam and replace the trestle over Shell Creek with a spillway to create a reservoir for a municipal water supply. It is today's primary source for the city.

Phosphate mines closer to Tampa, and modern highways, cut deeply into Seaboard's revenue. It merged with Atlantic Coast Line in July 1967. Thereafter, the merged lines became the Seaboard Coast Line. The old CH&N-Seaboard line to Boca Grande was discontinued in 1971 and abandoned in 1988.

Even the combination Seaboard Cost Line was not enough. Today, the former SCL trackage south of Arcadia is operated on a much reduced basis by the independent Seminole Gulf Railroad of Fort Myers.

Seaboard history is evident by the Punta Gorda reservoir, El Jobean fishing bridge over the Myakka River, and a stretch of roadbed in north Charlotte County which is slated to be connected to the Cape Haze Pioneer Trail. To enhance this project, the old C.H.& N. section crew bunk house at Placida will be restored as the Gault-Albritton Archaeology Study Center on the right-of-way where it bisects the important Coral Creek Indian Mound.

Ornery cattle inspired many tall tales. This 1895 illustration by Frederic Remington, shows two "crackers" trying to brand a wild bull.

Chapter 53

OLDTIMERS TOLD WHOPPERS

In the days before television, or even radio if you can imagine that, folks hereabouts amused themselves in their idle moments with "whoppers." These were improbable stories that were sometimes true, partly true, or figments of imagination. It didn't matter so long as they were extraordinary.

The acknowledged champion story teller was Morgan Bonaparte Mizell. He was ramrod for Cattle Baron Ziba King of Fort Ogden back when Charlotte and DeSoto counties were still part of Manatee County.

To Mizell's friends — and they were legion — the consummate Florida cowboy was better known as "Bone." As he became a legend in his own time, Bone dropped his given name and adopted that of Napoleon. He felt it added more "class."

Bone spoke with a decided lisp which enhanced both his story-telling prowess and his appeal as the subject of whoppers.

For example, a thief stole some of Bone's hogs one time, and Bone tracked the animals to a pen three miles away. Bone's ear notch — registered with the county clerk — had been freshly altered. Nevertheless, Bone drove the hogs back to his spread. The hog thief boldly swore out a warrant for Bone's arrest.

Bone got off on the wrong foot with the judge when he walked into the courtroom with his hat on. The judge demanded that Bone remove his hat.

229

Bone refused. "This here is a $10 Stetson; and there's a lot of thieves in here, not all of them accused." The judge relented and let Bone keep on his sombrero. When called to the witness stand, Bone was asked how long the hogs' ear notches had been changed. "About a moomph," he replied in his drawling lisp.

"What's a moomph?" the prosecuting attorney demanded.

"Why a moomph is firty days," said an astonished Bone. "I fought everybody knew what a moomph was."

Both cattle and hogs were marked with the owners' distinctive notches cut into ears and with brand marks on left, rear flanks.

On one round up, an ornery cow defied all attempts to brand her and ran off into a dense thicket. Buck King, foreman of the drive, announced in disgust, "Anyone who can catch her, and put his mark on her, can have her." Only Bone was brave enough to take up the chase into the thorny tangle of vines and palmettos.

The other cow hunters gathered to see how Bone would make out. There was a lot of crashing around, cursing and bellowing. Bye and bye, Bone staggered out alone — his clothes in tatters from the thorns and his hands and face not much better.

"What's the matter, Bone?" the cowmen taunted. "That old cow get the best of you?" "Not at all," said Bone. "I done put my notch in her ears." "How's that?" the men hooted. "You don't have a knife."

"Marked her wif my teef just as good as wif a knife," declared Bone. In disbelief, the cowboys circled the thicket and drove out the recalcitrant cow. Sure enough, Bone had bitten out a piece of each ear in the shape of his own notch.

On another drive, Bone signed up to help Willie Williams get a herd to market at Fort Pierce. That night the drive put up in a cow pen, and the men began to cook supper. Bone volunteered to get water for coffee from a nearby pond. Bone was gone, and gone, and gone. The other men started eating and were grouchy because they hadn't any coffee. Finally Bone appeared, carrying a couple of lard cans of water.

"Whatinell kept you?" his comrades demanded.

Said Bone in earnest tone: "Boy's, I just saw the damndest cat fight anybody ever saw. On the edge of that pond, two old bobcats was fighting and growling at one another. All at once, they stood up on their hind legs, clinched, and began to climb each other. I stood there and watched them until they clumb clear out of sight."

The "boys" weren't amused, being more interested at the moment in coffee than in whoppers.

After the cattle were delivered to Fort Pierce, the cowboys started home. Again they camped at the same pen where the celebrated cat fight had supposedly occurred. Also again, Bone volunteered to go for coffee water. "OK, but don't be so durn long this time," they said.

Bone came back promptly. One of his buddies inquired with a smirk, "See anything of those bobcats?" "No, boys," said Bone. "but I guess they're still a'fightin, as the fur is still a'fallin."

A whopper duel was hard to beat.

One day Bone and Cy McClellan were riding along on the 90-Mile Prairie east of Arcadia. Cy stopped his horse, stared intently at the horizon and pretended to see a ship. "Why, there's the Lily White," he said. "I think she's a mite off course."

Bone stopped also and shaded his eyes. "Yes, I see it; and there's a big horsefly on her mast."

" By gosh, you're right!" said Cy. "I just saw it blink an eye."

* * *

Another great spinner of whoppers was the Rev. George W. Gatewood — Methodist circuit rider for the southwest Florida settlements. As a minister, Rev. Gatewood respected the ninth commandment. However, as a renowned "exhorter," he could not resist embellishing a good yarn. His account of a hunting trip near his homestead in Bermont is an example.

"One day I was hunting in the eastern end of the county where the palmettos were thick. A deer jumped up and took flight. I went to shooting, not seeing any other human near. Guilford Lewis, though, was about 150 yards away. He could see me but did not see the deer. D.H. Huckeby, a Cleveland sawmill operator, also was about the same distance in another direction and could see all of us — me, Lewis and the deer.

"Lewis heard my bullets whistle through the air near him, and he thought I was shooting at him. Huckeby said Lewis outdistanced the deer, keeping ahead of it until he got out of breath. Fortunately, I did not hit either Lewis or the deer."

In a first-rate whopper, Rev. Gatewood let exhortation get the best of him: "J.W. Thomas, a blacksmith at Bermont, had a spring near his house. One afternoon, he went to get a pail of water and found a large soft-shell turtle taking a bath. As turtles of that kind make a choice dish, Tom took that one to a block and beheaded it. Then, he hung it up to bleed until the next day, since it takes a turtle a long time to die. In the morning, upon touching the turtle's flesh, it would jerk.

"When his neighbor, Pat Murphy, came over, Tom told him that a turtle had more lives than a cat. Pat said, 'No. The turtle is dead but not conscious of it.'

"That afternoon Tom began to prepare the turtle for cooking. Still, it jerked every time the knife touched it. By taking a pair of pliers in one hand and a butcher knife in the other, he finally got it cut up. Then, in the pot, the pieces got to jerking and kicking the water into a foam.

"Tom said he just couldn't stand it any longer. He jerked the pot off the stove and dumped its contents into the hog pen. The last he saw of that turtle, it was running around the pen in sections, the hogs chasing after."

At that time, A.C. Freeman owned and operated a hardware store at Punta Gorda and had a stock of coffins in the back room. Later he was mayor of the town and then sheriff of DeSoto County before Charlotte County was split away. Rev. Gatewood's favorite whopper involved a customer of Freeman's.

"A certain neighbor of mine, whom I will call Cox, used to go on periodical sprees with John Barleycorn," said the good reverend. "While on one of these toots, he wandered into Freeman's store and into the undertaking department unnoticed. Cox climbed into an open coffin that looked comfortable with its velvet lining. Unfortunately, he lay down with his head to the narrow foot of the casket and got wedged in. He couldn't get clear in, or pull himself out.

"Freeman's wife, who helped in the store, went to the back room for something and discovered a man's foot sticking out of the coffin. Horrified, she yelled for help. Freeman came a-running. He had to call for help to extricate the inebriated intruder.

"Cox became agitated, thinking they were trying to bury him. He kicked over every coffin in the place before they could calm him down."

* * *

Another famous whopper expert was Adrian P. Jordan, editor and publisher of the *Punta Gorda Herald* He specialized in fish stories which were widely reprinted throughout the state — "the truth of which the editor is prepared to support by the usual affidavits provided in such cases and warranted to keep in any climate."

"In these waters is a peculiar fish rarely over eight inches long. On the bottom of its stomach is a singular formation resembling the bottom of a lady's rubber overshoe. This little fish is called a sucker, from its habit of sucking itself, so to speak, onto the sides of other fish — fixing itself with greatest tenacity by means of the curious rubber pad.

"About a month ago, Henry Arrington (a thinly disguised spelling for Farrington, the 12-year-old son of a widow living near the bay shore) while fishing caught one of these queer fish. He tied a line around the fish's tail and tossed it into the water. In a moment, there was a tremendous pull on the line. The boy held on and finally pulled into his boat a large fish known as a snoot. It weighed about 30 pounds. Henry was greatly surprised to find the sucker sticking fast to the big fish.

"As young Henry touched the sucker, it released its hold. The sucker was tossed back into the water, and in a few minutes it caught more fish than the boy knew what to do with. Realizing that he had captured an aquatic fishing dog, so to speak, the boy carried the sucker home and put it in a barrel of bay water which he renews daily.

"Now, when he or his mother want fish, he takes his sucker and line down to the beach and tosses the little fish into the bay. Pretty soon the sucker catches all the fish wanted."

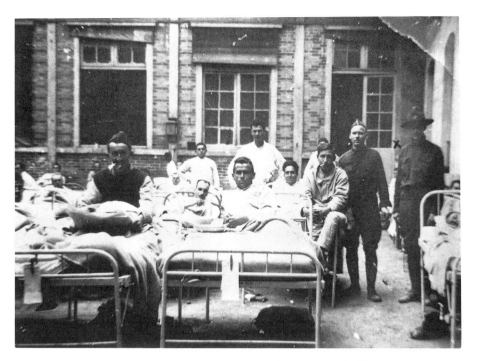

Neven Waltmiree, center, in Picardy Hospital was wounded but recovered.

Chapter 54

LETTERS FROM THE WAR FRONT

What today's history books call the First World War was the "European War" to Americans until soldiers from Punta Gorda, Charlotte Harbor Town and thousands of other United States communities joined the Allies in April 1917.

Then it became "The war to make the world safe for Democracy," or, "The war to end all wars." In short, it was a "popular" war. The Selective Service Act conscripted young men by lottery, but just as many volunteered in a fervor of patriotism. The first American soldiers saw action Nov. 30. Then a flood of fighting men began streaming to training camps — first step to active duty in the Allied Expeditionary Force under Gen. John "Black Jack" Pershing.

Local boys — "selects" and volunteers — marched off to great adventure. Sometimes to death or serious injury. Among the volunteers were two physicians, Dr. D.N. McQueen, and Dr. Archer Smith; and a dentist, Dr. Henry Carver. By May 1919, the *Punta Gorda Herald* published the names of 64 whites from Punta Gorda, five from Charlotte Harbor Town, and seven "colored" from Punta Gorda in training camps or enroute to the "battle lines of France." Embarkation of nine African-Americans was typical of the good-wishes accorded all the young men:

"Nine young colored men who had been selected for military service left here for the training camp Tuesday morning. They are Leonard Fulford, Bennie Coleman, Harrison Wadsworth, Lexie Bass, Jim Jackson, Ben Zachary, Ed Hayes, Lewis June, Will Martin, and Sellars O'Neal. They were given a great send-off by their friends, a large number of whom assembled at the depot to bid them a patriotic farewell.

"The nine were placed in line beside the railroad track. In front of them was a truck upon which their church pastors stood when addressing them. Rev. M.L. Cherry, pastor of St. Marks Progressive Baptist Church, was master of ceremonies. First, a large number of girls tastefully dressed in white, sang `America' beautifully. Then a patriotic, excellent address was made to the nine by Rev. W.W. Hamilton, pastor of the A.M.E. Church. This was followed by the singing of the 'Star Spangled Banner,' after which a prayer was said by Rev. T.W. Sanders of the Primitive Baptist Church.

"By this time, the train was waiting. The selects boarded it while the girls sang another song. As the train moved off, there was a great waving of hats and handkerchiefs .

"Dispatches from the battle line in France report that the colored troops there are covering themselves with glory. When our Punta Gorda colored men get over there, the dispatches will have more stories of valorous deeds to relate."

The *Herald* also persuaded its readers to share letters from their sons. The following excerpts from those personal communications provide an insight to that war since overshadowed by more recent conflicts — but poignant and instructive nevertheless.

Ferguson Jones, 112th Ammunition Train, 37th Division — "We had a nice trip across the pond, though two submarines caused some excitement. Both were sunk by the convoying destroyers. England is the prettiest country that I have ever seen. The English girls seem to think the American soldier is the only man in the world."

William E. Vecqueray, 1st Sgt. Co. C, 6th U.S. Engineers —"It is a peculiar thing, but unless there is too much cannon fire among your own guns, you can tell when a gun is fired by the enemy headed your direction.

"You can hear a dull thud, absolutely distinct from any of the other explosions. Almost immediately comes the whine of the shell coming toward you. Then you sit down close to the side of your trench, and wonder where it is going to hit. You get used to them in time, however, and seem to know automatically when it is time to take cover.

"On one occasion, some of the boys were under a poison gas attack for eight hours, but were lucky enough to come out of it with only a few of them very slightly gassed. Over 30,000 gas shells were fired."

Daniel W. Collins, Co. L, 28th Infantry —- "I was lucky enough to get through the big battle Saturday. I was shot about two inches above the left knee and right in the center. The bullet went only to the bone. I walked three miles after I was wounded. My leg is stiff, but I can walk without pain. I will be in the hospital two months.

"I don't want to be boastful, but I took two machine guns and killed six Germans before I got hurt. I was shot by an aviator in an aeroplane. We have put Kaiser Bill in mourning for awhile."

Editor Laments: Herald Publisher-Editor Adrian P. Jordan, whipped out an editorial in August to declare that the paper "now finds itself in a peck of trouble."

"The youngest son (Ivan) of the editor has been summoned to the colors and will leave for training camp tomorrow. He has been doing all the job printing, setting advertisements, making up the forms and putting them to press. No other one in the office can do the job. We had hoped, and confidently believed, that as the examining physicians had certified that a crippled leg rendered him unfit for military service, he would be exempted.

"This is not all, but is the worst of troubles inflicted upon the *Herald*. The increase in postage, and infliction of a zone delivery system upon newspapers, have been sufficiently discussed. Now comes some other government regulations which will impose serious burdens. These require that all subscribers who have not paid in advance shall be dropped from the subscription list; also, that the papers shall use 15 percent less paper.

"Newspapers not observing these regulations by the War Industries Board will have to cease publication because paper mills and ink companies will be forbidden to sell it supplies. All these things make the writer wish he had never gone into the newspaper business. It would have been more pleasant and profitable if he had devoted his life to raising chickens."

Two weeks later, Ivan Jordan wrote his father from Camp Wheeler at Macon, Ga. "I passed through the physical examination O.K. Thirteen of us were from DeSoto County (before Charlotte was split off), and only one man was turned down. I thought sure I was going to get home after I saw hundreds of big, husky fellows turned down, but it looks like they want me for the government printing office.

"Some of the poor fellows here are grieving over things too much. Four have committed suicide since I arrived. Two hung themselves, and two cut their throats. None of them were from Florida."

Raymon Ried, Transportation Battalion, A.E.F. — "As I told you, I was driving a truck at Deeize. Then I was one of eight men sent to Paris by train to pick up new trucks. The first thing that attracted our attention was an explosion. We did not know what it was but learned that it was a shell from the 76-mile German gun 'Big Bertha,' or, 'Fritz' as they call it. After that we heard the explosions every few minutes. There goes one now! They are nothing to worry about, as the French children laugh and make fun of it every time."

Big Bertha was the largest cannon barrel ever built up to that time. It was mounted on a special railroad car that at the high-water mark of German advance hurled projectiles into Paris. However, little damage was done because the shells fired were only 8.4 inches in diameter. Payload had to be sacrificed to achieve distance.

Constance Cook, R.N., — Dear Col. and Mrs. Charles A. Waltmire: I am writing for your son Robert, who is at present a patient in an American Red Cross hospital in the Picardy region. First, I must assure you that he is not seriously injured, and that he is progressing nicely. He has a minor injury of the right knee caused by a bullet wound; also, the left hand was penetrated by a machine-gun bullet.

"Robert went over the top in that splendid victory at the Soisson's sector of July 18th and 19th, when so many German prisoners were taken.

"It must have been very hard for you to see three of your sons leave for France with the First Division. It seems war was inevitable and that it was an absolute necessity for Americans to make their sacrifice along with the nations already long at war.

"We who have been privileged to do our part over here in France in active service are more than proud of the work done in the ranks by our own American boys. They deserve much credit.

"You have reason to be very proud of your sons — and of Robert in particular, perhaps. Do not worry about your boy. He will be up and around long before this letter reaches you. You should see your son now — sitting up for breakfast — with the aid of a backrest. I have helped him wash his face and hand, and he has scrubbed his teeth and combed his hair. I do not have to tell you how nice he looks now.

"As I happen to be the night nurse, I have cooked a pot of oatmeal on a queer little French coal-oil stove in the ward. The boys also have French coffee, bread with butter and jam, and oranges. Having finished breakfast, Robert proceeds to smoke a nice looking, but bad smelling — as you know — pipe and read a book."

Robert, better known by his middle name Nevin, and his two brothers Allred and Jack, were among the first Floridians to volunteer for Army service. They went with the first contingents to France.

Raleigh Whidden embraces his sister Ruth shortly before his death.

Chapter 55

RALEIGH WHIDDEN MORTALLY WOUNDED

As the First World war dragged on, letters of soldiers from the Charlotte Harbor area became ominous in tone. The following examples reprinted in the Punta Gorda Herald describe battle-field action in places that are remembered in history as decisive:

Pvt. Raleigh Whidden, Co. B, 9th Infantry — "Dear Sister Ruth: Although I have not had the chance to write you, as I have wished, you may be sure that home has a good share of my thoughts. These thoughts are just happy thoughts. I am not alone and stranded in France. Back of me and the other fellows is the great, old United States; and back of me is a good home. So, I feel glad to be on the job, putting on the finishing touches at teaching the kaiser a few things.

"Just now, I am having a short vacation. I was wounded a little, but the hospital gives me the best treatment. I am improving every day. Tell all the people that you have heard from me — especially my girl. Kiss my sweet baby for me, too."

Raleigh's "girl" was a Miss Nelson who lived on Harbor View Road in Charlotte Harbor Town. There was no bridge over the harbor at that time, so Raleigh frequently swam across just for the sport and, perhaps, to impress his sweetheart. He dragged along a lard can containing dry clothes. "Sweet baby" was his six-year-old niece, Mabel — daughter of Mr. and Mrs. Leslie and Ruth (Whidden) Lewis. The younger brothers of Ruth — Raleigh and Hudson — were taken in by her and husband Leslie when Mrs. Whidden died and Sylvanus Whidden remarried. The boys, therefore, had cherished baby Mabel from birth. Raleigh was only 16 when he volunteered for the Army — falsely stating he was 18.

Germany launched an all-out war on American shipping in late 1916. Many U.S. ships were sunk. Newly elected President Woodrow Wilson asked Congress on April 2, 1917, to recognize that a state of war existed between the United States and the German Empire.

This was enough inspiration for Raleigh — then a young fisherman for the John C. Lewis and Lorenzo T. Blocksom Fish Company. Two days later he joined the Florida National Guard which at that moment was the prerequisite for acceptance by the Army. Congress declared war on April 6. Raleigh was "called into active Army service" August 17 and left for Camp Wheeler Training Camp at Macon, Ga., on Sept. 16. By January 1918, Raleigh was at the front.

A week after Raleigh's optimistic letter to his sister, he wrote a grim one to Thomas "Shorty" Griggs, a friend:

"It will interest you to know that I have already been to the front and 'over the top.' I came back with one eye out and two pieces of shrapnel in my left knee, and two little holes in my chest; but I am getting along finely. My eye was not shot out. I was hit just above it and had to have it taken out. I will be given a glass eye shortly."

Over The Top Again

The full extent of Raleigh's injuries is described in a little diary he kept while in the hospital:

"I was injured in the battle of Chateau-Thierry on July l9, 1918. I fought hard all day. We went to a ravine to rest, then over the top again. I went about three-fourths of a mile wounded by shrapnel before I had sense enough to know I was hurt. I was carried to a first-aid station, then to Base Hospital at the city of Orleans. I was wounded in four places — right shoulder, left arm, eye and head. I also had two pieces of shrapnel in my knee. I had awful headaches for two weeks before an operation to take out my eye and install two silver plates in my skull. Then I was taken to another hospital and got a glass eye in readiness for discharge."

Raleigh returned to the Army Hospital at Cape May, N.J., two days before the Armistice of Nov. 11, 1919, was declared to end the war. He was there for a long time before being released.

He got a job working at the Punta Gorda ice factory, but the cold reacted with the silver plates in his head to cause excruciating headaches.

During this time, Raleigh went fishing with Shorty who fell into the harbor. Raleigh jumped in to assist his friend, and in the exertion lost his glass eye. The Army promptly sent him a new one.

Raleigh suffered seizures which increased in frequency and intensity for six months. He was sent to the military hospital at Carlstrom Air Field in Arcadia where he died. He is buried alongside Leslie and Ruth Lewis at Friendship Cemetery, Sweetwater, Fla.

Raymond Reid, standing, beside Army truck used as ambulance in France.

Other Letters

Dr. James Archer Smith, 1st Lt., Field Hospital 309, Sanitary Train 303 — "Villages and towns are all alike. Farmers live in little villages and have their barns and manure piles at the front door. A man's wealth over here is judged by the size of the manure pile. The streets are lined with them, and the odor is anything but pleasant. Every house has its wine cellar. I think the French exist entirely on wine and very seldom touch water.

"During the last five weeks I have not spent four nights in one place. On the move all the time. Have marched and rode trucks to my heart's content. When we finish one of these marches, especially at night, you just hunt a tree — if one can be found — double up in your trench coat, and sleep like the dead. Next morning you get up and erect a field hospital and be ready to take patients.

"A few days ago, I saw one of the greatest sights (artillery duel) that one can ever see in his life. Fourth of July has nothing on it. My field hospital was sent up farther than the rest. We were within one mile of the Boche lines. For 24 hours we lived fifty years. Talk about Hell on earth! You can get it over here. A man that says he isn't scared is either a fool or hasn't got good sense.

"Well, as to my work. Ours is designated a surgical hospital. That is, we handle all seriously wounded cases that cannot be sent on back and need immediate attention. Of course, our deaths are extremely high; but we must be this close up. If we can save a few lives of the very seriously wounded — who would die if they were sent farther back — then we have done a great deal.

"I am now in the receiving ward where patients come in and are sent to the operating room. I am on duty for 12 hours -- midnight to noon tomorrow. Tomorrow night I go in the operating room and give anesthetics for 24 hours on the stretch and then change back again. Home will be sweeter and dearer than ever to us all when we get back."

Braxton B. Blount, Jr. — "My Dear Wife: I know that you have been expecting a letter from me for a long time, but it was impossible for me to write. We were in the Argonne drive — the one that won the war. We have been on our feet, and on the move, every day since Nov. 1st (1918) until yesterday (Dec. 6) at noon.

From the 1st until the 8th we marched and built roads day and night. If we managed to get as much as three hours sleep out of 24 we were doing exceptionally well — and an awfully great amount of sleeping.

"MUD! My God, imagine the worst kind of gumbo pipe-clay eight to 10 inches deep. Then, multiply the stiffness of it by the fullest extent of your imagination and you will about have what we had to march through. This was day and night, day in and day out.

"Tired? Lordy, we were tired and muddy. Our uniforms were so covered with it that you couldn't tell their color. We never washed our faces and hands all this time. It was fairly good walking out on the farms to the sides of the roads. However, we couldn't walk there at night for the dead Germans. They were thick and covered miles and miles square of territory. I stumbled over dead — good — Boche and saw so many that it was as commonplace as going over a trampled-down rye field.

"I saw several peculiar coincidences. One German was sitting in a dug-out, on the ground, holding a cane in his hand between his knees. A 30-calibre ball took him between the eyes. His head was resting on his cane and knees as if he were nodding. Another was lying over his machine gun in the same position he was in when he last pulled the trigger. Another was lying over an armload of machine gun shells, in clips, that he was carrying to the one who was lying over the machine gun.

"We were in Verdun a few days. Oh! It's a great life. Our regiment was cited three times in the drives. Once in Alsace, and twice in the

240

Argonne Forest. I'm tired and sleepy. Will write more in a day or so. Our greatest hopes now are to board a steamer for the States. Your loving husband, Braxton."

Things Missed Back Home

It is interesting to note the things back home that the Charlotte Harbor area boys missed:

Jack Waltmire — "I am hungry for some American cantaloupes and Punta Gorda pineapples."

Coe Allen to his Mama on Dec. 11 — "We had a nice long hike getting to the Rhine River, but we arrived OK. Makes me homesick to see boats going up and down. Maybe I will be at home this Spring and see the boats on the bay. Hope to, anyway. I want to get back home for some real fried potatoes like those you make."

Tom Steele to his mother — "I guess you have heard lots about the Rhine River. I am now sleeping in a hotel that sits right on the banks. Can look out the window and see the boats. It makes me long to be in Punta Gorda. The German folks treat us fine. They cook for us and don't want to take any money, but we make them take it. They doctor the boys for colds."

William E. Vecqueray to Editor A.P. Jordan — "When our guns open up with a sudden barrage you can't hear yourself think. You fall asleep and dream you are in Florida and a big mosquito is buzzing around you. Then you wake up and find it is a flock of aeroplanes on their way to bomb the enemy's lines. When we get home again we will be able to sleep through a Florida thunderstorm and never know it.

William Mayes to his mother — "Had a bunch of prisoners down in a small village. The country around here is beautiful. See a lot of cricket moles. It puts me in mind of good old Florida. Got another issue of chewing tobacco today — good old American Star. It was a treat, as this French and English tobacco does not agree at all."

James M. Bryant, H.D.Q., 316 F.A. to his father, Milton — "Your letter of Sept. 23 just received. I am very well, but I would enjoy a fat mullet and some grits, as I have not seen any grits but once since I entered the army."

Everlas Casket Co. float for parade at opening of Barron Collier Bridge
promoted light-weight funery products made from palmetto roots.

Chapter 56

SECRET FORMULAS DIDN'T PAY OFF

Who hasn't, at one time or another, dreamed of discovering a secret formula for a product that would make you rich? At least four men in Punta Gorda during the last century turned such dreams into reality — with mixed success.

Consider the "extracts" of Dr. J.W. Best, for example. Punta Gorda in those days was not the edge of civilization, but local folks claimed "you could see it from here." Country doctors were accustomed to compounding their own prescriptions. To make his more palatable, Dr. Best developed extracts of fruit juices into which he mixed medicine.

In time he became as well known for his extracts as for his medical skill. Concentrated fruit juices could be mixed with water for a refreshing drink, or charged with nose-tickling carbonic gas produced by dripping carbolic acid onto marble chips. These ingredients could be obtained only from drug stores — doctors often owned them — which is why "soda fountains" were popular sidelines of drug stores then.

242

Dr. Best kept his extract formulas secret, but we can assume their base was "simple syrup" made from cane sugar. Into this was added strong fruit juice and a chemical preservative. Extracts from oranges and pineapples undoubtedly were early ingredients inasmuch as those fruits were plentiful here. It is clear that he produced several flavors.

Perhaps he experimented with peaches. His friend and partner was Perry McAdow, a prominent business man who planted a peach grove about this time on Burnt Store Road near Taylor Road. The peaches grew but did not bear commercially in the perpetually warm climate.

The flavors Dr. Best invented were of such quality that he entered them in state fairs and expositions — often winning blue ribbons.

The *Punta Gorda Herald* of April 1902 reported: "Mr. McAdow bought from Col. Trabue the business lot on Marion Avenue adjoining McLane and Oliver's store on the west (northwest) corner of Cross St. to erect a laboratory for the Fruit Extract Manufacturing Company. He and Dr. Best are the chief stockholders.

"It may be known that the fruit extracts made by Dr. Best took the highest awards at the Atlanta Exposition several years ago. It is hoped to have the laboratory in full operation by the middle of next month."

Dr. Best was born at Latrobe, Pa., in 1850. He was graduated from medical colleges at Meadville, Pa., and Cleveland, Ohio. He married Margaret Pratt in 1879 at Latrobe. They had a son Jodie, and a daughter Stella. Starting in 1890, they lived briefly at Lake City, Jacksonville, Arcadia and Charlotte Harbor Town before settling at Punta Gorda.

Unfortunately Dr. Best died suddenly on Aug. 28, 1902, of undisclosed cause, at his home. He was 52. He took the extract formula to his grave at Latrobe. His wife and children remained at Punta Gorda. She died in 1915 and is buried at Indian Springs Cemetery.

The *Herald* declared: "The untimely death of Dr. Best, who was to be the manufacturing chemist and local manager, has defeated the proposed organization of a company to manufacture fruit extracts. Everything was in readiness for the enterprise. The necessary building had been erected and equipped with requisite appliances, and the prospects were bright.

"Now, however, the enterprise has been abandoned, at least for the present. The building will be used for other purposes, possibly for a large up-to-date and very tony drug store."

Dr. Roberts' Tonic

Strangely, another secret formula was connected a few years later with the extract venture.

"Doctor" Walter A. Roberts was a pharmacist who came to Punta Gorda in 1892. His memory survives as the "first doctor" here although he was not a licensed physician. Druggists often were the only health care providers in frontier towns and were accorded the title of doctor.

Certainly Roberts had the first drug store. It was located in one of two buildings on the site of today's court house. Mrs. Trabue owned one, and it is likely Roberts occupied it after a general merchandise store failed there leaving counters and shelves in place. Marshal John Bowman lived in the other which had a "calaboose" jail nearby, off an alley now Herald Court.

Roberts compounded many patent medicines and probably filled prescriptions for Dr. Best using the latter's extracts. One of Roberts' popular medicines was "Roberts' 35-drop Wonder" for rheumatism. Another profitable concoction was said to be "666 Tonic" for malaria, then a common malady in mosquito-infested Florida.

Historian Byron Rhode says in his book *Punta Gorda Remembered* that "drug companies bought his secret formulas, and the famous 666 is still being sold by the Monticello Drug Company of Jacksonville."

Roberts died of tuberculosis at age 41. An obituary in the *Herald* stated: "For several months, Dr. W.A. Roberts had been in declining health. His condition had become to serious that on Oct. 23rd he was taken to the State Sanitarium to be given expert treatment. However, all efforts were unavailing. He passed away on Sunday, Nov. 1st and was brought here Tuesday for internment — just 16 years to the day since he first came to Punta Gorda.

"Born at Hamilton, Miss., Nov. 21, 1867, Dr. Roberts moved to Vaiden, Miss. until 1885. Then he came to Florida, locating first at Sumterville, where his parents had settled. Having held responsible positions in drug stores at Jacksonville, Tavares, Dade City and Tampa, he came to Punta Gorda Nov. 3, 1892, to engage in business for himself.

"He was married in this city on March 1st, 1893, to Miss Mattie Swift, and five children were born to them. Internment was at Creek Cemetery (Indian Springs)."

Rhode says that after Roberts' death, Mattie sold the drug business to Dr. Grover Cochran whose son Charlie managed it. About 1916, the Cochrans moved the drug store to west Marion Avenue in a building which later became now Bill's Bar. Mrs. Roberts moved to Miami with her sons.

Another Claim

In preparing this article, your writer interviewed Garnet Ashby, president of the Monticello Drug Co. to verify the local account of Walter Roberts' secret formula. According to company records, Dr. J.R. McEachern of Monticello, Fla., wrote a prescription for a patient with malaria. The patient had the prescription filled at a drug store operated by P.S. Roberts. The patient made such a complete and rapid recovery Roberts put up the prescription in bottles, naming it 666 which was the file number in his prescription book.

A corporation for volume production and distribution was formed March 14, 1908, by P.S. Roberts and his younger brother Thurston. Ashby is a descendent of Tharp Roberts, another brother. Later the company was moved to Jacksonville. As malaria was brought under control, the 666 formula was changed to a general tonic. The coincidence of names for druggists at Punta Gorda and Monticello, with secret formulas that became a commercial success, remains a tantalizing subject for speculation.

Lightweight Caskets

Not all secret formulas were sold in bottles. One of the strangest concoctions was invented by Clarence P. Wilhelm, a cement contractor who moved to Punta Gorda from Wheeling, W. Va., in 1913. He started the Punta Gorda Cement Products to construct casket vaults.

Cement vaults were expensive, and so heavy they had to be handled with cranes. To overcome these disadvantages, Wilhelm began experimenting with alternate materials. He finally settled on palmetto roots which grow so abundantly in south Florida.

Roots were easily gathered. After drying, they were shredded by machine, mixed with Wilhelm's secret binder, and pressed into a mould. The final vault was cheap, rugged, and easily handled by two men. He formed the Everlas (no T) Casket Co. — raising capital through the sale of stock, mostly to "out-of-towners."

Everlas was profitable and branched out into coffins and large funerary urns. Later Wilhelm produced whole house walls, and one for an automobile service station, still sturdy at the corner of Herald Court. Palmetto roots could be molded with smooth or pebbled surfaces, painted, and applied with ordinary carpenter tools.

The first Everlas factory was in a sheet-metal building next to the present post office site. Later the operation moved to a former laundry on Cooper Street near the railroad crossing. The Wilhelm family had their

Front wall of Bright Spot service station made of palmetto roots.

245

home on Alligator Creek south of town. The Everlas company reached its peak in 1931 when it entered a float in a parade celebrating the opening of the Barron Collier Bridge. Esther McCullough, who became executive director of the Chamber of Commerce in 1937, says the company was not in existence then.

It appears that Wilhelm suffered a serious decline in health. In any event, he moved with his wife Eliza to Englewood. He died in the Venice Hospital at age 85 in 1963. Historian U.S. Cleveland says Everlas stockholders came around ever so often trying to learn Wilhelm's secret formula for palmetto roots, but they never did. Wilhelm's will discloses he had assets of only 17 shares of capital stock in Seafood Inc., "a closed corporation" worth $4,500 and a Willis automobile valued at $100.

Lettuce Cigarettes

Gerald Schaflander, of Miami, invented a process for making cigarettes without nicotine from lettuce. He elected to build a factory for making the healthy product at Punta Gorda, then a center for the cultivation of winter vegetables. He expected the area could furnish lettuce year-round. The *Herald* of Nov. 14, 1963, announced the project in a front page splash:

"A completely new industry, the manufacture of non-tobacco cigarettes, is expected to employ 450 local workers. The Notob Products, Inc., went into operation Tuesday after an unprecedented seven-day conversion of a former skating rink into a factory.

"About 35 persons are presently employed, and production is estimated at worth about $10,000 per week. These figures do not include the potential income available to local growers who will be offered contracts and seed to plant and cultivate the black-seeded Simpson lettuce from which nicotine-free cigarettes are made. The new smoke will be marketed under the name Sentry. It will be introduced nationally in the greater Miami marketing area tomorrow."

The factory was a metal Quonset structure now a sign-painting studio on Tamiami Trail near Aqui Esta Drive. Joyce Hindman, a long-time resident of Punta Gorda, says the no-nicotine cigarette was ahead of its time. "No one would invest in it. After eight months or so, the company folded — owing everybody in town who had extended credit, including several hundred dollars for meals at a hamburger stand next door."

Mrs. Keith Austin, of Punta Gorda, remembers smoking a lettuce cigarette. "It was awful." By coincidence, there is a cigarette called Sentry now being sold, but it is composed of nicotine-loaded tobacco. Perhaps lettuce cigarettes might sell in today's health-conscious market, but Schaflander's secret process is unknown.

Arson was suspected cause of the 1915 Punta Gorda railroad dock fire.

Chapter 57

VOLUNTEER, OR ELSE!

A century ago at Punta Gorda, fire fighting was strictly voluntary — but you had better volunteer, or else! As with many small towns in America, still today, fire protection at Punt Gorda depended upon citizen cooperation when the dreaded emergency arose. Names of these oft heroic citizens are lost in the mists of history inasmuch as their calls to duty were infrequent and unofficial. Yet, they were vital guardians in the days of wood-burning stoves, open-flame lamps and buildings constructed of turpentine pines.

A minute or two delay in discovering incipient fire was fatal to structures — and some times to people. Courage and exertion was necessary simply to save nearby homes and stores.

Punta Gorda in its first few years after arrival of the Florida Southern Railway in 1886 was typical of a frontier boom-town. Flimsy buildings were thrown up hurriedly in a tight cluster. A bucket brigade was about the only defense against fire.

Punta Gorda's first blaze of note was that in Nov. 1895 of Gus Hart's ship Chandlery on the southeast corner of Retta Esplanade and Cross Street (Tamiami Trail south). It quickly spread to the *Herald* newspaper shop next door. Both buildings were consumed.

Thereafter, the need for a fire department was much discussed. Nevertheless, it was not until March 16, 1897, that the city council took action. Ordinance 129 gives us a quaint account of what constituted fire protection at that time:

"Be it ordained that there shall be organized a fire department to consist, for the present, of a hook and ladder company.

"The mayor and council shall appoint a fire marshal and first and second assistant fire marshals. It shall be the duty of the fire marshal to take control of all operations at every fire. All persons attending such fires shall be under his direction and shall obey his orders.

"The fire marshal shall drill the company so that it may be efficient. He shall have the care, custody and control of all fire apparatus that may be owned by the town.

"It shall be the duty of council's fire committee to purchase a set of hooks, ladders and buckets as soon as funds are raised. Also, to get estimates for construction of cisterns or reservoirs at the mouth of all streets opening onto Marian Ave. from the south, from King to Cross streets — not less than 10 feet square, as deep as can well be made — and at other places where they may be needed.

"And to purchase fire pumps to put into said reservoirs. Also, to contract for such hose as shall be necessary for use of said pumps.

"The fire marshal, or the assistants if in charge, shall during the time of a fire have the power to call on all citizens to aid in extinguishing such fire.

Fight Fire Or Pay

"It shall be the duty of all persons — when called upon or summoned by the marshal — to put himself under his control and obey his orders. Any person who fails, neglects or refuses shall be deemed guilty of a misdemeanor and be fined not less than $10 nor more than $50, or be imprisoned not more than 60 days.

"The fire marshals shall have the same police powers as the city marshal during a fire. They shall be authorized to arrest any and all persons guilty of violating any command, law or town ordinances during such fire. In order to carry the foregoing into force, a tax of four mills on the dollar, on the state valuation of property within the corporate limits of the town, shall be collected annually.

"Signed: Leo Taufkivch, President of Council; and George W. McLane, Mayor. Attest: Thomas R. Hector, Town Clerk."

The principal piece of equipment was a two-wheel hose cart with a T-tongue. Two men pulling and two men pushing trundled the cart to the reservoir nearest a fire. When cars came into common use after World War I, the cart was hitched to the first automobile arriving at the fire house. This primitive apparatus was still in use in the early 1920's.

The fire cart was stored in the small one-story town hall of concrete blocks constructed in 1899 on the site of today's city hall. An artesian well was drilled in back of the town hall to supply a rudimentary water main.

Water pressure was provided by the well itself. With this improvement, it was felt the fire reservoirs were not needed, and the fire marshals seem to have drifted into inactivity.

The *Punta Gorda Herald* of March 1902 noted: "A few years ago, seven large wells, each eight feet square, were dug for fire protection. They have become stagnant, and Council should fill them in." Council hired P.S. Cook to do so at a cost of $59.

Biggest Fire

The biggest fire of Punta Gorda's history broke out at 2 a.m. on March 18, 1905, in the H.W. Smith Bakery. The Smiths lived on the second floor and barely escaped with their lives. Within the hour, two blocks of stores were ablaze. (For details, see chapter 84, *Our Fascinating Past: Charlotte Harbor Early Years*).

Reported the *Herald*: "Progress of the conflagration was stopped at Register's place by extraordinary exertions of a throng of willing workers. This was accomplished by the help of apparatus at Hotel Punta Gorda. As soon as Manager Concannon was aroused, he had the hotel engines fired up and the hose ready. But there was only one line of hose available. This had to do double duty in protecting the hotel and throwing water on the burning buildings opposite. Otherwise, the fire might have been checked sooner. The disaster emphasizes the imperative need of fire protection. Everyone is agreed on this."

Council's first reaction was in June 1906 to construct a system of waterworks with a tower and 30,000-gallon steel tank at the corner of Virginia Ave. and King St. (now Tamiami Trail north). A year later, the town levied a "special fire department indebtedness tax" to expand the water mains and drill a second city well. The *Herald* said one was "to supply the public drinking fountain and the other to furnish fire protection through a main laid for the purpose."

Finally the "fire limits ordinance" was amended in 1908 to require all buildings on lots in blocks 4, 5, 6, 7, 31, 32, 33 and 34 --- the main business district "must be constructed of concrete, steel, iron, cement, brick or stone." These measures were not enough to minimize a series of destructive fires soon after.

A second great fire, in 1912, wiped out the main businesses that had escaped the 1905 disaster. Included were the King Commercial Hotel, and the Wotitzky General Merchandise Store.

The following year in October, a fire destroyed the Welch Block, livery stable, and Punta Gorda Hardware. The big Punta Gorda Cigar Factory, constructed in June, burned to the ground in December.

In January, fire destroyed the home of Mr. and Mrs. Jesse Sandlin on Sullivan Street. Said the *Herald*: "It is supposed the fire started from the kitchen flue, but the whole house was in flames when discovered. Mrs.

Sandlin was in the kitchen at the time, but was very busily engaged with her work and knew nothing of the fire until Mr. Sandlin and some friends rushed in to help fight the flames which rapidly consumed everything in spite of most desperate fighting.

"Good work was done in saving other nearby residences — which caught several times. Although men and boys, both white and colored, worked heroically, and accomplished good results, an organized, volunteer fire department would prove effective in these instances. A.H. Horn, the tailor, advocated in the board of trade a year ago that a fire department should be formed. It would have been better had it been done long ago."

Punta Gorda's first fire engines were kept in Hewitt's Garage. Men that can be identified in this 1926 photo are, from left, front row, first truck (a Seagrave)— Floyd Chadwick and Ira Atkinson. Back row, Chief Cleve Cleveland, Percy Wilhelm, unknown, unknown. Second truck (a LaFrance) — Arnold "Slim" Keys, unknown, Ebbie Rountree.

The council's fire and water committee came under heavy criticism for the recent, uncontrolled blazes. At the council meeting of Jan. 13, 1914, Councilor Norman Hewitt lashed out at Councilor Clay Chadwick.

Declared Hewitt: "In view of the fact that the people of Punta Gorda are condemning the town council for not providing some means of fire protection, I wish to place the blame where it belongs.

"After the Welch fire, I, being a member of the fire and water committee with Mr. (E.W.) Rountree, brought the matter up of connecting the water mains to the ice plant, which was agreed upon. I made arrangements with the hotel people and the ice factory to have immediate pressure on the whole city main — as soon as the alarm was given — by connecting to the hotel and shutting of the town well.

"Mr. Chadwick, when he finds the water cut off from his house — for which he has never paid any rent — forcibly enters the town hall and opens the valve on the city well, thereby making a pressure impossible until the valve should again be closed.

"As he was not a member of the fire and water committee at the time, and had no right to open the valve, I prefer charges (against Mr. Chadwick) of malfeasance and misfeasance while in office. Through his actions, water pressure could not be had until after the Sandlin property had burned down." Chadwick did not reply, and the matter never came up again.

Dock In Flames

Fortunately, the water pressure problems were solved before the great fire of June, 1915. Five fish-packing houses, five box cars, two skiffs, and a portion of the railroad dock were destroyed. It was not known how the fire started at 4 a.m., but arson by a disgruntled fisherman was suspected.

The *Herald* reported: "The alarm brought out all the people of the town. Men put forth heroic efforts to stop progress of the flames. Good work was done in saving the two packing houses that are left standing on the wharf, as well as several boats that were moored there.

"If it had not been for several sections of defective hose, even better work might have been done. A good pressure was kept on the water mains during the fire. However, much of the effect of it was lost in the bursting of weak hose and the leaking of other portions that were gotten hold of in the hurry to get a line to the fire.

"It is considered remarkable that the Standard Oil Company's supply tanks that are not very far from the railroad wharf, and were subjected to intense heat, did not blow up and burn."

251

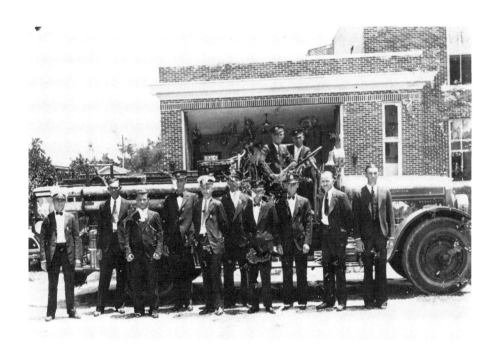

Punta Gorda firemen in 1931 at the new city hall station. From left: Elton Ingraham, Jude Forbes, Edgar Johnson, Arnold "Slim" Keys, Ira Atkinson, Percy Wilhelm, Carl Pittman, Kenneth Moriarity, John Jack, Elvin Rountree. On seat: Ebbie Rountree, Fred Bell.

Chapter 58

SEMI-PAID FIRE DEPARTMENT

The modern era of the Punta Gorda fire department began in 1922 when the city bought its first fire truck — a used, British-built Seagrave with right-hand drive. Cleve Cleveland, an electrician in charge of the city's power system for street lights, was appointed fire chief. The engine was kept in the shed behind the little, concrete-block city hall where the present city hall now stands.

Fires were reported to the ice factory at King Street (Tamiami Trail north) and Virginia Avenue. The engineer blew a long blast of the factory's big steam whistle — followed by a number of short blasts indicating the part of town where the fire was located.

Cleveland drove the fire engine to the fire and hooked up a hose while volunteers rushed to the scene — guided by smoke or glow in the sky.

The original city hall was demolished in 1926 to make way for today's structure. Included in the plans were larger offices, a two-truck fire station and a second-floor apartment for the fire engine driver. While the new city hall was under construction, the council reorganized the fire department.

252

Ordinance 46-1927 established once again a volunteer department — but this time with some compensation for the firemen.

The department consisted of a chief, assistant chief, and not less than 10 nor more than 20 firemen. All were issued badges. A fireman to be known as chief engineer had "exclusive charge of the fire engine and shall drive same under direction of the chief." The city made sure that the chief engineer earned his keep.

The ordinance specified that "his time during the customary working hours, when not required by the fire department, shall be at the service of the city, under direction of the City [Council]." For this special service, a regular salary of $125 per month was paid. Chief Cleveland was compensated at the rate of $25 per month — providing he did not fail to attend each fire alarm and practice drill. The assistant fire chief received $4 for each alarm and drill. Firemen received $3 for alarms and $1 for drills.

Mysterious Brush Fires

Pay for firemen was computed at the end of the month. Folks noticed that if there was no fire activity in the first three weeks or so of a month, mysterious grass fires occurred on the last day or two.

A suspicious city council then amended the ordinance to set up a salary scale — $15 per month for the assistant fire chief and $10 for firemen. The number of late-month brush fires dwindled remarkably.

Though the first, volunteer fire department was organized in 1897, the first fire chief of record is Cleve Cleveland, father of Historian U.S. Cleveland. Apparently city officials kept no records of firemen until they were put on the public payroll.

Chief Cleveland and other firemen were recognized in the *Punta Gorda Herald* of October 1926 for saving the Chadwick Apartments from destruction. The structure was built in 1896 as a full-grades school house, then converted to apartments in the early 1920s by Councilman Clay Chadwick. The building still stands on Goldstein St. and is listed on the National Register of Historic Places.

Reported the *Herald:* "Flames which rolled their dense smoke from the roof and windows for nearly a half-hour threatened destruction of the building and possibly several adjoining homes. The blaze was finally put under control by the local fire department.

"The fire fighters won the praise of the city for their prompt and efficient work which was declared to have not only demonstrated the value of the equipment when well handled, but to have paid for the initial cost of the engine several times over.

"The fire resulted from the flooding of a kerosene-oil cook stove on which Mrs. Burdell, who resides in the center apartment on the second floor, was cooking dinner. When the alarm was turned in, the fire had made considerable headway and had licked its way through the ceiling to rafters in the attic. In less than two minutes the engine was at the scene of the fire and in another minute a stream of water was being turned into the room where the fire started.

"Members of the fire department responded instantly to the alarm. Great credit is being given them. A roll call would show the following to have been on the job at their respective tasks, Elton Ingraham, I. Hart, C.E. Hurd, Floyd Chadwick, George Goff, William Duffie, O. Atkinson, and Ira Atkinson who took first charge of the fire; and Cleve Cleveland, chief." It appears that Ira Atkinson was either assistant fire chief, or operator of the fire engine — or both.

Reorganized volunteer firemen in 1949 were, front row from left: Robert Barley, Harry Mack, Victor Desquin, John Clement, Earle Davis, Victor Larrison, Jetson "Joe" Smith. On running board: Curtis MacConnell, Sam McCullough. At wheel: Chief Koon. At top: Bob Hendrickson, George Hill, Ed Hendrickson and Bud Ritter.

In another *Herald* story of October 1928 regarding fire prevention week, Cleveland is named as fire chief. Others mentioned are "Fire Truck Foreman Cassidy and J.C. Lastinger."

The new city hall was completed in 1928, and Cassidy was the first occupant of the fire department's city hall apartment. Lastinger may have been a bunk-mate of Cassidy and driver of the city's newly added second fire engine — a LaFrance with right-hand drive also.

When the fire engines roared out of the city hall, firemen dashed out of their businesses or homes — often in their night clothes or just pants — and ran to intercept the trucks.

Victor Desguin, a volunteer in later years, says, "people ran to the streets to watch firemen jump aboard the speeding engines. As the truck passed, they grabbed the rear-platform rail and held on for dear life —

literally," says Desguin. "Momentum of the truck jerked them nearly horizontal. They had to struggle to get aboard. It was daredevil stuff.

"I was getting a haircut one day when the alarm sounded, I ran out on Marion Avenue, still draped in the barber's apron, to catch the fire truck. I got my arms tangled in the apron and grabbed the rail with only one hand. It's a wonder I wasn't killed."

Ebby Rountree and Red Johnson, young bachelors, were the next fire-engine drivers, in 1933-35, to live at city hall. Johnson moved away, and Rountree gave up the live-in job to help manage the family's Coca Cola bottling plant. He married in 1937 and became fire chief a year later.

Henry Koon, with his wife and children, lived in the city hall for many years while he tended the fire engines. He continued as driver after being appointed chief — as did many chiefs thereafter.

Inasmuch as the Punta Gorda fire department was the only one in the county in the 1920's, the volunteers there were called on to fight fires out in the country. This was a futile exercise because there were no ponds or open wells from which to draw water in most cases — not that it would make much difference. Before the firemen could cover the distance, buildings were beyond saving.

Consequently, Punta Gorda in July 1927 adopted an ordinance "forbidding" the fire department to answer calls outside the city limits. Nevertheless, the department responded to two fires in Charlotte Harbor Town across the bridge. As usual, the fires were out of control when the Punta Gorda firemen arrived.

Only One Fireman

The Great Depression of the 1930's deprived municipalities of funds fire fighting equipment. Then the war drained away local volunteer firemen. Henry Koon was the only fireman on hand.

The *Herald* in May 1944 reported; "The fire department, disorganized for the last seven years, will be reorganized. Chief Henry Koon and James Oliver are employed on a part-time basis."

It was not until after World War II that Englewood, El Jobean, and Charlotte Harbor Town organized their own volunteer fire departments.

Also after World War II, Punta Gorda's fire department was expanded. Prime mover for a larger volunteer department was Cliff Daniels who came there in 1947 for his wife's health. His first job was pumping gasoline, but he soon opened a marine engineering firm.

Daniels had been here only a year when the Texaco bulk gasoline plant on Nesbit Street caught fire. He was shocked to see Koon pull up, alone, in the old Seagrave engine. The venerable fire fighter wrestled out the hose, dragged it to a hydrant and turned on the water. The hose writhed like a great snake, spewing water in all directions, until Koon raced to the nozzle and brought it to bear on the spectacular blaze.

Daniels went to Bert Sellin, superintendent of public works and suggested they recruit firemen. They asked the government for a gasoline tanker stored at the Punta Gorda Army Airfield, closed after the war, so they could convert it to a water tanker. The Army said it could release the '44 Chevrolet tanker only if it was used for the whole county. A used Mack fire engine was purchased from a Long Island, N.Y. fire department, and the old LaFrance truck sold to Bucky McQueen.

A new, enthusiastic band of firemen were given a week of training by the State fire marshal. Victor Desguin, one of the new volunteers, says they were anxious to demonstrate their skill and equipment.

"Chief Daniels cooked up a scheme we were sure would impress the town. At the time, I operated the movie theater on Marion Avenue. We thought we would stage a fire on a vacant lot across the street when the movie was over and a lot of people would be coming out.

Bonfire Backfires

"We dug a pit and filled it with lumber, old tires and crankcase oil. It was arranged that as the movie neared an end I would call Daniels, and the fire department would roar up to douse the flames.

"To make sure there were no hitches, we went out that afternoon to grease the hydrant cap and valve stem so they could be spun off by hand. Unfortunately, the waterworks supervisor came by later that day and noticed the hydrant dripping. He wrenched the cap and valve stem down tight, very tight.

"Upon my signal that night, a fireman lit the bonfire. A big crowd was on hand as we roared up. Try as hard as we might, we couldn't get the cap off or turn the valve stem. By the time we sent back for a bigger wrench, the fire burned out."

The roll of fire chiefs is difficult to compile because of lack of records. The following list incorporates memories of old-time firemen, but is believed to be accurate as to order of succession. Their dates, however, are incomplete:

Cleve Cleveland 1922-30, Ebby Rountree 1931, Bill Johns, Henry Koon 1938-47, Cliff Daniels 1948, Jetson "Joe" Smith 1951, Earle Davis 1960, Robert Barley 1961-66, Jetson "Joe" Smith second appointment 1966-70, George M. Hill 1971-77 (the last volunteer chief and first fully-salaried chief), Donald Romer 1977-88, Ed Keeler 1989-95 and William Dryburgh 1995-present.

The Florida panther is the largest American cat.

Chapter 59

LAST, UNREGULATED HUNT BAGS PANTHER

As the nation's last frontier, south Florida continued a commercial hunting and fishing haven well into the 20th Century. George Rhode, Punta Gorda postmaster from 1913 to 1921, gives us a graphic account of Everglades hunting in his fur-trapping expedition shortly after he retired

The hunt was one of the last before permits and limits were imposed to protect game — particularly endangered species.

Rhode was a young policeman at Tampa when he heard there was a promising opportunity at Punta Gorda for another grocery. He and another policeman, Henry Smith, moved their families here in 1906. Rhode went to work in the post office. Smith opened a bakery (for details, see Chap.. 4 *Our Fascinating Past — Early Years.*)

Upon leaving the post office, Rhode set out on a boyhood dream to explore and hunt in the Everglades wilderness. Alexander Kinsel, a Punta Gorda tanner and fur trader, offered to purchase all the pelts Rhode could bring in after a winter and spring of hunting. Rhode hired a young guide named John Bodiford to throw in with him. They packed a wagon with ammunition and supplies pulled by Rhode's mule, Frank; and Bodiford's horse, Peter. Accompanying them were several dogs: Rover, Florence,

Mutt, and Dixie. Enroute they bought two experienced coon dogs: Old Bull and Trixie.

After the successful expedition, Rhode wrote a highly readable account of his adventures. Following is his encounter with a panther:

Old Bull was guaranteed to kill the biggest coon in the 'glades single handed, to rout the fiercest wildcat and put him to tree. This is something that nothing but the best of dogs can do. A wildcat is extremely cunning, and his trail is very hard to follow. He has many smart and unexpected tricks to work on pursuing dogs. He will certainly confuse any dog that is not trained to understand them.

One thing a panther will do is to run at terrific speed for a mile or so. When he is at a sufficient distance ahead of the dogs, he will run up a tree, and jump from tree to tree 'til he has sometimes covered a distance of 50 yards or more. Then he will jump off as far as he can from the last tree, run on fast as he can to another, then do the same as before.

Tactics Of A Pursued Panther

The prairie is dotted with small hammocks covering from one to three acres each. It is to one of these that the cat generally goes when chased. If one is not within reach, he will run at top speed for a couple of miles, then turn abruptly on his trail and follow it back — almost track for track — for half a mile. After awhile he will rise and leap sometimes 25 feet straight to one side. Then, running at right angles, he will repeat the process over and over. When most dogs come to the place where the cat doubled back — unless they are well trained to know the difference — they think they are at the end of the trail and give up. But not so with Old Bull. He seemed to know from the first that he was expected to lead and instruct the other dogs. They immediately accepted his leadership as a matter of course.

Many an exhilarating and soul-stirring chase have we followed this pack through forest and glade — sometimes on horses, sometimes on foot — always at top speed and under the greatest excitement.

Sometimes the topography of the country was such that it would not permit horseback riding — especially in the marshes and glades. When we came to these, we would tie our mounts to a sapling and rush right in after the dogs.

On one occasion, as we were riding along on the edge of the timber line, all at once Old Bull opened up in his deep bass voice off about 200 yards to the right.

Immediately, Trixie, who was off in the marsh to the left, came by like a stone shot out of a catapult. In less time that it takes to tell, she had joined him — barking at every breath like her life depended on it. Then Florence and Rover took up the refrain. Such music none but lovers of the woods and the chase can appreciate.

258

It seemed like one bark could not get out fast enough for the others, and all going at once right down through the woods like a whirlwind. John and I followed at top speed for perhaps a mile.

We came up to the dogs all in a circle around a huge live oak, except Old Bull, all looking up the tree, jumping, barking, scratching and trying to climb the tree.

As we came dashing up, John said, "They've got him treed, sure as shooting!" But when I saw that Old Bull was not there taking part in the enthusiasm, I began to look for a reason. I saw at once he was running in a circle around the tree — off about 30 feet, not saying a word. He continued to run at break-neck speed around the harangue the others were making at the tree. Every circle got larger and larger. At every bound, his speed got faster and faster until Old Bull had reached a point about 100 yards from the oak. Then he broke loose in a wild ecstasy of yelps and barks and bounded away at top speed.

The other dogs at once forgot the tree and put every pound of strength and energy into the task of keeping up with Old Bull. They yelped like grim life depended on it, and with a different note in their voices representing every note in the scale. They had not gone more than 20 yards before they met Old Bull coming back, down the back-track.

Old Bull In Lead

In a few minutes, the whole pack passed us off in the south. Old Bull was still in the lead, eyes gleaming, nostrils extended and bristles raised, sides heaving. By that time, his voice had reached almost the intensity of a bass drum. At break-neck speed, the whole business plunged off into the marsh. We could hear the dogs making a beeline for the timber which they soon entered. The cat was periodically playing one of his confusing tricks to try to throw the dogs off.

However, Old Bull simply refused to be thrown off the scent. Each time the cat jumped from a tree, Old Bull he made one of his series of circles and came bounding back over the backtrack — with nose high in the air — to where the cat had sidetracked.

But always and ever, on and on, with the other dogs at his heel in vehement pursuit. In hot pursuit, I stumbled into rivulet of water and muck up to my chin. My shells and watch were ruined. John had to come back and rescue me.

When John and I reached the timber I could hear the dogs, half a mile away. With a thrill I suddenly realized that Old Bull had changed his bow-wow to boul-boul-w-l-l-!. I knew at once that he had treed. From the uproar and confusion of barks coming from the same vicinity, I knew the whole pack was there backing him up.

I yelled the news to John. At a time like this, one has to approach the tree stealthily or the cat will leap out and be gone before the hunter gets in range. I told John to go and shoot the cat, as my shells were all swelled up. He held out a handful of shells. With an "after-you-my-dear-Alphonse" tone in his voice, he insisted that I could shoot so much more accurately than he that he would not deprive me of the honor.

Now, if you have never approached a tree under similar conditions you will now know how to appreciate our spirit of unselfishness in each of us seeking to confer the privilege on the other. Realizing that we must take action at once — or the cat would get rested and again be dashing away — I took the shells and filled my Winchester shotgun full.

I carefully approached to within about a hundred yards; and then on my stomach, 'til I had worked myself up to within about 40 yards. There in a fork about 20 feet from the ground lay the cat — eyes green and glaring, hair all turned the wrong way, tail lashing on the tree from side to side, and emitting hair-raising screams and growls.

I raised my old gun. At the click of the lock the cat looked at me. I took careful sight between his eyes. At he crack of my gun he sprang into the air — I am satisfied it was 20 feet in my direction — with teeth bared and claws extended to their greatest length. Before the cat reached the ground I let him have another load of buckshot right behind the shoulder. When he hit the ground he was dead. I frantically beckoned for John to hurry. When he got to where he could see the animal and the dogs — who had turned tail in sudden terror and begun to run when the cat leaped. I said, "Look what a big wildcat!"

And he, looking in thunderstruck amazement, replied, "Good Lord, man, you've killed the biggest panther I ever saw!" If it hadn't been too late, I would have run even then. The panther measured nine feet from tip to tip. It was so heavy we could not get him to camp. We skinned him then and there. I sent the skin to Kinsel to make a rug for my wife's bedroom, where it has reposed ever since as a souvenir of our winter's stay in the 'glades.

"The bear was a monster, the first we had ever seen!"
Chapter 60

GAVE BEAR AND COONS MUCH RESPECT

Though the hunt and kill of a huge panther was exciting — as related in the preceding chapter — George Rhode and John Bodiford of Punta Gorda climaxed their winter-long expedition with greater adventure in an ordinary "cabbage hammock."

It was with great expectation that Rhode and Bodiford pitched camp in a large cabbage hammock. They cut out a number of cabbage buds for their supper of quail, rice, fried corn cakes and coffee. Rhode gives the recipe for swamp cabbage in his memoir of their 1921 hunt — one of the last before game limits were imposed:

"Use only the softest, tender part. The other is bitter. Cut it up fine, put it in a vessel, cover with water and boil thoroughly. Pour off the water and put in more cabbage. Stew thoroughly. Add a small piece of bacon and a little milk or butter to season. Then you have a vegetable dish as palatable as any you have ever tasted."

Alexander Kinsel, a Punta Gorda tanner and fur dealer, had offered to buy all the game pelts Rhode and Bodiford could bring back. The main quarry was raccoons. The animals were numerous and dangerous when cornered, but their pelts brought good prices.

The frontier methods of catching coons were trapping, chasing with dogs and "still hunting." Following is Rhode's story in his own words

One day while we were camped in a small hammock of pines and cabbage palms, up at the head of a little stream, I decided to go on a still hunt. That is, without any dogs who run down and tree coons for you. You go through the woods, looking into all the trees, especially the cabbages, and find coons lying on the limbs.

On this particular day, the dogs were all fagged out by virtue of having chased a wildcat and fox to the finish. The dogs' feet were worn out, and I wished to have them rest up for the next day. Accordingly, I tied them up to keep them from following.

Coon Asleep In Palm Top

I took my gun and strolled through the woods about a mile when I found the first coon. I noticed the top of a cabbage that was standing off by itself. A dark, thick place did not shine light through as clearly as it ought. When I got within 40 yards I spotted a coon, a big one, cuddled up in the bud of the cabbage as nice as you please, taking his morning nap.

I hated to interrupt his beauty rest but did not know any other way to get that fur coat he was wearing. So I leveled my old shotgun and blazed away. At the crack of the gun the coon didn't fall out as you might think. The fans and stalks of the tree were so thick he couldn't fall through. He simply sank down into them and died, lodged in the top about 20 feet from the ground. I wondered how to get the coon down. I decided to climb the palm and throw him out. I saw that I could easily shinny up to the top. Did you ever climb a cabbage? I did, that one. It was my first and also my last! I had heard that a bear would climb up and pull out the bud then turn loose and fall out. I never could understand, until my own experience, why a bear would risk a broken leg or neck rather than climb down. I found out the secret the hard way.

Going up was simple. I got hold of the old fellow by the leg and threw him to the ground. However, when I undertook the descent I met with a disagreeable surprise. I found out what I never knew before. The trunk of a cabbage palm is covered with tiny spikes, or "beards." They are something like fish hooks — all pointing upward. Climbing up is easy, but coming down is painful. If these spikes, or beards, pierce one's flesh, they are not nearly so easy to get rid of as they are to acquire. They are like the poet's flea — of which he said:

> *Larger fleas have smaller fleas*
> *Upon their backs to bite 'em,*
> *And smaller fleas have smaller fleas,*
> *and so on infinitum.*

262

Well, large cabbage palm beards have smaller beards. Their nature is to hold on and to work farther into the flesh. The more you try to remove it, the farther it is pushed in. It is necessary to cut the thing out bodily or let it stay in until you can poultice it out.

I soon found out that I could not hang there on the side of that tree indefinitely, for my strength would soon give out. Therefore, I struggled on up into the top foliage.

I settled down comfortably to try and figure out what to do next. Glancing over my shoulder, I discovered another old coon about four feet away among the fans. He was as ugly and vicious as you care to encounter. My intrusion did not seem to soothe his temper. He was already cocked and primed for a fight and was coming for me with all haste. I had only a second to decide what to do. I arose and grabbed about three or four fans and sailed out.

The fans swung me down about eight feet — giving me a chance to swing myself clear of the tree and jump. Luckily I landed on my feet unhurt, though shaken up.

Coon Lunged

I looked up and saw that the coon had made such a fierce lunge at me that he followed me clear out on the stems to which I had lately occupied. He was swinging and holding on for dear life. Quickly, I grabbed my gun and sent the usual remedy for such conditions up after him, viz, a load of number-four shot. I scored a fair hit, and he came tumbling to my feet.

Thus, I had two, big, nice coons whose pelts would add to my collection. To save the carcasses for the dogs, I swung the coons over one shoulder and my gun on the other. On the way to camp, I came square upon a soft-shell turtle — as fine a one as I ever saw. He had his head and neck run out about six inches. I threw my coons down and shot his head off. He was a dandy — must have weighed 20 pounds.

I tied the coons to each end of my rifle so I could carry the lot, Chinese style, on one shoulder. This freed my right hand to grasp the turtle. I had some difficulty grabbing one of his legs because a turtle will jump and jerk several hours after his head is cut off. Back at camp we dressed the turtle and carved off enough meat for supper. He made us four good meals. Turtle meat is sweet and tender. The flesh represents every imaginable kind of meat — chicken, quail, fish, steak, etc. Out of the forest or stream there comes no finer meat for food, and no better material for soup — especially with a mess of swamp cabbage.

Next day we took the dogs and walked up the creek in search of whatever we might be able to capture. A hundred yards from camp the dogs struck up a lively pace. Old Bull gave me the knowing howl which said "coon" just as plainly as words would have done. As we went breaking through the scrub of palmetto and gallberries, as high or higher than our heads, we came upon a cow trail where the dogs were running at top speed. Some were yelping, some howling, some whining, some screeching. They were after an object of contention.

We heard a big animal crashing through the bushes long before it hove into sight. My, what a racket! It sounded like a bunch of cattle — with the dogs in hot pursuit.

We stood with guns in hand, ready for any emergency we thought. All at once, there burst into view, about 20 feet from us in the trail, a big bear! He was a monster, the first that either of us had ever seen. The bear was fleeing at full speed from the dogs and had his whole mind and attention fixed on them. He was following the trail in order to increase his speed. We imagined the animal was coming down to get us. We had no idea whatever of offering any resistance.

John, in the lead, saw the bear first. I could not imagine what had come over him when he, without previous ceremony, dashed back toward me in the greatest excitement. He yelled, "Run, run! My Lord, Rhode, run!" Looking up, I saw the brute coming. I jumped aside just in time for John to pass. I took out after him. About the second jump, I stepped into a stump hole, turned my ankle over and hit the ground on my stomach so hard I bounced.

As I went down, I saw something making a streak through the gallberries. This I judged to be John; so I yelled out to him, "Oh, John, ain't you going to stay with me?"

Going My Way

He yelled over his shoulder with out slowing, "Yes, if you're going my way." I hobbled on and soon found John scaling a tall, slim sapling. He was going up that sapling like a squirrel.

I had to laugh, for as he climbed up, the sapling gradually bent over `til he was lying on the ground with his back in the grass. He was hugging the sapling tight in his arms and yelling for me to "Run! Run!" I limped over and peered down at him. With all the power of emphasis at this command, John shouted at me, "Don't come up here, you darned fool! Get yourself another tree. Can't you see this one won't hold both of us?"

I replied, "Well, John, the bear's gone. You can come down." He looked around cautiously to see if I was right. Then, he turned loose and got on his feet. I don't think he ever realized the ridiculous position he had presented. One thing sure, we never got the bear.

On the way back to camp, I said, "John, why were you running so from that bear?" He replied indignantly, "I wasn't running away. I was only going as fast as I could to try and head off the dogs."

Soon after this incident we decided to turn our course toward home, hunting as we went. We arrived back at Punta Gorda with 672 coon skins, 73 possums, 23 otters, and 12 foxes. These netted us $1,186.45.

Tom Ray examines the warning to moonshiners carved into a tree.

Chapter 61

MOONSHINERS RESPOND TO VOLSTEAD ACT

Moonshine stills have been popular money makers ever since the government started taxing whiskey in 1794 and brought on an insurrection of Pennsylvania farmers.

Early settlers here brewed alcohol with the same fervor — sheltered by the jungles of trees and palmettos. The Women's Christian Temperance, Union popularized by Carry Nation between 1900-1911 made secret distillation of tax-free whiskey immoral as well as illegal.

The famous saloon buster visited Punta Gorda and Arcadia but found no dens of inequity to trash. The WCTU had already persuaded DeSoto County voters, including those in what is now Charlotte, to go "dry."

Local option prohibition simply drove alcohol indulgence under ground to join the suppliers. Live and let live was the tacit understanding until the First World War. Congress then passed the Volstead Prohibition Enforcement Act as a war measure over the veto of President Woodrow Wilson.

A majority of states ratified it as the 18th Amendment to the Constitution in January 1919, but repealed it as a failed social experiment in Dec. 1933. During the 15 years of "prohibition," distillation of alcohol in strengths above 0.5 percent became big business throughout the nation — including Charlotte County. Oldtimers state, "There was a still behind every palmetto."

At first, "farming in the woods" was a minor infraction — of concern only to federal revenue agents. By the late 1920's, however, "revenuers" began offering rewards to local sheriffs for busting a still. The usual "commission" for raiding a still was $10, plus $40 for arresting and convicting an operator. In addition, the sheriff got to keep the expensive copper retorts and cooling coils which had a resale value of approximately $25 — a substantial sum in those days.

White Lightening Easy To Make

Ingredients for "White lightning" were easily available. Cracked corn was plentiful for chicken feed. Sugar cost 10 cents a pound in 100-pound sacks. Moonshiners were often recognized by their frequent purchases of corn and sugar in bulk. The corn was partly boiled into "mash." Then sugar, water and "starter yeast" from the preceding batch was added. After a couple weeks of fermentation, the fluid became a liquor of about 10 percent alcohol. The liquor was boiled. Alcohol evaporated first. This delectable steam was distilled into 200-proof "high shots" by passing it through a cooling coil commonly called a "worm."

A certain amount of poisonous "fusil oil" was distilled along with high shots. The longer the distilling process was carried out, the higher the concentration of fusil oil — and the most dangerous to drinkers. The best moonshiners then filtered high shots through hard-wood charcoal before cutting the 200-proof whiskey in half with water.

With revenue commissions available, Charlotte County Sheriff James H. Lipscomb and Deputy Ira Atkinson clamped down on moonshiners and bootleggers. The latter were distributors — mostly of imported liquors and wine.

The *Punta Gorda Herald* reported in Dec. 1926:

"What is said to have been the biggest haul of contraband liquor ever made in Charlotte County — by local or federal officers — was made Wednesday night by Deputy Sheriff C.B. Blizard and Hoyt Carlton of the

Punta Gorda Police department. They captured 610 gallons of alcohol which was being unloaded from a small boat and transferred to a Tampa bread truck. The capture was made in the vicinity of what is known as the old Long Dock, in the western part of the city, as the two men arrested were making the transfer from boat to truck. They were Percy Helveston and Charlie Longworth.

"The officers had been keeping an eye on the truck for some time — their suspicions having been aroused by the presence of the closed truck here without legitimate excuse or delivery of bread.

"The stuff captured is pure, grain alcohol put up in 5-gallon tin cans encased in wooden boxes without markings. Those familiar with such matters state that alcohol may be bought in Cuba for 95 cents a gallon, but that it brings $10 a gallon in Punta Gorda and $12 in Tampa. At the Punta Gorda price, the shipment is worth $6,100."

Local Stills Biggest

The two biggest moonshine raids occurred in late 1928. The *Punta Gorda Herald* reported the first in its issue of November:

"A 500-gallon still, used in one of the largest liquor plants ever unearthed in this section of the state, was confiscated by Sheriff Lipscomb and Deputy Atkinson who were accompanied on their Sunday night raiding party by officials from DeSoto County.

"Operators of the distillery had left when the officers arrived, but the plant was in operation with a hot fire under the retort. The still was first found by citizens of DeSoto county Sunday afternoon as they were wandering through the woods on the north side of Shell Creek near Burnt Bridge where they were having a picnic.

"Officers destroyed barrels containing over a thousand gallons of mash, and brought back a large number of 5-gallon demijohns of 'shine for evidence. Loss to the bootleggers was estimated at over a thousand dollars. It is believed destruction of the plant will somewhat cut down the flow of Christmas liquor into DeSoto County where bootleggers operating the still found the market for their product."

Peter Ray and his son now own a large grove of oranges on the south bank of Shell Creek containing remnants of the first bridge built across the stream about 1890. The wooden bridge was a rickety affair replaced a mile downstream by a steel bridge in 1909 — perhaps when the old wagon bridge burned. The steel bridge was replaced by today's concrete bridge carrying State Highway 17 over Shell creek.

Lipscomb's raid did not put the moonshiners out of business for long. They simply moved across the creek. Location on the stream apparently was important in order to move finished whiskey to market by motor launch. This new site was tipped off by someone who discovered it in 1930. Once again, Lipscomb and Atkinson raided the still.

The operators had built a dirt causeway along a tributary of the creek up to high ground. In addition to the usual equipment and 5-gallon glass jugs in wooden crates, the law officers noted an inscription carved on a tree: "I know you now boys so watch out, and where you live too. Mr. P." The cryptic initial probably alluded to Federal Revenue Commissioner Pinkerton at Tampa — before whom moonshiners and bootleggers were haled for trial.

The Rays have found several artifacts of the south-bank still — the door to a cast iron stove, fire bricks from a furnace holding the retort, metal hoops of barrels long ago rotted away, a brass gas-tank opener for a motor boat, and the bottom of a large, glass jug imprinted with the date 1930. Old piling that were part of the bridge construction are still visible.

Second Big Raid

The second big raid of 1928 occurred in December. Noted the *Herald:* "Two more big stills were found and demolished by Sheriff James Lipscomb and Deputies Ira Atkinson and Hoyt Carlton last week.

"The largest moonshine factory was located in the center of a swamp in Telegraph Cypress Swamp, near the southern boundary of the county. A 500-gallon plant had been constructed on an oak and palmetto island.

"It is thought that the still supplied an active trade in the Fort Myers territory. Not a single trail was found leading into it, yet, apparently it turned out more product than any other still in this section of the state. There were no signs of life — except that some of the coals were still warm, indicating that it had been operating the day before.

"There were three vats of 500-gallon capacity, all filled with mash. The worm, which is one of the most valuable parts of the equipment, had been taken away — either for repair or else hidden in case of a raid.

"The other still was discovered in a more open location close to Del Verde (an abandoned development near the intersection of state routes 31 and 74). It was declared by the sheriff as the filthiest plant he had ever seen. Later, when a shallow well from which water was obtained for the mash was examined, those inspecting the outfit found several dead rats and a decayed opossum in the bottom of the pit.

"It was concluded that the operators believed water with decomposed animal matter in it would create more active fermentation in the mash — thereby producing shine more readily, regardless of its deadly effect.

"The still at Del Verde utilized a 285-gallon gas tank as a boiler. Distillate was condensed in a long, tin pipe leading to a 5-gallon glass jug. Twenty six barrels of mash were close to the boiler, each one buried within a few inches of the top of the ground to avoid detection by hunters and other wanderers in the woods."

Byron Rhode, 14, was an active Boy Scout.

Chapter 62

GUM BALL MACHINE ATE PENNIES

You can take the boy out of the country, but you can't take Byron Rhode out of Punta Gorda.

This 92-year-old historian now lives in retirement in Charlotte Harbor. His powers of memory are phenomenal. Through his active correspondence with U.S. Cleveland, Esther McCullough and others, he still contributes fascinating anecdotes of his childhood and early adult life at Punta Gorda over a span of 35 years.

Rhode (no "s," please) was born in 1904 on a homestead farm near Williston, Fla. His parents, George D. and Docia (nee Cason) Rhode, moved to Punta Gorda with Byron when he was just two years old.

Some ten years ago Byron set down his vivid recollections in a book *Punta Gorda Remembered,* now out of print. Additional memories herein, give us insight to life in a time and place that is no more.

When my oldest sister and I were very small we used to walk to the Methodist Church and Sunday school. Old Grampa Griggs was the teacher. On the way we passed a sort of gum ball machine fastened outside to the front of Farmer King's store. Inside the machine was a toy, mechanical man. You put your penny in a slot. The little man would turn around and drop a piece of gum in a chute. This machine got all my Sunday school pennies until someone told my Dad. He tore by butt, and I stopped giving my pennies to the little man.

Later on we lived out on Taylor Road. Every Sunday us kids — by then Irma, Pauline and Lucille — used to hitch our old, black horse named Dock to the buggy and drive him to Sunday school. We always brought several other kids home with us to eat dinner.

Ice For Tea A Treat

On the way home we would go by the ice plant and buy a piece of ice for 10 cents so we could have iced tea for dinner.

We always had plenty to eat. We raised all kinds of vegetables and fruits. Mama canned a lot of stuff — guavas, jelly, marmalade. We raised pineapples, mangoes and avocados. We had a cane patch, and made our own syrup. We had chickens, ducks, turkeys, and guineas. Best of all, she made deep-dish guava pie — in my book the best ever.

My Dad was in the grocery business at first and then was postmaster. However, he felt we should be self sufficient. He built our house at night after work while I held the lantern.

Charlie Simmons was the local ice man. He delivered ice in a covered wagon pulled by a mule. Mr. Simmons sawed off what ever you needed from 300-pound blocks, carried the ice to your back door and put it in the kitchen ice-box. He hollered and came on in. Nobody locked their doors in those days. He tore off a pre-paid coupon from an ice-book hanging on the wall. In the meantime, the mule moved on down to the next house and would be waiting. He knew the route as well as Mr. Simmons.

There was an old Negro man named Sam Kennedy who used to push a wheelbarrow with dirt in it and a bucket of splinters. He had a small fire on the dirt. He would go from house to house at daybreak — or before — come in, and build a fire in your stove or fireplace for a small fee while you got a few extra minutes to snooze.

About the most exciting things were the minstrel shows that came to town for one-night stands — F.S. Wolcott's Rabbit Foot Show, Silas Green from New Orleans, etc. They used to set up their big tents on a vacant lot by Nettie John's Travelers' Hotel. Those Negro minstrels came in on the noon train, always had a parade. Then there were the road shows such as Jack King's Comedians, Williams' Stock Company, Great American Combined Railroad Show, and Kritchfield's Ten Nights In A Bar Room.

Carnivals had ferris wheels and merry-go-rounds powered by their own steam engines. The Chautauquas came and stayed a week, giving lectures on a variety of interesting subjects.

I think those road show parades induced Eddie Smith to organize a band. I used to beat the big, bass drum. We had a band stand down by the city dock at the foot of Sullivan St. The stand was a gift to us and the city by Judge William Fenimore Cooper from Chicago who had a beautiful winter home on Marion Avenue (now gone) He liked to hear us play, and gave us money from time to time for things the band needed.

The judge was asked to go somewhere one night, but he declined, saying, "Oh, no, I can't go, it's band practice night; and that's better than a three-ring circus."

We practiced in the little old concrete City Hall. At that time, the fire department was a shed on the side. The fire pump was sort of a two-wheel cart with a hose on it. It had a T-shaped tongue. Men would take hold of it and run to the fire. Later on they pulled it behind a car.

The fire alarm was a series of blasts from the steam whistle at the ice plant — whoo, whoo, whoo. Water for the pump was drawn at first from seven shallow wells dug for the purpose around town. When the water system was installed, water was drawn from the pipes.

A High Diving Tower

Before the Gilchrist Park seawall was built, the McAdow property (now Holiday Inn) extended into the bay with its own seawall. Later on the bay was dredged, the park filled in, and the seawall tied to McAdow's.

Us boys used to go over there, and go into McAdow's boat house. We changed into our bathing suits then walked the seawall to the Woman's Club bath house to swim. This way we saved 10 cents that it cost to use the bath house. On the edge of the channel was a tall diving tower that seemed 100 feet high (actually 25 feet). About every eight feet was a diving platform. You had it made when you could dive from the top.

There was a guy wire running from each corner and fastened to a piling. We used to take a piece of wire and bend it to fit over the guy wire with handles to hold onto. We would put it over the guy wire, hold onto the handle, an slide down to the water. Of course, you had to turn loose before you hit the post. One time Dick Cooper did not turn loose in time and like to have killed himself.

I remember the merchants downtown. Earnest had a dry goods store. He moved to Wauchula and Kirby Seward took over. Chadwick also had a dry goods store, Hewitt Brothers Hardware, Strong and J.S. Goff livery stables, Joe Meyerick's feed store, Benny's pool room, Henry Walker's

271

pressing club, A.J. Kinsel's first little shoe shop and later his tannery. H.W. Smith had a bakery where I worked for $60 a month, including room and board.

The town's little calaboose (jail) of two cages was located on Herald Court, as was the pound for stray cattle. You might look up Taylor Road and see Old Man (William) Duval coming to town from Acline with several yokes of oxen pulling a big wagon load of lumber.

A man named Wade had a drug store on the corner of Marion and Cross St. Out in the middle of the intersection was a big, round artesian fountain where horses and people could drink. A fish swam around in it.

The streets were just dirt. Wooden sidewalks. Stores had gas lights. The street lights were first kerosene, mounted on wooden posts at the corners. A lamp-lighter went around every evening to fill the lanterns and light them. Downtown people had outdoor privies. An old Negro named Alex Stephens went up and down the alleys — with a two-wheel cart and a white mule — cleaning out the privies for 50 cents a month.

Four-legged Gold

Cattlemen used to drive their herds down Marion Avenue to the cattle dock out near what is today's Fishermen's Village. The cattlemen would throw their saddle bags across the rail of the chutes. As a cow or steer went onto the boat, the Cuban or Spanish buyers would throw a gold piece into the open saddle bags. I have been told that when the old Punta Gorda Bank went broke, Mr. W. L. (Luther) Koon had enough gold coins stored in saddle bags at his home to reopen the bank. I knew him very well. He was a very wealthy man and president of this bank.

Although he was wealthy, he was happiest when out in the woods with his cowboys — sleeping under the stars with his saddle for a pillow and the saddle blanket to cover him and keep off the dew.

I have hunted cattle for him and camped out on his roundups. We had a little covered chuck wagon pulled by two little oxen. Food cooked out in the woods was really good. Biscuits baked in a Dutch oven over coals were out of this world.

During this time they often killed a yearling and sometimes a hog, ate some of it fresh and salted some of it down. What was left was made into beef jerky. They cut the beef into strips, then hung them on green oak limbs over a slow, smoke fire. The jerky would dry out and curl up like leather. To cook it we would cut it into chunks and boil it.

Most every cowboy had a small tin can with a wire bail tied to his saddle. When he was away from the chuck wagon, he used the can to make coffee or cook up some jerky, salt pork, or whatever he might have. Sweet potatoes were a favorite. They cooked these in the ground under the fire, cooked salt bacon on a stick over the coals, and made coffee in their little tin can.

For years, Mr. Koon kept what we called a Butcher Pen out south of town. He had a man there to butcher beef and haul it in a wagon to different markets around town. Near the pen was a pile of cow heads as big as a house — all rotting away and smelling terrible. I used to go out there to get horns and make rings to hold a Boy Scout neckerchief.

Mr. W.R. DeLoach (bank cashier) guarded Mr. Koon's money pretty well. If you needed to borrow a hundred dollars, he made you go and get two or three co-signers on your note. However, he was a friend, and I liked him.

When Dad died in 1927, Mama bought the old Charles Denham-Frank Blount house at the corner of Retta Esplanade and Cross Street (now demolished) from Cattle Baron A.C. Frizzell.

The house was painted yellow and had a porch all around the front. It had been built in 1902 by Charles Denham who was a real estate man who owned a pineapple farm and laid out a development at Charlotte Harbor Town. Frank Blount owned a grocery, and was brother to Dr. B.B. Blount and Chester who had a men's clothing store.

For years my mother lived there and operated what in those days was called a boarding house. She rented rooms and served meals for $10 a week. A few years ago I noticed the side porch had been taken off —to widen Cross Street for Tamiami Trail — and the house painted white.

Many times I have sat on the front porch there and watched the sun sink slowly down into the bay.

Baseball Fights

Punta Gorda had an amateur baseball team that played such places as Fort Ogden, Charlotte Harbor, Arcadia and Fort Myers. Lots of times these ended up in fights.

One Sunday afternoon Blanche [Byron's wife] and I went up to Fort Ogden with Harold and Olive Alexander to see a game. Mr. Rountree, his son Elvin our catcher, Johnnie Olsen, Elmer Barnhill and some others got into it. Pretty rough for awhile. Mr. Rountree's bald head got skinned up and bleeding.

As we were leaving, we passed a Fort Ogden girl. Harold, the politician, leaned out the car window and said, "How come when we come up here to play ball, you all jump on us and beat us up?"

"Beat you up?" she replied, "I wish you could see my poor old Daddy, he's all bunged up." And then she added, "But I enjoyed every minute of it!"

273

Boys hunted alligators two sell hides. These unidentified youngsters pose proudly with a trophy that could have eaten all three for dinner.

Chapter 63

KIDS HUNTED GATORS

Byron Rhode, the subject of the previous chapter, was a hard working jack-of-all-trades — typical of folks in Florida small towns emerging from the nineteenth century frontier.

In his book *Punta Gorda Remembered*, Byron lists the many jobs he held in this transition period when opportunities were scarce.

I had to quit school in the seventh grade to go to work delivering groceries for Baker Smith on my bicycle and help support my mother, sisters and invalid father. During my life I have worked in grocery stores, post office; fished with big commercial crews; been a shrimper; worked at saw mills; cut logs, snaked logs out of swamps with oxen for telegraph poles; cooked on boats and road camps; operated hotels, stores and restaurants, he writes.

His further recollections, gleaned from correspondence with old friends Esther McCullough and U.S. Cleveland, are continued here.

Twice Learned To Walk

My earliest memory of Punta Gorda was when I was about five. We were living where Irene Gatewood Adams now lives on Sullivan Street. Professor U.S. Whiteaker was assistant principal at the school on Goldstein Street (now an apartment house) and was raising hogs. I fell in love with the little pigs. Every night when I said my prayers, I would say, "God bless Mr. Whiteaker's little pigs." We later moved out to

Solana, just up the road from Five Points and across from Buttermilk Davis' place. I used to climb up to the kitchen sink to get a drink of water. One day I fell and hit my head.

I was unconscious for a time and went into a coma for about two months. When I came out of it, I was paralyzed from the waist down. My parents got a twin baby carriage to carry me around in.

After a month or so of this, I woke up one night and was so sleepy I forgot I was paralyzed. I tried to get up and go to my parents' bed but fell again. I struck my head; and great gobs of old, black blood came out my mouth, nose and ears. When the doctor came, he said, "This has done something an operation could not do! He will have to learn to walk again but will be OK." And I was.

Catching Alligators

Mr. A.J. Kinsel had a shoe shop in a little wooden building facing the RR track (in the middle of Tamiami Trail north), between Marion and Olympia avenues. He and his wife, Anna, lived in the back. Later on, Kinsel bought a lot across the railroad — between it and the ice track — down the alley. There he built a huge tin building for a tannery. You could not see the tannery, but you could sure smell it. Kinsel bought and tanned alligator hides from which he made shoes, wallets, ladies' hand bags, belts, etc. A man's belt sold for $1. Men's shoes that he sold for $5 sell for $200 or more today.

Down Burnt Store Road was a big pond called the Gator Hole. Any time of day that you went there, you could have walked across the pond stepping on gator heads. Money was tight, so Brant Lanier, Mac Whidden and I decided to make some extra money by catching alligators. We went out in the woods and cut a long cypress pole. After skinning it we cut a groove in the big end. Then we got a big meat hook and put it in the groove. We wrapped it with wire, soldering it tight. We cut a notch in the other end so we could tell which way the hook was turned.

Our other tools were a shovel, axe, and a long iron rod sharpened on one end. We cut the top out of a gasoline drum, bought a hundred-pound bag of salt and some bailing wire. We prowled the rivers and ponds, poking the iron rod along the banks to discover gator caves. When we found one, we dug a hole into the cave. Then we ran in our gator pole and jugged it around. If we felt the gator move, we tried to hook it.

After we hooked him, or her, all three of us grabbed the pole and pulled the gator out. Sometimes head first. Sometimes tail first. Sometimes doubled up. But always MAD! When we had it out, one of us grabbed the axe and chopped the gator between the eyes.

We skinned just the belly and let the carcass lay. We covered the skinned-out hide with salt. Starting at the tail, we rolled it up, bound the hide with bailing wire, and threw it into the barrel.

This was all legal, of course. Laws had not yet been made to protect alligators. We got a dollar per foot for the hides, but back then a dollar was worth something. We only sold our hides when we had a barrel full. As it took us two or three weeks, working weekends, to fill the barrel, those hides would really be smelling.

Really Messed Up

I was very friendly with Don Whiteaker. Along in the early 20's, I went with him up to Brownville where Don was courting the girl he married, Gertrude Pickering. I went to see a girl named Williams.

Neither of us had any money to speak of. We went up to Brownville on the morning train, spent the day, then came back on the night train. The fare each way was less than a dollar.

The trains did not stop at Brownville unless someone flagged it down. They had a catcher hook to pick up outgoing mail sacks on the run. The incoming mail sack was just thrown off as the train passed. As the train approached at night, we would roll up a piece of newspaper, strike a match and light the paper. Then we stood in the middle of the track and waved the torch. The engineer would give a little "toot-toot" with his whistle to let us know he would stop.

One time I was up there by myself. This Williams girl lived near the depot. I was sitting there on her porch talking to her after the train left Gardner. The engineer would blow for a couple of crossings before getting to Brownville. This alerted us that the train was coming.

I guess I got too interested in the girl this night because I didn't hear the whistle. Then I heard the steam engine coming down the track, chug-chug-chug. I jumped up and started running as fast as I could to the depot. It was a dark night. I couldn't see where I was going.

Suddenly something hit me across the knees. I fell sprawling. It was a cow lying in the road. Back then, cows and hogs ran loose. Well, I hit the ground and rolled over a couple of times. I had fallen in a pile of fresh cow manure. I was really messed up. In the meantime, the train roared on by.

There was water at the depot. I washed my self off the best I could, but I was soaking wet. I was ashamed to go back to the girl's house. I spent the night at that depot. It was winter time, and I like to have froze to death. There was a big chest affair on the platform. I got in and closed the lid to try and keep out of the wind until the morning train came and took me home.

In 1928 I went to work for the Punta Gorda Fish Company. It owned a big wooden hotel, store and post office down at Bokeelia. About a month later, some of us were sent down to Bokeelia to put a roof on the store and paint the hotel.

Painting With Toothbrush

Working in this store was a pretty, young girl, Blanche. George Mitchell, then cook on the company work boat, said to me, "We have got to paint the big hotel building." I said to him, "Is that girl going to be here?" He replied, "Yes, her sister owns the store." I said, "Well, that being the case, I will paint the whole thing myself — with a tooth brush."

I began to turn on all my good, Gemini charm. It got serious. I asked Blanche to marry me. She said, "I won't marry you as long as you are on that boat. What else can you do?" I said, "A lot of things. I do know a lot about the grocery business." She said, "I know some people who are opening stores — the Bevers with their B&B Cash Grocery chain. I will introduce you to them." These Bevers used to come into a her sister's drug store at Moore Haven for lunch and coffee.

I went to see them, to see if I could talk to them about opening a store in Punta Gorda. They asked me if I thought I could do a thousand dollars a week. I said, "Yes, that will be one hundred dollars a day and five hundred for Saturday." I didn't tell them I knew every fish crew on the coast. I was sure I could get that much business from the fishermen alone. So we made a deal. I quit the boat and opened the B&B — now the U-Save — in December 1928.

When I turned in my notice to Mr. Will Guthrie, he said, "Byron, what's the matter? Why are you quitting?" I said, "I want to get married." He said, "Well, you should keep your job. If, after you marry, you get along with your wife OK, you are home half the time. On the other hand, if you don't get along, you are gone half the time." Blanche and I got married in the Methodist Parsonage on Thursday night Feb. 7, 1929. We got along just fine. We were married almost 64 years. (Sadly, Blanche Rhode passed away in late 1992.)

Search For Pink Shrimp

The Depression was a tough time. I tried several things trying to improve my earnings. I left B&B to operate a filling station for the Standard Oil Company, then left them to work for Vasco Peeples' grocery market for $15 per week.

About this time the Home Supply Stores owned by the Lykes Brothers liquidated the chain, so Blanche and I mortgaged our home to buy the Punta Gorda store. We operated Home Supply for nine years. However, everything was credit. The city, county and state did business with scrip. No body paid us. We went broke. Then I sold insurance and operated a successful 100-seat restaurant in Fort Myers until a bank bought the building and kicked me out in 1950.

They had just discovered pink shrimp beds off Key West, and shrimping was paying big at that time. It was possible for a crew member to go out for six or seven days and make a hundred dollars a day. I got a job on a 75-foot trawler which worked the Tortugas and east coast, but not with much luck.

At Christmas we planned a short run to Tortugas. On the way, our skipper heard that shrimping was good off the Texas and Mexican coast. He turned and headed there. Forty one days later I was sitting on the stern — heading shrimp between drags — when we passed another shrimp boat with its ship-to-shore radio on full blast.

I heard my wife's voice loud and clear coming from the boat's speaker: "My name is Blanche Rhode. I am trying to locate my husband. His name is Byron Rhode and is supposed to be on the boat Lucky Strike. I have heard this boat was in a storm and lost."

We were in a bad storm, and some boats were lost. However, we came through. I got on the other boat and called her back. She said, "Come home NOW. Either get another job or another wife! I took you off a boat 20 years ago, and I'm not going to live like this." I took a job clerking for B&B in Fort Myers.

A year of so later, a salesman told me about a new chain of 39 grocery stores in Jacksonville and northern Florida owned by a Mr. Setzer and wanting a manager. I got on a bus and went up there to apply for the job. He said to me, in broken English, "Vat can you do in a grocery store?" I said, "Any damn thing you want done. I can run the store, relieve the manager, cut meat, stock shelves, order merchandise, run the office, or keep the books."

He hired me and really tried me out as a sort of trouble shooter for all his stores. After a year I received an offer as manager of a B&B store in Tampa. I told Mr. Setzer I would stay with him if he gave me a job in one place. He made me manager of his largest store in Jacksonville. I wound up my career there for 17 years.

Byron Rhode Scholarship

While I was with Setzer, I helped organize a small credit union for the employees. Setzer sold out to a national grocery chain which changed hands a couple of times and finally went broke. However, the credit union of grocery workers survived. In 1988, we were able to talk Winn Dixie into being our sponsor. They are a big outfit with over 1,200 stores. We now have a potential membership of over 100,000 members.

At our last annual meeting I was re-elected a director. The president got up to announce the credit union was establishing a Byron Rhode Scholarship "in appreciation of his many years of work and dedication to this organization."

It was a complete surprise to me. It made me very proud. Not bad for a dumb old country boy who never finished grade school!

Byron Rhode, Cleve Mays and Rev. B.F. Oswald's dog Max at Oswald's Solana pineapple packing house.

Chapter 64

PA LITTLE'S DOG HATED SHERIFFS

The best thing about Byron Rhode is that — at age 92 — events at Punta Gorda we consider history are fresh memories to him.

He was born in 1904 at Levy County, Florida, but came to Punta Gorda two years later with his parents. Blessed with a sharp memory still, his early recollections in a letter to Esther McCullough give us a vivid picture of life here at the turn of the century:

One of my early memories is of a fine, old colored man named Henry Little. His nickname was "Pa." In his younger days he was an animal trainer for a circus. He would put on parades with his trained dogs, cranes, and chickens. He sure did have them under control. They understood his commands — forward march, halt, etc.

When Little got too old to work, he bootlegged whiskey. He let his customers know a batch was ready by marching his big crane down

279

Marion Avenue. Pa lived in a one-room shack along that narrow railroad track used to haul ice down to fish dock at the foot of King Street (Tamiami Trail north). It was behind Frank Strohbar's bicycle shop.

Little had a small dog trained to climb up a special ladder to the roof and bark whenever any man in uniform came near. This was how Little got warning of approaching marshals or sheriff deputies.

Back in those days there was no welfare or Social Security. The only thing I knew that Pa Little did was to clean up, sweep out and empty cuspidors for old man Berry's pool room in a two-story building on the southeast corner of King and Marion. Berry lived upstairs.

Mr. Berry always wore the cleanest, whitest, starched and ironed shirts you ever saw. His clothes fit perfectly. I never saw him wear a coat, but sometimes a vest. He sported a big, gold watch with a large gold chain draped across his chest.

Sold Pool Room

When he sold his pool room and went back up north on the morning train, Little helped him on the Pullman with his luggage. Then Pa stood at attention in his old circus uniform — along with his chickens, poodles, and whooping cranes — as the train pulled out.

The place where Little lived used to fascinate me. He cooked, ate and slept in that one little room. At one end was a large figure of a black man with a crown on its head and sitting on a kind of throne. It was sort of like a shrine. I used to peep in the door at it.

Sometimes on a Sunday, Harry Dreggors would give me $5 to hitch our old horse to the buggy, go to town, pick him up and take him out to his orange grove on Alligator Creek. I always called him Mr. Harry.

In later years I worked for him again. I first started out as cook on the Harris Brothers, *a run boat for the Punta Gorda Fish Company which was partly owned by Mr. Harry. Roy Adams was the captain.*

There was no bridge to Pine Island, but several big orange groves were located there. About October each year the Harris Brothers *would be stationed at Bokeelia.*

The Punta Gorda Fish Co., had several big barges, some covered. We would load the boat and the barges — sometimes two of them — and go down through Pine Island Sound, then up the Caloosahatchee River to Fort Myers. Large packing houses used to line the waterfront there. This is where the oranges and grapefruit would be unloaded, packed and shipped north by train.

Many times Mr. Harry would meet the boat and eat breakfast with us. The channel up the river in certain places was very narrow and treacherous. Sometimes the tide would be very fast through these places. If you were not careful, the barges would come down on us, letting slack in the tow rope. This would get tangled up in the wheel (propeller).

This meant someone had to take off his clothes, dive under the boat, take a sharp knife and cut the rope out of the wheel. For some reason, that some one seemed always to be me. This was in the Fall and Winter, and the water was cold. I have been under this boat many times.

When we came to fast water, someone would be put on the stern of the boat to take up the slack. Usually it was Bill Stevens. Sometimes I thought he let the rope get tangled up just for meanness — to see me go overboard.

Later, Adams captained the Chase for the West Coast Fish Co., and I went with him as engineer. We had a double crew on the boat so we could run day and night down through the Ten Thousand Islands picking up citrus, pineapples and pompano for the packers.

At Punta Gorda, the oranges, pineapples and winter vegetables were packed seasonally in sheds near the railroad. Across LaVilla Road from the Clarence Brown/Aubrey Nelson place was a small depot, just a loading platform known as Pineapple Junction.

Pineapples grown in that area were a large, fancy variety as large as a gallon jug. The packers would leave space between them in the crates and stuff in excelsior — using a short, stubby stick to pack it just tight enough to hold the fruit steady in place but not so hard as to bruise the fruit and make it unsalable.

Miss Esther McCullough's father — Rev. B.F. Oswald — was another big pineapple grower at Solana. Across from their house a man had a packing shed. One of his best workers was a one-handed Negro man named Cleve Mays. His hand was cut off at the wrist, and he used the stub of his arm instead of a stick to stuff the excelsior down.

I thought he would bruise his arm that way but he didn't. We were good friends. His wife's name was Effie. They had a daughter named Elnora. She married George Hester. Cleve saved his money and bought two cottages formerly occupied by cigar makers for the El Palmetto Cigar Company — one for himself and wife and the other for Elnora.

Fastest Packer

The fastest packer was Belle, daughter of Lud McBean. He came to this country from Glasgow as a Salvation Army preacher. For years he was an ice house keeper for the Punta Gorda Fish Company at Carlos on the south end of Fort Myers Beach. Carlos was the end of our run for fish. We used to leave Punta Gorda at 7 a.m. on Monday, Wednesday and Friday. Then, return about noon or shortly thereafter on Tuesday, Thursday and Saturday.

We got down to Carlos in late afternoon, put off our ice, loaded fish and spent the night. We got up about 4 a.m. to head back to Punta Gorda and get there in time to unload our fish in daylight. I spent many an hour in the Carlos fish house listening to Mr. McBean's stories about Scotland.

Belle McBean married Fred Quednau who became Sheriff at Punta Gorda. Their daughter, Tosie Hindman, was supervisor of elections at Punta Gorda until recently.

Years ago, automobiles had brakes only on the back wheels. Then, they put brakes on all four wheels. Dale Meadows wanted a Buick which was so equipped. There were no Buick agents in Punta Gorda, so he wrote to Tampa for a salesman to come down and demonstrate a car. The salesman took the family for a ride, then back home.

He had some other prospects to call on, but Dale's nephew, Floyd Chadwick, wanted to ride some more and wouldn't get out. As they went up Marion Avenue, they looked up and saw a train roaring down King Street toward them. The salesman slammed on the brakes and managed to stop, burning rubber and squealing tires.

After that, you could ask Floyd, "Tell us about four-wheel brakes." Floyd did not talk plain. He would reply, "Me and man going down street, look up and see train tumming, man slam on brakes, stop quick. Man say to me, 'Smell that?' (meaning burning rubber). I say, 'I ought to — I sit in it.'" And Floyd did not mean burning rubber.

Ed Smith, Henry "Baker" Smith's son organized a little band. We had a band stand down near the old City Dock at the foot of Sullivan St. The stand was a gift to us and the city from William Fenimore Cooper, judge of the Juvenile Court of Cook County, Chicago.

Judge Cooper liked to hear us play. He spent his winters in Punta Gorda. His home (which burned down in 1994) was on Marion Ave. across from the Methodist Church.

Better Than Circus

He had a married couple working for him. The man drove his car and was a handy man. The woman was house keeper. I remember you (Esther McCullough) telling about one time you all were wanted to go somewhere, and you proposed a certain evening. The judge said, "Oh, no. I can't go then. It's band practice and that's better than a 3-ring circus." Also, I remember your talking about Ed, the leader, correcting J.T. Rose — God rest their souls — and J.T. said, "Who in hell is blowing this horn?"

Anyway, Judge Cooper and his household couple would often walk down and listen to us practice. They always applauded. When they did not walk down, we marched up the street and serenaded him. He always recognized us some way — either refreshments or a gift of money which we used for things the band needed. We were just boys, but when the judge met us on the street he hailed us, "Hi, Chief." It made us feel big.

He had some bird baths in his yard. Some numbskull from the city decided they bred mosquitoes, and made him get rid of them. This made Judge Cooper mad. He left and never came back. With all the marshes and swamps, around, what difference did a couple of bird baths make?

282

Rev. Gatewood in his senior years was distinguished in his white suit.

Chapter 65

MINISTER THRIVED ON HARDSHIP

Life in the Charlotte Harbor area — before the Florida Southern Railway made its way down the Peace River Valley in 1886 to Punta Gorda — was "hard and full of blisters." Yet, pioneers like the Reverend George W. Gatewood found satisfaction in wresting a living from a tropical wilderness.

A vivid account of those days was published serially in the *Punta Gorda Herald* under the heading, "A Kentuckian, 56 Years In Florida, Tells Of His Experiences." The columns were gathered into a booklet in 1939 when Rev. Gatewood retired to his home still standing on Sullivan Street and occupied by his daughter, Mrs. Irene Adams.

The following excerpts from his reminisces need no editing, though he modestly disavowed "literary ability."

Landing from a mule team in the winter of 1882, with few obligations and less money, I had youth and strength and a determination to make my way in this new land.

About all I knew was farming — the way it's done in Kentucky and Indiana. Of Florida farming I knew nothing. Its soil, climate, seasons and the methods of farming were all different. I got in, however, with a good farmer as a share cropper, followed his instructions and made a good crop of oats, corn and sweet potatoes.

Corn sold by the barrel at one dollar. A barrel was considered a bushel. It was left in the shuck to keep the weevils from eating it. The standard price for sweet potatoes was 50 cents a bushel.

Cattle and hogs — with their ears notched and sides branded so their owners could distinguish them from their neighbors' stock — grazed in the woods. Beef was sometimes butchered, cut in strips and dried in the sun. Sometime it was pickled in barrels for future use. Hogs were butchered, the bones taken out and the meat salted. Then it was left hanging in the smoke house to cure.

Flour By The Barrel

In those days, most folks bought flour by the barrel, meal and grits by the bushel, potatoes the same way. They thought it an extravagance to buy in small packages. They bought their coffee green and parched it themselves — in the oven of a wood-burning stove, in a dutch oven on the fireplace, or on a dirt platform outside the house.

Much of the furniture of poor people was homemade. The bottoms of most chairs were cowhide with the hair left on. Most of the people knew and practiced economy.

While eating dinner one day at a neighbor's, my host said to me that his son, who was about 17 years of age, would never have anything worthwhile. I asked him why he thought that way. "Well," he said, "don't you see that he sops his syrup on both sides of his bread?"

Oxen were used largely for draft animals because they could live on the range without grain better than could horses or mules. Also, they could manage better on the wet prairie during the rainy season.

Early settlers were satisfied with a simple living, their food being described as "Hog and hominy." A few vegetables were included. They had rice, sweet potatoes and sugarcane from their own fields.

There was, at that time, plenty of game in the woods and plenty of fish in the lakes and rivers. Wants of the people were few and easily supplied. Later, when people began to clamor for good roads, and all sorts of public improvements, taxes began to climb.

Ten, twelve and fifteen dollars a month — with board and washing — were the farm wages paid. The hours were not mentioned, but it usually meant from daylight until dark and sometimes much later.

The question was often asked by newcomers, "How do you make a living in this country?" I have never heard it answered satisfactorily. After living there 10 or 12 years, I could not have answered it myself. One man said "We skin gators in the summer and Yankees in the winter."

I was a licensed preacher and supply minister for the little Methodist churches in the Caloosahatchee circuit. My first assignment was Alva. After the stewards looked me over they said they had hoped they wouldn't have any preacher sent to them that year. I told them I thought they had gotten as near to nothing as possible. When they saw I had a sympathetic feeling for them, they began to cheer up.

It was in 1902 that I acquired a mercantile store in Punta Gorda to splice out my meager stipend as a minister. I was an enumerator in the federal census four times — 1900, 1910, 1920, and 1930. I did reportorial work on the Fort Myers Press, the DeSoto County News at Arcadia, and at different times for the Punta Gorda Herald.

After getting settled down in Punta Gorda, I was content to remain there until 1907. Then I became interested in the inducements offered by the federal government to get the public domain settled up. As a result, I embarked upon a homesteading venture.

Visiting Old Homestead

Visiting recently the old homestead, on what is known as Telegraph Cypress, in Charlotte County, vacated 21 years ago, there came to me many sweet memories of the ten years I and my family spent there — my wife, Minnie; and my children, Joe, Clarence, Nellie and Irene.

Although the buildings are now all gone, I could see on memory's screen the house and barn; and the store building in which, with the mercantile business I carried, the Bermont post office was once kept.

Still standing are the posts on which once rested our sugarcane grinding mill. The concrete cistern and parts of the lighterwood house blocks that didn't burn when woods fires destroyed the houses.

It was there that we learned how to do without things we thought necessary. It was there we were satisfied to live simply. It was there that the hardships of life made the blessings more appreciated.

The land of township 40, range 26, later known as Bermont Township, was put on the market in 1907, subject to homesteading. There were no good roads in that locality at that time. There was the old "wire road" which followed the route of the overseas telegraph line from Gainesville to Punta Rassa. That road crossed the Caloosahatchee at what was known as Bernizer's ferry.

While on the homestead, I was the Bermont postmaster, merchant, farmer, notary public, registration officer and almost anything that was required. I preached in a small, frame church that doubled as a school and community hall. It took it all to keep the wolf and wildcats from the door. Yet, it was the happiest period of my life.

When I pressed my cane and boiled syrup, I would have a big taffy pull party. Everyone came. After church we had a community picnic under the trees. It was all great fun.

Wildcats were plentiful. They are dreadful when they get started on a chicken roost; and they don't stop until they get the last one, unless you get them. I had to go to Sarasota on business; and, as we had been missing a hen every two or three nights, I told my wife to set some steel traps around the hen house. The first night she caught the thief — a large wildcat which had fattened on our chickens. He was standing up by the side of the coop, with one foot in the trap but otherwise unhurt. She was afraid to go near but got 22 rifle and put out his light. When I got home, she had his hide tacked up and drying. After that, the chickens had peaceful nights for awhile.

Skunk Was Loaded

Later, there came more trouble from the barnyard where we had a hen under a small coop to break her from setting. We had retired for the night when we heard her squalling as loud as she could. I jumped out of bed, grabbed my gun and started for the barnyard, my son, Joe, following, both of us in our scant night clothes. I raised the coop and there was a skunk ahold of the hen by her wing. He wouldn't turn loose after the coop was raised. I wanted to shoot him, but I couldn't without killing the hen, as well as the skunk. I grabbed the skunk by the tail and jerked him loose. After that, the battle was fierce. Joe and I didn't get over the effects of that scrap for several days. That skunk was loaded to the brim.

Wild turkey were quite plentiful right on our homestead in those days. Gobblers could make the woods ring early every spring. One morning, Joe slipped out back of our house and shot a gobbler so large that my wife cooked him in the sugar kettle because she couldn't get him in the oven.

State convicts at that time were often leased out to turpentine farms. One of these farms extended to the township where the homesteads were located. When a convict tried to escape, as happened now and then, he was almost sure to make for the cypress swamp adjoining my place. It was almost impossible to capture an escaped convict in that cypress if he could hold out against insects and hunger, notwithstanding they had bloodhounds for trailing them down.

286

I remember one Negro who escaped to the swamp, stood it several hours until the mosquitoes and starvation drove him out. He was captured at the only Negro cabin there was near the cypress.

Convicts in the turpentine camps and sawmills were a class of tough men and women. Sometimes they required rough handling. It was my lot as minister occasionally to visit the convicts in the stockade where they were housed. Sometimes I ate with them, partaking of the same rations they were given — good, plain, wholesome food.

At one time there was an abundance of oysters, clams, scallops and other shell fish. On one of my launch trips to little Methodist churches, I went up into Turtle Bay to get some oysters. It was about night when I loaded my oysters. As the weather was threatening, I camped in an empty fish house on the edge of the bay. I tied my boat to the little dock , then took my jug of water and a few other belongings into the fish shack.

That night there came a hard blow from the southwest, accompanied by a hard rain and high tide. My launch's stern line parted, and the next morning the boat was way up on the beach. The wind was still blowing almost a gale. My provisions were about gone, but I had plenty of oysters. I ate oysters from Monday evening to Saturday morning. Then I met the regular run-boat carrying fish to Punta Gorda which took me aboard and towed my launch in. Since that week's feasting on oysters I have had no great hankering for them.

Robinson Crusoe Notoriety

My folks were expecting me home Monday evening, and my delayed arrival might have caused them undue concern had they not long before learned not to worry when I did not return on schedule.

My week's experience eking out an existence with oysters as my only food, on that small island, brought me considerable newspaper publicity. A few days following my return, I saw myself characterized in various dailies as the Robinson Crusoe of the day.

I then remembered the way my friend of long standing, Adrian P. Jordan of the Punta Gorda Herald smiled when I had explained to him why I had no news that week for his paper. He had already made news of me, giving the Robinson Crusoe story first to several daily papers.

My family and I had been in Punta Gorda following our removal from our homestead, about seven years when the boom got underway in 1924. We had retained, however, a degree of the stamina and hardiness of our pioneer days that stood us well in hand when people and real estate prices went soaring. In the last analysis, we were little worse off after the boom than when it started — our worldly possessions were about the same when it ended as they were when it started.

Fourth of July 1909 fish fry was on Marion Ave. behind Hotel Punta Gorda —
looking east from Sullivan St. Seminole (Dade) Hotel on right.

Chapter 66

GLORIOUS FOURTH NEIGHBORLY

The "Glorious Fourth" was always a community holiday featuring food, games and patriotic oratory — but no pyrotechnic displays, it just wasn't a custom hereabouts at the turn of the century.

Big kids set off "penny crackers" — five cents for a package of 25 — little children twirled sparklers. But neighborliness was the bent.

Often a town, in a burst of enthusiasm, would invite the whole county to free feed and festivities.

Such an event was staged in 1902 by Arcadia, county seat of DeSoto which then included what is now Charlotte. The Florida Southern Railway ran a special excursion train from Punta Gorda to accommodate eager passengers.

Under the headline "A BRILLIANT SUCCESS," the *Punta Gorda Herald* gave it front-page treatment: Arcadia's celebration of the 4th of July would have reflected credit upon a town five times the size. The utmost good order prevailed throughout the day. Maybe this was because Arcadia is a "dry" town. But there seemed to be 2,000 people present.

"As it was, there was no disturbance and no unpleasantness — except the usual baseball logomachy which hurt nothing except the King's English.

"Even our baseball boys, who were licked 10-4, will acknowledge they had a good time. They console themselves with the belief that the victory was due to professional skill from Winter Park and a biased umpire.

"The third nine of the Punta Gorda Baseball Club utterly walloped the Arcadia boys — making a score of 13 to 8.

288

"The day was warm of course, but the sun was shaded by clouds. A breeze prevailed, and nobody suffered greatly from heat. About 200 people went up from this corner of the county. Before the train, which left at 7:30 a.m., reached Arcadia, not even standing room was left. The grand parade, headed by the Punta Gorda Brass Band in new duck uniforms, and playing patriotic airs, began at 10 a.m. Some of the floats were really superb and would have reflected credit upon a metropolitan city. After this came speeches by candidates. Judge Wall spoke first but did not allude to his candidacy. His remarks were national and patriotic. Although suffering from a painful physical disorder, he made a fine speech.

"He was followed by H. S. Phillips, Esq., in a similar patriotic strain which won him much applause. He proved himself an orator of splendid ability.

"Gen. Gilchrist (of Punta Gorda, elected governor six years later) spoke next. The applause given him clearly indicated his (Legislature primary) triumph next Tuesday. Upon the conclusion of his remarks, Mayor Jones of Arcadia got off a masterpiece of eloquence that moved the multitude — he announced dinner. The throng at once attacked the barbecue. There was an abundance of well cooked beef, mutton, pork and bread; and the big crowd had plenty to eat.

"After dinner there were bicycle races, a tournament, fruitless attempts by small boys to rescue a $5 bill from the top of a greased pole 30 feet high, baseball and more speaking.

"Candidate C.M. Johnson was the chief speaker of the afternoon. He acquitted himself with credit, but was handicapped by the audience being tired of speeches. So were four or five other county candidates who followed him. The tourney and baseball took off the crowd.

"The Hon. R. Hudson Burr was present and did not speak. We did not learn why. At night there was a brilliant ball which was attended by the young people and some of the older ones. Thus it was that Arcadia celebrated the 4th from dawn til midnight."

Bairdville's Fourth

A similar celebration was arranged in 1913 by the homesteaders at Bairdville and Bermont — new, tiny villages near Shell Creek east of the harbor. Meadowlark, correspondent there for the *Punta Gorda Herald,* announced in early June:

"COLONIAL CELEBRATION HERE FOURTH OF JULY. There will be a ball game and wheelbarrow race. Burro and ox will be ridden in a race in the afternoon. Jack Collins, who recently came from Texas where he had considerable experience lassoing cattle, will show the people how it is done by roping a Florida steer from a horse and then ride the steer. He has the trained horse, a saddle and a rope that were used in Texas. Be sure to see it!"

Within a couple of weeks, a spontaneous frolic had mushroomed into a major celebration. Committees were organized and a full day of activities planned. The formal program provides a Who's Who in east Charlotte County at that time, and an insight into the kinds of entertainment deemed appropriate for July 4.

Program -- A.M.

Place: the pine grove a few rods east of Bairdville post office, after colonial fashion.

Prayer by the Chaplain, Rev. G.W. Gatewood of Bermont.

Reading, Declaration of Independence, by F.N. Johnson of Bairdville.

Vocal music, national song, Mr. and Mrs. Gatewood.

George Washington's oration, by S.D. Huffman of Bairdville.

Martial music by Messrs. Sandford Blazer and Manness of Bermont.

Recitation by Miss Edna Huffman of Bairdville.

Vocal music by Mr. and Mrs. Gatewood.

Recitation by school children of Bermont and Bairdville.

Instrumental music by Sanford Blazer of Bermont

Program — P.M.

Ox and burro to be ridden in a race by two boys.

French cock fight open to all the boys.

Wheelbarrow race open to all.

Baseball game. Players bring your favorite ball and bat.

Committees For The Day

Flag decoration — Mesdames Graham and Stiles of Bermont, and Mrs. L.E. Huffman of Bairdville.

Vegetable and fruit display — Mr. and Mrs. Herzke of Willow Pens, Mr. and Mrs. Harn of Bermont.

Serving of luncheon — Mesdames Mercer, Blazer and Gatewood of Bermont; Collins and Kahl of Bairdville and Addison of Wolf City.

Entertainment committee to represent colonial personages — Messers Webster, Edmonds, Burke and Mercer; Mesdames Bailey, Edmonds and Burke of Bermont; Baird, Johnson and S.D. Huffman of Bairdville.

Program and grounds — L.E. Huffman and L.C. Baird of Bairdville.

Marshals of the Day — John Addison of Wolf City, Judge Blazer of Bermont.

Enclosed pasture for all who desire to turn their teams on the grass.

All are invited. As many as can conveniently do so should dress after colonial fashion. School children are requested to be barefoot.

As many as can, bring Kodak or camera.

Many people from Punta Gorda attended, including a *Herald* reporter identified only as "A Guest:"

"Quite a large body gathered at Bairdville to celebrate the 4th of July. Several boats, autos and carriages went from this place to enjoy themselves. The day was all that one could wish for — not too warm, and minus the usual rain on the great Fourth in this section.

"Too much praise cannot be given Mr. and Mrs. Baird and the different committees for their efforts to make every one enjoy themselves.

"Mr. Baird met the boats at the landing with a three-ox and one-horse team wagon, upon which he loaded the ladies; and they were off to the picnic ground with Mr. Baird astride one of the oxen. Mr. Huffman hauled the scribe out in a wagon to which was hitched a couple of Texas donkeys.

"At 12 o'clock, every one was summoned to dinner, which was spread out on tables under the trees and was a sumptuous one, plenty for every one. After the Rev. Fitzgerald of Punta Gorda saying grace, we were ordered to fall to. There were 150 to 200 people there, and they did justice to the good things to eat.

"Mr. Bailey of Bermont, the master of ceremonies, gave us a nice talk about the progress of the county. Then came several pieces said by little tots. I cannot give their names — or contestants in the 3-legged race, 100-yard dash, sack race, the donkey and O.K. races.

Good Old Dixie

"We had several songs by the Bermont choir of a natural character — among which was *My Florida,* and that good old never-to-be-forgotten Southern song, *Dixie.* Mr. C. Enguesser was there with a large Kodak taking pictures of the party.

"Mrs. Hershie of Willow Pens had a display that would do for any country. She has been there only 18 months. However, her display of fruit, vegetables, keifer corn, pineapples, sugar cane, figs, egg plant, pepper, onions and flowers, was simply grand.

"The party that went up in the boats had to leave early so as to get home. They had a delightful trip down the beautiful Shell Creek, one of the prettiest in the state."

Sam Houston Huffman, son of the S.D. Huffman mentioned prominently, was eight years old at the time. He recalls: "Mr. Collins got cold feet about roping and riding a steer, said he had gotten rusty since leaving Texas. My father agreed instead to rope the steer. It took him two tries, but he succeeded — to the cheers of the crowd. Even the cowboys from Arcadia were impressed. I was sure proud of him."

The villages of Bairdville and Bermont have been abandoned. (For additional details see *Our Fascinating Past, Vol 1.*) The location of Wolf City is unknown, as is the nature of a "French cock fight" by boys and an "O.K. race."

Solana Picnic

Not everyone in the county went to the Bairdville shindig. The village of Solana, just east of Punta Gorda, held its own community picnic at The Palms — described by the Herald as "the hospitable home" of Mrs. Mary K. Rankin. "The spacious porches were gaily and artistically decorated with flags and bunting," reported the Herald. "The dining room was festive with the National colors. Old Glory waved proudly from a flagstaff on the beautiful lawn to greet approaching guests.

"These, to the number of about 40 — some from the neighborhood and some from town (of Punta Gorda), old and young judiciously mingled — ranged in age from our snowy-haired hostess to little 2-year-old Cordelia Whitten.

"Various amusements were indulged in. Patriotic songs were sung. Younger members of the party engaged in an exciting flag-race on the lawn. When the low-descending sun indicated the hour for departure was at hand, the entire company assembled around the flagstaff and gave the National salute to the Flag: 'I give my head, my hand, and my heart to my country — One country, one people, one Flag.'"

Rev. George Gatewood and daughter Irene in 1924.

Chapter 67

CIRCUIT RIDER PREACHED TO INDIANS

When Rev. George Gatewood, accepted a "call" to Southwest Florida as Methodist supply minister, he found that his scattered congregations included a band of Seminole Indians. An account of this and other experiences in the frontier days here is included in his booklet *Ox Cart Days To Airplane Era* which he published in 1939 at age 77:

About the year 1887, while still a young man and unmarried, I applied to the quarterly conference of the Fort Dade circuit of the Methodist church for a license to preach. The following year I was sent to the Caloosahatchee circuit as a supply minister. Before I left Fort Dade, one man remarked — upon hearing that I said I was called to preach — that I had mistaken the voice of a hoot owl for that of the Lord.

Punta Gorda then was the southern terminus of the railroad. Travel south from there was by steamboat to Fort Myers. I reached my headquarters at Alva overland by team.

In 1888, as a Methodist circuit rider, I travelled this route on a Cuban pony. I carried feed for the pony and a morsel to eat for myself in my saddlebags and a couple of blankets on the back of my saddle.

As the homes were a long way apart, and the circuit about 100 miles in extent, I occasionally camped on the ground in the open. Once, when the weather was threatening and no house anywhere within reach, I gathered some Spanish moss, made a bed on the ground, and stuck my umbrella in the center of it. I coiled up around it as best I could and spent a night not many preachers nowadays would enjoy.

I organized a little group of Methodists at Everglades and built the first little church there long before the railroad came. I had the Indians for part of my congregation. The Indians, though, when they came to church refused to sit on the benches and sat cross legged on the floor.

Seminoles Remembered

I became personally acquainted with most of the Indians and occasionally invited them to eat with us. Among those I well remember were Squirrel Jumper, Water Turkey, Miami Billy, Tommy Osceola and Johnny Osceola. Johnny was an expert wrestler. He would wrestle with the white boys who were willing to tackle him. I think that he became chief of his tribe. At Alva I spliced out my meager stipend as a minister by operating a store for a man by the name of Luttrell. Then in 1892 I was asked to minister to the Ten Thousand Islands circuit out of Chokoloskee. It was at this time I married Minnie Clark of Leesburg. She was 17. She bore me four children: Clarence, Joe, Nellie and Irene.

(Note: Irene married William A. Adams and lives in Punta Gorda.)

In 1898 I went into the mercantile business in a small way as a "side line." I bought a store at Fort Myers and moved it to Sanibel Island. Subsequently I had a small store at New Prospect (now North Fort Myers) and then in 1902 at Punta Gorda. I was content to remain in Punta Gorda until 1907. At that time I became interested in the inducements offered by the federal government to get the public domain settled up. Consequently I embarked upon a homesteading venture for 10 years on what is known as the Telegraph Cypress Swamp.

Many sweet memories come to me of the decade that my wife, my children and I spent there. I can see on memory's screen the house and barn; and the store building in which, with the mercantile business I carried on and where the Bermont post office was once kept. They are now all gone. (Note: Bermont was a thriving village at the intersection of State Routes 74 and 31.)

In 1910 we had a very heavy storm. The wind blew down much of the heavy timber and some of the houses at Bermont. The storm roared so you couldn't hear the trees falling within a hundred yards of the house. I had a stock-feed storage shed built near the barn, all the posts of which were sunk deep in the ground. As our box-constructed house began to shake and quiver in the heavy downpour of rain, we made for the feed shed. There we stayed until daylight.

We were surprised next morning to see our house still standing. Much of the heavy timber of the ridge land around the house was lying on the ground. It seemed earth everywhere was covered with water. Fish actually were swimming in between the potato beds near our kitchen door

Some farmers with small orange groves didn't have titles to their lands. They said that if they got title they would have to pay taxes. Many lost their groves when speculators bought the land sight-unseen.

If their land was poor, they cow-penned it by putting cattle — sometimes a hundred head or more — on it in a pen at night. In the mornings they separated the calves from their mothers, driving the cows into the woods. The cows would come later to get their calves. Sometimes one family would milk 20 of those range cows to get two gallons of milk — taking only about a teacup of milk from each cow to keep from robbing the calves of their share.

Of course, fertilizer was the main object in penning cattle — not the milk. After penning a piece of ground for three or four weeks, the pens were moved to another plot of ground. Sugarcane, sweet potatoes or anything planted on it grew prolifically.

Cranes, curlews, wood ducks, gannets commonly called flintheads, and other pond birds came to that section in large flocks in those days. They often became very tame, so there was no need for a farmer who was scarce of meat to go hungry for very long — if he had a gun and ammunition and energy enough to pull the trigger.

Five Flintheads With One Shot

On one occasion there was a large flock of flintheads feeding around a pond. A grown flinthead is almost as large as a turkey. I wanted only one. I stooped down in my yard, and with a single shot from my rifle killed five of those large birds. The necks of three were shot off, and the ball went through the bodies of two others.

While on the homestead, I was the Bermont postmaster, merchant, farmer, notary public, registration officer and almost anything that was required. It took it all to keep the wolf and wildcats from the door. Yet, it was the happiest period of my whole life.

Rev. and Mrs. Gatewood gave up the rugged life at Bermont in 1917 and went into the real estate business at Punta Gorda just as the Land Boom got underway. In closing his memoir, Rev. Gatewood wrote, It has taken south Florida a long time to recover from the harmful effects of that period known as the Boom. In the last analysis, Minnie and I were little worse off after the boom than when it started. Our worldly possessions were about the same when it ended as they were originally.

Mrs. Gatewood died in 1944 and Rev. Gatewood three years later. Both are buried at Indian Springs Cemetery.

The Quednau home built in 1892 on West Marion Ave., Punta Gorda. Mrs. Belle Quednau, right, with friends and 3-year-old daughter Tosie. Top floor was removed and now is home of M/M Albert Quednau.

Chapter 68

OLD SOFTY ACTED TOUGH

Imagine the country town of Mayberry, and Sheriff Andy Taylor with a couple hundred extra pounds. Now you have Punta Gorda and Fred Quednau 54 years ago. Sheriff Quednau's daughter, Tosie, describes him as "a man's man, an old softy who acted tough."

"Oh, he was tough when he had to be," says Tosie Quednau Hindman. "He had only two deputies. One of these was Travis Parnell who with his wife, Maud, lived in the Court House to manage the jail on the second floor. The other deputy was Ira Atkinson. When there was trouble, Daddy had to take care of it.

"One time he brought in a tough hombre who was drunk and unruly. The troublemaker wouldn't walk up a half-flight of stairs to the jail. Daddy just grabbed the guy by the belt and collar and threw him up the stairs. Daddy weighed well over 300 pounds. Not many people wanted to tangle with him.

"Grandfather Fritz Quednau came here from Alsace-Lorraine in 1892 to start a cigar factory on West Marion Ave. His wife was Minnie (nee Gardner) from Germany. They had three boys — Arthur Fred, my Daddy, the oldest; Henry and George William. All were born here.

"While on a trip to Muncie, Ind., to drum up business Grandfather took pneumonia and died. It wasn't possible to ship bodies those days, so he was buried up there. Daddy was just four years old.

"Grandmother Minnie gave up the cigar business and converted the factory into a boarding house. She also did house work for Mrs. Isaac Trabue, wife of the town's founder; and Mrs. Perry McAdow, the town's social leader and prominent businesswoman.

"Daddy went to school on Goldstein Street — now an apartment building — until the third grade. One day he climbed out the school house window and never went back. Instead, he took odd jobs to help out with the family. It really didn't matter about the schooling. He was smart and could do anything.

"He ran errands down at the dock and shoveled fish for the run boats. He learned to pilot and had his own boat — a motor launch named *R.W. Powell* — when he was 16. A year later he qualified for a captain's license — the first man on the Gulf to do this at age 17. He carried cargo wherever anybody wanted it to go. Before Mamma and Daddy got married, ex-president Teddy Roosevelt came to Punta Gorda to catch a manta-ray. People called them devil fish. Daddy loaned Roosevelt the *R.W. Powell* for the week-long expedition.

Teddy Roosevelt Bellowed

"As the fishing party got ready to shove off — the whole town at the dock to wish it luck — Roosevelt bellowed, 'Where's the Kodak?' Nobody had remembered to bring a camera. Isabella 'Belle' McBean, then 22, the fastest fruit packer in town, said, 'I have one you can borrow. I'll go get it, only take a minute.' She hopped on her bicycle and fetched her Kodak Bantam. Roosevelt didn't return Mama's camera. Weeks later she received a package from Roosevelt containing a deluxe model Kodak and tripod. I have the tripod in my attic.

"Daddy married Belle, my Mamma, in 1919. She came to Punta Gorda with her parents, Ludovic and Maria (nee Mimms) McBean in 1912 from South Carolina. Grandfather McBean was a Scotsman. He kept the Punta Gorda Fish Company ice house and fish camp at San Carlos Bay.

"Daddy had the Standard Oil agency. He carried gasoline and oil down to Barron Collier's Everglades City. He also took along supplies to trade with the Seminoles for egret plumes. He stopped trading when he learned that egrets died when their fancy plumes were pulled out.

"Nevertheless, he retained respect from the Seminoles throughout his life. They sometimes came to Punta Gorda and always stopped by to see us. They called Mama 'Pale Face.'

"Daddy didn't like to stay away from home. When I was six, I fell out a two-story window at the old home place and dislocated my shoulder. He was on a trip to Everglades City at the time. He was upset when he got back and found out about my fall. 'Seems like every time something bad happens, I'm down the bay.'

"This is why he gave up the freight business in 1928 and opened a restaurant down-town on Marion Avenue. The place was just one counter and stools called Fred's Quick Lunch. Mama did most of the cooking at home and carried it down to the restaurant in our black Whippet auto.

"Daddy stayed open until 9 or 10 at night, depending upon business. After work he often went with other businessmen to skinny-dip in the Hotel Charlotte Harbor's huge swimming pool. After the hotel burned in 1959, the pool was filled in for the Howard Johnson Motel parking lot.

"The Great Depression hit in 1929. Daddy didn't make much money at the restaurant because he gave too much food for too little money — not to mention the free lunches he gave down-and-outers.

"Back then, Tamiami Trail, U.S. 41, came across the harbor on the first bridge at Nesbit Street. It was a narrow bridge just big enough for two Model-T Fords or one bus. If you got caught on the bridge with a bus, it wasn't the bus that backed up.

"While the second bridge was under construction in 1928-30, the Trail turned west on Marion Avenue to Shreve Street then south at our house. One day I noticed a man hitch hiking with a little girl in a red coat with red hood. They weren't having any luck.

" There were only about 20 cars a day traveling the Trail in those days.

SHERIFF FRED QUEDNAU

I thought at first they were headed for the tourist cabins and gas station operated by Louis Stallo and his wife, Mason, at the corner of Shreve and Charlotte streets. I watched, but the man and girl walked on by.

"I felt sorry for them because it was getting dark and spitting rain. I called Daddy at the restaurant. 'Come home right away!' 'Why?' he asked. 'Never mind, just get here as quick as you can,' I declared. Daddy jumped into the Whippet and rushed home, thinking there was a great emergency.

"I told him about the man and Little Red Riding Hood. Daddy took out and found them trudging along. Daddy said that when he stopped, the girl jumped in like a little jack rabbit. He brought them back to our house where he and Mama put them up for two days.

"The man explained that his wife had died in Illinois. He was out of work and unable to provide for his daughter. They were on their way to

Homestead where he had a sister who would take care of her niece until he could get back on his feet. Six years later, Daddy got a letter from the man enclosing a money order for $200.

"Daddy joined the Fraternal Order of Odd Fellows and became president of the Rotary Club. In 1934 he was elected to the city commission which ran both the county and Punta Gorda. He served six years, and twice was chosen by his fellow commissioners to complete unexpired mayoralty terms. In 1940, Daddy was elected sheriff and served 16 years. He was the second sheriff after James H. Lipscomb who was elected in 1921 when Charlotte County split off from DeSoto.

"Daddy never carried a gun — just like the TV Andy Taylor — but he had one near by if he needed it. He said he didn't wear a sidearm because a drummer (travelling salesman) came into the restaurant one day in disgust and wanted to know what kind of town Punta Gorda was? Said the first three people he saw had pistols on their hips. He had seen Sheriff Lipscomb with two deputies.

"I was 17 at the time of Daddy's election and on my way to Florida State University at Tallahassee. I got so homesick I couldn't stand it so came home and married Jack Hindman. Then I went along with Daddy on of ficial business every chance I could.

I Went With Daddy

"When Daddy had to take a woman to the prison at Raiford, the law required a deputized woman go along. One time we were transporting a woman and passed a man walking along the road near Murdock. I was driving. Daddy had me stop and back up to the hiker.

"'Where you going?' said Daddy. 'Sarasota or Venice" said the man. He said he was a drummer and had run out of gas. We took him back to a stalled car to make sure he was out of gas, and he was.

"We drove on up to Sarasota, and Daddy nudged me to turn into town. He gave me directions until he had me stop in front of the jail. With this the man we had picked up shook his head. 'Captain Fred, I know you know who I am. I'm the one who broke out of the Pine Island Road Camp this morning. I knew I would end up with you.'

"'That's right,' said Daddy. 'We've been hunting you.' The stranded 'drummer' was Conch Sawyer who killed a man at Everglades City and had been sentenced to life imprisonment. When he escaped he stole the real drummer's car. 'Well" said Conch, 'I just wanted to see my Mama. Now I'm ready to go back.'

"Once Daddy was asked to arrest a boy who had been caught shoplifting. 'Why did you do it?' asked Daddy. 'Because I never had a penny,' the boy replied. 'Well, I'm going to let you go on one condition — that you come to my house every Friday.' The boy came, and Daddy gave him two dollars.

"A bunch of boys came to our house every Friday to get little handouts of money until they got old enough to earn spending money on their own.

"On Christmas Eve, Daddy would let prisoners go home if they promised to get back to jail by 5 o'clock the next day. There never was a defector. On Easter we made little baskets with candy eggs for the prisoners. They really appreciated it.

"Willy Wells, a retarded man who lived in a tin shack at Hammock Pond, shot a neighbor couple — killing the wife and wounding the husband. After the shooting, the killer ran into the woods. Daddy took a deputy, and they went out to capture Willy. It was getting dark and foggy. Willy's brother implored Daddy not to go in the woods after Willy. 'He or you probably would get killed. Leave him to me and I'll bring him in tomorrow morning.' They were sitting on the Courthouse steps, waiting, when Daddy came to work at 6 a.m.

Gave Only Suit

"That's why even prisoners respected Daddy. He was a good judge of character and treated people right. Because of his size, Daddy had only one dress suit. He gave that away when a poor man of equal size died and the family didn't have a decent suit to bury him in.

"After the jail was federalized, the U.S. marshal one time brought in a Chinaman who was a big-time bank robber up north somewhere. The Chinaman slept in beautiful silk pajamas. When the marshal came to get his prisoner, the Chinaman said to Daddy, 'Sheriff, I'm going to give you something to remember me by.' It was a pair of silk pajamas. Daddy never wore them. Said it was indecent.

"No one ever broke out of Daddy's jail. Prisoners liked Mrs. Parnell's cooking, and didn't want to embarrass my father. Daddy's fine reputation led to his being elected president of the Florida Sheriffs Association.

"Daddy retired in 1956, but many of the celebrities who came here when he was sheriff would call on him. One time, Arthur Godfrey, Rudy Vallé, and Senator Claude Pepper came to go fishing with Daddy. He had fitted out a large barge as a house boat. Daddy wouldn't move the boat because a couple of sparrows had a nest under an overhang. Instead he rented another smaller, leaky, house boat for his guests

"Burl Ives, the folk singer, and a bunch of people from Hollywood came to Florida in 1958 to shoot the movie *Winds Over The Everglades*. They wanted Daddy to go down there for several months to work with the Seminoles. He wouldn't do it, though, because he didn't want to leave home. I was so disappointed that he wasn't going to be in the movie.

"Daddy died in November 1968. A man from Sarasota came to the funeral and told Mama, 'When I was a boy, Captain Fred used to give me money every Friday upon my promise to stay out of trouble. I owe my life to him!'"

Spinster sisters Euphemia (left) and Dr. Mary Green in 1918.

Chapter 69

TWO SPINSTERS START MOTHERS CLUB

Curiously, the Lemon Bay Mother's Club was proposed by two spinster sisters — Euphemia and Dr. Mary Green who became its first officers. It is not clear whether the club was organized by 12 ladies in February of 1918 to support mobilization for the War To End All Wars, encouraging education, boosting Englewood — or for all three.

Its charter set forth the goals "to promote civic, community and child welfare." The first endeavor was to sew for the Red Cross at Sarasota and to arrange a Fourth of July celebration in 1918 just as American soldiers began arriving in France.

The Green sisters were true pioneers, coming to Englewood at the turn of the century from New York State according to local Historian Bob

Cashatt. Euphemia operated the Latonia Gift Shop on Dearborn Street for many years. Mary had a doctorate in education and was the only teacher at Englewood.

A newspaper story of Feb. 7, 1918, reporting the event, reads like a "Who's Who" of early Englewood matrons: "The meeting for forming a Mother's Club in Englewood was postponed from the second Friday in January, because of stormy weather, to last Friday. At the meeting it was unanimously decided to give the club the name of 'The Lemon Bay Mothers's Club.' Officers elected were: President, Miss E.M. Green; lst vice-president, Mrs. B.E. Miller; 2nd vice-president, Mrs. W.H. Lampp; 3rd vice-president, Mrs. Josh Platt; recording secretary, Mrs. A. Stanley Lampp; treasurer, Mrs. P.W. Buchan; historian, Mrs. J.D. Kinney.

"Chairmen of standing committees were appointed: auditing, Mrs. J.T. Lampp; program, Miss Mary W. Green; entertainment, Mrs. Walter H. Green; press, Mrs. A. Stanley Lampp; decorating, Mrs. S.L. Kelly. Constitution and by-laws for the Club, as drawn up by the committee, were accepted as a whole and the committee discharged.

"The club will meet the second Friday of each month at the school house (corner Dearborn and Elm streets) unless otherwise stated."

Met At Buchan's Pavilion

Charter members met at Buchan's Pavilion over his general store. Every woman was made an officer. Mrs. A. Stanley Lampp, Winifred, was assigned two duties. She and Stanley operated the Tamiami Lodge for many years, platted several subdivisions and gave land for the Englewood school. They had the first automobile in town. Mrs. Walter Green, Hallie, no relation to Euphemia and Mary, was a bibliophile whose interest was in establishing libraries for the school and the public. Hallie and Walter had moved to Sarasota in 1914, then to Englewood three years later where he became a real estate broker. They came from New York state in a canoe — via the Erie Canal, Great Lakes, Mississippi River, and Gulf of Mexico.

The Lampp and Platt families came to Englewood in the late 1890s, the Buchans in 1902.

By June 1918, the newspaper noted that the ladies were already active in public service: "The work that was being done for the Red Cross, consisting of three dozen shirts, was turned in completed to Mrs. Halton, of Sarasota, who had sent the work to Englewood through Miss Mary W. Green. It was decided to ask for more work that could be done in the homes. It also was decided to hold a picnic the 4th of July in Englewood. Three new members were elected — Mrs. T.V. Donneli, Miss Anna Gottfried, and Mrs. Herbert Ainger."

By 1922, the library committee had obtained, covered and indexed 200 books for the school. Three tables were built by a Mr. Jenkins for $35. The ladies thought this price excessive, but Jenkins would not accept less.

A second-hand piano for the school was purchased that same year from the Hermitage on Manasota Key for $125 and shipped to Englewood by boat. Hallie Green donated $80, and the club made up the balance. A piano tuner came two weeks later to reset the strings, charging $32 and overnight lodging for the job.

Other school improvements in 1922 included a flag pole, fence, and a rain tank "to provide drinking water for pupils." The club thereafter kept the school supplied with paper cups.

Programs featured nature, world affairs, and problems of raising children "with nothing to do." Money was raised to pay for bed linen at Venice Hospital and for cleaning the Englewood cemetery — although husbands were pressed to volunteer.

When Mrs. Anna Gottfried, another pioneer died, the family was unable to provide a grave marker. The club, therefore took up a collection of $5 to buy a tomb stone for her resting place.

The need for a community hall was apparent. Mr. and Mrs. Stanley Lampp donated two lots in their subdivision in 1924 for a club house where other groups could meet. The site was at the corner of Coconut Avenue and Maple Street.

With this, the membership changed its name to the Lemon Bay Woman's Club and began a drive to raise money for a building. Mrs. D.O. Clark gave the first $25. Dances, fish fries, quiltings, card parties and a variety of other fund raising activities were conducted.

A building committee was appointed. It was comprised of Mrs. Stanley Lampp, chair; assisted by Mrs. Walter Green, Mrs. A. Darling, Mrs. A.G. Weatherall and Mrs. C. Burgess.

Architects Gave Plans

Noted architects Clare C. Hosmer and Thomas Reed Martin, both of Sarasota, provided plans free of charge. The design they chose was "prairie" style which was popular at the time. Hosmer lived for a short time at Englewood during the Land Boom. A street was named after him.

By late 1925, the ladies had raised $613 in cash and more than $2,000 in pledges. This was deemed enough for the hard pine lumber needed. Three contractors, husbands or friends of members, donated their labor.

The Woodmere Lumber Company, largest in south Florida, near Englewood, refused to furnish lumber that came to $3,123 on the basis of pledges. Several hundred dollars in additional pledges were collected quickly; and Mrs. E.C. Willetts, a club member, loaned $2,000 on mortgage against the new building.

Carpenters were Roy Bastedo, Frank Clark and Pat Lampp. The structure consisted of a large meeting room, semi-circular stage, fireplace and long porch. An outhouse was donated by an anonymous friend. A house-warming was held Feb. 19, 1926. Two hundred persons attended.

Among them were Mayor John P. Rampe, Chamber of Commerce President H.L. Horton and Architect Hosmer.

A year later, the Woman's Club incorporated. Officers were Mrs. Charlotte Wellington, president; Mrs. Emily V. Merryman, first vice-president; Mrs. Olive Brown, second vice-president; Mrs. Mabelle Horton, recording secretary; Mrs. Laura E. Semple, corresponding secretary; and Mrs. Wilhelmina Bastedo, treasurer.

The club-community hall was the hub of social and civic activity. It was the original home of 10 churches — the first being Englewood Community Church from 1926 to 1928, now Englewood Methodist.

Among many other groups meeting there regularly were the American Legion, Boy Scouts, Lions, Oddfellows, Eastern Star, and Rotary.

Hard Times

The Great Depression of 1929-32 brought an end to the Florida Land Boom. Englewood, gave up its city charter. Real estate subdivisions reverted to weeds. The Englewood State Bank closed with the Woman's Club savings of $37.

Despite hard times, the club continued paying off its mortgage — though at reduced payments. The last payment in March 1938 was celebrated with a big mortgage-burning party. Unfortunately, Mrs. Willetts had died by this time, and final payments were made to her heirs.

During World War II, the ladies again turned to Red Cross work. Three sewing machines were kept busy. By 1944 the club had provided 29,914 surgical dressings to Dr. Fred Albee's hospital serving the Venice Army Air Base.

Contributions of books to the school continued until the club acquired its own building. At that time the Board of Education began furnishing school libraries, and the Woman's Club collection was returned. The club then opened a public lending library for the two-county area. Books were added steadily under the guidance of Hallie Green until her death in 1952. By 1958, the collection had grown to 2,500 volumes.

Charlotte and Sarasota counties opened public libraries in vacant stores at Englewood in 1962. Mrs. Harriet Ives, librarian of the Elsie Quirk library, remembers that the Woman's Club donated the major part of its library to the Else Quirk Library of 3,500 books. A large number of books also were donated to the Charlotte County Library. A few of the old, original books are still on the shelves.

The Legislature in 1972 adopted laws requiring liability insurance for public meeting facilities. The cost was prohibitive so club rentals to outside organizations were discontinued. There is no record of Euphemia's death, but Dr. Mary Green continued an inspiration to the club until she resigned in 1975 and died shortly after. The Woman's Club was placed on the National Register of Historical Places in 1988.

Major George Ola, commander of the Door and Carlstrom airfields at Arcadia during World War II, was photographed in a Stearman bi-plane.

Chapter 70

AIRFIELD TRAINED BRITISH CADETS

The two airfields east of Arcadia that trained American and French pilots during the First World War — then were abandoned to palmettos — were resurrected for World War II by a remarkable entrepreneur named John Paul Riddle.

During the Great Depression, Congress in 1935 took up legislation to expand the Army Air Force and build new military airfields to help create jobs. State Rep. C.H. Smith of Arcadia, and State Sen. Henry G. Murphy of Zolfo Springs, hopped a train for Washington, D.C. to urge reopening of Carlstrom and Dorr Fields. DeSoto County commissioners offered to sweeten the deal with 10,000 additional acres. The Florida Legislature got behind the effort with a supportive "memorial" to Congress and President Franklin D. Roosevelt. The Florida delegation was cordially received, but Congress funnelled money instead to civilian projects.

John Paul Riddle had trained as an Army Air Cadet at Carlstrom Field in 1922, its last year. Five years later he teamed up with T. Higbee Embry

305

of Cleveland, Ohio, to create the first air express line. The partners sold out to American Air Lines in 1924. Riddle invested his share of $325 million with Brazil's first air line which went broke — the only investment that ever went sour for him.

Riddle formed a new Embry-Riddle Corporation — though his former partner was not associated with it — and obtained a contract to teach flying at the University of Miami. He opened schools also at Opa Locka and Daytona Beach and reorganized as Riddle Aeronautical Institute.

Nazi Germany invaded Poland in 1939. All Europe plunged into war. The United States proclaimed neutrality but adopted a "cash-and-carry" plan by which the western allies could buy guns and carry them in their own ships. Anticipating involvement in what then was called the European War, the U.S. launched a free Civilian Air Training Program (CAT) for college students. Riddle was in perfect position to capitalize on this sudden expansion of flight training. With the backing of Florida Senator Claude Pepper, Riddle obtained government contracts to rebuild Carlstrom and Dorr fields, and then train Army pilots. Renovator of the Arcadia fields was C.F. Wheeler of Miami. He was a major contractor who worked closely with Riddle and was the first father-in-law of Arcadia Historian Claude Jones.

Dedicated To Perfection

"Riddle and Wheeler were fine men, dedicated to perfection in all things," says Jones. "They built with concrete block so the main buildings would last. The Arcadia fields were known throughout the service as 'country clubs.' They had a large swimming pool, tennis courts, and a well-stocked canteen with scarce ice-cream.

"Barracks were constructed in colonial style, four cadets to room, metal bunks, a large study table and matching chairs. New-fangled florescent ceiling fixtures provided light. Each room had a tiled shower and toilet. Each man had an 8-foot closet. Well-prepared meals were served under covered dishes, family style, in a large dining hall. Class rooms were air conditioned, a rare luxury in those days."

Upon completion of the fields in early 1941, Riddle leased them for $5,760 each. He provided one civilian instructor for every five students under supervision of Army officers — first to CAT reservists called up for active duty as Air Cadets, then to volunteers. General manager of the two fields for Riddle was Len Povey who had organized the Cuban Air Force.

The first class of 49 cadets began training in March 1941. Capt. Stanley Donovan was commanding officer at Carlstrom. Lt. William S. Boyd was commanding officer at Dorr. Donovan was transferred in September 1941 and succeeded by his engineering officer, Second Lt. George Ola promoted to First Lt. for the job. Shortly after the fields were opened, General Ralph Royce, commander of the Southeastern Army Air

Training Center at Maxwell Field, Alabama, came to the Arcadia fields to conduct an inspection. He had been commandant at Carlstrom Field during the First World War, so base personnel were anxious to make a good impression.

"That was an outstanding event," says Jones. "Public officials and many Army brass were invited for a barbeque. Among the guests was Sally Rand, a famous dancer who had been a sensation at the 1932 Chicago World's Fair. She performed with two ostrich-plume fans and seemingly nothing else. As she twirled you saw a lot of arm and leg — and expected at any moment to see a lot more, but never did. She was beautiful and graceful so you were disappointed but appreciative. The arrangements committee put her up at the old Plaza Hotel.

"The hotel manager was anxious to make a good impression so had Miss Rand's bathroom painted with white enamel. On the evening before the barbeque, Miss Rand used the facilities. Unfortunately the paint was not completely dry and she stuck to the toilet seat. A couple of maids were called to pry her loose, but some skin didn't make it.

"Nevertheless, Miss Rand gave a memorable performance. Everyone admired her for giving her all to the service."

British Cadets Predominate

Ola, now a retired colonel living a stone-throw from the former Carlstrom field, is most closely connected to the World War II training center. "Our operation was unusual inasmuch as British Royal Air Force cadets were sent to us for primary flight training after the U.S. entered the war in December of 1941," Ola relates. The Brits were fine young men, diligent in their studies. Their nation was under relentless air attack by German bombers and needed defense pilots desperately.

"However, the English lads were difficult to train. Most of them had never even driven an automobile. They had no sense of speed or depth perception. This hampered their flight judgment. Every six weeks we received about 350 students at each field, and they trained 12 weeks. About a fourth were Americans and the rest British. Together, we had 1,400 trainees on the two bases at any given time. We had a fleet of 600 Steerman PT-17 bi-planes designed specifically for training purposes. They were easy to fly. Half would be in the air while the rest were being serviced. We needed two fields to keep air traffic manageable.

"During the nearly six years one or both fields were in operation, 23 British cadets lost their lives in automobile accidents, by diseases, and one by drowning. None were killed in flight accidents.

"Those RAF cadets who lost their lives here were buried in a dedicated plot at Arcadia's Oak Ridge Cemetery. There the Union Jack flies and bagpipes are played on special occasions — such as the Memorial Day ceremony attended by British and American officials.

"Our safety record surpassed those of the other primary training fields. More than 100,000 flights by learners were lofted in the short time the Arcadia fields were in operation. Of these, only one resulted in a fatality.

"U.S.Cadet Edward J. Haines was killed in March, 1944, when his Steerman collided with another. Haines' craft was cut in half by the other plane's propellor. The civilian instructor, Henry P. Donell, was thrown from the crippled plane and was able to deploy his parachute. He suffered a broken ankle. The other plane landed safely.

"Night flying began at the fields in March 1942. Portable lights and smudge pots outlined the runway. We did not have radios, so essential communication was by 'biscuit guns' which projected red, white, or green light. Town folks pitched in to help with the war-time slogan of 'Keep `Em Flying.' Civilians provided mechanics, dispatchers, guards, and maintenance men. Ladies packed parachutes and worked in the offices. Both men and women staffed the huge kitchen and mess halls. We couldn't have done it without them," Col. Ola declares.

New Missions

Col. Ola is a distinguished example of military soldierly. After graduation from college, he joined the Army Air Corps in 1934 as a mechanic at Panama. He earned the privilege of entering flight training four years later and was commissioned Second Lt. in 1939. While at Carlstrom, Ola was advanced in rank three times to major. He fell in love with Miss Ruth Pemberton, a former Miss Arcadia. They were married before he was transferred in December 1942 to Fort Leavenworth, Kansas. He returned to Florida in 1944, being assigned as executive officer for the 3rd Fighter Command at Sarasota which included the fields at Arcadia, Punta Gorda, and Fort Myers. Thereafter he saw service in Panama, Central America, South America, Canada, England, South Korea and six United States. He was awarded the Air Medal, Bronze Star, Distinguished Flying Cross, Commendation Ribbon with three battle stars, and South Korean Military Merit Medal with silver star.

Upon surrender of Germany on VE Day (Victory In Europe) May 7, 1944, Dorr Field was deactivated in November. Carlstrom Field continued training pilots for the Pacific War until Japan surrendered on VJ Day (Victory in Japan) Aug. 14, 1945.

Once again the fields seemed headed for oblivion. This time, however, Florida prevailed upon the Army in Dec. 1946 to sell the fields for a token $1. Hangars were dismantled, but the concrete-block buildings were converted to a branch of the Chatahoochee State Mental Hospital. In 1967, state patients were confined at Carlstrom. Dorr became part of the Sunland Training Center for mentally handicapped youth. In a few years, Dorr was revamped for the DeSoto Correctional Institute. Carlstrom became G. Pierce Wood Memorial Hospital.

Kettering's Bug was self-guiding "aerial torpedo" launched from rails.

Chapter 71

FIRST GUIDED MISSILE TESTED 1919

Adolph Hitler, dictator of Nazi Germany, unleashed his "secret weapon" during the closing months of World War II in a desperate attempt to defeat Great Britain. The device was an unmanned airplane carrying a one-ton bomb. Upon reaching its pre-selected target area, the engine shut off; and the flying bomb dived to destruction.

Britishers called it a "buzz bomb" for the sputtering sound of its air-breathing ram-jet engine. Hundreds were launched but many were shot down over farm fields by Royal Air Force pilots.

In recent wars, rocket propelled missiles have been employed that are uncannily accurate and devastating. Intercontinental missiles are capable of spanning the oceans to exploded a nuclear bombs within five yards of a target. The U.S. cruise missile, with a TV camera in its nose, flies a photographed path and can dive down a smokestack. It was a decisive weapon during the Persian Gulf War.

Few people know that the prototype guided missile was invented during the First World War by an American named Charles F. Kettering — and successfully tested in DeSoto county which then included today's Charlotte County. Germany declared war against the other European nations in 1914. The United States attempted to stay neutral. However, it broke off diplomatic relations in early 1917 when the Germans sank the U.S.S. Housatonic. President Woodrow Wilson asked France how the U.S. could help. French authorities replied: "Invent new weapons and train our soldiers to fly." The airplane, perfected by the Wright Brothers of Dayton, Ohio, then was in its infancy.

A French delegation came to Florida immediately to help find a suitable air field for their cadets. The big prairie east of Arcadia was ideal because of its flat, treeless terrain and year-round flying weather. The U.S. Army chose a site southeast of Arcadia. The Atlantic Coast Line Railroad built a spur from its main track to bring in building materials. Construction was barely underway when the United States entered the war in April 1917. An airflight training center for American pilots was designated due east of Arcadia, and the rail line extended there. Wooden hangars and barracks with corrugated steel roofs were constructed hurriedly.

The first field was named in honor of U.S. Army Air Corps Pilot Victor Carlstrom killed in a flying accident up North. The companion field was named for Stephen H. Dorr, Jr., also killed in a training accident elsewhere two days after enlisting in August of 1917.

While the French and American fields were being built, the Navy Consulting Board convened to study possible new weapons. An "aerial torpedo" seemed promising. The Army Chief Signal Officer appointed a committee to study the Navy suggestion. A majority report rejected the concept of "automatic flying" as impractical for military use.

Kettering Report Okayed

However, a minority report by Kettering — a Dayton, Ohio, electrical engineer newly appointed vice-president of General Motors Research — persuaded the Army to let him develop a flying bomb.

What Kettering proposed was a complete little biplane made of cardboard and sticks. Orville Wright, co-inventor of the first, practical airplane, designed the fuselage and 12-foot wings. Ralph de Palma, a racer and engine designer for Ford Motor Co., built a 4-cylinder 2-cycle motor to turn the propeller. Elmer Sperry, inventor of the gyroscopic stabilizer, donated blueprints of his device and sent his son Lawrence to supersize installation by C.F. Harding of the Dayton Metal Products Co. F.W. Warner of the Aeolian Organ Company contributed pneumatic controls.

The flimsy contraption weighed only 300 pounds but carried an equal payload. Workers called the machine "Kettering's Bug." First test of the craft was held at Wright-Patterson Field in Dayton.

It is reported that the flimsy plane rose about 150 feet, then whipped around to dive at the crew that had just launched it. Subsequent, short tests were more promising. The Army ordered 36 aerial torpedoes for testing under field conditions.

Col. H.H. "Hap" Arnold, was enthusiastic about the potential of the flying bomb. He went to France in Oct. 1918 to brief Gen. John J. "Black Jack" Pershing, head of the American Expeditionary Force. Germany surrendered Nov. 11. Thus, Kettering's Bug was not put to combat use. Nevertheless, the Army wanted to evaluate the aerial torpedo's practical applications. Twelve were shipped in the Fall of 1919 to Carlstrom field where their flights could be easily monitored over the prairie.

Tests began Oct. 21, 1919. Army, Navy and civilian observers came to watch The missiles were mounted on a carriage that ran down a long rail track. At takeoff speed, the plane lifted away from the carriage.

Distance to the target and wind speed were calculated, then the launching tracks properly aimed. An electrically driven gyroscope, linked to an altimeter sensitive to atmospheric pressure, maintained level flight. An odometer coupled to the motor's crank shaft activated electric motors after a pre-determined number of revolutions. These drew out bolts holding on the wings. With this, the fuselage and payload — a 300-pound chunk of concrete — plunged to earth.

Variables Daunting

The number of variables to accommodate were daunting. The first several flights were erratic which frustrated Kettering. When one missile failed to level off and instead climbed out of sight, Kettering muttered, "Leave the damn thing up there," and stalked off the field. Crewmen in a Model-T Ford started across the prairie in the direction the pilotless plane was heading. They found it 21 miles away.

Finally, one of the flights proved satisfactory. The missile travelled its programed 15 miles and simulated bombing only two degrees off course. Historian Gene M. Burnett records in his book *Florida's Past* that among the observers was a young lieutenant named Jimmy Doolittle. As a Colonel in World War II, he led the first air raid against Japan. Doolittle's report on the Arcadia field tests was pessimistic: "The torpedo took off in a zoom, climbed to 200 feet, fell off and crashed. Torpedo flew 1 ¾ miles and crashed due to motor failure. The last torpedo, constructed from salvaged parts of previous wrecks, flew about 16 miles. It was approximately on its course, the proper altitude was adhered to, and the crash was caused by motor trouble. The motor is not sufficiently reliable to permit the torpedo flying over friendly troops."

Tests completed, the aerial torpedo project was discontinued by the Army. The Navy continued experiments under the supervision of Lawrence Sperry. He solved the accuracy problem by remote, radio control — then the pilotless bomber finally was shelved.

Malcolm Simons of Port Charlotte now is able to reveal how the pilotless bomber was revived by the U.S. Navy during World War II:

"During the Battle of Midway in June 1943, the tide of Japanese advance was halted by an aerial torpedo sqauadron of 15 piloted planes. They pursued the enemy carriers relentlessly. The squadron sank or disabled four carriers and a heavy cruiser — a fatal blow to Japanese ambition. However, the entire squadron was was shot down by the heavy curtain of anti-aircraft fire.

"Only one American pilot, picked up a day later at sea, survived the intital attack. U.S. dive bombers took up the battle the next three days and also suffered heavy casualties. The Navy then decided to revive development of pilotless war planes in order to reduce the heavy toll of fliers. I was assigned to the Special Air Task Force, Stag l, 2, and 3, to come up with such a weapon. We were based at Clinton, Oklahoma. I was part of Stag 2. We concentrated on drone airplanes with then-secret television cameras in the nose cones. 'Mother planes,' flying 25 miles behind, controlled the drones through 'joy stick' radio.

"Of course, this operation was top-secret. The natural curiosity of folks in Clinton about what was going on gave us problems. For example, one of our experimental planes crashed in a field. MPs in jeeps managed to get to the scene and cordon it off before a crowd of locals arrived. After awhile, we sent an ambulance — sirens screaming and lights flashing. The medics reached into the crashed fuselage, covered a 6-foot piece of wreckage with a blanket, placed it on a stretcher, and rushed off. When newspapers and concerned citizens called to inquire about the 'pilot,' we said he was badly injured but recovering.

Retrieves Bomb

"As experiments proceeded, they were transferred to Houma, Louisana — then to Eaglemount, Texas — for tests with live, 100-pound practice bombs. Several drones crashed. On one occasion, I had to dive down in shallow water of the Gulf of Mexico to retrive an unexploded bomb.

"The project was discontinued in 1944 when the Japanese Navy was largely sunk. Some of our people were trasferred to the U.S. Army Air Corps in England to cope with Hitler's "V-2" (vengence) guided missiles. There was no defense against these. The Vs were manufactured at Peeneumnde, on the Baltic coast — the most heavily fortified center in all Germany. We lost many planes and pilots trying to neutralize the place.

"Navy Special Project technicians installed TV, radar, and remote radio controls on Liberator bombers loaded with explosives. These were crash-dived into Peenemunde. This reduced V2 production to the point it could damage, but not defeat, Great Britain."

First World War air fields Carlstrom and Dorr continued as flight training schools until 1922. The best cadets formed the Carlstrom Aerial Circus which performed for crowds in Victory Bond drives.

A prize student at Carlstrom in the post-war period was Lt. Colonel Charles H. Danforth. He was assigned Commander of Langley Air Field, Virginia, in 1920 but did not know how to fly. Consequently he was detailed to Carlstrom for basic flight training. He soloed in six months. During Danforth's flights from Carlstrom he noticed beautiful Shell Point on the lower Peace River now in Charlotte County. Shortly before retirement in 1936, Danforth bought Shell Point acreage and built a lovely home there. Charlotte County purchased the structure in 1966 for a public meeting facility. Upon being closed down, the DeSoto air fields offered their "Ox-Jenny" Curtiss JN4D planes with OX 5 engines to buyers at cut-rate prices. The *Arcadia Enterprise* noted:

Carlstrom air cadets pose with their Curtiss "OX-Jenny" bi-planes.

"You can buy an army plane now for a pittance of $400. Uncle Sam has a flock of them at Dorr Field that he is offering to firstcomers. Sportively inclined folks hereabouts who have been hankering for an air flivver of their own need only line up now at the bargain counter."

Historian Claude Jones of Arcadia recalls that a man named Simmons bought one of the obsolete planes and taught himself how to fly. "I and a buddy liked to hike out to his place and watch him take off and land. One day he asked us if we would like a ride. We were thrilled. I was afraid to tell my father about our adventure because he and other townspeople thought Simmons was a nut to risk his life in such a primitive plane. He eventually heard about it and was the maddest I ever saw him. He threatened to give me a whipping I would never forget if I ever flew again.

"Some of the buildings out at the fields were sold and moved. Some were dismantled for materials. The remainder just fell apart from neglect. Weeds grew up in the old runways."

An American 14-inch cannon pounds a German
rail center 20 miles away.

Chapter 72

CELEBRATE WITH DYNAMITE

Of the 100 or so local soldiers who fought in the First World War, only two died as a result of enemy action — though a third man who never saw Florida is named also on a memorial plaque in front of the Charlotte County Memorial Auditorium.

The first native son killed outright was Augustine Willis of Charlotte Harbor Town, as reported by the *Punta Gorda Herald* in Oct. 1918:

"Mr. and Mrs. Garrison L. Willis received Monday the heart-breaking news that their son, Augustine, had been killed in one of the fearful battles being fought in France. He was one of the noblest young men of DeSoto County [Charlotte was not split from DeSoto until 1921] and was warmly esteemed by all who knew him.

"His parents and other kindred have the heartfelt sympathy of this entire community as well as that of their many friends north of the bay. They have received a very tender, sympathetic letter from their son's comrade, Harry L. Loar, who was with Augustine when he fell.

"The letter which was dated Sept. 8, 1918, gives no particulars, but abounds in fervent expressions of sympathy for the bereaved parents and of praise for the dead youth. The following are extracts from it:

"'I am writing you for the remembrance of your son, Augustine, who was at my side when he met his death. His manly form is always before me as I sit and ponder through the long evenings. He was, and is yet in a way, my dearest friend and chum. He at all times commanded the respect of everyone with whom he came in contact.

"'He met his death a few minutes after we had promised each other that should one of us be killed, the other would write to the bereaved parents and tell them the sad news. It is in fulfillment of this promise that I am writing. I can almost see him as I write, and it fills me with grief to think of the death of so brave and noble a comrade.

"'Of course you will mourn for him, but you must be brave and be comforted by the fact that he met his death with head up and fighting while encouraging his weaker comrades. His name will always be spoken with reverence by those who knew him, and it will go down as that of one whose military and personal record was without a stain. His last words to me were --- 'Write mother and father if I get killed.'"

Augustine and his father, Garrison, were gill-net fishermen at Charlotte Harbor Town. There were three Willis families there — Garrison, Mott and Emmett — not all related.

Augustine was buried in the American Cemetery at Flanders, France.

Second Death

The second military death here was that of Raleigh Whidden of Punta Gorda who was mortally wounded seven weeks before Augustine Willis was killed — as related in the preceding chapter. Notice of Whidden's death appeared in the Jan. 15, 1920, edition of the *Herald*. The paper noted that he died at Carlstrom Air Field, Arcadia, where he was taken for treatment after his Army discharge.

His obituary pointed out that Raleigh was a charter member of Punta Gorda post of the American Legion. His death was the first of the organization's veterans. Braxton Blount, representing the post, drove to Gardner, Fla., to assist in burial arrangements. Raleigh was buried in the family plot there between his foster parents.

The American Legion Post was formed in the early Fall of 1919. After Whidden's death, the post was renamed for Willis and Whidden. Unfortunately there were not enough veterans to sustain membership, and the post's charter lapsed. Then a Veterans of Foreign War post was established and named after Willis and Whidden. It, too, faded and was succeeded later by a new VFW post.

A new American Legion Post 103 was chartered Jan. 8, 1926, and named for Dr. David Norman McQueen who had served with the 2nd Infantry Medical Detachment and recently died.

Home folks also knew death — from the worldwide epidemic of "Spanish Influenza" propagated by soldiers travelling back and forth. The disease killed more people, and faster, than any epidemic in history. Because the war commanded everyone's attention, the 1918 flu epidemic was little noted. Yet, it claimed more American lives than the combined battle deaths of World War I, WW II, Korea, and Vietnam.

At its height in October, Gen. John Pershing, commander of the American Expedition Force, refused to accept that month's draft of 142,000 recruits. More than 21 million deaths were known to have occurred, but thousands more were never reported.

The *Herald* published warnings of flu symptoms and distributed 200 copies of the Surgeon General's instructions for quarantine. Big cities and military camps were hard hit. The Charlotte Harbor area suffered many cases but few deaths because of the scattered population.

War Ends

When the World War ended on the eleventh hour, of the eleventh day, of the eleventh month of 1918, the *Herald* proclaimed the victory in the largest type it had. This was followed with a sub-head summarizing the ensuing, spontaneous celebration:

"PEOPLE SHOUT AND FIRE GUNS AND DYNAMITE, WHISTLES BLOW, BELLS RING, SINGING CHILDREN PARADE THE STREETS, MEN MAKE SPEECHES AND EVERYBODY REJOICES!

"The news came first by way of Fort Myers whence the conductor of the north-bound train and his passengers brought it here.

"At the same time, it was confirmed by a special dispatch to the *Herald* from Jacksonville. As soon as people realized the truth of the glorious news, bedlam broke loose, and there was an uproar of rejoicing. The engine of the out-going passenger train whistled with all its might. The ice factory joined in with its tremendous voice, and then the church bells sent forth a joyous chorus.

"Everybody that could shout, did so. Even ye scribe, who for 40 years had not been able to yell, made such a desperate effort to do so that he ruined his voice for singing.

"Men and boys fired guns and pistols. Fire crackers, which no one thought could be found in town, mysteriously and suddenly came forth and were exploded by hilarious boys. Dynamite, in lieu of cannon, was set off along the waterfront, sending out a sound of thunder for miles around.

"The dozens of automobiles running about the streets kept their horns sounding at full blast. Everybody tried to make the loudest noise possible. Tin horns, cornets and other implements of noise added to the din.

"Old Glory suddenly made its appearance all about town, particularly along Marion Avenue, and its graceful folds floated proudly to the breezes. Two big flags swung over the center of Marion Avenue in front of Goldstein's furniture store. Another was suspended between the Seminole

Hotel and the Cooper hardware store. Two, with the royal ensign of Great Britain between them, swayed to the breezes between the Plaza Theatre and Ed Wotitzky's store.

"Everybody who could get one either wore or carried a small flag, and the automobiles were decorated with them.

"About 10:30 a.m. the high school was dismissed. Teachers and pupils, carrying small flags and singing patriotic songs, marched down Taylor street to the Seminole Hotel. There they halted under the leadership of Miss Gladys Martin, and continued singing. A great, enthusiastic crowd gathered around and cheered them lustily.

"Meanwhile, all along the main street and the bay front, dynamite continued to roar, and pistols and guns kept up a constant fusillade.

"After singing on the corner, the children — followed by the crowd — marched to the railway depot and greeted with songs the passengers on the train arriving at 11 o'clock.

"At 3 p.m., all the business houses closed and the people assembled in the Methodist church to participate in a splendid patriotic service conducted by the evangelist Rev. F.P. McCall. This service, which was very impressive and inspiring, closed at 4 p.m.

Hold Elaborate Celebration

"At 7 p.m., a rather elaborate celebration was held in front of the Plaza Theatre, where the crowd filled the street. The lobby of the Theatre was converted into a stage and was gaily decorated with the national colors illumined by big electric lights.

"The Theatre orchestra furnished inspiring music. Mrs.J.B. Washington played the piano while that brilliant artist, Harry Goldstein, with his violin, and Mrs. Goldstein with her cello, executed music that thrilled the crowd.

"The Home Guards in force, in full uniform with gleaming rifles, stood at attention back of the crowd. Prof. Donahue presided over the meeting and called out the numbers on the program. These included stirring addresses by Mayor S.F.J. Trabue, Col. Waltmire, Col Hancock, Prof. Bell and Evangelist McCall; inspiring songs by Miss Gladys Martin and Prof. M.L. Lifsey; fighting-front dialect recitations by Miss Norma Pepper; and choruses by the audience.

"The exercises, which lasted for two hours, were highly impressive. Upon their conclusion, the crowd entered the Theatre and enjoyed a first-class picture show. Thus ended Punta Gorda's great fete day — greatest in the town's history."

John Davis, a resident of Gardine, Montana, is memorialized at Punta Gorda for his World War service because of the persistence of his loving wife — the former Pearl Johnson, daughter of Capt. and Mrs. William H. Johnson. Capt. Johnson came to Punta Gorda in 1900 and dabbled in real estate. Pearl was born shortly thereafter. Later, Johnson became a pilot at Boca Grande.

According to the *Herald* of Sept. 1919, Mrs. Davis and her baby boy arrived at Punta Gorda from Asheville, N.C., where she spent the summer. Said the report: "In the Fall of 1917 she was married to John F. Davis of Montana. The couple lived there until her husband enlisted in the Army and was sent to France. He served in the Quartermaster Corps until his death Feb. 2 this year.

"Meantime Mrs. Davis returned to her parents' home at South Boca Grande where on Feb. 22, 1919, her son was born. She was graduated by Charlotte High School and finished a course at Columbia College in Lake City, Fla. After a short time she will return to her parent's home."

Oldtimers say Pearl fell madly in love with John Davis, a cowboy, while on a visit out west. He died of "black fever" (typhoid, a serious affliction common to soldiers in the field).

Having died in a French military hospital, with his body intact, John's body was shipped back to his home for burial. It is believed his grave is in the Custer Military Cemetery near Hardin, Montana.

In respect for his wife, Pearl, and for his father-in-law, Capt. Johnson, John Davis was listed on the first Punta Gorda American Legion Post 103 honor roll of soldiers who died overseas. And there his name was when a subsequent generation three wars later transferred the honor roll to a bronze plaque where it remains today.

Soldiers man machine gun in decisive Meuse-Argonne battle.

Anson Gaskill in retirement tends his orange trees.

Chapter 73

OWES HIS LIFE TO SECRET HERB

Thanks to a secret, Indian herb gathered from the Everglades by a friend, 82-year-old Anson Gaskill is still around to tell us about the old days in Charlotte Harbor and Punta Gorda.

"My daddy, Harry, came here with the great emigration of 1902 by North Carolina fishermen," says Anson. The number of fish in Charlotte Harbor was unbelievable. A modern ice plant at Punta Gorda opened a vast market up north for mullet, snapper, oysters and such like.

"A dozen or so fish packing companies started up, but there weren't enough fishermen to supply the demand. Consequently the Punta Gorda Fish Co., and the Florida Fish and Produce Co., sent agents up to North Carolina to recruit fishermen. They offered good prices for catches and paid to transport the families. Folks with furniture were given a box car in which men, wives and kids could go to the end of the railroad and then live in the cars until they could build a home. Young bachelors and teenagers like my father, he was 16, rode in passenger cars. When they arrived they lived in tents or in company fish camps down the bay."

According to the *Punta Gorda Herald* of August 1, 1902: "Nearly 100 fishermen are daily expected to arrive from North Carolina." Subsequent issues reported that 80 families came in the first wave, and 23 in the next.

"Other families came individually for the next few years," Anson relates. "Whenever companies needed fishermen they telegraphed help-wanted messages to North Carolina sea-coast towns. Telegraphers posted the messages in their windows. Within a week the companies would have new fishermen.

"Daddy stayed at a camp near Boca Grande Pass. On weekends, when fishing was suspended, he would row over to the quarantine station on Cayo Costa, or the light house on Gasparilla Island, for company. The light house had been in operation since 1890 under the keep of William Lester. His assistant was a Norwegian named Eric Danielson. He married a local girl named Clara Sapp, and they had a daughter named Bertha. She was really the attraction for my Daddy.

"They got married and built a house on the beach at Charlotte Harbor. It was next door to where the Snapper lawn mower shop is today. There they raised seven children — Elta, Reba, me and my twin sister Anna, Bertha Lee, Harry, and Philip. I was born May 21, 1912. Austin Groves built us two fireplaces so we kept warmer than most people back then. Mama cooked on a big, black, cast-iron stove. It was my job as a boy to cut wood for the stove and fireplaces. I had to hustle to keep up.

Guided Campbell Soup President

"Daddy at this time was a fishing guide and an independent fisherman. In the winter season, when wealthy sportsmen came to fish, he would be gone two or three weeks at a time. Several seasons he guided for the president of the Campbell Soup Company. On those occasions, he would bring home two or three cases of soup left over from their overnight fishing trips. When Daddy was gone for extended periods, Mama took us to the lighthouse to stay with Grand Dad. One night during a bad storm, the light's rotation system broke down. The family took turns turning the light by hand. It wasn't difficult, even the little kids took a turn. Two, big phosphate ships came in that night, depending on our light. Mr. Lester and Grand-dad were tickled at our faithfulness.

"I started to school at the new Charlotte Harbor building when it was still under construction in 1920. They hauled sand from the beach to the school site by ox carts. The school was torn down a couple of years ago for a shopping center.

"My teacher was Mrs. Sam Knight. She was a good teacher, but strict. All teachers kept big switches on their desks, and they didn't hesitate to use them. Mrs. Knight had one made from the spine of a cabbage palm frond. I got a taste of it one day during recess. I climbed up in one of the big oaks in the yard to smoke a cigarette. Mrs. Knight caught me and tore me up. I never did that again.

"We had a terrible hurricane in 1921. It blew into the harbor, raising the highest tide I have ever seen. Daddy woke us at 3 a.m. and said he had to leave because the water was coming into the house. We gathered up some clothes and bedding and started for the school which was made of brick and had a second floor. I waded in water up to my waist. All the Charlotte Harbor folks came. We crowded up to the second floor in the dark and listened to the wind howl, rain beat down, and waves crash against buildings

"We had to stay there that night, the next day, and the next night before the water went down enough for us to go home. There was two feet of water in the school's first floor — two and a half feet in our house. However, no one was killed or drowned.

"When I was 12, Daddy wanted a car but he didn't know how to drive. I had learned on a Model-T Ford owned by the father of one of my buddies. One Saturday, Daddy got him and me a ride over to Punta Gorda where he said he would buy any car I could drive. We settled on a Ford because I could drive that. They had one that had just come out with an electric starter, a fancy top and a muffler cut-out. I chose that one so people could hear me coming.

"The harbor bridge was just wide enough for two Fords if you squeezed close to the railing. While we were crossing, I had to get over for another car. I got too close to the side and tore off a fender brace. Daddy said, 'Never mind that, you're doing swell.'

Daddy Dies

"I slept with my father. Mamma slept with the girls. A few months later Mama woke me and said there was something wrong with Daddy. I was a deep sleeper and hadn't been awakened by him, but she had heard him from the next bedroom gasping for air. She said to go get Doctor [D.N.] McQueen in Punta Gorda. I got Doc McQueen, but Daddy died of a heart attack before we got to him. My baby brother, Philip, was only three months old. I had to quit school after the 11th grade — the highest taught at Charlotte Harbor School — to help support the family. All of us had to do something. I took a job on one of Joe Goulding's (Pete's father) stop-net crews. Later I fished with my Uncle Ott Danielson down around Sanibel Island. My brother, Harry, was a crabber.

"Charlotte Harbor [town] in the late twenties got real prosperous. We were incorporated. Lem Barnhill was mayor, P.C. O'Haver city manager and Kid Laney was our speed cop with a motorcycle. I paid city taxes for one year. Then the Great Depression struck, and nobody could pay taxes. We gave up our city charter. During the Depression you couldn't get enough money for fish to buy nets or gasoline for your boat. I got a government job with the Works Progress Administration (WPA) for 75 cents a day making little rocks out of big rocks.

"Aubrey Nelson came to me one day and said he had recommended me as a boat captain to a wealthy winter visitor at the Hotel Charlotte Harbor. I hurried to see him and got the job at $10 a day — big money even for good times.

"He was Morehouse Stevens of South Bend, IN., who had inherited a lot of stock in railroads. He was not an old man but had a bad heart. When the big hotel at Punta Gorda closed for the summer, he rented the McGuire place at Fort Myers — across the street from Thomas Alva Edison. The chauffeur and I had an apartment over the garage.

"When we caught a big fish I had to trundle it in a wheelbarrow over to show Mr. Edison. He would get his camera and take pictures.

"Wherever Mr. Stevens went he wanted to go fast, and he liked Scotch whiskey. He had some kind of pull with the railroad, because they would let him run the locomotive. He always drove the train as fast as it would go. One time I was driving him back from a speakeasy, in my 1928 Chevrolet. He was drunk, and I had a few myself. It was driving rain. As usual, Mr. Stevens urged me to drive faster. I was speeding across the Caloosahatchee bridge when a policeman stopped us. Mr. Stevens asked to know the fine. The cop said, 'Fifteen dollars.' Mr. Stevens handed the cop thirty dollars and said, 'Here, take this, we're coming back this way real soon.' He died soon after of a heart attack.

"Then I took the job of fishing guide for the Eagle's Nest Lodge — now owned by the Elks Club — at Solana east of Punta Gorda.

"When World War II started I tried to join the Navy at age 28. I knew boats and liked the idea of carrying your bed with you in battle. Doctors turned me down twice because they said I had heart trouble. Finally I got a certificate from my local doctor that I was OK, and they let me in.

Fought at Iwo Jima

"Because of my boating ability, they made me a petty officer second class boatswain's mate. I taught sailing for awhile at Port Everglades and Key West. Then they promoted me to Chief Boatswain and sent me to the Pacific to operate a landing craft. I took part in the Iwo Jima and Okinawa campaigns. After the war, I became the fishing guide and boat captain for Lou Calder at his luxurious Allapatchee Lodge on Alligator creek. Joe Washington was the hunting guide and dog trainer. Mr. Calder was head of Perkins-Goodwin, a New York City investment firm. He kept the best guides, boats and dogs any where around for his friends and customers.

"Mr. Calder went back to New York during the summers. I took him there in his 34-foot cruiser *Loula* He paid my salary and all expenses while we were in New York. In the Fall I brought him back. He was a fine man who contributed generously to the Punta Gorda Library building fund and the Boy Scout Community Center in Gilchrist park.

"I worked for Mr. Calder 27 years. Toward the end he developed heart trouble and moved to Long Boat Key where he could be near his doctor. I used to go see Mr. Calder nearly every Sunday, the last time was with Doc [Nathaniel] McQueen, an old friend of his. Mr. Calder died the following week. He left me $5,000 in his will. He left the lodge, by then

322

vacant and vandalized, to the University of Miami. It sold the land to Al Johns for the Burnt Store Isles development.

"Also after the war, in 1949, I married Helen Inghram, a divorcee with a sweet, 18-month-old daughter named Gail. Helen managed Bob's Place, now the Slip Not Lounge. She was a wonderful woman who didn't drink or smoke. After we were married I stopped, too. She said she lost her best customer. She bore me two children, Nancy and Kenneth.

"We bought the Maytag Highlander self-serve laundry on Taylor Street near Scotty's home supply store when Mr. Calder closed the lodge. We worked at the laundry everyday, servicing the machines and doing laundry for folks who were unable to do it themselves. I developed colon cancer in 1973. When discovered, the malignancy was in its final stage. My doctor removed my lower bowel but said he couldn't get all the cancer and so I had only six months to live. Harry Miller, a friend, told me he knew of an Indian herb that grows in the Everglades and cures cancer. I was in great pain, and no prospects of getting better. I asked him to get me some of the herb. In a few days he brought me sack of chopped up, green plant I was supposed to chew and swallow the juice.

"At the time I had lost all my lower teeth because of dental surgery. There was no way I could chew anything. Helen, bless her soul, got a meat grinder and reduced the herb to pulp. She tried to get empty capsules from the drug stores to put it in. However, no one would sell to her — they thought she was peddling narcotics, even called the cops. Helen went to the A&P and bought capsuled gelatin. She poured out the gelatin and filled the capsule with the herb.

Saw Three Of Everything

"The first capsule I swallowed didn't do anything so a half-hour later I took a second one. Harry said, 'Take it easy. That herb is potent.' This time the pain stopped — that was a welcome relief — but everything seemed to turn upside down. I saw three of everything.

"Helen led me to bed. Next morning I looked out the window and saw six of everything. Harry said to take one capsule a day for 10 days, or until my eyes crossed. I took the capsules for 10 days and felt fine. I went back to the doctor and he was amazed. All the cancer was gone.

"My wife came down with lung cancer last year. Nothing helped her. My friend, Harry, had died. I tried to find an Indian who knew about the herb, but couldn't. We had a little of the dried herb saved from 21 years ago. I boiled it for tea, but it didn't help. When I lost Helen, I lost my right arm.

"Perhaps the old herb had lost its potency, or it acted only on colon cancer. I've heard there is some man over at Boca Raton who is growing the herb and trying to get it tested. If it works he will make a fortune. I would lay in a supply for myself, just in case."

Whitten stood with his neck in the noose, but trap was never sprung.

Chapter 74

HOW WHITTEN CHEATED THE GALLOWS

The hangman's gallows built for Bernard Whitten at Arcadia — when it was the seat of DeSoto County that included today's Charlotte — stood in the jail yard for two years waiting for its victim.

Circumstances of a sensational murder that led to construction of the lethal device in 1920 was related 13 years later in a memoir by Chester Dishong who was a deputy sheriff then but later a U.S. marshal. Reporter Gene Plowden recorded it for historical reference:

" Mid pleasures and palaces, though we may roam; be it e'er
so humble, there's no place like home."

* * *

Lizzie Whitten, comely bride of four months, sang that old familiar song as she played the organ in the parlor of her parents' home in Wauchula on that fateful Saturday night in April, 1920.

A sinister shadow moved past the open window. The mellow light from an oil lamp streaked through the drizzling rain. Rain drops glinted like diamonds as they flipped through the light and pelted down on the soft, warm earth.

Lizzie reached the end of the first verse. The shadow paused. Then it crouched beneath the window sill, as if to escape the light. Lizzie hesitated, and the shadow seemed to melt in the dripping rain. Slowly, the organ started again, and Lizzie began the words of the second verse.

324

The shadow rose again, poking an ugly head above the window sill. The barrel of a rifle glinted in the lamp light. It pointed toward Lizzie Whitten — the finger of death. "Spang!" The rifle spoke. Its sharp bark mingled with the strains of organ music.

Lizzie's hands rose from the keys; she gasped, then turned and twisted her body before slumping to the floor. The sudden cessation of music and Lizzie's singing brought her parents who gathered the girl up in tender, loving arms, imploring her to speak. But Lizzie was limp and silent, her lips sealed forever.

Dr. J.E. Garner, the family physician, was called. He found the girl had been shot once, with a .22 caliber rifle. The bullet had entered the back of her neck and passed through the spine.

A stunned crowd gathered at the little, unpainted house where Lizzie's parents lived. Among the first to arrive was Chief of Police D.E. Gillette, veteran peace officer of South Florida who spent most of his life as a policeman and deputy sheriff.

Chief Gillette made a hurried search of the premises, gathering what clues he could in the rush and excitement that followed the shooting.

Discovered Tracks

He found some tracks in the soft sand under the window. One of the tracks was made by a deformed foot, else the owner had done a clever job of walking on the toes of one foot while using all of the other. Lizzie's new husband was known to have a deformed foot.

The chief also discovered bicycle tracks leading from beside a tree in the yard. They trailed off toward Main Street, a block away. It was easy to follow them in the soft sand along the unpaved street.

Dozens of men were quick to volunteer their services in a hunt for the killer. Chief Gillette deputized several of them to watch railroad trestles, highway intersections and bridges. A cordon was quickly thrown around the town of 2,500 inhabitants who by this time were thoroughly aroused over the brutal murder.

There were scores of bicycles in the town, and nobody reported one missing. It was still raining, but not hard enough to erase the bicycle tracks. Gillette asked one of his posse, Fred Brown, to help him follow the bicycle tracks.

They followed the tracks by car north to Bowling Green, Fort Meade and Brewster — 21 miles in all. There the tracks vanished. Gillette and Brown continued to hunt, stopping at farm houses, waking occupants, learning nothing.

Meanwhile, my brother, DeSoto Sheriff J.L. Dishong, drove up from Arcadia and organized another search party. About mid-day Monday, they came to an abandoned farm house where they found tracks coinciding with those at the murder scene.

325

A pitcher pump on the back porch was wet, as if someone had just drunk from a tin cup hanging on a nail. From the house, the tracks led off across a freshly-plowed field and vanished in a palmetto swamp beyond. The suspect apparently had abandoned his bicycle and was now traveling on foot. The officers had missed him by minutes.

Lizzie was buried Monday. That added fuel to the fire of bitterness that was raging against the suspected slayer. That afternoon Chief Gillette came to my home in Wauchula to discuss plans to apprehend the suspect which we believed was Lizzie Whitten's new husband whom she had recently left after only four months of marriage. A telephone call from Bowling Green advised us the suspect was seen headed south, toward Wauchula.

We were discussing how we might apprehend him and then outwit a mob, and get him out of town, when Wesley Easters walked up. "I just saw the S_O_B_ walking down the railroad track toward the Negro quarters," he said.

Will Pyler, night policeman at Wauchula, went with me to the Negro quarters which were less than two miles from the scene of the crime. In less than ten minutes we were searching the cabins with the help of Dave Dickson, fireman at a nearby mill.

Finally we came to the shack where Adam Adkisson, an ex-slave who claimed to be 100 years old, lived alone. I sent Will and Dave to the rear of the cabin and knocked on the front door. The door was locked, but I heard the aged Negro shuffle to the door. "Who dat?" he asked.

Open This Door!

"It's Ches Dishong, the sheriff," I said loudly. "Open this door!"

Adkisson shuffled his feet a few times, shoved boxes and chairs aside, fumbled with the latch, and eased the door open inches at a time. I met him with my pistol. I searched under the bed an in darkened corners while the old Negro stuttered stout denials that anyone was hiding there.

A partition ran through the center of the shack, and a door was cut in the middle. I walked over to this door, shoved it open and poked my flashlight inside. The light picked out a youth about 21 years old. He was skinny, with a sallow complexion and of slight build. It was Lizzie's husband, Bernard. He trembled when he saw me.

He raised his arms, and a rifle barrel gleamed in the light, but my pistol covered him before he had a chance to level the gun. "Drop that rifle," I commanded. A sneer crept over his face, but the weapon crashed to the floor.

Dave went back to his work, but Will and I hustled the prisoner into my automobile. We started for the county jail at Arcadia. Less than half a mile down the road, a mob was waiting for us. If they stopped us, our prisoner would never be brought to trial.

326

I put on speed and drove like mad. The mob stood in the middle of the road, waving their arms and yelling at us to stop. Instead, I swerved the car to the side of the road to avoid hitting them. We tore down a section of wire fence, then careened back into the ruts beyond the mob.

The mob surged behind us. Some members climbed into an automobile and chased us, gaining on us every mile of the way. I decided to take a desperate chance. As we turned a curve in the road, I swung off onto a side road, drove for a mile or two through the woods, and stopped in a clump of palmettoes.

We sat there for two hours before venturing out onto the main highway again. Thus we outwitted the mob and landed our man in jail.

* * *

Arraigned in open court, Bernard Whitten pleaded "guilty" to the charge. Under Florida law, however, the court could not accept it. The plea was changed to "not guilty."

His parents lived in Georgia and could not be present at the trial. Inasmuch as Whitten was a few weeks short of 21 years, the law required that a guardian be appointed for him. The court named Louis Robbins and J.A. Timberlake as counsel and guardians.

Evidence brought out at the trial showed that Bernard Whitten had deliberately planned to murder Lizzie. They had married the previous Christmas, and she had left him only a few days before the crime. The Saturday when she was killed, he had bought a rifle at a Wauchula hardware store and practiced marksmanship for two hours. He told some acquaintances he was going to kill his wife.

Murder In The First Degree

The jury brought in a verdict of "guilty of murder in the first degree." The judge sentenced Whitten to be hanged in the jail yard at Arcadia on July 30, 1920. Whitten sat in his cell and watched carpenters erect the scaffold outside the window.

The afternoon before he was to die, his sister employed W.D. Bell, Arcadia attorney and later state senator and judge, to appeal the case to the State Supreme Court. The time was short, but Bell hopped on a train and rushed to the court at Tallahassee. Invitations to the hanging had already been delivered.

At the designated hour the next morning, a crowd from all parts of the county gathered to see Bernard Whitten pay for his crime. A large delegation came from Punta Gorda.

Rudyard Kipling Bell, W.D. Bell's six-year-old son, wanted to see the hanging with some other young friends. Mrs. Bell would not consent, despite much youthful begging. At the appointed time, High Sheriff J.L. Dishong led Whitten out into the jail yard. The noose was ready. Whitten mounted the gallows.

A Western Union messenger boy pushed his way through the crowd, shouting "Stop! Stop!" He handed the sheriff a telegram. The Supreme Court had stayed the execution. Simultaneously, W.D. Bell in Tallahassee called his family to give them the news. Little Rudy's pleading had been unnecessary after all.

Whitten was led back to his cell to await the next act in this human drama. He did not have long to wait.

Timberlake, his attorney and guardian, was handling a divorce case. When the husband of the woman suing for divorce heard about it, he walked into Timberlake's office, shot the lawyer dead, and then killed himself. Attorney Bell filed a "writ of error" and won a new trial.

Before the trial could come up, DeSoto county in 1921 was divided into five parts. Wauchula became the seat of Hardee County, and the case was transferred there. It was at this time that Charlotte County also was split off from DeSoto.

Escaped

Whitten was tried at Wauchula Oct. 26, 1921, and was again sentenced to hang. Again his sentence was appealed. Months passed. On the night of May 4, 1922, he and four other prisoners fled jail in a wholesale break for freedom.

The next day, Deputy Sheriff Ed Garner started out to look for the escaped prisoners. In the village of Buchanan, a man stepped out onto the road and waved Garner down for a lift. It was Bernard Whitten. Garner hustled him back to jail.

A few months later, the gallows at Arcadia was taken down. The structure was becoming weather worn. Besides, there were no prisoners on the docket awaiting trial for a capital offense. There has never been an execution in DeSoto County.

The State Pardon Board commuted Whitten's sentence to life imprisonment in August 1924. Over the years, he escaped four more times from work camps. He was recaptured three times, and on one other occasion turned himself in for unexplained reasons. Though the gallons was cheated, the prison was not.

Chapter 75

CHASED BY GOBLINS

Ghost stories vied with fish tales for local gossip in the old days —
encouraged by Adrian P. Jordan, publisher-editor of the *Punta Gorda
Herald*, who was noted for his tongue-in-cheek articles.

Readers of this series will remember serious accounts by early
residents of supernatural events. There is the Sandlin house in Punta
Gorda haunted by the ghost of young Mary Sandlin. She was burned to
death by a malfunctioning, gasoline-fueled clothes iron, and now is said on
occasion to flit about during the night strewing laundry through the house.

The Hermitage house at Englewood was said by various owners to be visited by the spirit of Grandma Johansen slamming her bedroom window and tipping over her old chair. Supposedly she is searching for her "sacred lead" which she burned in life to cure sickness.

Then there is the Charlotte Harbor Town restaurant built over an old African-American cemetery. Workers say the place is plagued by mischievous fires, napkins that fly through the air, and dishes that crash to the floor when no one is looking.

To these stories can be added two more. The first involves Dick Windham, a shady Punta Gorda character at the turn of the century. He was accused, but absolved, of complicity in the assassination of Marshal John H. Bowman in 1903. He also was said to the be the lover of Mrs. "Ma" McGraw, proprietor of the notorious "Bloody Bucket" road house, whose husband was shot to death under mysterious circumstances in 1931.

Here is Editor Jordan's report of Sept. 12, 1902, before Windham had come to be feared by local folks. The judge mentioned apparently was a travelling salesman who hired a buggy to take him to Fort Myers and back.

A GHOST STORY

Dick Windham Saw a Goblin

As fish stories are getting rather scarce, here is an "o'er true tale" of a genuine boogie having been encountered about 9 o'clock Monday night by Richard S. Windham, a livery-man of this city, and Judge S.A. Murden, a commercial tourist those home is at Leesburg.

Both these gentlemen are well known for veracity. Indeed, who ever did know a drummer or a horse swapper to tell anything but the truth? If, however, there had been any doubt of the truth of the story, the pallid countenances of the two gentlemen next day would have dispelled any want of faith in their narrative.

But, here is the story as they tell it. At the hour mentioned, they were returning from Fort Myers in a top buggy drawn by two staunch mules. They had reached a point in the road about ten miles south of Punta Gorda and far from any habitation. Windham was driving. The judge was dozing. Suddenly the former observed a very white something — the size of a tall man — lying full length close beside the road. The mules were moving pretty briskly. As they approached the object, it rose up under the noses of the animals. This caused them to dash aside in terror.

In swerving, the buggy grazed a pine tree. The jolt aroused the judge. He opened his eyes to see a tall, white apparition standing straight up beside the buggy and as high as the buggy top.

The judge yelled, "Who are you?"

By this time, the mules, frantic with terror, were running away. Windham had all he could do to keep them in the road. The judge kept his eyes fixed on the boogie and was horrified to observe it glide into the road behind the buggy and follow along with the greatest ease — although the vehicle was going at the utmost speed of the mules.

In a moment or so the thing glided up to the back of the buggy and seemed to peer earnestly within. Then it uttered an unearthly, blood-curdling shriek, stood still in the road for a second or so and suddenly vanished.

After the mules had run a mile or more, Windham succeeded in checking them up. Then he proposed to drive back and try to ascertain what the thing was. However, the judge had seen enough and insisted on coming to town, which they did.

Both gentlemen say the apparition had the appearance of a very tall man wrapped in a sheet; but they cannot imagine what could prompt any man to wrap up that way and go out all alone ten miles into the wilderness and lie down beside the road.

In fact, they do not believe it was a man. They scout the idea of its having been a cow or a white bear. The judge says he is coming back here shortly to see if he can solve the mystery.

The Kissimmee Gazette, which is an expert on Florida ghosts and ghost stories, might throw some light on the subject.

Spook Contest

The second example of "other world spirits," reported by the *New York Times* in December 1908, describes a proposal by Punta Gorda Judge Francis Kemper Adams to test clairvoyance.

The story was headlined: *"SPOOK CONTEST SPIRITS TRICKY."* *The Metropolitan Psychical Society of New York City announced that it had received "literally thousands of applications" to claim an offer of $10,000 to any medium who could describe the nature and number of oranges "carelessly spilled" behind their back.*

Society President James L. Kellog said, "It soon become evident that the spirit fakers and guessers had to be separated from those who sincerely claimed supernatural power of connection with the spirits of the departed.

"Only one has made a correct answer, and she in one particular only," said Kellog. "However, Judge Adams has written an uncommonly interesting letter proposing a test which will be undertaken by wire. Judge Adams tells of two women of his acquaintance who have done remarkable things. He says: 'Five years ago, while I was a judge at Punta Gorda, my deputy sheriff was shot in the dark by unknown parties. The following year, the women declared who did it, and it was correct.

"'Another attempted killing was also told, and it also was correct. Deaths have been foretold, and very many unforeseen events here have been correctly told which none who knew ever supposed would occur.

331

"'Now, I am not a believer of these things, but I must acknowledge that many things occurred that could not in any possibility have been known to the persons foretelling them.

"'Could not this experiment be performed? Have five of your society meet some evening in New York, bringing your oranges. Write me the date. It takes three days usually for mail. I will have the two ladies meet and get their spirits to inform them of what you do — number of oranges, style of bag or receptacle, and so on.'"

Kellog sent the following reply to Judge Adams: "Your experiences are interesting. Later we will arrange some experiments to be tried and recorded at each end of the wire."

Spiritualism Popular

Spiritualism was widely discussed and believed at that time. The deputy sheriff mentioned by Judge Adams was Marshal John H. Bowman who was assassinated Jan 29, 1903, by a shotgun blast through an open window. A deed that at first implicated Dick Windham. The lady "seers" later singled out Isiah E. Cooper (See Vol. 1).

Cooper stoutly denied guilt but was arrested, tried, and convicted to be hanged. After several appeals, the sentence was commuted to life imprisonment. Ten years later he escaped from a work gang and was never seen again.

The "attempted killing" mentioned by Judge Adams was that against Capt. Albert F. Dewey, a prominent marine towing and dredging engineer. His assailant fired a rifle through an open door, but the bullet was deflected by brace on the screen and shattered Dewey's left leg (See Vol. 1).

It is interesting to speculate that one of the clairvoyants might have been Mrs. Marian McAdow, a wealthy and socially prominent matron of Punta Gorda. She was an ardent believer in spiritualism and took up the hobby of photography — including darkroom processes — in an attempt to capture materialized spirits on film.

Mrs. McAdow also was an accomplished painter. She and her husband, Perry, made a pact that the first one to "pass to the other side" would return and tilt a painting she had made of Col. Isaac Trabue's original waterfront cabin.

After Perry McAdow died, the painting hung undisturbed in a hallway for many years. Marion finally gave it to a friend, Willie White, the telegrapher. A few years ago, Mr. and Mrs. Marlon and Terry Runkle rescued the painting from discarded articles in the garage at Mrs. White's former home. Today it hangs in the Runkle's living room — happily straight and true.

The Bat Hotel

Chapter 76

BAT HOTELS SCORNED BY TRANSPLANTS

There was a time in old Punta Gorda when folks earnestly cultivated bats in their belfries. The reason is aptly explained by the number of Florida mosquitos and the attempt 70 years ago to control them with "bat towers."

Actually there were two bat towers — or "bat hotels" as they were dubbed by local wags. The structures were built in 1923 by Dr. David N. McQueen, county health inspector; and Harry Dreggors, president of the Smith & Dreggors Fish Co. (later Punta Gorda Fish Co.)

Dr. McQueen owned a vegetable farm southwest of the Shreve and Henry street intersection. Dreggors owned a citrus grove farther west on Henry St. where the Punta Gorda utility department is now located.

Beyond the Dreggors grove there was nothing but marshy "sand flats" — ideal breeding ground for mosquitos of heroic dimensions.

Shortly before the Civil War, local fishermen and cattlemen developed a brisk trade with Cuba. When Col. Isaac Trabue persuaded the Florida Southern Railway to extend its line to the south shore of Charlotte Harbor in 1886, farmers expanded the Cuban connection.

An important commodity obtained from Cuba was guano — the droppings of bats. It was very high in nitrogen and unexcelled as fertilizer — but expensive. After the First World War, state health officials emphasized the dangers of mosquitos which transmitted malaria. The disease was a scourge in the low, flooded lands around Charlotte Harbor.

McQueen and Dreggors hit upon the bat hotel scheme which they believed would get rid of mosquitos and simultaneously create a free source of guano. Each man — with the technical assistance of Dell Huckeby, a Cleveland sawmill operator and citrus grove owner — built slotted 40-foot towers to provide homes for the bats.

Each tower was comprised of a tall pine log at each corner, tapering slightly toward the top for stability. The roof was pyramidal and wooden shingled. The upper 10 feet was slotted like over-size venetian blinds through which bats could enter. A maze of rafters braced the structure and provided roosts.

Remainder of the tower was enclosed to within five feet of the ground. The lower portion was left open so guano could be removed. The towers were well engineered for they withstood the devastating hurricane of 1926 when scores of smaller buildings in the area were destroyed.

Cuban Bats Captured

With all in readiness McQueen, Dreggors and Huckeby went to Cuba for a colony of bats. Local farmers climbed around in caves to capture several boxes of "bull bats" — a large species that feeds mainly on mosquitos.

The bats were brought here and released inside the towers, and all went well for the first year. The mosquito population was noticeably smaller, and the guano was a welcome byproduct.

At first, boys would hike out to the towers to see the bats, but their curiosity was quickly satisfied. The rain of bat droppings made visits inside the towers unpleasant — especially if the bats were disturbed.

Unfortunately the bats did not reproduce as in their homeland. Perhaps the towers were not as cool and dark as the bats' normal habitat. They flew away one by one, nobody knows where.

Within a few years, all the flying animals were gone and the towers demolished to make way for Punta Gorda Isles — which is just as well because owners there take a dim view of bats.

Charles Cerny, white shirt, gets help in plowing his field with oxen.

Chapter 77

DEFIED BUZZARDS

When Charlie Cerny saw buzzards "wrangling" outside his isolated homestead cabin at Bermont, he knew he had to get up from his sick bed and summon help. "You won't get me," he muttered!. He had a severe case of malaria, high fever and was too weak to prepare a meal — not that he felt like eating. He had not taken food for two days. .

Painfully he struggled to the door, pulling along the sheet from his bed. He waved the sheet weakly at the buzzards. They squawked and retreated to nearby tree limbs to keep close watch. Charlie reached a pine sapling he had skinned for a flag pole a year earlier. He tied the sheet to the halyard and slowly hoisted a signal of distress.

Charlie didn't remember how he made it back to the house. He was just thankful he didn't pass out in the yard circled by beady-eyed buzzards. As he slipped into unconsciousness he hoped some one would find him before it was too late. Nearest neighbors were Mr. and Mrs. Vanselow, a mile and a half away across the desolate prairie. As Mrs. Vanselow hung out her wash that day, she noticed a flutter of white in the distance. There it was again. She watched carefully. Yes, it was a signal for help. She called her son Oswald who agreed he should check on his best friend.

Oswald brought back Charlie in an ox cart, the only reliable means of transportation in the rough and wet countryside. Mrs. Vanselow nursed Charlie back to health.

Bouts of malaria, spread by clouds of mosquitos, were not the only hardships endured by settlers 20 miles east of Punta Gorda. The area was opened to homesteading in 1905 — the last to be offered because it was poorly drained and dotted with swamps. The area would have remained a "wet and dry" prairie if it had not been for an energetic promoter at Chicago. He advertised that for $200 he would move a family to Florida and guarantee a homestead claim.

About 80 percent of settlers ultimately taking up land were city folks from Illinois yearning for an independent life in tropical paradise.

Unfortunately they did not realize the difficulties of farming Florida wet land. They lived in tents until a portable saw mill was brought in and cut timber for cabins. Bermont and the neighboring community of Sparkman (named for the surveyor who laid out the section lines) peaked in 1915 at approximately 250 families. Today, a blinking traffic light at the intersection of State Roads 74 and 31 is the only marker of the once thriving community of Bermont. Sparkman today is open fields.

In their heyday, each village had a school, church, general store, post office and baseball team. Then, young men went off to the First World War. Many older folks drifted back to Chicago where the war-time economy provided good pay.

Chicago Emigrants

In Chicago at this time was Frank and Anna Cerny. He was an immigrant from Bohemia, skilled as a coppersmith. She was a native of Prague. They had four children born in the United States: Frank, Bertha, Charles and Jerome. Frank became an attorney for the Illinois Central Railroad, Jerome an architect, and Bertha married well.

Charles, born in 1899, apprenticed as a machinist, spent the war turning out armaments. He worked the next four years in the railroad machine shop, but sought greener fields — literally. Thus, in 1922 he and another railroad machinist, Jerry Leiner, quit their jobs and went to Florida to visit their old Chicago buddy, Oswald "Van" Vanselow. The latter's parents had taken up a homestead at Bermont.

Charlie and Jerry stayed with the Vanselows three months while looking for jobs as machinists. Southwest Florida then was still a sparsely settled country of ranchers, fishermen and farmers. There were no jobs for machinists. Reluctantly they decided to go back.

Oswald was not enamored of the hard life of a hard-scrabble farmer so he joined his friends. The trio set out in Oswald's 1917 Chevrolet. They stopped at the village of Gainesville to earn travel money by doing odd jobs. Gainesville was the office of the United States homestead agent. The Florida Land Boom was just getting underway, and Oswald said free homestead land would be worth a lot a money in the near future. He urged his friends to file a claim which cost only $13.

Jerry wasn't interested, but Charlie invested his last bit of cash on the last homestead available at Bermont — a tract adjacent to the Vanselow place. He reasoned he might be able to sell the claim before the five-year proving-out period expired. The young men drove on to Jacksonville hoping to find work in the railroad yards. However, none was available. Oswald was disillusioned about job prospects. Inasmuch as he had enough money for gas to get back to Bermont, he gave up and returned.

The railroad roundhouse men arranged for the stranded Charlie and Jerry to deadhead by rail to Chicago. In addition, they took up a collection which was enough for two "pie cards" good for six meals each at railroad restaurants along the way. Such cards, bought in advance at a discount, had numbers which were punched out as used.

Charlie went back to work at the Illinois Central shop and to live with his parents. Yet, he could not get the Florida sand out of his shoes. Shortly before his homestead claim was due to expire he left once more, this time to try farming. Oswald, with his ox cart, met Charlie at Arcadia. The 20-mile trip to Bermont in the rain took 12 hours. Charlie was dismayed to see his land ankle deep in water. He stayed with the Vanselows until he could build an 8-by-10-foot corrugated-iron shack that barely met the homestead requirement of a habitable dwelling.

Crop Washed Out

Charlie invested in a yoke of oxen, plow, axe, cross-cut saw, and gun. He cleared three acres — the minimum required — and planted oats. The grain had barely germinated when a rain storm washed away the seedlings. He did get in a little vegetable garden for food. The only meat was that he could obtain by hunting — mostly rabbits. In later years, when he jumped in his sleep, his wife joked it must be because he had eaten so many rabbits.

He once said he would have starved if he hadn't occasionally fixed someone's' farm equipment and been paid in foodstuff. What little cash he earned came from pulling cars stuck in the sandy trails that ran to Arcadia, Punta Gorda and Fort Myers. Every five weeks, Charlie and Oswald hitched up an ox cart and went to Arcadia for supplies. The rate of travel was just two miles per hour, so the men camped at Arcadia overnight.

As a young bachelor, surviving alone for three years, Charlie had to learn to cook for himself. His guide was a recipe book which came free with a sack of flour. His first attempt at baking bread was a dismal failure.

"The scrawny loaf was hard as a rock," he related later. "I threw it out in the yard for the wild hogs and birds, but they wouldn't eat it either. It took a month before it went to pieces.

"I kept on trying and finally was able to make myself a couple of birthday cakes with sugar-water icing, and wild tomatoes instead of cherries for decoration. I invited the Vanselows and a couple of other friends in for a party. Everyone said my cakes were delicious."

Partying was what Charlie and Oswald liked best. Charlie played the saxophone, and Oswald the fiddle. They were in constant demand for dances and church suppers where food was plentiful. Rev. George Gatewood, earliest Methodist preacher and a fiddle player, joined in.

When things got lonely out on the prairie, Charlie would sit on his door step and play his saxophone. "Cattle gathered around my fence to hear my music," he said. "I reckon they didn't know what kind of an animal made sounds like that."

It was an event when an adventurous motorist came by. There were no bridges and so cars got bogged down often. The usual method of fording creeks was to cover the car's radiator with a blanket and make a running charge at the crossing. Usually the car's momentum would carry it through before the motor stalled. When they didn't make it, Charlie pulled them out with his oxen and was rewarded with a dollar or two. One grateful man gave him $6 for rescuing him — the most Charlie ever got for the service.

Charlie Cerny, third from left in front of his homestead, proudly displays the birthday cakes he made for himself. Oswald Vanselow is next right. Couple next right is unknown. M/M Vanselow are far left.

During the rainy season, Charlie would hear bawling cattle stuck in the swamps. He pulled them out also. Once he noticed buzzards circling and went out to investigate. He found a new-born calf by its dead mother. He took the calf home and hand fed it until it was old enough to forage.

Cash money was hard to come by, but with his mechanical and musical ability, Charlie was well prepared to take advantage of every opportunity. One time he was hired by Lee Evans, who operated a turpentine still, to make a coffin for a leased convict who had died. "I not only made the coffin, I buried the man," declared Charlie years later. "Evans told me he would pay $10 for the job. Now Evans is dead, and I never got my $10."

During the five months each year that homesteaders could leave their claims, Charlie hired out as machinist on a dredge at Useppa Island. Advertising and hotel magnate Barron Collier was building a resort hotel.

After three years, Charlie wrote the land office saying he was ready to prove up. The inspector first questioned neighbors about Charlie and noted that he had let his claim expire. The inspector arrived tired, hungry, and dubious at Charlie's little tin cabin. His doubts disappeared when Charlie served him fried rabbit, dumplings and fresh-ground coffee. Charlie didn't have much of a farm, but he had learned to cook. This, and favorable reports by his neighbors, earned homestead approval easily.

Received His Deed Patent

When Charlie received his deed patent, he went to Punta Gorda to work as engineer at Collier's Hotel Charlotte Harbor. There in 1925, Charlie met the lovely Margaret Goetz on a work vacation from New York. She and other girls had arrived by steamship around the Keys.

Charlie was smitten and lost no time in dating Margaret. They were frequent dance patrons at the fashionable Log Cabin. Before she left for home, they were engaged. Miss Goetz' parents insisted Charlie find "more suitable employment," so he took a job in Collier's New York offices.

The couple married in 1928, honeymooned at Niagara Falls, and returned to Punta Gorda. Charlie and Oswald bought the Hewitt Machine Shop just west of today's post office. Vanselow was a "mechanical genius," but a recluse who never married. Van retired to the old home place when Charlie built a new shop, the Cerny Garage and Machine Shop, now a marine repair shop at Tamiami Trail and Charlotte Avenue.

The Cernys bought a home at Solana and had three children — John, Robert and Elizabeth Ann. John made family records available to us for this story. When the Depression hit in the 30s, Cerny lost his old homestead. but was able to buy it back later under the Murphy Bill.

Charlie retired in 1968 and built a beautiful home on Alligator Creek. John and Elizabeth had moved away, so he turned over the business to Robert and wife, Jane. Both men are now deceased, but Jane is still active in community affairs — unconcerned about the buzzards of Bermont.

Highlight of 25th anniversary of Scout troop 5 as investiture of four tenderfoot scouts by torchlight along Alligator Creek. Scoutmaster U.S. Cleveland, without torch, facing camera, administers the Scout oath to, from left, Richard Salmon, Eddie Mann, Jimmy Nordlund and Freddie Rye.

Chapter 78

SCOUT TROOP OLDEST IN FLORIDA

Early Boy Scouts of Punta Gorda remember with fondness and awe the visits of Uncle Dan Beard, national Chief Scout, who treated them to rattlesnake meat and taught them how to throw a tomahawk.

Oldest Scout troop in Florida is Punta Gorda 5 — having been chartered April 21, 1921. It was, however, successor of Punta Gorda Troop 1, organized in 1918 but let its charter lapse after two years.

J.H. Albert was the first scoutmaster and served only five months. He was succeeded by W.D. Wilson who served out the year. Assistant scoutmaster was Frank M. Cooper. To the best of our knowledge, only one member of Troop 1 is still living. That is Byron L. Rhode.

There was no sponsor that first year. A committee consisting of Cooper, F.R. Blount, Charles Cochran, H.B. Blazer, J.H. Lipscomb and Leslie L. Lewis provided what little financial support was needed.

Just 13 boys signed up: Edwin Smith, Joseph Rutterer, Charles M. Cooper, James C. Goff, Harry B. Blazer, Furman B. Moodie, Byron Rhode, John T. Rose, Jr., Wheeler Sheffield, C.M. McWilliams, Hy W. Massey, Burland Lewis and Charles E. Midgett.

Edwin Rountree and Lamar Rose joined the following year along with 14 other boys. Cochran was scoutmaster for the second year, but the little troop faded when he resigned to operate the family drug store.

Troop 5 was organized under the leadership of J.H. Sutherland. Records list the sponsor as "a group of citizens." Edwin Rountree and J.T. Rose were the only scouts from Troop 1 to enter the new one, but they were joined by many others whose names were to become well known. Its roster over the years reads like a "Who's Who" for Punta Gorda. Pick any prominent professional or business man who grew up in Punta Gorda, and you are almost certain to find his name in one of the early rosters.

Scoutmaster with the longest tenure is U. S. Cleveland, now president of the Charlotte Harbor Area Historical Society. He served 12 years from 1946 to 1958 after six years as assistant scoutmaster. For this and other service to the council, Cleveland was awarded the Silver Beaver medal, highest honor awarded by local councils to Scout leaders.

"Those were wonderful years," says Cleveland. "I joined Troop 5 in 1931. The motto in those days was 'Keep the out in scouting.' We went on weekend camp-outs in the wild every month and one-day field trips in between. Two meetings a month were devoted to study for merit badges.

Uncle Dan Beard

"Uncle Dan Beard in his declining years came to Florida in the winters. He spent several seasons at the Hotel Charlotte Harbor. Uncle Dan would come to our meetings and show us how to throw a tomahawk and spear. We were mightily impressed and the envy of other boys in town who did not have such an exotic skill.

"We used to have father-son banquets in the hotel every year while Uncle Dan was here. At one of these banquets, he brought along a 'special treat' which he said he had prepared himself. It consisted of white, delicious meat chopped fine in a relish dressing on crackers.

"After everybody proclaimed the appetizers the best they had ever eaten, he announced it was rattlesnake meat. What a time we had the next day boasting to our friends about what we had eaten and assuring one and all it was delicious.

"I became scoutmaster just in time to observe the Silver Anniversary of Troop 5 in 1946. We celebrated with a community party and Scout field meet March 30-31.

"A highlight of the event was the investiture of four tenderfoot scouts in a solemn ceremony by torch light in the woods at the dam in Alligator Creek. Sheriff Fred Quednau prepared a tasty 'slumgullion' stew for supper that evening. He would not tells us his 'secret recipe,' and we wondered if it also had rattlesnake for an ingredient.

"After the ceremony we sang songs and put on stunts around a big bonfire like we did at camp. As the fire died down we had more solemn moments, and climaxed the evening with ghost stories. One of the boys' favorite was about a wealthy woman in Punta Gorda who dressed in blue denim, upholstered her furniture in blue denim, draped her windows with blue denim, and even had blue denim seat covers in her Cadillac. Her explanation of where she got all the blue denim was the unbelievable part.

"While on the train from Lakeland, she met a drummer no one else could see, and she only out of the corner of her eye. The drummer explained he was a ghost who years earlier had promised not to return to his company until he had sold a truck load of blue denim for the firm. Unfortunately he fell under the wheels of the train while running to catch it after a fruitless stop in Wauchula. He begged the lady to buy some denim to help him escape riding the train through eternity.

"Believing the apparition long dead with no way to deliver her order, the lady ordered a whole truck load of blue denim. A week later the denim manufacturer delivered the huge quantity of material, and she spent the rest of her life trying to use it up.

"Such yarns, told around the embers of a campfire in the woods, is an experience youngsters of today rarely have an opportunity to enjoy," stated Cleveland.

First Scout Cabin

American Legion Post 103 sponsored the troop for several years during the "boom" and in 1931 built a scout cabin in an abandoned orange grove at Harbor View on the north shore of the bay. It had 20 double bunks with plank bottoms. Boys had to bring their own bedding and food. Cooking was over open fires outdoors.

The Punta Gorda Kiwanis Club became sponsor for Troop 5 in 1939. The cabin across the bay was little used during World War II because of the strict rationing of gasoline. It was difficult get together enough gas to transport the troop to its cabin. Consequently, Kiwanis moved the cabin to Gilchrist Park at Punta Gorda.

The frame cabin started showing its age, so Kiwanis raised money in 1952 to replace it with a larger, concrete structure. Within two years, it was too small, so Kiwanis more than doubled its size. Principal contributor toward this effort was Lou Calder, a retired New York City detective who owned a luxurious hunting lodge on 500 acres along Alligator Creek, now the Burnt Store Isles golf course. Because of Calder's generosity, the Boy Scout meeting hall, now also a community center owned by the city, was named after him.

Troop 5 today is sponsored jointly by the Kiwanis Club of Punta Gorda and The Congregational Church of Christ. All are proud of the Troop's heritage of duty to God and Country.

Two bathing beauties test flooded Marion Ave. after 1926 hurricane.

Chapter 79

HURRICANE EMPTIES CHARLOTTE HARB0R

The Florida hurricane of 1926 blew the water of Lake Okeechobee against the southwestern dike, breached it, and within 10 minutes flooded the town of Moore Haven to a depth of seven feet. The official report listed 130 residents of Moore Haven drowned, but dozens of others were unaccounted for. Throughout south Florida, 373 persons were killed and 6,281 injured. More than 17,000 persons suffered loss of, or severe damage to, their homes.

Charlotte County counted two dead. The 4-year-old daughter of Mr. and Mrs. Tom Joiner — caretakers for a fishing company camp on Captiva Island — was drowned when their cabin on a barge was swept into the harbor. Jerome Grizzard, one of a gang of workmen from Georgia brought in to repair the many power lines blown down, was electrocuted when he brushed against a high tension line.

The Good Shepherd Episcopal Church was blown off its foundation and its bell tower toppled. Johnny Brown's blacksmith shop was demolished, prompting him to give up the declining trade and open a machine shop.

The most curious effect of the hurricane was blowing all water out of upper Charlotte Harbor as the storm approached — then blowing it back to flood Punta Gorda and Charlotte Harbor Town as it passed.

Dr. Kenneth Oakley, a keen-witted 93-year-old ophthalmologist in retirement at Bend Oregon, recalls his adventures during the hurricane.

343

His experience also illustrates the frenzy of speculation spawned by the Florida Land Boom of the 1920s. At age 22, he began his remarkable careers at Punta Gorda in 1925 at the height of the boom as a civil engineer and surveyor.

"When my temporary $150 monthly job at Springfield, Ill., with the highway department was finished I repaid my unnamed benefactor in Waco, Texas, for a $400 student loan," states Dr. Oakley. "Then I made a $100 down payment on a beautiful Stutz Bearcat touring car.

"I expected to drive the car for 30 days with the joy involved and then return it. I ended up driving it to Florida with a friend named Bert Shackleton. An old Army buddy had retired to Punta Gorda and wrote that Bert should come on down because the land boom was in progress. Bert said he would handle the gasoline bill, which he did only partly, if I would drive down with my Stutz. Upon arriving, the demands for a surveying engineer paid me a salary of $375 monthly. My large contract was with a group of New York millionaires sub-dividing 520 acres along Alligator Creek into lots called Radair Park. It was named after H.H. Raymond, a shipping magnate, and William T. Adair of World Book Syndicate. Organizer of the consortium was Lou Calder, president of Perkins-Goodwin Investment Co. and owner of the luxurious Allapatchee hunting lodge on Alligator Creek. Calder finally paid off their $8,000 debt to me with company stock which later proved worthless.

"Meanwhile, the boom came to a sudden, fatal collapse. I was busted. I owed Parson Woods, a civil engineer and grand guy, his last salary of $200 — and still do.

Follow The Money

"I borrowed $100 from Mayor Bertie Hatch. I was getting a 25-cent shave and 50-cent haircut from Grover Cleveland with the last of it when the thought occurred to me that to make money, one goes to where money is being spent. Charlotte County had just sold two million dollars worth of road construction bonds. Broadbent Construction Company of Wauchula, Fla, had the contract. I left immediately with my fresh barbering for Wauchula. It took George Broadbent and me about thirty minutes to agree on a contract for me to construct culverts.

"On Saturday morning, Sept. 15, 1926, I and my African-American crew were installing a 36-inch diameter tin-whistle (corrugated) pipe at Punta Gorda. The sky was overcast, with increasing gusty wind from the east. There was occasional slight mist and a rapid cooling.

"I noticed my crew was shrinking. I found most of my men crouched inside the pipe where they had taken refuge from the wind, mist and cold. It was then I realized a tropical storm was approaching, so we went home. Ultimately, the wind was clocked at nearly 200 miles per hour before the anemometer was blown away.

"Beverly Smith decided to get out of Punta Gorda in his Ford touring car before the storm worsened. He started over the bridge to Charlotte Harbor Town. Halfway over, he found the draw had been left open to permit boats to pass. The wind tore the hood cover off his car and dropped it onto a bridge girder. Somehow, he climbed down the girders, pulled the cover loose and one-handed climbed back up to the road. He threw the cover on the back seat and putting the car in neutral let the wind blow him back to Punta Gorda.

"I had gotten jobs at Charlotte County for three civil engineers from the Illinois highway department, and the state surveyor from Tampa was in town to check my section corners for Radair Park. All of us took refuge from the storm in the big Hotel Charlotte Harbor at Punta Gorda and had ourselves a hurricane party.

"We drank 'shine; and, boy, did we get drunk that night. Abbie Burns wandered around the hotel trying to find his room. He went into the wrong bedroom and discovered a woman rolling a drunk (searching his pockets) at the height of the storm.

"After three days of storm, Mrs. Willie White, telegraph operator at Western Union, received news about the disaster at Moore Haven. The information was relayed by the Atlantic Coast Line railroad wire which was the only line left open. Willie said folks at Moore Haven requested doctors and drinking water.

"I contacted Dr. L.W. Martin in Punta Gorda and asked if he was willing to go help. Dr. B.B. Blount had already packed up all the medical supplies he had and drove with them to Sebring where emergency shelters were being set up for Moore Haven survivors.

"Dr. Martin quickly agreed to my suggestion, so we loaded the Stutz and headed for Fort Myers on the gravel road. Mrs. White wired Fort Myers to get a boat ready with jugs of water to go up the Caloosahatchee River to Moore Haven.

Bridges Washed Out

""There were 15 wooden bridges between Punta Gorda and Fort Myers. Approaches to the first one were washed out so we returned to Punta Gorda and got two 10-foot heavy planks — carrying them in the car with the top down. We laid the planks down at the bridge approach, drove the car onto the bridge, picked up the planks and carried then across to the other side, drove across and picked up our planks. We had to do this several times on our journey.

"We reached Fort Myers that evening. Mack Mickle had an open boat which was ready to go. He, the doctor and I left immediately. The river was eight feet above its banks and choked with hyacinths uprooted by the high water. We reached the Atlantic Coast Line railroad bridge but could go no farther. Hyacinths had packed up against the bridge like a dam. I pulled at the tangled mass of vegetation without result. I even climbed out onto the packed hyacinths they were so solid. Finally I threw the boat's anchor forward and Mack put the engine in reverse. Thus we were able to dislodge a section of debris. We repeated the process until we had cleared an opening large enough to pass through. We burned out the reverse gear, but we didn't need it to get of Moore Haven.

"We got to Moore Haven at 10 o'clock the next morning. Folks there were desperate for water and bread. There was no sight of dry land. The stench of foul air filled our nostrils with every gust of wind. Dead cattle, chickens and hogs floated everywhere and were strewn along the banks of drainage ditches. I was drafted immediately to help carry an injured black man in for treatment. I found I was too exhausted to do any more and got some rest. Dr. Martin was plenty busy though, even delivered a baby. The rest of the expedition was quiet. We returned to Fort Myers in a few days — leaving the doctor but bringing a nurse back with us."

The *Punta Gorda Herald* of Sept. 20, 1926, reported the relief efforts of other Punta Gordans. As Oakley and his party left Moore Haven, they met a second expedition arriving from Punta Gorda. It was headed by Walter Helveston whose mother, father, sister and two brothers lived at Moore Haven. Helveston, Paul Hughes and Frank Lowe made it to the stricken village in Helveston's 48-foot cruiser. His family was unharmed but among the 200 homeless people.

Children Cling To Boards

When the Helveston party left that same afternoon it carried 85 refugees back to Fort Myers. As the boat went through the Okeechobee canal, three bodies were seen floating. They had to leave them to their watery grave. Two children were picked up when the boat came through Lake Hicpotchee. They had been clinging to boards, and without food, since the storm.

Punta Gordans gathered a cash purse of $1,546 for the Red Cross of Sebring overseeing emergency relief.

The folks at Moore Haven rebuilt their stricken town only to have it flattened again two years later by another hurricane which breached the southeastern Okeechobee dike.

This time, more than 1,800 people there and at Miami were killed — making that storm the worst in history. Charlotte County experienced only mild flooding.

Kenneth Oakley was impressed with the dedication of doctors in the 1926 disaster and resolved to become a physician himself. He went to summer school at Emory University and obtained his medical degree at the University of Michigan. He married and took up practice in Oregon where he now lives.

Dredge had to throw up a grade just to survey Tamiami Trail route.

Chapter 80

TOWN SURVEYOR SET TAMIAMI TRAIL

The Tamiami Trail — from Tampa to Miami via Charlotte Harbor — was recently four-laned, divided, access-limited all the way. Lost in congratulatory ceremonies was the participation of Charlotte County folks in its construction. Concept of a highway linking southwest Florida to the southeast coast was that of J.F. Jaudon, formerly tax assessor of Dade County and in 1915 a land developer. Helping him sell the idea was a Miami Herald reporter named William Stuart Hill.

Enthusiastic supporters on the west coast were the residents of Charlotte Harbor Town, Punta Gorda, Fort Myers and Naples. They saw the proposed road as the key to attracting tourists who would become home owners, customers and entrepreneurs. Chief booster on the west coast was Barron Collier, a wealthy New York business man who made a fortune selling poster advertising on street cars. He came to Useppa Island on vacation in 1911 and fell in love with the scenic, largely undeveloped southwest coastal area. Collier saw the possibility of a still larger fortune in real estate and tourism opened up by easy access. He began buying land in southern Lee County. Later he renovated the Hotel Punta Gorda.

At Charlotte Harbor Town and Punta Gorda, then part of DeSoto County, Commissioner John Hagan agitated for a bridge across the bay to accommodate Tamiami Trail rather than see the road swing inland.

Collier, DeSoto County, and Lee County contributed money for survey of an Everglades route starting from the west. Jaudon and Dade County raised funds for a simultaneous survey from the east.

347

One of the surveyors from the west was Kelly B. Harvey of Punta Gorda. He was active throughout southwest Florida as early as 1878 for railroads and developers. He laid out Punta Gorda in 1885 for Col. Trabue, Southland (El Jobean) in 1887 for Daniel MacPherson, and Boca Grande in 1897 for himself — speculating in real estate all the time.

During the survey and initial work on Tamiami Trail in 1916, Harvey described the difficulties in an interview for the *American Eagle* newspaper at Estero Bay: "The route was obstructed by a mass of trees of all kinds and sizes. Thousands of switches, poles, brush, and ferns all woven together with bamboo, rattan, and vines. Perhaps several hundred would be chopped off at the ground before the mass would fall so that it could be chipped apart with brush axes," he said. "Think of leaves on trees trembling, and the whole mass of muck and sand for hundreds of feet in each direction quivering like a mass of jelly with each vibration of the dredge engine. Then, think of putting a 40,000-pound engine across it, with muck and marl 12 feet deep, and chancing that the slightest mistake would make it a buried and tangled wreck of steel and machinery."

This effort, directed by Harvey, used mats of brush as a road foundation. Unfortunately the technique didn't work. Whole sections sank overnight. Work was abandoned during the First World War.

Bridge Difficulties

Meanwhile, Hagan was having similar difficulties building the first bridge between Charlotte Harbor Town and Punta Gorda. Only half the structure was completed when work stopped because of a shortage of materials needed for the war effort. Construction of the Charlotte Harbor Bridge resumed in 1921 when Charlotte County was split from DeSoto. Commissioner William M. Whitten advanced several thousand dollars of his own money to get things moving.

Last section of the Charlotte Harbor bridge was poured June 28, 1921; and a grand opening was held July 4. The public was invited to a free fish fry. More than 6,000 people showed up. With this, Collier redoubled his efforts to resume work on the Everglades section of Tamiami Trail. He spent his own money to build the western leg at $25,000 a mile — a large sum in those days. Progress was slow because of the hardships involved.

A group of Trail promoters — anxious to prove the Everglades could be conquered — set out on April 4, 1923, to traverse the approximate survey grade with a motorcade of 10 automobiles. The adventurers called themselves the Trail Blazers and expected to make the trip in three days. The party consisted of 24 men from Tampa, Sarasota, Fort Myers, Everglades City and Estero — accompanied by two Seminole guides named Abraham Lincoln (Assumhachee) and Little Billie (Cornapatchee).

The fleet was eight Model-T Fords, an Overland and an Elcar. The Overland and a Ford became hopelessly mired and were abandoned along the way. Seven Fords and the Elcar made it to Miami 17 days later with the help of tractors sent out to assist them. F.S. Lewis, editor of the *American Eagle*, was a member of the Trail Blazers and recorded the event. Following are a few entries from his log:

Lewis' Log

Notwithstanding predictions of failure on the part of those who claimed to best know the country, a little motorcade mostly of Fords set out from Fort Myers on April 4. We were determined to blaze the way through the trackless wilderness lying between Fort Myers and Miami along the approximate survey of the Tamiami Trail.

At Bonita Springs, where a short stop was made, a wag in the party introduced George Dunham to several of the inhabitants as Henry Ford himself. This was rather sudden, but George always tries to deliver the goods. Before leaving, he promised to finance the building of a 15-story hotel at the Springs. He also secured the promises of several enthusiastic ladies to support him in his race for the presidency. From Marco Junction east to Royal Palm Hammock, the road for some distance is heavy sand and difficult to negotiate. Then, for a few miles, a poor grade of marl is found in the wheel ruts which facilitates travel somewhat.

Going east from Royal Palm, the wooded hammocks give way more and more to open marsh country where tall reeds, switch grass and aquatic birds are seen. The road grade for long distances is overgrown with tall grass, weeds and bushes to such an extent that the car ahead is soon lost to sight to the observer in the rear.

With the encountering of marl soil, this heavy growth diminished, making better going. However, here a new difficulty was encountered in numerous washouts — some 12 to 14 in all. These had to be detoured or, more frequently, bridged. For this purpose heavy planking was employed which was sometimes carried forward to the next washout. Thus we destroyed, if we did not literally burn, our bridges behind us.

Gasped Its Last

About a mile before the end of the grade was reached, George Dunham's car gasped its last, due to some serious internal trouble. After a consultation of the Ford doctors present, it was decided that a new engine was necessary. As it had been neglected to carry one in the tool box, the car was left where it died, to be salvaged at some future time.

Camp was made the first night at the end of the road grade. Speculation was indulged in as to our proximity to the little settlement of Everglades. Guns were fired, and spotlights trained on the sky in that direction. It later developed that no one saw or heard our signals.

When we went into Everglades to get supplies and get help for our mired vehicles, we met Capt. George Storter, and old-time resident and pioneer. He told us that the Collier Company had a tractor at a logging camp which we arranged to use. The tractors performed marvelously to get our mired cars to more firm ground. Our next camp was made a mile or more west of Deep Lake Railway (a short-line logging spur). The ground being damp, we cut cabbage palm fans to sleep on.

Going was heavy the next day with much pushing and shoving of the cars before we reached the railroad grade about noon near a hammock called Lemon Camp. We rechristened it Seminole City. The train arrived from Everglades with gas, oil and provisions which had been ordered the previous night by telephone. After spending the night at Everglades, we returned to camp and told Mr. Giles we could no longer take the time for his 3200-pound car which was often in trouble.

Before reaching Turner's River, we came onto an Indian camp where the mother of our guide, Abe Lincoln, lived. Members of the party took their pictures and bought Seminole Indian dolls at $1.50 each.

At Turner's we ran into the problem of having to cut some stumps to facilitate the passage of the cars. Some towing was required through several boggy places. This is where we left another car because the front wheel had shattered when it hit a stump.

Some 98.8 miles from Fort Myers, a well was dug since this was said to be last place for miles where we could get fresh water. A deer was spotted galloping off, and Little Billie left us to go hunting. He never rejoined the party.

Early Monday we sent a scouting party to skirmish out a feasible crossing of the next cypress (swamp). The ox trail had vanished, and it was up to us to cut a new pathway through the uncharted wilderness.

The intrepid Trail Blazers of 1923 gather at Fort Myers before setting forth across the Everglades on the unpaved grade. Faithful Seminole guide, Abraham Lincoln, is second from right in back row.

350

The strenuous work of chopping trees and stumps, lifting and pushing cars — together with the uncertainty as to just where we were — was beginning to tell on all of us. The heat in the midst of the cypress, the unsatisfying drinking water, and frequent shortage of rations added to our discomfort.

Imagine our feeling when we heard a shout up ahead, and our scouts — Maurice Ayrer, George Prime and Abe — gathered around the camp fire to tell us they found a survey stake with figures of Township 54, Range 33, Sec. 7. This meant we were only 50 or 60 miles from Miami.

On Wednesday, just one week from Fort Myers, we decided to send a scouting party on foot to Miami to send messages to anxious relatives and forward provisions to the motorcade. The scouts struck a car trail some miles on, and Abe (their Seminole guide) returned to camp. The others — George H. Hunt, John P. Cosden, and Ora E. Chapin — proceeded to the end of the car trail where they secured a car at a construction camp and arrived in Miami at 1 a.m. Thursday.

Heard Airplane

Back at camp, work was resumed with a will. The motor of an airplane was heard, but apparently the pilot did not see the big smoke we put up. Just one mile of cutting had been done that day.

Abe brought in a deer, and shortly after supper Porter Richards of Everglades came into camp saying that Mr. Giles and Joe Taylor were a mile back with the Elcar and a tractor. He said they were about famished for lack of food. They had followed our tracks from Everglades with two tractors, one of which had broken down. He was given half the deer and returned to his companions. We had cut our way through to the scrub cypress when we heard a shout and saw a big smoke. In a few minutes we were met by a rescuing party of three from Billy Roberts' camp. We soon reached their truck with its load of gas.

We bumped over rough, rocky prairie in which it was impossible to run for long in high gear. In the muck a few miles farther on, we mired to our axles. However, by dint of hard pushing, prying and laying cypress boughs in the ruts, two of the cars were extricated shortly after dark and made their way to Roberts' Camp.

Friday morning began the rescue of the cars from the mire. Shortly after 9 a.m. a plane from Miami went by high overhead, circled the glades and came back to land at the camp. It brought a generous supply of provisions which were very welcome. However, he brought only one quart of whiskey for 23 men. The pilot, Capt. W.A. Carr, said he had observed our progress and did not see how we could have improved the route.

Saturday we began on the last boggy marsh land between us and the end of the grade — fully confident that we could manage to cover the five and a half miles before nightfall. But the short distance very nearly *became our Waterloo as we were mired in it for a week. Only then we were extricated by Herculean efforts. Each driver plunged into the mire, going as far as he could before being strangled by the mud. The tractor finally rounded all the cars together about three and a half miles from destination. There we stayed from Saturday to Saturday. Food was getting scarce, so six of us walked to McCreary's construction camp on the grade. Several others came in during the day. The camp was on rocky ground. The rain which had been threatening came down in a heavy shower, and the wind was chill.*

On Sunday, a car came out from Miami, taking several men back, and Erben Cook arrived with provisions he had brought for us. The rain lessened our chance of release from the mire.

It was the suggestion of Mr. Cook that extra rims and tires be bolted to each wheel that the cars eventually came out of the mire mostly under their own power. Nevertheless, it took the united efforts of 30 white men, Negroes and Indians — together with a tractor pulling on a rope — to dislodge some of them.

All Hands Arrive

All hands arrived in Miami April 21 with the cars which were placed in the local Ford Garage. On Sunday morning, members of the party donned old clothes and motored to Coconut Grove to enact realistic stunts for the moving picture man.

That afternoon we paraded down Flagler Street to the city park where we were welcomed by the mayor. Immediately after the ceremony, three of the cars pulled out for the homeward journey to Fort Myers by way of Fort Pierce, Okeechobee City, Palmdale and LaBelle.

Though some Trail Blazers rushed home, Ora Chapin, a prominent member of the Fort Myers Board of Trade, stayed in Miami several more days to publicize the event. He sat in a hotel room with his feet in a tub of ice, his lips swelled for lack of water, and dictated page after page of the adventure to a stenographer. His account flashed around the nation and Europe on news wires.

A fellow member of the expedition, Grover Hackney, said, "Ora was responsible for the world-wide publicity we got. The Ford people were delighted. They told us to bring the cars in and they'd put them back in shape just like they were when they left."

Tamiami Trail motorcade of March 6, 1922, from Fort Myers (top) made their way over trail through woods, welcomed by Punta Gorda citizens. Additional cars at Punta Gorda joined the tour to Tampa.

Chapter 81

COLLIER BOUGHT HIMSELF A COUNTY

Barron Collier, the wealthy advertising executive who had pushed for the cross-Florida highway since its inception in 1916, was impressed with the Trail Blazer feat. He had bought a million acres of southern Lee County before the First World War in anticipation of a land boom to be sparked by the Trail. Now he used his considerable influence to persuade the Florida Legislature to establish a new county named for himself a month after the Blazers came home in triumph.

"I am anxious to do some big developing in Collier County," Collier said in May 1923. "I felt I could do it much better with a friendly county

353

administration than I could with one that was more interested in Fort Myers and other parts of the county than they were in the section I am trying to develop. I intend to build the Tamiami Trail just as fast as it is possible to do so."

Basil J. Scott, Collier's chief engineer, said, "I am under instruction from Mr. Collier to proceed day and night to the Dade County line. Just give me a year and we will show you something!" This was over-enthusiasm similar to that of the Trail Blazers. Five years of arduous labor would be required to finish the road. While Collier's crew worked east, The Chevelier Corporation with 207,000 acres in Dade County pushed west. A rivalry developed between the two groups to see which could build the most miles. A good day's work was 150 feet.

Collier won the contest by spending $25,000 a mile for his end of the road. In time, he had eight huge dredges digging a canal and throwing up the spoil for highway foundation. Common laborers were paid $1.50 a day — generous for the time — plus meals and a bed in barracks on wheels. Dredge operators were paid $150 a month.

Largest Consumer Of Dynamite

The limestone bed of the Everglades was blasted with dynamite to produce rock ballast. At the height of construction, the Trail project was the third largest consumer in the nation of dynamite. That explosive cost 15 cents a pound at first, but grew to 30 cents as western miners, railroads and other contractors vied for the output. Approximately 20,000 pounds of dynamite per mile was required when the going was easy. Twice that was needed when blasting through the rocky spine of Florida. Surprisingly only one man was killed during construction.

Tamiami Trail was completed in 1928 amid celebrations at towns along the way. Caravans of cars were popular among residents who marveled that you could, with a little luck and some hard driving, travel the 263 miles between Tampa and Miami in one day. Collier expanded his enterprises to capitalize on expected growth. He bought the *Fort Myers Press*, telephone companies and resort hotels. Among the latter was the defunct Hotel Punta Gorda which he renovated with a fifth-floor ball room, giant swimming pool, tennis courts, skeet range, and baths for every room. He bought all the memberships of the Punta Gorda Golf Club so hotel guests would have a place to play.

One of the stipulations he demanded from Punta Gorda was a new bridge across the harbor to accommodate automobiles. The original bridge had been designed for automobiles of 1915. Cars could cross the bridge at the same time only when one would pull against the railing so the other could pass. Large trucks and busses could not cross simultaneously even with this maneuver. Fights were common between truck drivers at the middle of the bridge to see which would have to back up.

The new bridge, named for Collier, was opened July 4, 1931, with a free fish fry even bigger than that which marked the opening of the first bridge exactly 10 years earlier. Collier brought a number of Seminoles to entrance the crowd with their colorful dress.

The late Carpenter Guthrie as a boy recalled that the Tamiami Trail through Charlotte Harbor Town and Punta Gorda was merely a shell-topped marl road. "It followed the U.S. 41 route generally, but at Charlotte Harbor it turned sharply south along Larsen Street (now renamed Laura) to Bay Shore Drive," said Guthrie. "My grandfather, Will Guthrie, had a store, gasoline filling station and post office on Bay Shore which served many travelers on Tamiami Trail. Mrs. Bennett had a tea room at the corner of Larsen and Bay Shore that was popular with tourists. She served good food, and so much you couldn't eat it all.

For Crying Out Loud

"Mrs. Bennett was a dear lady who was active in getting the schoolhouse and church built. She wore her hair curled in a bun. One time we had a program at school, and Mrs. Bennett had a featured part. She let her long, grey hair down and combed it while she sang 'Silver Threads Among the Gold.' Her husband began snorting and choking to keep from crying out loud. This started the rest of us snorting and choking to keep from laughing out loud.

"Tamiami Trail made another sharp turn to get across the new bridge. It still was pretty narrow by today's standard. Skimmer straw hats were the style, and the Model-T Fords had convertible tops. As men drove by, fishermen on the bridge would swing their cane poles — as if to cast — and knock off the skimmers. These 'accidents' often ended in fights.

"The bridge was concrete, but the road was just marl. After a rain, the sharp turn at the Charlotte Harbor Town end gouged out a deep rut. There was a man with four mules who staked out the spot and made good money pulling motorists out of the mud," said Guthrie with a chuckle.

Unfortunately, the stock market crash of 1929 and following Great Depression choked off the growth anticipated of Tamiami Trail. Collier lost his fortune but left a legacy of land for his heirs living today at Naples.

The Guthrie store and Bennett's tea room were demolished. Hotel Charlotte Harbor in Punta Gorda was sold as a mineral-water spa called Charlotte Harbor Spa, but it burned in 1959 — some say of arson in order to collect insurance on what had become a losing proposition.

Tamiami Trail lived up to expectations after World War II but soon became inadequate for modern traffic. Today, "Alligator Alley" (I-75) from Naples to Fort Lauderdale is the high-speed route across southern Florida. Nevertheless, the Trail is preferred by visitors who enjoy a more leisurely and picturesque route.

The Trail Blazers would applaud.

Joe Addison, left, strikes a boxing pose for his friends.

Chapter 82

BOY SCOUT WINS TITLE FIGHT

Joe Addison won the Punta Gorda-Arcadia light-weight prize fight of 1924 but had to split the $21 purse with Tommy Gaskins, 60-40.

"The fight was the main event of Punta Gorda's annual Midsummer Carnival that year," recalls Joe, a life-long native of Punta Gorda. "We were seniors in high school and fellow Boy Scouts. My father and my Uncle Charlie Cochran were amateur boxers. I just naturally got interested in fisticuffs as a boy.

"Uncle Charlie owned the drugstore next to the *Herald* newspaper offices on West Marion Ave. He started the first Boy Scout troop, and we made a room in back of the drug store our headquarters. There was a punching bag and a heavy body-bag back there and enough room to box. Uncle Charlie coached us. We got pretty good.

"I only weighed about 120 pounds back then, but I was handy with my fists and pretty cocky. My uncle used to take me with him to Tampa to see prize fights at Benjamin Field's Arena. Mostly the fighters were Cubans working in the cigar factories.

"I felt sure I could beat them and asked Uncle Charlie to get me a fight with them. He would'nt do it. He said, 'You leave those Cubans alone. They'll clean your clock.'

"Scoutmaster Covington at Arcadia also was a boxing fan and had developed some good fighters. He had one fighter, Tommy Gaskins who was said to be dynamite. They set up a match for us. I had heard about his reputation so was a little scared.

"My mother didn't like me fighting. 'I just hope he doesn't beat the tar out of you,' she said. She got the law after me to have me jailed until after the Carnival. City Commissioner Mayo Sturgeon hid me in his Bay City Grocery in the Smith Hotel across the street from today's post office.

"An hour or so before the fight, Commissioner Sturgeon came and got me. He said, 'Don't worry. I won't let the marshal get you.'

"The arena was set up in the Ford Garage where the post office now is. It was the largest building in town, the first to have a clear-span truss roof. Folks feared the roof would cave in because it had no sup-porting posts. However, it went

Uncle Charlie, cyclist, and Joe.

through several hurricanes and was torn down to build the post office.

"The ring was just a wooden platform, and the seats were all kinds of chairs from people's houses. There were 300 or 400 people there — most everyone from Punta Gorda and Arcadia it seemed like. We got a referee from Fort Myers so there wouldn't be any favoritism.

"We were scheduled to fight five three-minute rounds. Uncle Charlie was my manager. He told me, 'I can't talk to you while you're fighting, but when I see you can take him, I'll pound on the floor. You can feel the vibrations with your feet. That will be the signal to finish him off!'

"When I saw Tommy get into the ring, I knew I could take him. We sparred lightly in the first round, checking out the other guy's moves. Uncle Charlie told me at the break, 'Be careful. Don't get over confident. He may be faking, and when you let your guard down he will whip you.'

"About half way through the second round, Uncle Charlie began pounding on the floor. I had taken a liking to Tommy so I clinched and told him, 'I'm gonna take you, but I'm not going to knock you out or let you hurt me. This purse isn't worth it.'

357

"During the second-round break, Uncle Charlie said, 'Why didn't you put him away? Didn't you feel my pounding?' I said I did but wasn't going to knock out a Scout buddy for a measly $12.60. Uncle Charlie was disgusted. He stalked away, saying, 'I'm through with you.'

"We boxed the last three rounds right smartly, and the referee decided the match. I got the decision, but the Arcadia people felt their fighter should have won. However, I still have a letter from Mr. Covington commending me for not taking advantage of Tommy.

"My girl friend, June Williams, thought I was pretty special, but mother said, 'That's enough.' I still fought for fun but gave up any thoughts of a career as a prize fighter. Tommy got into the business of making things out of cypress knees over on U.S. 27.

"I stayed in scouting for several years after that. We had a lot of good times. I especially remember a camping trip over the Christmas holidays to Salt Springs (Warm Mineral Springs). It was way out in the 'boondocks' and uninhabited then.

"Byron Rhode, in his book *Punta Gorda Remembered*, wrote about that trip and blamed me for something I didn't do.

A Tempting Target

"One day while some of us were skinny dipping in the spring, Harry Blakely got out of the water and bent over to pick up his clothes. Just then, another boy who had been out hunting quail came into the clearing and spotted Harry's bald rear across the pond — an irresistible target. The boy with the shotgun, I don't remember his name, thought he was far enough away that the bird shot would just sting Harry. He aimed and fired. Unfortunately the target was closer than he thought. Harry yelled and started running. We had to catch him, and Uncle Charlie pried out several shot with his pen knife. Harry slept on his stomach and ate standing up for a couple of days. Uncle Charlie gave the hunter holy Hell. But I didn't do it. I didn't even own a gun.

"Those were tough times. The Florida land boom went bust, and after that came the Great Depression. Jobs were scarce. I was pretty good with the drums so I started a little jazz band. We played at restaurants, parties, bars, festivals and dances. Finally I got a job with the post office. The other fellows got regular jobs too. I worked for the post office for 44 years, first as clerk and later as a rural carrier..

"Boxing was a clean, wholesome sport, popular with young men in those days. It taught us sportsmanship and discipline. Too bad it has gone out of style," sighed Joe.

Granny Rhode on her 100th birthday with son Frank and his wife Maxine.

Chapter 83

GRANNY HIDES UNDER THE BED

"That's God's worry!" Explains Mrs. Ruth "Granny" Rhode of Punta Gorda when asked how she lived to be 100 years old. Descendants, including six great-children — and a host of friends at the Life Care Center where she lives — gathered Jan. 2, 1996, at the First Baptist Church to celebrate what she calls her first century. She says she is shooting for 110.

Mrs. Rhode came to the Bermont area with her parents, Isaiah and Jennie (nee Howell) Patrick, in 1909 at age 13. Lands east of Punta Gorda had been opened to settlers in 1908. It was the last frontier.

Patrick filed a homestead claim on which to raise vegetables. His 160 acres consisted of the southeast quarter of section 21 in township 41 range 26. Today, the site is part of the Babcock-Webb Wildlife Management Area. Then, it was 6 miles by trail from the store, post office, and school known as Bermont at the intersection of state routes 31 and 74. Tucker's Grade and State Route 31 were constructed in 1915, making the Patrick homestead more accessible. Normally, homesteads were "proved out" in three to five years. However, Patrick didn't call for his official inspection until 1920. His certificate of ownership was dated June 2 of that year.

"The land was wild frontier back in 1909," recalls Mrs. Rhode. "Rattlesnakes everywhere. Mosquitos terrible. Water was ankle deep when it rained. However, the virgin soil grew bumper crops.

"Occasionally we heard panthers scream at night but they were no problem. Next to rattlesnakes, we were most concerned about bobcats. They would catch chickens that roosted outside. We kept our chickens in strong coops at night because we could get a penny each for eggs.

"My sister-in-law, Laura Rhode, was particularly careful to watch out for rattlesnakes. Once she killed one six feet long with 21 rattles. She also shot a turkey in her yard. There were lots of deer. Once we walked right past one lying in our garden. It startled us when it bounded away.

"Pine trees were an important crop. Mr. Addison had a sawmill at Bermont, and Mr. McAdow had a turpentine still down near the Lee County line. Papa leased his pines to the Evans Turpentine Company for $500. We had to be self-sufficient those days. Women helped in the gardens, but they were busy most of the time having babies and taking care of them. We had no doctors, so women helped each other deliver babies.

"Mama made a wonderful salve that cured most everything. Its main ingredient was aloe, but I can't remember the rest. I wish I could for it would be a money maker. She also made her own soap out of old bacon grease and lye. She scrubbed everything with it.

Kids Slept on Pallets

"Christmas was a family holiday. Kids usually got just one present. We celebrated by going to church and setting off fireworks. When family came overnight, kids slept cross-wise on beds or on a quilt pallet on the floor. One time, 10 children huddled on one bed.

"In addition to Bermont, there were two other villages nearby — Sparkman two miles north of Bermont center, and Bairdville two miles west. We knew the Bairds. They were retired from up north and had a small ranch where he kept milk cows and experimented with pasture grass. He rode around on a big, bull ox.

"Others took up homesteads near Mr. Baird, and the settlement was known as Bairdville. It was mostly settled by the Huffmans from Texas. They dug a big ditch to drain a swamp there and it soon had lots of brim (fish). We would scoop them out and cook them on the spot in a kettle.

"Bermont had a little, combination meeting house and school where we attended a couple of years. One day, Papa threw a bucket of boiling water out a window on to me as I passed by. It burned me badly. I missed several weeks of school to treat my burns with Mama's salve.

"My uncle, George D. Rhode of Punta Gorda, was very religious — not an ordained minister — and came out to preach about once a month. Rev. George Gatewood, who had the store and post office at Bermont, was a Methodist lay preacher and conducted services at other times. Folks came from miles around to hear the preaching and have a picnic. The Sparkman and Bermont boys each had a baseball team, and after eating would play a game. It was quite a rivalry. We had fun cheering them on.

360

"Once or twice a year the men and boys got a work gang together and ditched a section of road. When it stormed, the few cars around were useless. Even in dry weather, a horse and wagon were more efficient.

"I married Walter Lee Rhode in 1920. We called him Lee. We set up housekeeping in Punta Gorda out on First Street (now Airport Road) near Jack Collins who was the engineer for the ice company (Punta Gorda Ice and Electric Company; now, Florida Power and Light Co.). Punta Gorda was a small town with dirt streets. The big Hotel Punta Gorda was the main building. Railroad tracks ran down the middle of King Street to the depot and fish docks across from the hotel.

"Lee worked on a lot of interesting jobs. He was camp cook for the work crew grubbing out Tucker's Grade. He worked in a rope factory at St. James City on Pine Island, a shark-hide leather factory on Sanibel Island, and kept an ice house down the bay for a fish company. He helped build the first bridge across the harbor shortly after we were married. They had a big fish-fry at Gilchrist park to commemorate the opening. Fish were cooked in big sugar pans. Lee's permanent job was with the post office.

Boom Underway

"The big Florida land boom got underway about 1923. It seemed that everybody was getting rich buying and selling land. My parents had bought land, all along. They got in on the boom by purchasing land and a store at Bermont. Papa ran the store and Mama was the postmaster. Papa gave up the store in 1925 and bought a small farm at Punta Gorda near us where he raised vegetables and water melons for sale to local markets."

According to DeSoto County deed records, Patrick bought 360 acres at Bermont's center in 1923 from Carey Carlton for $6,000 — a goodly sum — but the area was being platted into city lots named Del Verde. He sold the homestead in 1925, to Norman Hewitt for a sum camouflaged by the legal minimum of $5. Patrick immediately bought another 340 acres from two sellers for an amount exceeding $2,000. However, few lots were sold. The boom collapsed with the stock market crash of 1929 heralding the Great Depression. All traces of Bermont are now gone.

Mrs. Rhode is especially proud of her family of 19 descendants. "Our first son, Raymond, died at age two. Then came Roy, Walter and the twins Frank and Fred. Our twins were born in September of 1926. I went to my sister-in-law Laura's house to deliver them.

"Two weeks later, a terrible hurricane struck south Florida. It blew the water out of Lake Okeechobee and drowned hundreds of people. At Punta Gorda, it rained and blew for two days straight. Our place was in low land, and water flooded up to our door. The wind was clocked at 125 miles per hour. Our house rocked and finally was knocked off its foundation blocks.

"I was really scared for my two-week-old twins. Lee and I waded with them, in waist-deep water, to my mother's and father's house. Lee went into town to find safe shelter for us. Meanwhile, the storm grew worse and my folk's house began to rock. They decided it was best to go into town. I was still weak from delivering Frank and Fred, and I didn't want to be gone when Lee returned to get us.

"Before my father and mother left, they tucked me and the twins under a bedstead with pillows and quilts to provide us some protection from falling timbers if the house blew down.

"Lee came back in a few hours and was alarmed to find the house empty. He searched frantically and found us still under the bedstead — cold and wet but safe.

"Many houses were knocked askew in that storm, but no one was hurt. Folks ran boats up and down Marion Avenue. We got our house back on its blocks, none the worse for wear.

"Our boys served in the military during World War II. The twins, Frank and Fred, joined the Navy. Walter served in the Army and Roy in the Coast Guard. My husband, Lee, died in 1948 and is buried at Indian Springs Then, I got a job for years helping Mrs. Shepherd who had a day-care service for babies and toddlers. I enjoyed it. I guess we took care of half the kids in Punta Gorda. That's why they call me 'Granny.'"

Mighty Good Melons

U.S. Cleveland attests to the superior water melons raised by Isaiah Patrick. "Back in 1937, the Charlotte High School senior class of 13 students had a chaperoned slumber party at May Durrance's Spanish House in Charlotte Harbor Town — boys and girls in different bedrooms, of course. It was in late winter when watermelons were starting to get ripe. We got to talking about how much we enjoyed the first watermelons of the season. I had the use of the family Ford that night so Jimmy Thomas and I decided to poach a few melons from Mr. Patrick's field.

"We drove across the bridge and out to the Patrick place, then the edge of town. I parked along U.S. 41 and cut off the car's headlights, but Mr. Patrick detected us anyway. He kept a sharp eye on his melons when they ripened. Jimmy and I walked across the railroad and crawled through a barbed-wire fence into his field. We selected four melons — one for each of our arms. As we started to leave, Mr. Patrick cut loose with a shot-gun.

"We had been told he patrolled his field with a shot-gun loaded with rock salt. A direct hit was not fatal, but the salt would break skin and sting painfully. Consequently, Jimmy and I tore out as fast as possible — weighted down with four, big melons. 'Bam! Bam!' Rock salt peppered the ground all around us, but we hop-scotched marvelously out of danger.

"Looking back on the escapade, we couldn't remember how we got past that barbed-wire fence on the way out. As excited as we were, we possibly high-jumped it — melons and all. Anyway, the melons were delicious. Jimmy and I were a big hit with the girls that night ."

The Punta Gorda Kiwanis team that challenged the Baltimore Orioles. Frank Smoak, Sr., stands far right. Other identifiable Pelicans standing are John Swinney next to Smoak, and Vassa Jones far left. Seated are Paul Garret, editor of the *Punta Gorda Herald* far left, Dr. Ralph Martin third from left, Fred King fourth from left and Edwin Parker far right. Frank Smoak, Jr., center with mascot Bob.

Chapter 84

ORIOLES SPRING TRAINING A DISASTER

The return of the Texas Rangers reminds Oldtimers of their youth when the Baltimore Orioles came to Punta Gorda in 1926 for spring training. "It was an exciting event that nearly ruined the town," says Esther McCullough. "Chester Blount lost his house over it!"

Starr Matthews, sports writer for the *Baltimore American*, arrived first on the scene that year. He wrote a glowing account of the town and construction of a baseball park at the end of Carmalita Street — now the county Little League fields, BMX bicycle track and horse show ring.

"This place is a delightful feast for the eyes with its fragrant orange blossoms, trees with the golden fruit weighing down the branches, the flaming red poinsettias, and the wide-spreading banyan of which the town boasts. The grandstand, painted a vivid green, is almost finished. It will seat about 1,000 cash customers. There are two bleachers. Surrounding

363

the park is a fence 600 feet from home plate which is hard to see with the naked eye. Anyone who hits the ball over the boards will be a home run king of immense proportions.

"Just inside this barrier, some time or other, there will be a half-mile race track, because it is to be the fair grounds. A couple of months ago it was a rough bit of land covered by palmettos and other scrub. The field has been leveled and covered with special clay brought from Arcadia.

"Beneath the grandstand is the club house. They have been particular about this. Five showers, electricity, about 48 lockers and a private office for manager Jack Dunn have been installed.

"The movement to bring the Orioles here was started by President W.S. Whitfield of the Rotary Club. The Chamber of Commerce, of which E.P. Gage is president, is taking a very active part in the preparations. The city is spending $25,000 in this form of advertising. It is paying the Orioles $5,000 to come here, and Punta Gorda is taking the gate receipts.

"There are only 3,500 people here at best, but Fort Myers, where there are to be many games between the Orioles and Athletics, is expected to visit Punta Gorda. Between these cities there are smaller towns, and Arcadia is not far away. So, the whole section is rooting for either the Birds or the White Elephants.

Merchants Backed Venture

"From the pocketbooks of the baseball lovers of these cities and towns, Punta Gorda must get back $52,000 — or as much of it as it hopes to put back into the treasuries of the local merchants and those backing the venture." To finance the promotion, a group of civic leaders first formed the Charlotte Amusement Co. As enthusiasm grew, the Charlotte County Fair Association was incorporated to sell stock and build a permanent baseball facility with other uses.

Officers of the association — all large stockholders — were President John Pelzel, First Vice-President W.H. Johnson; Second Vice-President Ernest Pearce; Secretary Treasurer Mose Darst; Directors W.S. Whitfield, Frank Smoak and R. Chester Blount. A prominent "propagandist" for the project was William Grafston.

The Orioles were scheduled to arrive on the morning of Feb. 22, and be welcomed by a band and parade. However, they were 45 hours enroute and delayed 14 hours until late that night by a wrecked freight train blocking the line. Only a few officers of the Fair Association were on hand to greet the players. The *Punta Gorda Herald* reported: "The ceremony of handing over the keys of the city took place about noon the day following. Col. Francis Bent, newly appointed secretary of the Chamber of Commerce, had a key of adequate proportions to turn the lock on the huge gates of any city which he presented to Dunn — at the same time making a short speech of welcome."

Dunn was manager, president, and majority stockholder of the Orioles. Under his leadership, the team had won the past seven pennants. The Orioles at that time were associated with the International League — and had close ties with the Philadelphia Athletics.

Baltimore and three other teams had been dropped from the National League in 1899 for lack of attendance — despite three Oriole championship pennants in 1984-86 and a 1897 Temple Cup victory. The latter was a post-season game between the first and second National League teams. There was no second, major league yet, hence no World Series. The Orioles were taken into the American League when it was organized in 1901. However, its franchise and best players were moved to New York City two years later to form the Knickerbocker Yankees.

Though classed as a "minor league" team, the revamped Baltimore Orioles played superior baseball. The club is remembered as the major league originators of "scientific baseball." Among their new techniques were the hit-and-run, bunt and hook-slide. They returned to the American League during its 1954 expansion.

Volunteer Taxi Service

The 1926 team at Punta Gorda spring training was quartered at the newly built Charlotte Bay Hotel where the Professional Building on Marion Ave. is now located. The athletes were driven by volunteers to and from the baseball park each morning and afternoon.

For the opening game March 5 with the Athletics, Punta Gorda Mayor John R. Jack declared a half-holiday so the whole town could attend. To celebrate an expected victory, a dance at the Charlotte Bay Hotel would feature a special attraction — a "Charleston contest with $50 prize for the couple showing the greatest skill at this newest expression of the terpsichorean art."

"Everything started off right," reported the *Herald*, "when Mayor Jack heaved the first ball in the general direction of north-by-east. Assisted by a pair of wings, a butterfly net and step ladder, McKee might have been able to catch it. As it was, the mayor was charged with an error."

A crowd of 1,000 spectators saw the Orioles beaten 5-3. March 16 was designated Punta Gorda Day at the baseball park. Said the *Herald*: "A picked team from the city will meet the Orioles to decide the city championship. Some even predict a 1 to 0 score in favor the locals.

Known as the Pelicans, the team was comprised mostly of Kiwanis Club members. The grandstand was full of Punta Gordans to cheer them on, but the final score was 13-1 in favor of the Orioles. The *Herald* provided details: "The Punta Gorda Pelicans went down with wings flapping in defeat. Jim Cooper started on the rubber for the locals but was bumped hard for the first three innings, allowing all the runs. Various big league scouts on hand to sign him up, went away disappointed.

"As was predicted, several of the players slated to don Pelican flannels, developed cases of measles, or were cutting teeth, for they failed to appear. A few players were borrowed from Jack Dunn's squad to replace the various fatalities in the Pelican ranks. Poole replaced Cooper in the box after the third inning.

"Not dismayed by the big lead obtained by their foemen, the Pelicans kept pecking away during the entire game and even managed at times to get on base. A feature of the game was not presented until the seventh inning when Frank Smoak, pinch hitting for Artigiani (an Oriole fill-in), clouted the horsehide for a terrific blow — almost to third base.

"Tillie Walker made a vain effort to catch it, but he overran ten yards. By the time he had gone back for the ball, Smoak had streaked to first. Walker's throw to the base was wild. While Monahan juggled the pill, Smoak took second. Speeding around the bases with the speed of black light during an eclipse of the moon on a cloudy night, Smoak rounded third. The stands, stormed to him to go home. All but exhausted, he dove for the plate and beat the ball by the skin of an onion. Alberts, Oriole catcher, passed up the best chance to get him by missing the third baseman's peg, who had come nearly home to make the throw.

"Soon after Smoak's spectacular run, the game ended, for the next two players were unable to duplicate the feat."

Final Record

The Orioles ended their spring training with a victory over the Athletics at the Punta Gorda ball park. The Birds played 14 games during their 7-week sojourn in Punta Gorda. They won five — three from the Athletics, one from the Buffalo Bisons, and one from the Philadelphia Phillies. They lost nine games — eight to the Athletics and one to the New York Giants.

The Orioles never came back because the visit was a financial disaster for Punta Gorda. Gate receipts failed to meet expenses by $5,000 so the stockholders lost their investments. The loss was covered by a note from the bank, pledged by five local businessmen — Frank Smoak, R. Chester Blount, Capt. Johnson and two other men whose names are not known.

The Great Florida Land Boom collapsed that year, followed by the Great Depression in 1929. The men who pledged the note could not make payments. Blount lost his home. Only Smoak, later Punta Gorda Mayor, was able to make partial payments with difficulty. Finally, the bank forgave the balance, settling for 20 cents on the dollar.

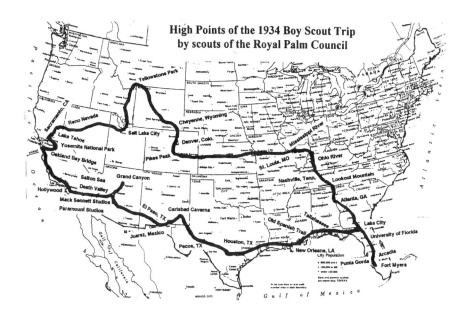

High Points of the 1934 Boy Scout Trip
by scouts of the Royal Palm Council

Chapter 85

BOY SCOUT TOUR OF WEST MEMORABLE

Former members of Punta Gorda Boy Scout Troop 5 got a little misty-eyed in April when they gathered to celebrate its 75th anniversary. Old men sometimes get that way when recalling their carefree boyhood.

Of all the yarns recounted, none was more compelling than the adventures experienced during a seven-week, 9,500-mile, circuitous, tour "out west" in the summer of 1934.

The Royal Palm Council — which consisted of Charlotte, DeSoto, Lee and Hendry counties — organized the motorcade. Making the trip for a fee of $75 each were 31 boys, four scout adults and two little girls.

The scout adults were H.O. Kight, council executive from Fort Myers; William Persons, Punta Gorda scoutmaster; a Mr. King, scoutmaster from Clewiston; Edward Cassels, Arcadia scoutmaster; and William A. Neal, a troop sponsor from Arcadia who took along his wife and two daughters Cynthia and Dea. Another adult was "a fine colored man" hired to cook.

The caravan had two busses. The largest was a bus furnished by Barron Collier. He was a wealthy advertising tycoon, prominent citizen of the Florida county named for him, and owner of Hotel Charlotte Harbor in Punta Gorda. This bus was renovated by Mrs. Francis (Louisa) Crowninshield of Boca Grande, a noted philanthropist and social leader of the winter "beach colony" at Gasparilla Island. She once gave a new Chevrolet car to Kight who fainted from surprise.

The bus seats were replaced with wooden benches having canvas seats that served also for makeshift beds. Each person had a personal locker. A "kitchenette" at the rear furnished sandwiches on the run. "Chef" prepared campfire meals at night and breakfast when the boys slept on the ground under tarpaulins attached to each side of the bus. The Neals enlarged their pick-up truck to a screened camper for themselves.

Punta Gorda boys were the brothers Howard "Corky" and Nathaniel "Doc" McQueen, James "Sammy" McCullough and Arthur Johnson.

The Arcadia boys were Claude Jones, John Johns, Bobby Bevis, Buck Carlton, Harry Gold, Virgil Christ and William Gaskins.

Scoutmaster Keeps Diary

Arcadia scoutmaster Cassels kept a diary of the trip and once a week sent his entries to the Arcadia, Punta Gorda and Fort Myers newspapers. Those published in the *Punta Gorda Herald* were kept in a scrapbook by Howard and Nathaniel's mother. Following are interesting highlights — omitting enthusiastic descriptions of familiar tourist attractions:

July 6

Just as we were leaving Fort Myers, we were delayed a few hours to make repairs to our bus. We left Arcadia about 10:30 a.m. We had a good joke played on us when the bus ran out of gas about 100 yards from a service station north of Leesburg. Arrived at Gainesville at 6:30 p.m. Billy Neal made arrangements with the University superintendent to pitch our tents on the parade grounds.

Mr. Kight assigned Buck Carlton as milk boy. When we go into camp he has to nose around and find a dairy and place an order for five gallons of milk for breakfast. William Persons and Doc McQueen pack and unpack equipment on top of the bus. Miller, McGrath, H. McQueen and Case hang and stack tarpaulins. Johnson and McCullough set up the chef's tent and cot. Billy Neal is in charge of the water supply.

Doc McQueen is the tire-pressure expert who tests the tires twice a day. William Gaskins supervises windshield wipers. Prior, K. Hand, Bevis, Gold, Jones, Johnson, DeLancy and Pearle keep the camp clean. I have to look after many of these things as inspector, and what a job!

July 7

They have a lot of pretty girls in Georgia, if our boys are judges, and we saw many. When in Atlanta, we took on another boy, Neal Kirby, Mr. Neal's Nephew. A few miles out of Atlanta, we began to see mountains. John Johns was very much thrilled as they were his first. Claude Jones asked me many times when we would come to the mountains.

On entering Tennessee, we rode on a concrete highway which gave us better running time. Everyone was thrilled as we traveled through a mountain, via tunnel, entering Chattanooga.

After passing through, we started for Lookout Mountain. Several of us had the thrill of walking up most of the way. But we were glad when Mr. Neal came along and picked us up.

July 9

Up at 6 a.m. After breakfast, Claude Jones, John Johns, Henry Gold, Buck Carlton, Dea and Cynthia had a big time hiking down the mountain. We would get to going so fast that we were obliged to grab a tree to slow us down.

In Jasper, Tenn., we picked up Bobby Bevis, Bill Neal and Buck Carlton who had hitch-hiked on ahead while the bus was being worked on near Lookout Mountain.

July 10

Stopped in Manchester for gas and Mr. Neal invited me to ride with them. Their little bus is very comfortable. My ride ended rather abruptly because a tire blew out 20 miles south of Nashville.

Arrived in Nashville at noon. While Mr. Kight made arrangements to get us a swim at the YMCA, the chef served us sandwiches. Everyone enjoyed a shower and swim. With a change of clothes we felt better.

Had a good ride through the mountains of Kentucky. Saw some of the coal mines. Pitched our tents at Young's tourist camp at Madisonville. Several boys went into town.

July 11

Stopped at the U.S. Royal Tire Co. in Evansville, Ind., where the boys discovered an ice cream parlor where ice cream was 15 cents a pint. Billy Neal has the record of eating the most ice cream. In Alvia, we picked up one of the fellows who had left us the night before with some friends.

A sand storm came up on us about 5 o'clock, which was followed by rain and lightning. Several trees were blown down. We got an idea of the force of the wind when we had to retie the tarpaulins on top the bus. It rained on us on into St. Louis.

July 12

Motored over the Mississippi River to the White Truck Agency at St. Louis to get a couple of spacers between our rear wheels. After touring the Lindbergh Trophy museum, and the zoo, we were informed that we would not be able to leave St. Louis until the next day.

We had been very uncomfortable from the heat and found out that it was 105 in the shade. Just after supper, John Smith, Buck Carlton and I found a 15-cent picture show where we could rest some. All slept around the bus.

July 13

Reason Hampton and Henry Gold started a laundry and made some extra money from the boys who didn't want to wash their own clothes. It was so hot we were almost like wild people waiting for the bus. Several of the boys had two or three cold showers during the day.

We left St. Louis at 8:30 p.m. It was much cooler riding along at night. We stopped briefly at midnight for coffee.

July 17

On setting up camp at Colorado Springs, Mr. King with Bevis, Jones, Rich and Ballard, left just before supper to see a picture show. Leaving the theater, they found one boy missing. A lady reported that a Scout boy was asleep in the show. All ran in and found Claude Jones asleep. They hid behind a pillar, and Mr. King shook him. What a surprised boy Claude was when he awoke and found the theater empty.

July 18

After breakfast, and everything packed, the bus carried us to the foot of Pike's Peak. About 10:30 we started hiking up the peak along the track of the cog railroad — nine miles of climbing.

Jones and I were the last to get started. Shortly we came up with a school teacher and some children from Oklahoma. Claude Jones decided he didn't want to make the climb and went back with the teacher.

About 2 o'clock Bevis began to feel sick for a little while. Late in the afternoon we reached Windy Point where one of the railroad men lived. He served us coffee which pepped us up for the air was cool.

Joe Prior got sick. Walter Ballard and I supported him taking about 20 steps and stopping for a rest so that he could lie down. We resumed the climb and made the peak about 11 p.m. Upon reaching the top we were at an elevation of 14,019 feet. Every boy was about frozen. Mr. Neal's outfit had arrived in the afternoon with Mr. Kight. Doc McQueen told me several boys took the burro train and stopped at a cabin, sick.

(Note: The boys from flat Southwest Florida probably suffered from altitude sickness, a common discomfort for first-time climbers.)

We were so tired and cold that I thought it best to stay at the bunk house, though the cost was $1.50.

July 19

The caretaker called us at 3 a.m. to see the sunrise. The other boys were so sleepy they did not care to get up. When I joined the crowd on the cog tracks, there were a lot of people waiting to see the sunrise. It was a little cloudy so it wasn't so good. Mr. Kight said they had seen better in Florida, and I agreed.

After some of the others had gotten up, we took photos of each other sitting in the snow.

Mr. Kight asked me to look after the fellows hiking down. There were eight of us, and we decided to go down the burro trail. It is longer, but you get to see the best scenery. It was a very tiresome hike, with many stops.

On reaching the bottom, none of us wanted to make the hike up and down Pikes Peak again.

Thrilled Scouts gathered around actress for a group photo.

Automobiles in 1934 were not engineered for 9,000-mile trouble-free journeys over mostly gravel roads. The Scouts accepted breakdowns as part of the adventure, and the adults knew that breakdowns and flat tires were inevitable on long trips with cars of the day. Collier's bus had seen better days on his Tamiami Trail Tours bus line of southwest Florida.

After hiking up and down Pikes Peak in two days, the caravan stopped at Denver to replace a broken axle. Adult drivers often drove through the night to make up lost time while the boys and two little girls, Cynthia and Dea Neal of Arcadia, slept in their improvised seat beds.

One man drove while the other "rode shotgun" on the emergency brake. The boys and men had to get out and walk up steep grades as the big bus had insufficient power to propel itself and a load up the steep mountain roads..

We again pick up the diary of Arcadia Scoutmaster Edward Cassels:

371

July 22

Ran out of gas about 5 a.m. in front of a filling station. Stopped on the plains for breakfast. Entered the Rockies at Wind River Canyon.

Had a grand swim at Hot Springs Park in Thermopolis, Wyoming. The caretaker of the pool showed us how to "placer" mine — just in case we had time to hunt for gold.

July 23

The grade leading up to Shoshone Dam was steep, and all the boys had to spend some time walking up. A landslide had covered the side of the road. Workmen cleared it just as we reached it.

A mile east of Yellowstone Park, Mr. Kight announced he would give a nickel to the boy who saw the first bear. Ten minutes later, Lester Hand saw one along side the road. The chef handed me some bread, and I fed the bear from the bus window. I could hardly believe that the bear could be so tame. He stood on his hind legs and took bread from my hand.

While setting up camp and eating supper, the boys joked one another about bears coming into camp. The chef sleeps under a tarpaulin at the end of the bus. They told him the bears would get him.

Upon arriving at Mammoth lodge, Mr. Neal went to the post office for our mail. Pitched camp, and it began to rain. Some of us got pretty wet.

July 25

After Breakfast, J. Smith and I took Bevis to the hospital to be looked over. He had some bad sores on him. (Claude Jones, a Scout on the trip, now retired at Arcadia, says his friend Bevis got into a fight with another Scout who bit him. The bites became infected.)

Arrived at "Old Faithful" geyser about 30 minutes before it emptied itself. What a thrill we had when it did shoot into the air about 150 feet.

After supper, most of us went to a dance at Old Faithful Lodge.

July 26

Shortly after breakfast, the boys reported at Old Faithful in uniform to have our pictures taken standing near as it emptied. Immediately after the eruption we started on a 2-mile hike with a ranger as guide.

July 28

We arrived in Salt Lake City at 6:30 p.m. After some delay pitched camp back of a service station.

It was decided that we would spend Saturday looking over the city, attend services at a Mormon church Sunday morning, and have a swim in Salt Lake on our way out to California.

Leaving the bus, most of us began looking for a barber shop and a good shower. Several barber shops we entered failed to have showers.

A man told us that the police station could accommodate us. Away we went, not to be outdone. A patrolman told us to go in and see the captain. He said "Okay." Our shower felt fine, even though it lacked soap and towels. Several of the fellows guyed us about going to the police station

372

for a shower, but we saved a quarter which we spent at Kress' for a sandwich and at a theater seeing Will Rogers in "Handy Andy."

July 29

Our first stop after breakfast was at one of the Mormon churches. As we marched in and sat down, an official saw Mr. Neal and asked him where we were from. He must have misunderstood Mr. Neal to say we were all from Arcadia for he announced the Scouts were from there. The Punta Gorda and Fort Myers boys did a little grumbling.

On reaching the bus, it was decided we would have time to attend afternoon services at the Great Mormon Temple. It looked like there were about 300 people in the choir.

Arrived at Salt Lake for a swim at Sunset Beach about 4 p.m. We just couldn't sink. Our feet would bob up in that salty water. As we came out, our faces and bodies were salty all over. We looked like we had been in a flour barrel.

Rode all night over the Salt Lake Desert, for it is very hot crossing during the day. About midnight it became very cold. We stopped at Welles City for coffee and pie.

August 1

Arrived at Sacramento about 7:30 p.m. and pitched our tents at Scout Camp. This camp has a clubhouse given by the Sacramento Lions Club. Any time the boys want to use it, day or night, it is kept open by a caretaker.

Supper over, some of the boys went to bed. Others went to a nearby fruit stand. They told us that cantaloupes were 50 cents per crate, and grapes 24 cents a lug.

August 2

For breakfast we had a large cantaloupe apiece and all the cereal and milk as usual. My, but those boys can eat! At noon we stopped at a fruit stand where Mr. Kight gave us all the watermelons we could eat. Little John Johns sure is a melon eater for his size.

August 10

Spent the previous night in the American Legion Hall in front of the Mack Sennett Movie Studio near Hollywood. We saw two or three actors that play in western pictures. Going to the Electric garage for a generator part, we passed Fox, Warner and Universal studios but couldn't get in.

While waiting for the bus, William Gaskins phoned a friend who was living in Hollywood and indirectly connected with the studios. He said he was sure arrangements could be made for us to visit Paramount studios.

August 11

During breakfast at the bus, a phone call came in saying we would go through the Paramount studio. Gaskins friend, Mr. Butler, would be at the bus in a few minutes. We quickly got into our uniforms.

A photographer and a young man from the press department showed us about the studio grounds. On our tour we passed a large draw bridge on a set that was used in the picture "Cleopatra" finished a couple of weeks before.

Baby Leroy was working on a picture, but it made him nervous to see a group, and we were unable to see him. Cary Grant was on the lot but unable to come out.

Miss Evelyn Venable came out dressed in a costume she was wearing for "Mrs. Wiggs of the Cabbage Patch." Had two pictures taken with her — one with Eagle Scouts Howard McQueen and Waldo Farabee.

Leaving Paramount, we headed for Beverly Hills to see some movie stars' homes. Mary Pickford's home is known as Pickfair and was very beautiful. We also stopped in Santa Monica where Shirley Temple, the little girl actress, was born and where Marian Davis and Buster Keaton have homes.

A man told Mr. Kight the radio said two of our boys were (left behind) at Long Beach. Mr. Kight phoned the police station there and instructed them to meet us in Pasadena. The boys on the bus gave Neal Jr. and Grace the razz as they entered the bus.

In Arcadia, California, we saw a lot of orange groves, lime groves and grape vineyards.

August 14
We arrived at Grand Canyon at 3 a.m. Up at 7 a.m. Chef made sandwiches for us, as dinner time would catch us on the trail into the canyon. Some boys rushed on without sandwiches.

It is nearly 16 miles down and back to the rim. We left the top at 11 a.m. We arrived at the Colorado River at 2:30 p.m. Jerry Fugate met us on the trail and said he had hiked eight miles to see a muddy river and wash his feet. We didn't fail to do likewise as our feet were very tired.

One of the girls felt sick as we left, so our climb was much slower. We expected to get a drink of water at one of the two fountains on the way up. We were very dry and considerably disappointed at finding no water.

It began to get cloudy and lightning. I suggested we better stay together because it was getting dark and the trail couldn't be seen very well.

On one of the turns of the trail we saw a light ahead moving fast toward us. We stood on the side. To our pleasant surprise it was Corky McQueen and Reason Hampton with wine and water to warm and quench our thirst. The water made us feel lots better.

We arrived at the rim at 11 p.m. It was a very tired bunch that reached the top.

August 18
We camped at a service station just outside El Paso, Texas. Breakfast over, we started for the Mexican Border. Mr. Kight instructed the boys

to be very careful and not say anything to the Mexicans that might in any way irritate them, for they would be jailed for the slightest offense.

I thought it would cost considerably more than 2 cents to cross the border, but that was the cost either way. We entered at Juarez.

Just outside a souvenir store, some little Mexican boys offered to shine our shoes for a penny. Bevis told me to wait for him. Just after he sat down in the chair, the man inside told me not to let the boys shine our shoes because they would charge a quarter before we left the chair. Two boys were shinning Bobby's shoes.

When he left the chair he paid his penny. The boys refused it, saying "We want two bits." Bobby told them "A nickel apiece is all I have." That taught us a lesson that we had to be very careful buying things.

August 24

Leaving New Orleans, I pointed out a sign marked 672 miles to Tampa, Florida. Mr. Kight remarked that the distance wasn't very far for us to travel.

We were riding in Alabama after lunch where we saw our first scattered palmettos. We knew then that Florida was not far away. On entering Florida, the boys gave a big cheer.

August 26

We passed through Tallahassee at 3:30 in the morning. The nearer home, the better the bus ran. We stopped in Lakeland to wire home. Arrived in Arcadia at 7 p.m. A wonderful tour but a bit too ambitious that kept the boys away from home too long.

The Tower Bar
Chapter 86

TOWER LAST RELIC OF LAND BOOM

The tragic death by drowning in Charlotte Harbor of Howard "Chris" Kristyensen, owner of the Tower Bar east of Punta Gorda, focused attention on his unique landmark. Dr. Charles W. Fambrough of Port Charlotte Beach reveals heretofore unknown facts about the 30-foot tower — last relic here of the Great Florida Land Boom.

"The tower was built in 1921, at the start of the land speculation, by William W. Wilson, a developer and vice-president of the Punta Gorda State Bank," states Dr. Fambrough, 84, now retired. "W.W. owned a two-story home on a large tract on Shell Creek. He platted this in lots to cash in on the land fever that began after the first World War. He extended Riverside Drive from Cleveland and built the tower as a sales office at the intersection with Highway 17.

"The area was a long way from town, so W.W. also installed a gas pump to reassure folks they wouldn't be stuck out there. The tower was meant to attract attention and provide a vantage point for prospective customers to look over the terrain. It was a pretty spot on Hobson Branch flowing into Shell Creek and the Peace River.

376

"Lots weren't selling well so W.W. leased out the tower in 1925 to my sister Lillian and her husband Chauncey Headley as a home and part-time business. They were both teachers in Punta Gorda and operated the filling station — as gas stations were called then — in the evenings and on weekends.

"The Headleys had their bedroom on the second floor of the tower. However, Lillian was pregnant; and she thought the room was too small and inconvenient. Therefore, P.C. O'Haver and I built a one-room cottage behind the tower for maternal quarters. A daughter was born which the Headleys named Marjorie Jean. She now is married to the Rev. Richard McEuen, a Presbyterian minister at Jacksonville. The little cottage later was rented as a tourist cabin.

"I had just been graduated from Charlotte High School and taken a job laying tile for a company in Tampa. I got sick, however, and came home to get well. We lived in the Freeman House (now restored and listed on the National Register of Historic Places) at Punta Gorda.

Mrs. Blazer's Boarding House

"My mother, Lena, Mrs. Thomas Fambrough, ran Mrs. Harry Blazer's boarding house near the Baptist Church (now Rebekah Lodge). Her cooking was known throughout Charlotte, DeSoto and Lee Counties. The dining room had three tables with ten chairs each.

"In addition to the few boarders, my mother served 90 meals a day in three sittings at 35 cents per plate --- 50 cents on Sundays. You had to make a reservation in order to get a seat. Mother's regular menu was meat and seven vegetables. My father bought the groceries at Vasco Peeples' store. Vasco said we were his best customers.

"I got well on mother's cooking, and my sister suggested I stay home and operate the tower during the day while she and Chauncey were teaching. I agreed. I sold Texaco gas at 19 cents per gallon from a hand-operated pump. Years later, new owners switched to American Gas, now Amoco, and added five more cabins. We carried soda pop, candy bars, cigarettes, canned milk, bread and a few other staples. We also had a slot machine on the counter. I used to open a can of Eagle brand condensed milk for lunch and developed a fondness for the thick, sweet concoction.

"There was a vacant lot across the street, and we dug a pit there over which to barbecue a pig on Friday nights. Charley Edwards, who lived in the Sans Souci subdivision nearby, would come and turn the pig all night. On Saturday mornings, people from Punta Gorda and Arcadia would drive out and buy roast pork for 20 cents a pound. It was delicious.

"The road to Arcadia at that time was one lane with a marl (shell and clay) surface. In the summer of 1926, the state sent a construction crew to widen the road. They had a tent camp on the same lot as the barbecue pit.

A tremendous hurricane in 1926 blew away the tents, and the workmen took refuge in the first floor of the tower building," says Dr. Fambrough.

"The hurricane of Sept. 17-18 that year, was the worst to that time to hit Florida. Wind instruments in Miami were blown away at 125 miles per hour. Thousands of homes in Miami and Fort Lauderdale were destroyed. The wind blew all the water out of Lake Okeechobee, drowning 18,000 people! Bodies were scattered in windrows throughout the Everglades.

"The tower shook so badly in the storm, our only shelter, I backed my Ford roadster against it to keep the structure upright," Dr. Fambrough recalls. "The hurricane blew the water out of Charlotte Harbor. You could throw a baseball across the channel. When the eye passed over, the wind reversed and blew so much water back into the harbor it flooded Punta Gorda. People ran boats on Marion Avenue," declares Dr. Fambrough.

The hurricane and attendant deaths shocked the country. People were afraid to live in Florida. That was the beginning of the collapse of the land boom. The stock market crash of 1929 and subsequent Great Depression finished the speculation, which made many millionaires and as many paupers.

Dr. Fambrough managed the tower for two years until he decided to go to college in Iowa and become a chiropractor. The Headleys gave up their lease shortly afterward and moved back to town. Wilson sold the tower to Jeff Limear. He built five more "tourist cabins" in back and switched to Sinclair gasoline.

Bicycle Races

U.S. Cleveland, of Punta Gorda, remembers that the Boy Scouts of Troop 5 used meet the Second-Class requirement for a "14-mile hike" by hiking out to the tower in the morning, eating lunch, and returning in the afternoon. The favorite route made a loop, going by Route 17 and returning by Riverside Drive. On the Fourth of July the town would stage a bicycle race to the tower and back. The tower cabins were popular during World War II with the families of cadets at the Punta Gorda Army Air Base.

After the repeal of prohibition, either Limear or another owner named Sam Curtis turned the filling station into a bar, most likely the latter. Kristyensen, a retired butcher from Long Island, N.Y., bought the bar from Curtis in 1979 and filled it with automobile memorabilia. Old license plates are dated as far back as 1913. Model cars fill shelves. Old theater posters decorate the walls. The original gas pump is still upright. A real traffic light tells patrons by the color of lights whether the bar is open, closed or at "last call."

Water cascading from a pipe meant for oil attracted bathers but not buyers for lots. Note sign far left displaying 97-degree temperature.

Chapter 87

HOT WATER LEGACY OF OIL BOOM

When Frank W. Warren of Waukesha, Wisconsin, wrote his brother in 1930 — about overdue taxes on 160 acres of family land in Charlotte County — he had no inkling of the oil boom about to begin.

Frank wanted no part in paying his $23 one-fourth share of several years back taxes totaling $92: "I will just pass and drop out of the picture. For the life of me, I can't see any future for this property. There is so much more just like it you can't give away." All Frank wanted was one of the four shawls their late mother had knitted. His brother, L.L., at Louisville, Ky., agreed to pay the taxes — and to forgive a personal loan of $1,000 — in return for Frank's supposedly worthless interest in the property.

It should be remembered that the Great Depression was underway. A few dollars had greater import then than now.

The parcel suffering from unpaid taxes was the north half of section 16, township 42, range 23 near Burnt Store Road south of Tropical Gulf Acres. Owners in addition to Frank and L.L., was another brother J. Sutcliffe, and a sister Fanny.

L.L. was executor for the estate of their father Clarence A. Warren that included several Florida properties purchased in 1885 by their grandfather Eugene C. Warren of Louisville, Ky. The latter bought all of section 16 (one square mile) from the Florida Board of Education for $1.25 per acre — apparently for speculation.

379

Sections 16 of all townships were earmarked by federal survey "for the benefit of education." Proceeds from sales of such sections generally were used to build state colleges.

A few years after Frank signed off, geologists discovered that southern Florida was sitting on a giant "anti-cline" — a dome of subterranean rock that traps oil and gas. Prospectors began putting down test wells to determine the extent of the anti-cline.

The Peninsular Oil and Refining Co. drilled a well to 10,006 feet in Collier County that brought in salt water. This sometimes indicates the edge of a lens of oil which floats on water. Drillers rushed in all directions attempting to find the apex of the dome and the middle layer of oil between water and gas.

William O. Blanchard and Associates drilled to a depth of 10,284 feet near the Tamiami Trail 44 miles west of Miami. Humble Oil Co., a subsidiary of Standard Oil of Kentucky, went to 11,789 feet for a test in Dade County. Republic Oil drilled on an over-water location off Key Largo. Pure Oil Company drilled four holes in Gulf County to depths of 8,708 feet. Hunt Oil put down four wells in Madison County ranging from 3,000 to 5,400 feet. Stanolind Oil Co. went to a depth of 6,580 feet in Leon County. Magnolia Petroleum Co. put a test well down to 7,003 feet in Bay County near Panama City.

Humble was the first to strike oil in 1943 at Sunniland between LaBelle and Everglades City. The oil was of poor quality and accompanied by salt water. Nevertheless, it proved the anti-cline did contain oil.

Two Miles Down

The Humble well was more than two miles down. The drill had moved up the anti-cline but still had not found the pure oil layer. Oil fever was kindled by Humble's report that the oil was coming from a strata corresponding to the Glen Rose — a high-producing formation in Texas.

With this, the hunt moved north into Charlotte and Highland Counties where the anti-cline apex was expected to be discovered. Black Gold fever gripped property owners as company agents scurried to lease rights.

Family letters suggest that Frank wished he had not been so hasty in ducking his share of their property.

The Peninsular Oil Co. offered L.L. Warren a lease that included the Burnt Store Road parcel and another 80 acres north of the present Charlotte County Airport. Wrote Agent A.D. Hunter in March, 1940:

"We are trying to assemble a block of leases in the vicinity of your land and are paying a consideration of 7½ cents per acre when the lease is signed. The primary term of ten years is contingent upon our either commencing drilling operations on your land — paying an annual rental of five cents per acre — or producing oil, gas, sulphur or other mineral therefrom.

"In the event of production we pay you a royalty of one-eighth on oil and gas, 50 cents per long ton on sulphur and one-tenth of all other minerals." L.L. was a shrewd negotiator. He turned down the offer and waited for a better one. He got it from Humble Oil.

We obtain an insight into oil boom negotiations in a letter from W.E. Cross, an official of Standard Oil of Kentucky, to its agent at Sarasota, Fla., in Feb. 1943:

"Our agent at Punta Gorda, Mr. T.I. Kennedy, and his brother-in- law Mr. A.C, Frizzell, are both large land owners in Charlotte County. They have both signed the oil leases after same were examined by their attorney, Mr. Earl Farr, who is also County Attorney. From other information I can get, am advised that practically all land owners in Charlotte County have signed the oil leases so far. The representative of Peninsular Oil Company states it is leasing land for the purpose of drilling a test well, and that it was not a stock-selling scheme as there is no stock for sale. In other words, I find that the people of Charlotte County are making a real effort to get all property owners to sign. A thorough investigation was made by Mr. Farr who has approved the leasing of this land.

Airport Land Sought

"Now, as to the airport in Charlotte County, located next to Mr. L.L. Warren's property. The contract was let for construction of this airport on or about January 1st.. The John E. Ballenger Construction Co. of Lakeland was successful bidder. The airport, with two runways and taxi strips, should be completed within 90 days after work is started. This project was let under the Civil Aeronautics Authority in Atlanta, Ga. When the airport is finished, it will be used for the time being at least by the Gunnery School Training Center at Fort Myers as an auxiliary field. As competition among oil companies for leases intensified, the *Punta Gorda Herald* took notice. It reported the frenzy with a front-page story in June 1944:

"More than half the 440,000-acre area of Charlotte County has been leased for oil exploration at prices ranging from five to 50 cents an acre, according to oil leases recorded in the office of Circuit Clerk E.H. Scott up to Monday of this week. Total acreage now under lease is 234,492.

"Leasing started in this county in 1939, when the average price paid was five cents an acre. The price has risen steadily — large areas being under lease at 10 cents and the more recent leases providing for greater sums. Greatest single financial transaction was the leasing by A.C. Frizzell of more than 30,000 acres in the western part of the county, at 35 cents an acre, to the Sinclair Prairie Co. The figures on leasing activity in this county indicate that interest is greater here than in nearly any other area.

"Prices are rising for the leases, and those now being recorded are largely at 50 cents. If past trends are continued, the prices will increase even further. It is indicated that the interest in this particular area, where test holes have been drilled over long periods of time, is at fever pitch.

"The biggest companies — Humble Oil, an affiliate of Standard Oil; Sinclair; Gulf; Texas; and others — have obtained leases in the county. Leases thus far signed give no indication as to when drilling operations will begin; but with the huge investments made here, predictions were being freely made that the time is not far distant."

The Warren heirs finally jumped on the bandwagon and signed a one-year lease with Humble in January 1945. They split a bonus of $600 plus one-eighth royalty right on any oil produced.

The largest benefactor of the oil lease boom was the huge Babcock Ranch in east Charlotte county all the way down to the Lee County boundary. It signed with Shell Oil for a bonus of $1 million, according to Larry Campbell, manager of the Babcock-Webb Wild Life Management Area which includes former Babcock Ranch land.

Shell's first well was drilled east of I-75 and north of Tucker's Grade. At 11,000 feet the crew gave up and moved farther south to a spot east of U.S. 41 where Oil Well Road ends. Campbell says the company built the road and parallel canal to bring in its heavy equipment. This time, the pipe was pushed down 13,000 feet — a deep well even by Texas standards. However, it also was dry. With this, Shell moved to Highlands County. The company brought in a "doodle-bug" truck and crew to prospect by dynamite-sounding the "Bear's Den" intersection of U.S. 27 and S.R. 70 — so named for a popular roadside restaurant there.

Another Oil Well Road

Another Oil Well Road — in South Gulf Cove in west Charlotte County — recalls an unsuccessful drilling effort there on vast acreage owned by the Vanderbilt family.

A unique reminder of the heady 1940's is Hot Springs on Burnt Store Road south of Punta Gorda. A deep drill for oil there failed to find black gold but did tap a reservoir of 97-degree mineral water. In disgust, the well was capped and forgotten.

King-Miller Corp. of Cape Coral in early 1967 bought the well and surrounding property for a development featuring the curative power of hot mineral water. The site was platted into home-size lots. People came to swim in a pool fed by a fountain atop the old oil pipe. However, few lots were sold and no homes were built. After a year or so, the project was abandoned.

After a decade of dry wells, the oil companies gave up. Dreams by local land owners of wealth evaporated. Humble Oil abrogated its Warren Family lease in April 1947. The brothers and sisters divided up Mrs. Warren's old shawls, and Frank had the last laugh.

!PHOTO CENSORED!

Chapter 88

ENGLEWOOD'S GOOSE-BUMP NUDIST CAMPS

Nudists frolicked on Manasota Key beaches back in the 1920s and 1930s. Englewood oldtimers recall them with amusement.

When the Lemon Bay Historical Society kicked off their programs for the 1995 season on Feb. 13, highlight of the program was an informal exchange of reminisces by Jack Tate, L.A. Ainger and Larry Evans.

Jack's family came into the area in 1926, and he married Margaret Buchan, only child of Mr. and Mrs. Peter Buchan who arrived in 1902.

L.A.'s parents, Mr. and Mrs. Lorin Ainger settled at Grove City in 1898, and he married Merle McRae whose family homesteaded at Fort Winder at the turn of the century.

Larry's father was a commercial fisherman who moved his family to Lemon Bay in 1920 to harvest the bountiful mullet there.

Diana Harris, program director for the society, introduced the speakers. She encouraged them with well directed questions about the nudist "camps" that once flourished here. The trio passed a microphone back and forth as memories nearly forgotten flooded back in bits and pieces. Their own words say it best.

JACK:

"The camps — some called them colonies — got started in the late 1920s when Cornell University at Ithaca, N.Y., pushed family nudism as good for physical and mental health. There were several colonies south of Sarasota — three on Manasota Key.

"I was invited by Bill Hewitt, a friend who adopted nudism, to visit him at the Hermitage camp and have dinner. I went on a Sunday afternoon, and Bill greeted me au naturelle at the door.

"There were two ladies cooking dinner in the kitchen. They did wear shorts — a wise precaution around the stove — but nothing else. I wasn't sure where to look when I talked to them. Bill put on his shorts when we sat down to eat.

"The Hermitage camp was called the Sea Island Sanctuary. It was started by a Mr. Feinstein and other German people from New York City.

"When I was a teenager, we boys used to go out to the Hermitage which was abandoned at that time. We went Friday afternoon after school — taking along oysters and fish and other food. We went skinny dipping in the Gulf, so I guess we were the first nudist camp there."

383

L.A.:

"There was another nudist camp at Knight's Pass. A retired dentist from Arcadia built a two-story store there, and he lived upstairs.

"New Yorkers came down on 2-week trips. Every two weeks they changed — groups, not partners. They spent a lot of time sunning themselves on the beach. They didn't have sun-tan lotions in those days, so they smeared themselves with olive oil.

"Nudists came to Sarasota or Punta Gorda by train then took a bus to Englewood and a boat across the bay. Some camps had their own busses.

"A man I met in my store invited me to visit him on the island. I took Merle with me, but we were not yet married. We didn't have TV in those days, so we didn't know what sex was. My acquaintance, in the nude, answered the door but right away wrapped a towel around his waist. We spent a pleasant afternoon sipping coffee.

"All the camps were family oriented — men, women and children. They were interested in nature — trees, sun and the like. The people usually dressed when they ate and said a prayer. Otherwise they wore no clothes, except the women wore hats to protect their hair-dos. They played volley ball all the time."

LARRY:

"When I was 14 or 15, Bill Hewitt took me along on an expedition to find a camping place for some nudists from New York. Their leader was a short middle-aged man who looked like a barrel. He was escorting an attractive young lady about 30. We showed them Thornton's Island south of Stump Pass, this side of Knight's Pass. There was an empty 2-room house there built a few years earlier by Mr. Thornton.

"It was next door to Doc. Flint's old house which was badly rotted. He had died in the early 1930s, and the house had not been maintained.

"When we pulled up to Thornton's dock, the old man jumped out and shucked his clothes he was so anxious to get started. Mosquitoes liked to be eating him alive, but he didn't care. The lady took off part of her clothes. The old man wanted to inspect Flint's house, but we warned him it wasn't safe. He didn't pay any attention. He stepped on the porch which gave way — plunging him between some joists. He was wedged in tight. Luckily, he didn't straddle a joist. That would have fixed him up for life.

"Bill and I had to rescue him. We got him out, but he had no skin from his knees to his navel. There was another nudist camp on Little Gasparilla Island. After that my parents sent me away to school."

L.A.:

"The camps operated mostly in the winter. The nudists ran around with goose bumps, but they thought it was great. Back home it was snowing.

384

"Late winter was the run season for mullet. One commercial fishing crew once caught 136,000 pounds of big mullet. They also caught many small fish but threw these back. The fishermen seemed to like to cast their nets around Knight's pass where the nudists ran up and down the beach like no one was around. We ought to have sold tickets.

"Lemon Bay was deeper in those days. Big schooners brought supplies from Tampa. Now, with canals, the bay has filled in a lot.

"It is true that the nudists consisted mainly of families. They conducted daily religious ceremonies that included sun worship. There was a moonshine still on Thornton's Island, but the nudists never indulged.

"When Doc Flint died, I went over during a storm with some other men to bring him back. He had been dead three days.

"As the youngest, I was directed to get on the bed with the corpse and roll him to the edge. There was air in the deceased's stomach, and when I rolled him over he groaned. This scared all of us. We took him to Ponger's Funeral Home in Punta Gorda."

LARRY:

"I lived on Thornton's Island in 1930 when I was in the second grade. My Dad was catching shrimp in those days for the Northerners. We wouldn't eat shrimp because they looked liked worms.

""Not many folks would eat snook either. If you don't skin them, they taste like bar soap. Skinned they taste good.

"Doc. Flint told Dad to catch some shrimp and he would show us what you could do with them. Dad got a bucket full and took them to Doc who put them on to boil. After they got going real good, Flint said to put in two or three garlics he had there.

"We were used to eating onions so threw in three whole garlic bulbs, not the little cloves Doc Flint had in mind. It was a powerful stew which stunk us up pretty good.

"During World War II, the German nudists stopped coming. There was a scare story going around that German submarines were putting spies ashore on Manasota beaches. We organized night patrols to catch them. We had a .22 rifle and a .410 shotgun. These might had killed the spies laughing, but we never saw any.

"After the war, the Chamber of Commerce got hold of a nudist directory printed in Germany that said Englewood had the finest nudist beaches in the world. The Chamber was upset. Apparently the directory was compiled from old pre-war accounts."

JACK:

"I want to make it clear that when we boys spent weekends at the Hermitage skinny dipping we didn't have any women along."

Gus Cole's stilt-house. Grandmother Mary Jane Cole stands with Lois **and Ralph.** Tanks stored rainwater for household use.

Chapter 89

A LINK BETWEEN PIONEERS AND PRESENT

Lois Peeples, 86 at this writing — matriarch of the Peeples family and seemingly the entire city of Punta Gorda — is a living link between the pioneer days of yore and the present era of space flight.

"The most interesting thing I have seen is the steady progress the county has made since the coming of the railroads," says Mrs. Peeples, widow of the late Vasco Peeples. "Progress is good for everybody."

Mr. and Mrs. Vasco Peeples are descended from hardy pioneer stock and were active in building Punta Gorda from the first day they arrived there in 1933 to take over the IGA Grocery. Prior to that they were doing the same for their native Florida elsewhere.

How their ancestors opened up America's last frontier — to the Florida we know today — is part of everyone's legacy. Lois' maternal great-grandfather, Narciso DeNoda, as a young sailor emigrated in 1848 from the Canary Islands to Palma Sola, Florida (near Bradenton). He moved back to the Canary Islands but returned to Palma Sola in 1870 with a wife, Mary Concepcion. He was a ship rigger and she a teacher. They home-steaded 38 acres at Palma Sola, proving out their claim in 1889 and gaining U.S. citizenship in 1894. The DeNoda's had one daughter, Carmen, who married Solomon Switzer of Palma Sola — a patent medicine salesman and orange grove owner . They had a daughter named Abbie.

Lois' paternal grandparents were Martin and Mary Jane Cole of Arkansas whose son was Gus. The family moved to the village of Tampa, Florida, in 1887, when Martin's health declined. The trip by wagon was an arduous 1,300 miles. Cole didn't stay long in Tampa because a great yellow fever epidemic broke out there a year later. Fearful of his weak health and the safety of his family, Martin packed up to move to St.Petersburg across the bay. This trip took three months. They were halted around the bay by a blockade which quarantined the Coles in camp until it was certain they did not carry the dreaded disease.

Martin opened another store but died in 1890. His widow, Mary Jane, took Gus to Palmetto where they built a palm-thatched cabin. Mrs. Cole took in washing, and Gus dropped out of second grade to work in Whitehead's general store. It was a practical substitute for school. He learned how to compute customers' bills, divide weights and keep inventory. Gus became a commercial fisher at age 15.

Upon reaching adulthood, Gus married Abbie Switzer. They lived in one of three stilt-houses on Tidy Island — so named because it was out of the water only at low tide. Today the island has been filled in for a development of exclusive homes. Lois was born there in 1907. She has no birth certificate because it had to be mailed to the county seat, and Tidy Island was not claimed by any post office. Two years later Cole bought half of a 3-acre island north of Gasparilla Island. He moved his family there because the fishing at Charlotte Harbor was better.

Stilt House Over Water

Gus built a stilt house over the water so he could bring his boat up to the front door. Rainwater was collected in barrels for drinking and household use. He built a walkway to his part of the island — today enlarged to 20 acres and known as Cole Island — where he built a net shed. A few years later he built a cabin home there for the aged DeNodas. Eventually he bought the other half of the island.

Though Lois was barely two years old, she remembers the trip by sailboat from Palma Sola. "The water was rough, and we had to sail south of Gasparilla Island and back north to reach the place my father had selected near the best fishing grounds," says Mrs. Peeples.

"My next memory is of a Thanksgiving there in 1910 when I was not yet four. There was a hurricane that September that blew all the water out of the bay. My father was worried about our house being blown into the water so he took us and the DeNodas to the net storage building on the center of our island. I was impressed because my great-grandparents walked on the bottom of the bay. Mrs. DeNoda was afraid we were all going to drown. She insisted that my brother Ralph and I should be dressed in our best clothes so we would be presentable if found later floating in the harbor.

"That Thanksgiving we all had dinner in our home which survived the storm. The only food I can remember was collard greens, though there was much more. I was thankful because I could look out the window and see water around our house.

"Once, a boat-load of great-grandfather DeNoda's relatives sailed up from Cuba for a visit. They only stayed one day and night. Great- grandfather died in 1919 and Mary Concepcion in 1922. Their funeral processions were by boats to Englewood where they were buried in the old cemetery. Great-grandmother had brought her funeral clothes from Spain many years before.

"Grandmother Mary Jane Cole lived with us for about three years and never left Cole Island until she went to live with her other daughter at Palma Sola.

Lois Cole holds diploma.

"My father and mother, Gus and Abbie Cole, were good managers. They saved money and invested it in Vicker's general store on Gasparilla Island along the Charlotte Harbor and Northern Railroad. The CH&N was built in 1907-08 to haul phosphate from the Peace River to the dock at South Boca Grande. The railroad also built 16 houses at the north end of Gasparilla Island for renting to fishermen. Other fishermen and a fish packing house came to create a nice little village called Gasparilla.

"Mr. Vickers was hit by a sting-ray in 1919 and died of blood poison. Father bought out the widow's interest and obtained a post office for the colony. He moved the store and post office to Placida in 1944 when a road was built there. I started helping out in the store at age 12. When I was 13, I sent away to the U.S. School of Music for a correspondence course on the piano so I could play for Sunday School. I learned enough in a few months to accompany my Sunday school class in a Christmas program of 35 numbers. I was no virtuoso, but I got the job done.

"I saved enough money by the time I was 14 to buy 10 acres of land near Englewood. I held it for 49 years as a sort of emergency resource. I went to Tampa Business College when I was 16. I signed up for a 2-year course — everything they offered except telegraphy. Father wanted me to finish as soon as possible so I could come back to the store. I stayed with an aunt and spent all my time studying. Thus, I was able to finish in 10 months. I got 93 to 100 in all my subjects except orthography (writing with correct spelling and grammar). I got only 79 in that. My shorthand was good, and I still use it.

"While I was in business college, Vasco Peeples was hired by father, a member of the school board, to teach at Gasparilla for a season. The following year Vasco came to visit father, and we met. It was love at first sight for both of us. We were married in August 1926.

"We took jobs with the McAlpin school in north Florida — he as principal and teacher, I as a teacher. You didn't have to hold a teaching degree in those days if you could pass the state exam. I had no trouble with the test because of my business college study. Times were tough, and the school year was only seven months long. Our first daughter, Carmen, was born there. Then we moved to Live Oak and opened a grocery store."

Elected State Representative

"Vasco was elected State Representative from Suwanee County — serving from 1928-1930. His grandfather, William L. Peeples, served in the Florida House 1885-87. His great-grandfather, Daniel Bell, served in the 1839 Territorial Legislature and the first state Senate elected in 1845.

"The Great Depression hit in 1929, and most of the Legislature failed to be re-elected as people desperately sought a change. Vasco returned to the grocery business full time, but it was tough going because of the economy. Vernon, now a fourth-generation state legislator, was born there in 1930.

"In 1933 we received a telegram from my father: BOUGHT STORE IN PUNTA GORDA. COME PLAY BALL. J.T. Griggs, owner of the IGA Grocery there, had died. The store was available for a very fair price. No one had much money.

"Vasco and I came with our two children and moved the store to the old Goldstein building at the northeast corner of Marion Avenue and Cross Street. We lived upstairs where Gussie was born.

"We became active in First Presbyterian Church, and Vasco was president of Punta Gorda Rotary. Even in the Depression, he insisted that at least 75 cents be kept in the cash register for his weekly Rotary lunch. He had 49 years perfect attendance. I was involved with the Business and Professional Women's Club.

"Both of us were also active in the Democratic Party. We served on the county executive committee, the state Democratic Committee and attended several national conventions as voting delegates.

"Operating a grocery during the Depression and World War II — before supermarkets became popular — required substantial risk. Independent stores had to extend credit, but often the customer simply could not pay at the end of the month. It was painful to cut off credit, but more painful to take the loss. Stores stayed open to midnight on Saturdays when the fishermen were home with their families and three weeks' pay.

"Fishermen worked a 3-week "set of tides" at a "fish camp" on stilts or on "lighters" near good net grounds. To compensate for the long Saturday, stores closed Wednesday afternoons. No one operated on Sunday. Monday and Thursday mornings were especially busy because merchants were filling orders for fishermen down the bay. Merchandise was delivered to run boats delivering ice and supplies and bringing back fish.

"During World War II, Vasco — very patriotic — volunteered for the Army Corps of Engineers even though he was 38 years old and had four children. He built bases for three years in Brazil and the Azores. While he was gone, the rest of the family pitched in to run the store. Little Gussie helped even though she could barely see over the counter.

Lois Cole Peeples, widow of Vasco, as elder, First Presbyterian Church.

"When Vasco returned, he was elected to the County Commission for eight years — all as the chairman. We sold the grocery in 1952, and had time for civic affairs. I accepted presidencies of the Punta Gorda Woman's Club, Business and Professional Women's Club, and Charlotte County Parent-Teacher Association. I become a deacon and Sunday school teacher at First Presbyterian. I've had a full life."

What Mrs. Peeples did not mention is her achievements and honors after the death of Vasco in 1985. She became manager of her son's insurance and real estate business when he was elected to the Legislature. She also was elected a ruling Elder of her church. Mrs. Peeples is especially proud of being the first woman in the county to be inducted into a Rotary Club — that of Punta Gorda, the oldest service club in the County, where Vasco had been president.

She should say, "I have a full life."

Lois died September 14, 1994 and is buried at Indian Springs Cemetery

The 1935-36 Charlotte High football squad. Front row, from left: David Root, Virgil Mulholland, Alfred Larrison, Joy Duggar, U.S. Cleveland, Benny Malone, Chidester Johnson. Second row: Sidney Parnell, J.A. "Sammy" McCullough, Coach Taylor, Frank Smoak, Marshal Robinson.

Chapter 90

STATE'S FIRST WOMAN SCHOOL SUPERINTENDENT

The most popular young woman at Punta Gorda in 1913 demonstrably was Miss Sallie Jones, a senior at the high school. She was destined to become the first woman in Florida to hold the position of county school superintendent, and the only one of her gender ever in Charlotte County.

The Kadel-Kritchfield Road Show came to town in January for a six-day engagement and as a promotion conducted a popularity contest for "maidens." Reported the *Punta Gorda Herald:* "The voting contest last week developed great interest and a friendly rivalry amongst the friends of the several competing young ladies. This interest ran high on the last night, and the balloting was close. On the final count, however, Miss Sallie Jones was declared the winner and awarded a handsome set of silverware."

Upon graduation, Miss Sallie attended the state six-week training course for a certificate to teach primary grades. Her first job was at Chokoloskee, and the following school year at Pine Island. Then she obtained a teaching position at her alma mater.

In the summers she attended Florida Southern College, majoring in education. She and a fellow student fell in love, but he was killed in an automobile accident. Heart broken, she never married. She dedicated her life to other peoples' children. After obtaining her degree, Miss Sallie taught English, history and science in the higher grades.

Charlotte County's modern school system began in 1921 when DeSoto County was divided into five parts. The only high school was at Punta Gorda on Taylor Street. There were "rural" elementary schools at Charlotte Harbor Town, Gasparilla, Vineland-San Cassa, McCall,

Murdock, Placida, Bairdville, Bermont, Sparkman and Acline. Early teachers at these schools have been mentioned previously.

Upon division of DeSoto County, Governor Hardee appointed the first county officials. Among them was W.E. Bell, formerly DeSoto County superintendent, as the same official here. The Board of Public Instruction was comprised of Thomas S. Knight, Charles A. Cantwell, and W.H. Mason. Supt. Bell complained in his first report to the Board that he had inherited a pro-rata deficit of $8,500 from the DeSoto County school indebtedness. The school year was set at eight months. In his 1924 report, Bell recommended that students failing to comply with the Florida compulsory attendance law be jailed.

Simultaneously with county status, the first bridge across the harbor, between Punta Gorda and Charlotte Harbor Town, was opened. This made it possible to bus students from rural schools to the junior high school at Charlotte Harbor Town built in 1917, and the Punta Gorda combined grammar and high school built in 1911 on Taylor Street. The *Herald* of August 1927 reported the cost of operating six buses totaled $2,500 — or $30 per pupil per semester. The routes give us a good picture of the county population distribution.

"Harold Aber, who so ably handled the main transportation route from the DeSoto County line through Cleveland and Solana to the Punta Gorda School, will have charge next year over the same route. H.W. Placier will carry the children in from Acline. James Rockwell will bring them from the Whidden, Washington territory on upper Shell Creek. Alonzo Sias will cover the Murdock, Charlotte Harbor section, bringing lower grade pupils to the Charlotte Harbor Town School; and high school students into the county school here. Children living along the mainland and on the islands down the bay will be brought to the Gasparilla School by Mack Brawner. Mrs. J.D. Mercer will transport pupils to the school at Bermont."

Charlotte High School

Bussing and construction of a non-accredited junior high school at Charlotte Harbor Town swelled Punta Gorda Combined School enrollment dramatically. Thus, it became necessary to build a larger school there. A site was chosen in the Forest Park subdivision on Cooper Street, and construction bonds of $180,000 were issued to a Toledo investment firm. Work began in April of 1926.

That same year, the state Department of Public Instruction raised salaries for "rural" teachers. The average for a teacher in schools of one or two rooms was $615 annually; in schools of three to 10 rooms was $766; and in schools of more than ten rooms was $933. Charlotte County paid the highest salaries in the state, according to the report. By this time, bussing had reduced the number of rural schools here to five of one room, and one of two rooms. Rural teachers in one-room schools (serving first through third grades) received $1,000 annually. Teachers in two-room schools (serving six grades) were paid $1,200.

Work on the new Charlotte High School did not progress as rapidly as hoped, but commencement exercises for June 1927 were held in the school auditorium — though classrooms were not yet completed.

The building had been planned to house the full range of grades 1 through 12. However, enrollment for the 1927-28 school year was so large, the first three grades at Punta Gorda School had to remain there. Total enrollment for the county was 1,000 students.

Charlotte County High School opened to public inspection Aug. 19, 1927; and to classes Sept. 5. Principal W.E. Riley announced assignments for 21 teachers — among them was Miss Sallies Jones teaching English and science. Reelected to the Board of Public Instruction was W.E. Mobley, chairman, T.S. Knight and J.W. Brawner.

"Professor" Riley is said to have held a strict hand over the student body. His wife taught the eighth grade and also was a disciplinarian. Teachers influenced their pupils by their good character and excellent example. During this time, home economics became a required subject for girls. Varsity football, basketball and baseball teams were organized for boys — basketball and tennis for girls.

The class of 1927-28 — the first to attend and matriculate from Charlotte High School — also printed the first annual book. It was named *The Silver King* edited by Gladys Roberts.

The Great Depression of the 1930's hit all schools hard nationwide. The school year in Charlotte County was shortened to seven months, and teachers taught the last month of the semester without pay. Salaries were paid in "scrip" — promissory notes which could be exchanged for goods and services with merchants. Women teachers with husbands were laid off so male teachers with families could work. Many older students dropped out of school in order to help support their families.

Bell resigned as county school superintendent in 1933 and was succeeded by Paul Eddy who served four years. Miss Sallie then was

Charlotte High School shortly after opening in 1927.

elected in 1937. She served with distinction for 16 years — the longest period in the history of the Charlotte County school system. The superintendent's office was in the court house. She had one administrative employee, a secretary, the late Maud Mauck.

Miss Sallie set the policy that all teachers had to be professionally qualified. She introduced the first school lunch rooms. Her role was especially challenging because some members of the all-male Board of Public Instruction believed a woman could not govern effectively — an attitude she overcame with tact and ability.

She retired on the last day of 1953 after 31 years as an educator. When a new elementary school was built four years later across the street from the high school, the Board named it in her honor.

Sallie Jones Elementary School consisted of only six rooms at first. It was expanded quickly when the old Taylor Street school burned in October 1958. Fortunately the children had been excused that day so they could attend a circus.

Edith Jones, a niece of Miss Sallie, describes her in an interview as "a bushel of fun who loved to entertain us. She played games with us, sang to us and took us to the movies and the beach — whatever we wanted to do. She was dedicated to education. Her whole life was teaching."

Mrs. Lynn Harrell Jones (no relation) recalls as a child living next door to Miss Sallie. "I first saw

MISS SALLIE JONES

Miss Sallie strolling along with a parrot on her shoulder. They were talking to each other. I was dumbfounded. She invited me to her home for lemonade. She entranced me, pointing out plants with their botanical names and explaining the mythology of statues in our gardens."

Miss Sallie was a goodwill ambassador for the schools to the community. She was president of the American Legion Auxiliary, proud that her brother Ferg had served in World War I. She also was president of the Business and Professional Women's Club; Matron of the Order of Eastern Star; member of Delta Kappa Gamma, an education sorority; and superintendent of First Presbyterian Sunday School. Miss Sallie died Oct. 21, 1960, after months of illness. She is buried at Indian Springs Cemetery. Her house was demolished to make room for expansion of Medical Center Hospital, now Charlotte Regional.

Homer L. Jones (no relation) was elected school superintendent after Miss Sallie. He was followed by W.S. Hancock in 1961.

The citizens of Florida in 1962 voted by public referendum to appoint county school superintendents. Hancock served out his four-year term and then gave way to Dr. A. Hugh Adams 1965-68; Dr. James W. Longstreth 1968-72; Dr. Thomas E. Brenner, Jr., 1972-77; James B. Lawless 1977-81; and Robert L. Bedford since 1981.

A major change in the administration of Florida's public schools occurred in 1947 when the Legislature superseded local school districts by adopting the Minimum Foundation Act. This funded improvements in school buildings and equipment and set standards for curricula.

Charlotte Harbor primary and intermediate school was closed in 1950 and students bussed to Punta Gorda. The stately structure was razed in 1990 for a shopping center. Two, huge residential developments by General Development Corp., forerunner of Atlantic-Gulf Communities; and Punta Gorda Isles, Corp., sparked explosive growth in population and rapid expansion of the school system.

Explosive Growth

Some notable examples: Peace River Elementary 1961, Lemon Bay K-9 grades 1962, Charlotte Junior High grades added to Charlotte High 1962, East Elementary 1964, all schools integrated and Baker Academy converted to a pre-school center 1964-66, Neil Armstrong Elementary 1970, Port Charlotte Junior High 1971, Punta Gorda Junior High 1971, Meadow Park Elementary 1975, grades 10-12 added to Lemon Bay High 1979, Charlotte Harbor Special school 1980, Charlotte Vocational-Technical Center 1980, Port Charlotte High 1984, L.A. Ainger Junior High 1984, Liberty Elementary 1986, Vineland Elementary 1986, Murdock Junior High 1989.

The oldest parochial private school, St. Charles Boromeo, was established for Roman Catholic students in 1960. The first principal was Sister Mary Fides. Several other church-affiliated schools have opened in more recent years and are listed in the telephone directory.

An extensive adult education program began in 1960 as an activity for retirees at the Port Charlotte Cultural Center dedicated to the public by General Development Corporation. The first director was James E. Baldwin, a retired high school principal from Indiana. The complex was presented to the county in November 1971, and adult education supervised by the Board of Education.

An important education facility is Edison Community College which opened at Port Charlotte in rented quarters in 1974. Now the college under direction of Dr. Richard Yarger occupies a 180-acre campus on Airport Road just east of Punta Gorda on land donated by the county.

Allapatchee Lodge in its heyday,

Chapter 91

RICH MAN'S PLAYHOUSE

Not all shakers and movers of Punta Gorda were residents — Louis Calder being an outstanding example.

Octogenarian Esther McCullough knew him well. "Mr. Calder was an extremely generous man," she recalls. "He was a tall, handsome and well-built man who loved to hunt and fish. He spent every winter at Punta Gorda pursuing his favorite sports. His wife, Lucille, often came with him. Mr. Calder was a wealthy man active in the Florida land boom of the roaring 1920's. He had lots of friends and customers who also were outdoor men.

"They would come down together and stay at Mr. Calder's luxurious, rustic lodge on the Allapatchee River, meaning Alligator Creek in Seminole. In those days there were lots of game and fish in the area."

Calder was president of the Perkins-Goodwin Investment Co. of New York City, a director of Standard Oil, and part of a consortium of financiers seeking greater wealth in Florida real estate.

The consortium incorporated as the Punta Gorda Finance Co., and engaged Ernest Pearce, a local developer, as vice-president and general manager. The group in 1925 bought 550 acres along Alligator Creek to lay out 439 home sites with good sized gardens.

The Punta Gorda Finance Co. was typical of speculators at that time. Other members in addition to Calder were H.H. Raymond, president Mallory & Clyde Steamship Co., N.Y.; William T. Adair, president World Syndicate Co., N.Y.; Calvin Austin, president Eastern Steamship Lines,

Boston; J.A. Coates, vice-president Old Dominion and Eastern Steamship Lines, N.Y.; Joe Mitchell Chapple, editor National Magazine, Boston; Eldridge Henderson, real estate, N.Y.; Major A.P. Duval, St. Petersburg; Farquson Johnson, president American Business Builders, N.Y.; and William T. Bidwell, Punta Gorda, developer and Buick dealer.

Their development was named Radair — a contraction of the names of directors Raymond and Adair, major stockholders. The Radair sales office was in the Pearce Building on Taylor Street opposite the big Hotel Charlotte Harbor.

A 4-page folder advertising the development was printed with the slogan: "If it's in Florida, it's good. If on the West Coast, it's better. If at Punta Gorda, it's best."

Calder was captivated by the Florida climate and the wilderness then easily accessible for hunting. Courthouse records reveal that in July 1926 he bought a large plot in Radair Park along the river for himself. Calder also bought 100 shares of $100 par-value Punta Gorda Finance Co. stock from Bidwell for $2,500.

Calder then built the Allapatchee Lodge as a country club to accommodate his friends and prospective Radair Park buyers. A swimming pool and golf course were planned but never built. Radair Park was designed for "gardens of strawberries, peppers, tomatoes, chickens and every table necessity" — according to the *Punta Gorda Herald* of September 1926.

Rustic Style

The *Herald* reported the lodge, then under construction, "contains 36 bedrooms, each equipped with shower bath and hot and cold running water" — a luxury even the Hotel Charlotte Harbor could not yet boast about. "It is furnished throughout in rustic trim, and contains one of the finest lounge rooms of any country club in the state. The fireplace in the center of the room is a massive structure of cemented boulders, open each side. It speaks of the many romantic stories of south sea island adventures that will be related before the fireplace during coming winter evenings.

"The lobby opens onto a broad veranda which is on the edge of a lagoon opening out on the waters of the river. The lagoon is to be cleaned out. The island between it and the river, already covered with a natural growth of tropical plants, will be beautified.

"The English oak dining room will seat 125 guests and is connected with a kitchen equipped with modern hotel cooking apparatus. Food for the dining room will come directly from the Radair Park gardens."

First manager of the lodge was Pearce who was active at the time in organizing the Punta Gorda Lions Club. Four small parties were held at the Lodge in December, but the grand opening was a banquet in January 1927 for the Lions Club. The event celebrated the presentation of the club charter by Col. C.M.R. Graham of Miami, state president of Lions.

Allapatchee Lodge hired the best cooks and was a popular hostelry for wealthy winter visitors for many years. An early chef was Alfred Ballard.

Calder kept kennels of well trained hunting dogs and comfortable boats for the fishermen. Anson Gaskill was the boat captain and fishing guide. Joe Washington was the dog trainer and hunting guide.

"Joe was the best guide in the state and a Cracker-Jack marksman," Anson recalls. "He also was an independent cuss. A pompous guest once kept giving Joe a hard time. When loading up his truck with dogs and equipment for the next hunting trip, Joe rubbed the guest's snake leggings on a bitch in heat. Upon arrival at the hunting area, the guest put on the leggings and Joe opened the dog cages — there were 12 or 14. One by one, all ran up to the guest and urinated on his legs.

"Joe could shoot the eye out of a fly. He would entertain lodge guests with trick shooting. He routinely shot down coins tossed in the air, or simultaneously with two pistols shoot the heads off two matches stuck on a fence post. I saw him with a 20-gauge Winchester shotgun break six eggs tossed in the air at the same time. After the lodge shut down during the Depression, Joe and his wife went around the country for the Winchester Gun Company putting on shooting exhibitions.

Singing At The Depot

"The grounds keeper was 'Preacher' (Richard) Robinson, African-American minister at Macedonia Missionary Baptist Church. Mr. Calder gave him a donation for the church every year. When Mr. Calder arrived and left on the Pullman sleeper, Rev. Robinson brought the Macedonia choir to the depot to sing for him. I and other workers at the lodge joined in. It was a regular hullabaloo. Mr. Calder liked that.

"One summer, I took Mr. Calder on his big, cabin cruiser up through the intracoastal waterway to his home in New York. In the fall I brought him back down again.

He asked me what church I belonged to. I told him First Methodist. Then he wrote out a check to the Church for $500, a lot of money back then, and handed it to me. 'There,' he said, 'that ought to pay your dues for a long time.'

Mrs. McCullough also emphasizes the generosity of Calder toward Punta Gorda. "He was modest about his contributions," says Mrs. McCullough. "He usually gave through someone associated with a worthy project. For example, he gave $500 to Mrs. Clark, a hostess at the lodge, for the First Methodist Church. On another occasion he did the same through me.

"Mr. Calder made a generous donation to the Women's Club through Mary Maxwell for the first public library building in Punta Gorda, now the Adventure Museum building next door to the Memorial Auditorium. Both she and I were invited to the opening."

Despite his desire for anonymity, Calder was publicly recognized for his large contribution to the Boy Scout clubhouse in Gilchrist Park. Kiwanis Club members led a drive to replace the original wooden bunkhouse with the present masonry building in 1952. Six years later Calder gave a large sum to double its size. Grateful Scouts and their Kiwanian sponsors named the new center after their benefactor, but the city now calls it the Bay Front Center.

During the Depression of the 1930's, there was not enough patronage for the lodge. Adair and his wife Helen took over management but they gave up after a couple of years. However, Calder and a few friends continued to winter at the lodge until 1960. Thereafter, vandals trashed the empty building. Calder sold the property in 1971 to Al Johns, developer of Punta Gorda Isles, for a twin canal-laced neighborhood called Burnt Store Isles.

However, Calder wanted proceeds from the sale to go to the University of Miami. He assigned the deed to U.M. which in turn transferred it to Johns for cash. The sagging lodge was burned down to make way for the seventh hole of Burnt Store Isles golf course.

MAYORS OF PUNTA GORDA TOWN

William H. Simmons (temporary) 12/3/1887
Dr. W.H. Burland -- 1887
James L. Sandlin
Sumner Hinckley
William B. Hardee
John Dreggors
George W. McLane -- 1895-7
John Sullivan
A.K. Demere
Charles G. Davis
John C. Pepper
R.L. Earnest
A.C. Freeman
John H. Concanon -- 1903-4
M.V. Williams -- 1905-6
C.L. Porter -- 1907-8

R. Chester Blount -- 1909
R.J. Spence -- 1910
Charles A. Davis -- 1911
S.H. Morton -- 1912
B.Hugh Mobley -- 1913
George S. Stone -- 1914
Edwin W. Smith -- 1915-6
S.F.J. Trabue --1917-8
James N. Sikes -- 1919-20
Max Charles Price -

Town re-incorporated as a city when Charlotte County erected from DeSoto County in 1921. First city mayor was J.N. Sikes.

Aerial view of Florida Power and Light plant shows new diesel engine building and fuel tank at right shortly after construction in 1929. Note that King St. (Tamiami Trail) had not yet been extended there though a sidewalk was in place. Church upper right is St. Mark Baptist.

Chapter 92

ICE MAKER SHAKES WHOLE TOWN

When Mr. and Mrs. George and Grace Day — 93 and 86 respectively — sit on their front porch and watch traffic whiz by on Cooper Street, they marvel that the village of Punta Gorda grew into a city while they watched.

"Punta Gorda was a nice little place but had nothing going for it after the big, old hotel closed and the fish got scarce," say the vigorous couple who recently celebrated their 69th wedding anniversary.

"Then in 1958, Al Johns and Bud Cole built Punta Gorda Isles out on the sand flats where the water came in at high tide and millions of fiddler crabs swarmed at low tide."

"Everybody thought the developers were crazy to think they could build houses out there. However, it was a great undertaking. They dug canals to get fill to raise the ground level four feet. Folks went around exclaiming, 'Why didn't I think of that?'"

George was born at Cottoncon, Ala., near Fort Benning, Ga. "I worked on the family farm at first," he says, "but when the cotton played out I drove lumber trucks at night. It was hard, lonely work so I was glad to head for Fort Lauderdale, Fla., in 1925 when a friend wrote that work there was plentiful.

"I arrived by train on a Sunday afternoon. My buddy put me up at his boarding house. He said the Phoenix Utility Company was building lines for the Florida Power and Light Company of Miami and needed able-bodied men. Bright and early Monday morning I went out to the construction camp. They handed me a shovel and put me to work.

"Back then there wasn't much north of Miami, but the Great Florida Land Boom was at its peak. People were moving down from up north expecting to live in luxury while making a fortune. Fort Lauderdale then was smaller than Punta Gorda today.

"Phoenix completed its contract by Christmas. All the construction workers were laid off. The foreman said, though, that FPL wanted eight men to patrol the lines we had just built. Two others in addition to myself accepted the offer. I should have known by the few number who volunteered that there was a catch in it.

"I was assigned 15 miles of line from Fort Lauderdale to Deerfield. That area today is solid homes and businesses along two major highways. It was a miserable stretch of palmettos, rattlesnakes and alligator holes. Every time I waded waist deep through a pond I wondered if a hungry gator might like to taste me.

"I got a room at Deerfield where I could catch a morning bus to Fort Lauderdale the walk the line back home. My job was to examine insulators through binoculars and report any that were cracked.

Cracked Insulators

"After two months of this I was sick of it and wrote the FPL superintendent at Miami to consider me for other work. He wrote back that I could split the patrol if I could find a buddy to take the half I didn't want. I replied that no one would take even half the route because the territory was plain hell. A couple of days later I received a telegram from him which said: 'COME TO MIAMI FOR OTHER WORK.' I was put with three other experienced transmission workers as their 'grunt' or ground man.

"Our main responsibility was to remove Spanish moss, limbs and kite strings from the lines. When those things got wet and caught on an insulator they would short out the lines. We often worked 48 hours straight through without going to bed.

"Nevertheless, I have always been grateful for that job in Miami because that is where I met and married Grace in November of 1925."

Mrs. Day's experience in Florida were not as arduous or dangerous, but equally satisfying. "I was born on a farm in Georgia but came to

Miami with my sister who had been hired as a teacher. I got a job working in the principal's office. Very soon I fell in love with George and married him. We had two children there — George James and Billie Jean."

When the Great Depression hit, and workers were laid off, the young family went to Cottoncon where they raised chickens. "Things picked up a little in 1932, and I was hired back by FPL to operate sub-stations," says George. "I worked at several stations — Hialeah, West Palm Beach, and the trolley railway station at Miami to convert AC power to DC for the city's street cars.

"Our son, Richard, was born at West Palm Beach. I was transferred to Punta Gorda in 1937 as a division load dispatcher for FPL."

Mrs. Day relates, "We rented a little house out in Forest Park east of Cooper Street where we could have a garden. The Steele brothers, Charlie and Harry, built several houses there. We bought our present home from Harry who had built it of cypress for himself.

"The Steele brothers were go-getters. They had a downtown 'beer garden' with a pool table during Prohibition — selling soft drinks and non-alcoholic 'near beer.' Later they started making cigars on the second floor of a tin building on the corner of Marion and King streets.

Curdled Soap Suds

"We loved our house except for the well which furnished our water. The water had so much sulphur, soap suds curdled in it. We got our drinking water from the ice plant, carrying it home in a 5-gallon can.

"When we came to Punta Gorda, FPL was still making ice at its King Street location — now on the National Register of Historic Places. I could tell when they were making ice. That took a lot of electricity. George would start the second of two, huge diesel engines to run the generators. The engines were said to be the largest in the world. I could feel the ground shake way out at our place when both engines were running.

"Every house had an ice-box. An ice man in a horse drawn wagon came around every day to deliver. You indicated how much you wanted by posting a card in your front window. You put the payment on the ice-box where it was handy for the delivery man.

"No one locked their doors in those days. The ice man just walked into your back door, took his money — leaving change if necessary — and put ice in the box. Melted ice drained into a pan underneath the box and had to be emptied every day without fail lest the pan run over.

"Marshal Robinson was the ice-man. When refrigerators came in he switched to selling real estate and did very well at it.

"Down Cooper Street a block or so was a large field where the county fair was held for many years. In between fairs, Charlie Steele's daughter grazed her horse there. The annual fair was a big event. Prize citrus, vegetables, cattle, hogs, and horses were displayed. Ladies showed quilts, preserves and cakes. A midway of amusement rides was a popular diversion, but not as much as today. Country produce was the main attraction. One year our daughter Billie Jean — then a young teacher at what was known as the 'little school' on Taylor Street — was chosen Tarpon Queen for the fair.

"Saturday night was the big shopping and social event. Downtown stores were crowded. Vic Desquin's mother and dad had a movie theater where kids could get in for 9 cents — plus a one-cent tax in effect at that time. Adults were admitted for 25 cents plus one cent.

Haircuts 35¢

"Haircuts for men were 35 cents, and for boys 25 cents. Bread was 10 cents a loaf. Fred Quednau, our sheriff, also had a restaurant where you could get a full plate of food for 35 cents.

"I was a 'home-room mother' for the high school — which mostly meant I went along on picnics and trips to chaperon and furnish refreshments. The favorite picnic spots were Warm Mineral Springs and Prairie Creek.

"The old hotel was run-down and catered mostly to old folks down here for the winter. It had a huge swimming pool where our kids got swimming lessons for 25 cents. The junior-senior banquets were held there. The hotel burned in a spectacular fire in 1959. Folks said it probably was arson."

George fondly remembers hunting in A.C. Frizzell's woods across the bay — now Port Charlotte. "There were plenty of turkeys there," he recalls. "A.C. also operated a saw mill there. Rough lumber was only $1 per hundred board feet, planed boards were $2 per hundred board feet. I bought some lumber from him to build a garage and a louvered, ventilation window for our attic. The 1947 hurricane blew rain through the louvers, flooding our attic. Water which, of course, dripped through our ceiling. All the wall paper came loose. What a mess!"

Today, the Day home is attractive and comfortable — a proper background for photographs of the Day's eight grand children and 20 great-grandchildren.

Punta Gorda Air Field personnel lived in "hutments." Lt. Glenn Herd, right, was a fighter pilot instructor, later a Brigadier General.

Chapter 93

COUNTY AIRPORT BEGAN AS ARMY BASE

There was great excitement at Punta Gorda in Sept. 1942 when Florida Senator Claude Pepper announced that the Civil Aeronautics Authority had decided to build an Army Air Force training center there.

The United States was fully engaged in the European and Asiatic theaters of World War II, and large numbers of fighter pilots were urgently needed. In those days, there was not yet a separate, strategic air force. Each branch of the military had its own air arm.

County Attorney Earl D. Farr told the *Punta Gorda Herald* that the CAA had earmarked $700,000 for the facility. It was to be built on 1,720 acres east of the "county stockade" (prison) at the corner of Carmelita and Florida streets. Construction got underway on county-owned land in July 1943. A 3-mile asphalt road was built to the site, and another three and a half miles were laid within the base — all at Army expense. Punta Gorda extended its water main. Florida Power brought in electricity, and the phone company installed six circuits. The army installed its own sewage treatment plant and fire fighting equipment.

Army personnel began to arrive in Dec. 1943 with their wives and children. However there was a shortage of rooms for them in the little town. Maj. Forrest H. Munger, commanding officer of the new base, appealed to local residents for rooms to rent. The *Herald* relayed the appeal in a rare, front-page editorial: "Greetings to the Army! Punta Gorda became an army town this week as troops moved in to prepare for activation of the new airbase here.

"It was a spectacular change from the quiet community of a week ago when 10 lonely soldiers arrived to do some of the ordinary jobs. Streets that had not been crowded, except on Saturday nights, are filled with soldiers and their families.

"Speaking of families, the statement that the United States Army is 'the marrying-est army in the history of the world' is evident here. A very large percentage of the men are married. Many of their wives and children are here with them. Rooms and apartments here have already been snapped up. Real estate and rental agencies are urged that more accommodations be made available. There also was quickly shown a serious shortage of eating places. Steps already are underway to open more restaurants. We have the greatest opportunity in our history to serve a group of soldiers — and at the same time leave a favorable impression with them that will carry into the post-war period and bring them back as 'visitors.'"

Everyone "Swell"

A month later, Lt. W.J. DeLaney, construction engineer of the Punta Gorda air field, completed the initial building phase. "I have never been on a job where the people worked as well with me," DeLaney declared. "Everyone has been swell."

Mentioned particularly for their "100 percent co-operation" were Farr and the board of county commissioners; city officials; "Doc" R.S. Maxwell, a druggist and member of the committee helping the base; Manager E.H. Smith of the electric company; Superintendent C.E. Hurd of the waterworks department; Mayor W.H. Monson; and Sheriff Fred Quednau.

Formal dedication of the Punta Gorda Army Air Field — a "sub-base" of the Venice Army Air Field " took place March 19, 1944. Florida's U.S. Senator Claude Pepper delivered the leading address before a crowd of 1,000 civilians and soldiers. Sen. and Mrs. Pepper arrived at the field by special airplane and was met in the air by a fighter-plane escort led by Lt.Col. Fred Hook.

Senator Pepper praised the leadership of President Roosevelt as commander-in-chief of the armed forces and credited him with doing a "masterful job." He said, "United Nations leadership excels that of the enemy — from the top leaders to the officers directing activities of the services in the training camps and on the war fronts."

Note the term "United Nations" which Roosevelt had used in the Atlantic Charter of Jan. 1942 to describe the allies. The United Nations Organization we know today was not chartered until 1945.

Maj. Munger was master of ceremonies. Mayor W.H. Monson and County Chairman W.R. Sparks extended a welcome to the field personnel. Farr introduced the speaker. Col. V.B. Dixon of Venice, commander of the Sarasota, Venice and Punta Gorda fields, thanked people of the area for their cooperation.

Training at the air field settled into a hurry-up routine. Replacements for front-line fatalities were urgently needed. Principal reason for choosing Florida for training fields was the predominantly good weather for flying. An unusual, but highly efficient, runway consisted of three 5,000-foot strips of asphalt in triangular configuration. Only one other such pattern was built. The strips were 150 feet wide with 8-foot packed-marl shoulders. Heavy oil for mixing asphalt 1 1/2 inches thick was purchased from Mexico. U.S. oil was reserved for gasoline essential to the war effort.

The original runways are still in use, though two were re-surfaced in recent years. A spur was added to one of these in 1986 — lengthening it to 6,500 feet for large jet planes. Eighty-one P40 airplanes and 22 various other craft served an average of 200 pilots in two squadrons — the 502nd Fighter-bomber, and the 490th Fighter. Forty-four assigned officers and 1,097 enlisted men kept the squadrons flying. Later the P40s were replaced with new P51s. There were 61 service buildings — hangars, repair shops, mess halls, etc. Personnel lived in 268 "hutments" consisting of wooden lower halves and canvas tops. A 20-foot control tower on open-work steel beams sorted out the 500 flights monthly.

Brig.Gen.(Ret.) Glenn Herd, of Deep Creek, was an aviation cadet at the field in 1944 and was retained as an instructor. He says sand-filled practice bombs were dropped on a target at the Cecil Webb Wildlife

First fighter planes at Punta Gorda in World War II were P-40's, above.

Management Area south of the field. Air-to-air gunnery was conducted over the Gulf. The war ended before Herd got overseas, but he stayed in the Army. He flew 100 combat missions during the Korean War and flew cargo missions in the Vietnam War.

Major Munger turned over command to Maj. J.K. Coughlan and in doing so complained that local landlords were over-charging families of base personnel.

This prompted the city council to call a special meeting to investigate the matter. Former Mayor E.M. Parker presided in the absence of Mayor W.H. Monson. Maj. Coughlin and Lt. Alfred James, public relations officer, told council: "The rental situation, as a whole, is not bad. However, there are a few flagrant situations in which unreasonably high rents are charged army personnel."

Council appointed a Fair Rents Committee to handle complaints. Chairman was E.H. Smith, district manager of Florida Power, and immediate past president of the Chamber of Commerce. Other members were Earl Farr, S.M. Dismukes, W.F. Rigell, and Elmer Oswald. Such disputes were common nationwide until Congress established the Office of Price Administration and rolled back rents.

Friction Dispelled

Despite some friction over rents, relations between airmen and local residents were warm and friendly. Enlisted men of the 490th Fighter Squadron in December 1943 appealed for furniture, reading materials and recreation equipment for an off duty "day room" at the field. Local folks responded quickly. Plans for a non-commissioned officers club in town were already underway. Farr organized a United Service Organization (USO) center at Punta Gorda and The Punta Gorda Womans Club agreed operate it in their building on Sullivan St. The first USO Blue Circuit travelling show of "pretty girls, music and song" was presented to a full house in January 1944. Max Baer, then world-champion heavyweight boxer, came to talk about the importance of physical fitness. Rotary volunteers distributed refreshments and cigarettes. Farr, resigned as USO chairman in March — mission completed. He turned over a check for $660, a two-month allotment for the local center.

Mrs. May D. Durrance, active for more than a year in the informal enlisted men's day room, was elected chairwoman to succeed Farr. Others elected were Rev. W.M. Mulllen, vice-president, Mrs; Fred M. Johnson, treasurer; and Mrs. Cecelia Thames, secretary. Mrs. Sadie B. Farrington was chosen house chairwoman for the USO center and Mrs. Elliott Paul was appointed director. Mrs. Paul's salary was set at $100 per month and Mrs. Farrington was allotted $60 monthly for expenses. The Womans Club received $50 a month for use of the building. Rotary Club, Womans Club and various church members volunteered to provide servers.

The non-commissioned officers' club moved into its downtown location in July 1944. It was located on the north side of Marion Avenue adjacent to the New Theater between Cross and Sullivan streets.

Occasionally there would be surprise "air raids" on the Punta Gorda field to spray tear-gas in order to familiarize the men with gas masks and how to function in a gas attack.

On Sept. 7,1944, a sudden shift of wind carried fumes into Punta Gorda. The result was reported by the *Herald:*

"All Punta Gorda, and some surrounding territory, dissolved in tears about nine o'clock this morning — real, honest to goodness tears that welled from the eyes and trickled down the cheeks of all citizens.

"School was disrupted for some 30 minutes. A.S. Taylor and his high-line crew of the Florida Power Company had to suspend operations. In fact, everything in the city came to a standstill while the citizens had a good cry.

"Capt. R.H. Rehlm, base adjutant, said the field was having its monthly gas alert. Everyone there had gas masks. Here, there were none. This was the first time the tear gas — which results in temporary discomfort but no injury to the eyes — has gone wild. Officers say it won't happen again."

Tear gas thereafter was discharged from "jeeps" — small, rugged vehicles widely used during World War II.

New Command

Lt.Col. R.A. Hanes took over command of the airfield in Sept. 1944. At that time, the field's designation was changed from Replacement Training Unit (fighter) to Combat Crew Training Station (fighter). New P5ls replaced the old P40s. Instructors now were mostly decorated, combat veterans rotated to the states.

The year 1944 brought the first casualties at the field. A portion of the city pier had been taken over for a crash-boat operation, but was of no help in the three fatalities.

Flight Officer Edward B. Harrison, a trainee officer pilot, crashed after engine trouble developed on a demolition bombing mission March 9.

Capt. Dorrance C. Zabriskie crashed on a dive-bombing exercise and was instantly killed March 31. Ironically he was operations officer on the staff of the 490th Fighter Squadron and presided over the Crash Investigation Board.

Lt. Harris L. Kimble, an officer trainee, was killed in a crash during a routine training flight June 1. Search parties found the plane and body on sand flats six miles west of the field. He was 19.

Punta Gorda west on Marion Ave. from Taylor St. in 1944. Dependents of Army Air Force personnel filled Princess Hotel, left. Soda fountain of Seminole Pharmacy, right, was popular hangout for servicemen.

Chapter 94

POISON GAS BURIED AT AIR FIELD

When VE-Day (Victory in Europe) occurred May 7, 1945, activity at the Punta Gorda Army Air Field slowed but did not stop. The Pacific air war was fought largely by carrier-based Navy planes and long-range Army bombers. Army fighter pilots were not as urgently needed, but the United States was not ready to disarm.

VJ-Day (Victory over Japan) on Aug. 15, 1945, brought gunnery training at Punta Gorda to a sudden halt. A banner headline of the *Punta Gorda Herald* proclaimed on Aug. 30: "AIR FIELD ACTIVITIES HALTED HERE." The air field had been in service only 22 months but had graduated 800 fighter pilots crucial to victory in Europe.

Lt.Col. R.A. Hanes, base commander, declared the field "surplus" in November. Then began a hectic race to dismantle the base.

With the help of several German prisoners of war recently assigned to the field to do routine maintenance, the men at Punta Gorda Air Field began disposing of all movable equipment. Tools and furniture were smashed with sledge hammers to prevent the material from flooding civilian markets or attracting vandals to abandoned warehouses. Air planes were flown to McDill Air Field at Tampa.

409

It was not until 1980 that extent of the dismantling was fully known. Fred Farris, editor of the fledgling *Charlotte Sun* interviewed several local men who had worked at the field as civilians during its last days.

The late Earle Davis, a fireman at the base and a watchman during the dismantling period, declared he had seen German prisoners breaking up tools. He said: "I saw all sorts of supplies loaded aboard trucks, then taken away and buried. There are lots of very expensive tools and materials buried out there. I saw men loading canisters of tear gas and other chemical agents onto a truck. They told me they were labeled secret and known to exist by few people except chemical officers."

Editor Farris wrote that Davis's account was verified by another "informant" who asked to remain anonymous. The informant said he had seen "poison gases" buried at the airport, but he had "been afraid to speak up for personal reasons."

***

Your present writer can attest to the haste with which war material was junked after the war. I was attached to U.S.S. Eagle 27 (sonar trainer) which was being decommissioned at Charleston Navy Yard the day Japan surrendered. German prisoners, with PW stenciled on their shirts, moved unguarded throughout the yard on work details.

Two days later, the decommissioning officer came aboard and said he wouldn't be displeased if everything aboard ship not welded down was removed before he arrived the next morning to take inventory. As men went ashore on liberty that evening, they staggered under the loads of tools, pistols and portable apparatus tucked into sea bags.

Within the month I was discharged and accepted a job as reporter for the *Detroit Free Press*. My first assignment was to investigate tips of wholesale junking of valuable war material. I found that the practice was widespread — so much so that my editor considered the story worth only four paragraphs on an inside page. The manager of the Grand Blanc (Mich.) Tank Plant begged me to publicize the fact that he had five thousand 12-volt batteries available at $1 each — the value of lead in them. Cars in those days used 6-volt batteries.

***

Military personnel at the Punta Gorda Air Field were required to don gas masks and walk through a shed infused with tear gas to learn how to function in an attack. They also were taught to identify by smell tiny whiffs of other gases that might be used against them.

Thus, the stories of war prisoners, wholesale scrapping of material, and poison gas would not be unusual at the Punta Gorda Air Field. The amount of residual gas that might leak from a buried canister, if it hasn't already, would be undetectable today.

Cindy Anderson, administrative assistant at the airport, says the Army Corps of Engineers came to the field in 1985 and made a thorough search for buried junk by magnetic detectors. Several pits were dug, but no gas canisters were found.

The County Commission in 1943 assembled land for the air field — and later enlarged it to a total of 2,560 acres — by purchasing private property through the power of eminent domain. After the war, the county had a first class airport on its hands. Similar fields in Lee County and elsewhere were bulldozed to bare earth. Charlotte commissioners decided the facility had possibilities of attracting industries and so held onto it.

The airport was turned over to the county on April 21, 1947, along with its sewage plant, a complete water distribution system, fire fighting equipment and all buildings.

Then began a raid on the facility. The sewage treatment plant was dug up and leased to the city of Punta Gorda for 99 years for $1. The dollar was never paid. Some buildings were sold and moved off the site.

For the next few years the field was leased by the county to a variety of private operators — none of whom succeeded. When aviation interest waned, it was leased for a giant trailer park in 1950, then for a farm in 1951. A huge water tank was sold for $377 that same year.

A Chevrolet fire truck — left by the Army to protect materials stored by the War Assets Administration — was given to Punta Gorda by the county on condition the vehicle would be used to fight fires south of the harbor also. The Civil Aeronautics Administration — holder of a 99-year lease on the field — forced the county to buy a replacement.

P-51 was advanced fighter plane. Control tower in background.

There was further hanky-panky in 1952. A county resident convinced commissioners they should pay his way to Washington, D.C., so he could try and get the base reactivated for the Korean war. The Commission paid his expenses, not knowing he had other business there to attend to for a client. Upon returning he said more land was needed at the airport. Whereupon he sold the county 80 acres owned by the client. The field was not reactivated.

Single-prop bi-plane was a stable trainer.

County Commissioner Vasco Peeples in 1956 pushed through a proposal to build a new hangar at the field to try and get the county back into the aviation business. Other commissioners wanted to break up the parking apron and taxiways for road ballast. Peeples prevailed and a new hangar built. The old one was sold for $1 to get it moved off the field.

All the fire hydrants at the airport were uprooted in April 1958 and given to Punta Gorda. At the same time, commissioners appointed a Development Committee to try and attract industry at the field.

Encouraging progress was made. The field was again leased to a private flying service. Other tenants were manufacturers of folding doors, sheet metal products, building trusses, battery terminals, and aluminum extrusions. A local partnership in 1960 leased a large part of the air field with intention to build a development of pre-fabricated aluminum houses.

Prospects for the airport appeared bright. The county asked the CAA to surrender its claims to the airport. The CAA refused. Without firm claim to their factories, the tenants moved away, and the housing project was abandoned. The Development Committee was abolished.

Commissioners again petitioned the CAA to cancel its reversion clause that would allow the government to reclaim the airport in the event of a national emergency. They asserted the reversion clause inhibited industrialization of the field.

The CAA firmly informed the county that airports were for flying and that any revenue derived from any source at the airport had to be used for airport improvements. Florida Air Taxi and Southeastern Airlines took leases in 1962 but could not make their services profitable. When Southeastern folded, one of its pilots, Andy Crane, was hired as airport manager. He began developing the airport for private aviation. Crane went on to become pilot for F. Lee Bailey, the nationally known lawyer. Bob Hill, a former race driver and pilot, was hired to replace Crane. Hill, also, pushed private aviation and taught scores of local people to fly.

Civil Air Patrol Organized

From this cadre of enthusiasts, a Civil Air Patrol squadron was organized by the late Col. W.W. "Mouse" Moore. He had served as base safety officer at the Army Air Field during WW II. With the help of federal aid, the airport was upgraded for night operation by installation of lights along its main runway. Prior to lighting the runway, night landings were made by lining up a plane with a lighted telephone booth.

Fred Watts, present manager for the Authority, says the Florida Legislator in 1963 adopted a measure creating Development Authorities of 11 members with limited taxing power.

Charlotte County commissioners immediately established a Development Authority and finally persuaded the CAA to revoke the reversion clause. The airport was deeded to the Development Authority by county commissioners in October 1969. The Authority board was reduced to five members — one for each commission district, in 1973. The Authority is the only one remaining of three originally established. The Charlotte County Airport in the early 1980s was considered for expansion into a southwest regional airport. Ray Peach, a CAA engineer who had supervised building the Punta Gorda Army Air Field in 1943, had become a top man with the CAA. He advised that the Charlotte County Airport was ideally situated for the huge, new facility.

However, the two members from Charlotte County who served on the search committee voted for Fort Myers. They didn't want jet engine noise at Punta Gorda. Today the airport is self-supporting though it no longer has any taxing power. It has several large and financially strong industries. Ken Williams is administrator of both the field and industrial park. The airport in a typical year logs approximately 70,000 operations — takeoffs and landings — by private and commercial planes. The annual air show for charity held there is considered one of 10 largest in the nation. The field's elevation, 25 feet above sea level, is among the highest in Charlotte County. It is a "regional recovery center" for refuge in hurricanes.

Wars have come and gone, but the airport is still serving.

413

German flyer Maj. Von Hagen, center, barn-stormed the United States after the First World War and posed with Col. Danforth, right.

Chapter 95

AIR FORCE GENERAL MADE HARBOUR HEIGHTS

It is no coincidence that Charlotte County's congregate dining building, pool and picnic park at Harbour Heights are located opposite the best fishing hole in the Peace River. Early pioneers called the spot Shell Point and took large tarpon there before phosphate mines in the river bed destroyed all marine life for many years.

Shell Point was homesteaded by Neil Larsen, an Iowa farmer who migrated here to grow oranges. The tax roll of 1882 shows that he owned 73 acres, three of which had been "improved" with a dwelling appraised for $250. He acquired 230 additional acres nearby about five years later.

The 1900 census gives Larsen's age as 51 -- head of a household that included his wife Eliza, 44, and a son Neil, 8. A dirt trail linked Larsen's Shell Point home with Nathan DeCoster's Harbor View subdivision and the little cattle town of Hickory Bluff — now called Charlotte Harbor town. When DeSoto County was erected in 1887, he was elected commissioner.

Most of the land north of the bay was owned by the Florida Internal Improvement Fund. Purpose of the fund was to reward construction of railroads and induce settlers to take up land.

The Florida Southern Railway completed its line from Bartow to the newly platted town of Trabue — now Punta Gorda — in 1886. As part of its prize, the line took sections 15 and 21 — minus Larsen's holdings — at what is now Harbour Heights.

The railroad sold its land there the following year to John Brewer, a financier of Bingham, Mass. Brewer and his descendants leased the land to the Consolidated Naval Stores Company for the bleeding of pine trees for turpentine — valuable in those days of wooden sailing ships. When the pines had been bled to death in 1912, the property was leased to the Russ Lumber Company of Arcadia for the taking of timber. The land was sold in 1920 to the Bay Shore Company of Punta Gorda.

The Florida Land Boom was just getting underway. Bay Shore expected its land would become priceless when roads were extended to Shell Point. Neil Larsen sold his homestead to Bay Shore in 1925 at the height of the boom and moved to Charlotte Harbor Town.

The speculation bubble burst in 1929. Land was worthless. Unable to pay taxes which had skyrocketed when land values soared, owners let hundreds of thousands of acres revert to the state. Shell Point was one of the properties abandoned. Shell Point lay idle during the ensuing Great Depression until 1934. At that time, it was picked up for $107.24 in back taxes and another $300 in interest and court expenses.

The purchaser was a retired U.S. Army Air Corps general named Charles H. Danforth. He had a remarkable military career in the fledgling Air Force when it was struggling to prove its military potential. Eventually it became the separate U.S. Air Force.

Private to General

Danforth enlisted as a private in 1898 with the U.S. Volunteer Infantry at age 22. He rose through the ranks to second lieutenant in three years. He served in Cuba, Philippines and Mexico between 1898 and 1914.

During World War I, he was assigned to train National Guard troops at St. Paul, Minn., and Baton Rouge, La. In 1920, as a lieutenant colonel, he was detailed to the Army Air Service and sent to Carlstrom Field at Arcadia to learn how to fly.

He soloed in six months and then was transferred to Kelly Field, Texas, for bombardment experience. Upon completion of this training, Danforth was appointed commanding officer at Langley Field, Va. There he became a staunch supporter of Gen. Billy Mitchell's crusade for air power.

It was during Danforth's tour at Arcadia that he noticed Shell Point from the air. Years later he said he was entranced with the climate and with the wilderness so close to civilization and vowed to return some day.

Danforth bought Shell Point two years before retiring in 1936 and leased grazing rights to R.W. Garner, an Arcadia cattleman. He then built a "mansion" patterned after the officers' club at Panama. He named the place Shell Point Ranch. The general liked good food and drink — and an attentive audience. Historian Byron Rhode relates in his book, *Punta Gorda Remembered*, that Danforth was a special customer of Rhode's Home Supply Grocery in the Post Office Arcade.

"Mr. Danforth would send in an order by some of his help," writes Rhode. "No matter what he needed, he would send the order to me. We had this understanding — if he wanted anything other than groceries or meat, I would go out and buy it, charge it to him, and deliver it. Being in the Army all those years, he was used to getting what he wanted.

"Once in a while, he might request a salesman to come and see him. The man was told to come to my store and I would take him over there. I would always be invited to come in and have a drink. Over the years he told me many tales of old Army days."

U.S. Cleveland, was a mail clerk at the Post Office in the old Arcade, and recalls another example of Gen. Danforth's demanding ways.

"Mr. Danforth had a large mail box that was near the floor where all the large boxes were located. He was a portly gentleman who had trouble reaching below his belt buckle.

"One day he came to the service window and brusquely ordered Hugh MacGibbon, later the postmaster, 'Hand me my mail, boy!'

"Mac had just returned from World War II in which he had been ordered around enough. 'Get it yourself, boy!' said Mac. The general sputtered, 'Damn it, I can't bend over.' Mac promptly brought his mail. After reaching that understanding, plus learning that both were Air Corps veterans, they became good friends."

Ranch Sold

Danforth contracted Parkinson disease and moved to Arcadia where he could be near medical care. He sold his beloved Shell Point Ranch in 1953 to the Federal Realty and Development Co. of Lee County.

The general died Sept. 25, 1958. An obituary in the *Punta Gorda Herald* recorded the highlights of his military career and his association with the Presbyterian Church and various Masonic orders.

"He has no near relatives, and his funeral arrangements were made by Mrs. Mert McLeon who has been his housekeeper, nurse and companion for the past several years. Burial will be at the National Cemetery."

Shell Point Ranch was resold in 1955 to the Charlotte County Land and Title Company of Miami, Fla. The firm dug canals, installed an Olympic-size swimming pool, converted Danforth's home into a club house and developed Shell Point Ranch into "Fashionable Harbour Heights."

It folded when the local manager embezzled clients' purchase money and went to prison for his misdeeds. The club house and swimming pool fell into disrepair and was purchased by the county for a public facility in 1966 after a campaign by Rebecca Neal Owen, a member of the Council on Aging. The facility now is named after her.

John Bass' personal laboratory and office at New Point Comfort.

Chapter 96

THE FIRST MARINE LABORATORY

John Foster Bass, Jr., lived and worked at New Point Comfort in west Charlotte County for only seven years, 1933 to 1939, but in that short time left a legacy of scientific achievement in marine biology.

Bass was a colorful personality who inherited wealth enabling him to establish the Bass Biological Laboratory on the shore of Gottfried Creek. In the brief period of its existence, the facility was recognized world wide as the center of marine research.

Dr. Ernest D. Estevez, ecologist for Mote Marine Laboratories says the privately owned Bass Laboratory pre-dates all university marine stations in Florida. "The Carnegie Institute operated an earlier one on a seasonal basis at Fort Jefferson on the Dry Tortugas, but the Bass Laboratory is the first full-time marine station in Florida — if not the nation."

Bass was the only son of the Chicago Tribune's war correspondent at Athens, Greece, where his father was headquartered during the Crimean War of 1897. His mother was named Abba. In later years, Bass senior was appointed to the U.S. diplomatic service and attended the Versailles peace conference ending the First World War. Bass, Jr., completing his military service, accompanied his father as aide-de-camp.

Because of his father's interesting occupations, young Bass traveled widely and acquired an international outlook.

At the outbreak of the European War — as the First World War was originally called — Bass, Jr., joined the French Foreign Legion in order to fight for democracy. When the United States entered the conflict in 1917, Bass was allowed to transfer to the American volunteer Lafayette Escadrille Aero Squadron.

The Bass family acquired its wealth initially through the sale of the family farm in the heart of what is now the city of Chicago. Prudent investments in downtown commercial buildings increased the fortune. Bass senior died in 1931 after having set up a trust for "scientific pursuits" with his son as administrator. Bass junior took over management of the real estate business, but his primary interest was marine biology.

While recuperating from a glider accident, Bass heard about the fabulous fish population of Lemon Bay. He came on crutches to investigate. Finding the reports true, Bass bought part of the original Gottfried estate. There he built a complex of laboratories and "cookie" cabins to house distinguished scientists from around the world. Several structures survive despite the demolition of many in 1990 to clear the site of Merchants Crossing shopping center.

No Gender Gap

Bass provided three-month "fellowships" from the family trust for visiting scholars that included travel expenses, board, and living quarters. A faded visitor's register of 58 signatures is a veritable Who's Who of the leading marine biologists of that day. There was no gender gap at Bass labs. It was the first such facility to go co-educational.

Mrs. Dorothy Dekle of Englewood, now 90 and former secretary for Bass, recalls her duties: "At Mr. Bass' direction, I wrote letters offering fellowships to every university in the United States and most of those in Europe. Of course, we got more responses that we could handle. Therefore, Mr. Bass chose only those with best credentials.

The guest cabins and principal laboratories were constructed of disks cut from pine logs about ten inches in diameter and stacked on edge in cement mortar. They looked like cookies. Though the laboratory was not affiliated with any university, students accompanying visiting professors were allowed credits toward their degrees.

To assist in the study and collection of sea organisms, Bass purchased a 2-masted schooner named *Virginia*. The ship was in sad shape but was overhauled at great expense. Captain of the beautiful vessel was Bill Davis, Sr.. The *Virginia* was said to have been a dispatch boat for Union naval forces during the Civil War battle of Mobile Bay — an historic event remembered for Admiral David Farragut's declaration: "Damn the torpedoes! Full speed ahead."

By all reports, Bass loved to socialize with the noted scientists who took advantage of his generosity. After a strenuous day aboard the *Virginia*, or dissecting specimens, everyone would join in a communal meal to discus findings and experiences. The evening meal was more a party that mere dinner.

Dr. Estevez, who now has custody of Bass' records, states: "At least 50, and perhaps 75, scientists came to New Point Comfort to collect specimens, measure the environment, and write reports in the fields of anatomy, embryology, endocrinology, natural history, systematics, taxonomy and other subjects." Bass acquired his interest in research while in college. He became an assistant to McGuchi, a renowned herpetologist and venom biochemist. The two went to Central and South America to collect poisonous snakes. Thus, Bass turned to natural history, specializing in the study of sharks, parasites, sea worms and conservation. He is credited with

Bass aboard his schooner.

identifying the Chadwick (Englewood) Beach Mouse.

"The New Point Comfort facility was a stopover and staging area for many of Florida's own scientific leaders, such as John Davis, Jr., and Archie Carr," says Dr. Estevez. "Bass also employed Donald Zinn and Steward Springer as successive directors who went on to distinguished careers in biology after World War II."

Tragedy struck Bass labs on Dec. 10, 1939. Bass and his wife Else (nee Jensen) went to Mexico City in July of that year for an extended vacation. They wished to see if the hot, dry climate there would ease his recently developed "lung congestion." Stewart Springer was left in charge of the labs.

Mrs. Bass returned home in early December in expectation Bass would soon follow. On the fateful day, Bass went for an airplane ride. The change of air pressure fatally reduced his oxygen intake, and he died of asphyxiation at the age of 42. Springer flew to Mexico City and had Bass' body cremated in order to return the remains.

Impressive funeral services for Bass were held on the lawn of his New Point Comfort home. Dr. A.W. Johnstone officiated. At sundown, the ashes were interred in the Englewood Cemetery while Homer Hebb sounded taps. He was survived by his widow, son John F. Bass, III, and by his mother Mrs. Abba Bass.

Over his grave, the family erected an arch supporting a ship's bell engraved: *"Provincia de Pampanga, Anno de 1859,"* It is believed to have been the bell of the schooner *Virginia*. The ship was sold. When last seen in 1972 at a Miami boat yard, the historic vessel had fallen once more into disrepair.

The laboratory ceased to function without its guiding hand. Family descendants occupy the remaining buildings.

Ten years after Bass' untimely death, another wealthy patron of marine biology, Eugenia Clark, established a similar research facility at Placida. It was called the Cape Haze Marine Laboratory.

Mote Connection

In an autobiography titled *The Lady And The Sharks*, she noted a significant connection with the Bass Laboratory: "One day, the Basses came over and found me looking over my books trying to identify an odd jellyfish that Beryl had found floating in the bay. Johnny Bass asked, 'I think we've still got some books in my father's lab. Do you want to look them over?' We drove over to the old buildings of the Bass Biological Station and opened doors and drawers that hadn't been touched in years.

"Under cobwebs and dust we found dozens of valuable books, series of scientific journals, and publications on fishes, jellyfishes, worms, etc., sent to Johnny's father by scientist friends form all over the world.

"Beryl and I had to come back another day to haul away all the items we could use at the lab which the Basses offered us. There was laboratory glassware, many unopened bottles of chemicals, and various instruments of the kind useful at a marine laboratory.

"Johnny's mother also was pleased that the lab could use this material. She asked if I wanted to glance through the records her husband had kept. I began to get a good picture of how the Bass Biological Station had operated, and how useful it had been to scientists, teachers and students."

The Cape Haze Marine Laboratory subsequently was moved to Sarasota and renamed Mote Marine Laboratory. Thus, the work of John Bass, Jr., continues to benefit science.

Crescent-B cowboys round up bison.

Chapter 97

THE AXLETREE OF CRESCENT-B

Fred C. Babcock, axletree of the vast Crescent-B Ranch in east Charlotte County, is a modest man who shuns the limelight. Thus, it is understandable why it took the state of Florida 54 years to discover his major role in helping assemble the 63,000-acre Cecil M. Webb Wildlife Management Area near the ranch.

Nevertheless, overdue recognition came in May 1995 by Gov. Lawton Chiles at a governor's mansion reception in Tallahassee. It was attended by a hundred friends and family of Babcock and by dignitaries of the Florida Game and Fresh Water Fish Commission.

The commission now has re-named the Charlotte County facility as the Fred C. Babcock & Cecil M. Webb Wildlife Management Area.

Gov. Chiles commended the Babcock family for "wise management of its property — conserving, renewing and improving natural resources while harvesting its bounty commercially." The ranch is nationally known for its multi-use production of beef cattle, calves, beefalo, lumber, limestone, vegetables, seed corn, native plants, and sod.

In responding to Chiles' praise, Babcock said, "Taking care of the land is just common sense because of the benefits it returns." He pointed out

421

that Florida from the beginning has been "the doorway of America, and is destined to be more so in the future. The state has the longest coast line of any American state," he declared. "It is farther from Pensacola to Key West than from Jacksonville to Philadelphia." Gov. Chiles interjected, "And that's a long way to walk!" Laughter by guests indicated they recalled Gov. Chiles' famous walk from city to city during his campaign for the U.S. Senate.

Babcock said "Florida is blessed with an abundance of natural resources which we must enlarge and improve for future generations." His philosophy is simple: "Put more into the land than you take out. Always allow seeds for additional growth. Take care of the soil, and it will take care of you. It is in the best interests of cattlemen and farmers to be careful stewards of the land so they can pass it on."

Cecil M. Webb was a prominent miller of Tampa who maintained a hunting lodge along Tucker's Grade in southern Charlotte County. As chairman of the Game Commission, Webb pushed

FRED C. BABCOCK

for a wildlife preserve where ordinary hunters could pursue the sport.

Fred Babcock, and his father Edward Vose Babcock, avid hunters, supported the proposal enthusiastically. They bought a large tract of land for back taxes and deeded it to the Game Commission. Later, they donated 23,000 acres of the ranch. The preserve was opened to the public in 1942. Today, the Babcock-Webb preserve is self supporting from the sale of permits, leases of pasture, and selective lumbering.

While managing Crescent-B as a conventional ranch, Babcock experiments with new products and techniques. A unique example is the "ecological-tours" of the 140-square-mile ranch. These enable the public to see firsthand what is going on in the natural surroundings of the pasture, forest and swamp lands. Tour guides are biologists who explain the sights on a working ranch amidst pastures, forests and a huge cypress swamp. From the safety and comfort of open-air busses, visitors view snakes, bison, alligators, turkeys, deer and wild pigs — as well as cattle and horses. Cowboys seen are the real thing.

Babcock was the first rancher in Florida licensed for commercial harvesting of alligators. Since introduction of careful management, the number of wild gators has increased considerably. In the wild, only 10 percent of newly born gators survive. When alligator eggs are collected and incubated, more than 90 percent of hatchlings survive.

Possibly the most important environmental improvement is the control and conservation of surface water. A system of low dams save water for the dry season and prevent flooding during summer storms.

Babcock has devoted a lifetime to prudent management of land as chief executive officer of the Babcock Lumber Company of Pittsburgh, Babcock Florida Co. of Punta Gorda, Babcock Enterprises, Bayvue, Inc., Davis Supply Co., and Earthsource, Inc. In addition, he is a director of several non-related companies.

Among his many honors, are the Florida Environmental Stewardship Award (1993), the Florida and National Cattleman's associations' stewardship awards (1992), and the Florida Tree Farmer of 1987.

Began in 1914

Fred's father came to Punta Gorda in 1912 to hunt and fish. He was owner of the Babcock Lumber Company and mayor of Pittsburgh. Later he was elected a commissioner of Allegheny County.

E. V. Babcock was so impressed with the area here he bought several townships in 1914 from C. M. Carrier, a timber scout who had leased the land from a Punta Gorda entrepreneur named Perry McAdow. After leasing the lumber rights to the Roux Crate and Lumber Co., of Bartow, Fla., E.V. Babcock converted the stump land to pasture.

Fred Babcock came to the new Crescent-B Ranch in 1927 at age 14 to learn the family business — having already worked in the Babcock sawmills in Pennsylvania as a laborer. The family built a town house in Punta Gorda on Sullivan St. next door to the Womans Club. He became an airplane pilot in 1928 when aviation was in its infancy and was grad-uated from Dartmouth in 1936. He has travelled extensively, and explored wilderness areas on medical research projects.

He and Miss Marion Barnes, a graduate of Mt. Holyoke College, were married in 1936. They have four daughters and eight grand-children.

Fred Babcock is only the second chief executive of the Babcock Lumber Co. — now in its 108th year as this is written. The company is rated 35th in size in the United States. He is retired from active management but continues as chairman of the board.

Mr. and Mrs. Babcock are noted philanthropists whose many contributions to educational, cultural and medical projects — here and in other states — are by their wish little publicized. However, it is known locally that they were major donors to the Charlotte County Art Guild Visual Arts Center, Crossroads Wilderness Institute on Bermont Road for less-fortunate boys, Boca Grande Health Clinic, Medical Center Hospital of Punta Gorda, and Boy Scouts.

The Charlotte Hospital shortly after construction at Punta Gorda.

Chapter 98

CONTROVERSY SURROUNDS HOSPITAL

Until after World War II, the nearest hospitals for folks of Charlotte County were at Arcadia and Fort Myers. The Punta Gorda Rotary Club had discussed building a hospital, but plans were thwarted by a war-time shortage of materials.

One of the Rotarians enthused over the proposal was Dr. Walter B. Clement. He came to Punta Gorda in 1936, and established an extensive practice. When the war started he turned over his practice to another physician and joined the 101st Airborne Division as a flight surgeon.

Dr. Clement broke his back landing by parachute in Normandy, which limited his service thereafter. Nevertheless, he resumed his practice and was appointed by Rotary to spearhead a drive for a hospital.

The Charlotte Hospital Association was formed consisting of all who contributed money, work or materials to the project. The 2-year effort involved civic leaders on both sides of the harbor.

Finally, a little 22-bed hospital, plus five bassinets, was opened in Aug. of 1947 on land purchased 20 years earlier from Mrs. C.C. Carlton, widow of a prominent fruit packer. The price of $1,000 was considerably less than it was worth. The first patient was a little girl named Gussie, daughter of Vasco Peeples, a Rotary Club president. She had her tonsils removed.

Dr. Clement related background information to his Rotary Club years later. Reported the *Herald* in March, 1969: Dr. Clement said that only last December he had paid off the mortgage on his home, taken out years ago to help build a new wing on Medical Center Hospital. He said the hospital was conceived at a Rotary Club meeting before World War II and brought up again after the war. Rotarians were the first contributors.

Among the original founders of the hospital were Judge J.T. Rose, J.T. Manning, Johnny Jack, Lamar Rose, Ebby Rountree and Pharmacist R.S. Maxwell. In those days of shortages, permits to build had to be

424

obtained from the War Assets Administration. Dr. Clement took many trips to Tampa to get paper work done.

The foundation had been laid, walls up, and lintel poured before the permit finally came. Clement's brother in Arcadia got electric supplies at cost. Construction efforts were by D.B. Malone and C.P. Wilhelm. Men made building blocks on the site.

Ebby Rountree and the Coca Cola bottling company made $1,000 donations. Several contributions of $500 and $1,000 were made by winter visitors. Bingo parties were held in the trailer park.

Dr. Clement's cousin, Joe, came here from Tampa with a work crew to put up tile ceiling at cost. A firm at Sarasota provided doors at wholesale prices. X-ray and laboratory equipment came from his own office. Operating room equipment came from an uncle who had died.

Shortly thereafter, says Dr. Clement, he got tired and resigned from the board. But when the hospital was $14,000 in debt he came back, told the board he would take charge and straighten matters out. It was two hard years, he said, but he paid off the debts.

Dr. Clement told of hiring R.O. Bruce as hospital administrator and Leo Wotitzky as secretary to the board. "Hospital care just went down and down," said Dr. Clement. "I complained but to no avail.

"Finally they got tired of me and hired a lawyer in Fort Myers. They told me one night they had a trial in the courthouse, and I was no longer to be around in the hospital.

Voted Out

Oldtimers today say Dr. Clement had a possessive attitude about the hospital and goaded both the board of directors and staff doctors to the point they voted him out unanimously.

The hospital was a success and grew steadily. However, it suffered from chronic financial difficulties in those days before widespread Medicare, Medicaid and health insurance. By 1969 there were 14 physicians accredited to the medical staff.

A dispute arose in March of that year over billing for work performed at the hospital by Dr. Carl Reilly, radiologist of Port Charlotte. This triggered a movement by the medical staff to take over control of the hospital by exclusive right to select staff doctors.

Reported the *Punta Gorda Herald* : "A cold war is being waged at the Punta Gorda Medical Center. Members of the medical staff voted at their regular monthly meeting to appoint a committee to investigate possibilities of incorporating the staff. Such a move, if legal, would give staff members the power to decide which doctors they may or may no accept as members. This is one of the skirmish lines in a battle between the staff, or at least some of the staff, and the board of directors of the Charlotte Hospital Association, Inc., chaired by Leo Wotitzky."

Two weeks later, the board of directors revoked Dr. Reilly's privileges as a member of the hospital medical staff. He retaliated by filing a slander suit against the Board for damage to his reputation.

An attempt in September by the doctors and the Board of directors to reconcile differences failed. With this, the Board began searching for a not-for-profit religious group to take over the hospital as a special mission. The Catholic, Baptist and Seventh Day Adventist churches were approached. The Adventists agreed to accept.

A transfer of management   not ownership   took place on Sunday, October 19, 1969, at a meeting of the Charlotte Hospital Association and the Southern Adventist Health and Hospital System, Inc.

One by one, the 12 members of the Hospital Association board of directors resigned and an Adventist trustee was elected. Twenty minutes later, the Adventists had full control.

Robert Bruce was replaced as administrator by Jack Weisberger, assistant administrator for the Florida Sanitarium at Orlando. Donald W. Welch, president of Southern Adventist, assumed chairmanship of the Charlotte Hospital Association.

The *Herald* reported that H.H. Schmidt replaced Wotitzky as president of the board. Other officers are Donald W. Welch, vice-president to succeed Vernon Peeples, and Weisberger secretary-treasurer replacing Earl Hadley.

The Seventh Day Adventists adopted the Medical Center as one of its official projects, reported the *Herald*. "It will have the support of the church organization, and its earnings will be used exclusively to expand the hospital and improve its services.

"It would appear the medical hassle in the county may be nearing an end, except for the loose ends, including numerous lawsuits initiated by both the hospital and Dr. Reilly whose March 19 firing set off the crisis."

Indeed, the crisis was over. The new Board invited all physicians to join the medical staff. All lawsuits were dropped; and Dr. Reilly founded his own out-patient clinic, Intermedic, at Port Charlotte.

Still Another Controversy

When the non-profit Adventist Health Systems offered to sell its Medical Center Hospital at Punta Gorda in the Fall of 1992 to a for- profit buyer, the community protested strenuously.

Bidding was fierce by several prospects. Legal problems were tangled. Finally, Health Management Associates, Inc., of Naples was approved by the state. Exempted from the sale was $2 million of donations by local residents into a Medical Center Foundation for hospital improvements. An independent Charlotte County Foundation was established to continue receiving gifts and fund local health and education projects under the direction of the Foundation board with Jack Price as executive director.

426

Light house was attraction for Mackle Brothers development at Port Charlotte bisected by Elkcam Waterway — Mackle spelled backward.

Chapter 99

PORT CHARLOTTE INCORPORATION FAILS

Controversy in 1995 over the cost of sewer lines for parts of Port Charlotte, stir sentiments once more for incorporation and freedom from county commission control.

Realtor Monroe Randol asserts the multi-million-dollar project is a "terrible destruction of property values." Estimated hook-up costs range from $5,000 to $7,000 for residences — plus monthly charges — and $12,000 to $20,000 for businesses.

The state mandated central sewer systems in 1983, and the Commission hired the Camp, Dresser & McKee engineering firm to design a $315 million project for Charlotte County. When home owners objected strenuously, the scope was reduced to Charlotte Harbor Town, nearby businesses on Tamiami Trail (U.S. 41) and the Whidden industrial area on Harbor View Road.

New total cost was $14.3 million, but Camp, Dresser & McKee submitted a bill of $17 million for unused design work. Now, the Charlotte Harbor Town Community Redevelopment Advisory board wants to scrap the whole plan unless some way can be found to reduce costs.

427

Commissioners Max Farrell and Sue Dudley support the sewer line project on the basis it has been mandated by the Legislature for environmental protection. They say septic tanks must be disconnected sooner or later, and later would be still more expensive.

Aalarmed residents suggest incorporation as a way to escape commission dictates. The proposal is not new. A move by Port Charlotte to secede from county government began in 1958. This was only two years after the Mackle brothers of Miami, built the first homes in what had been Arthur C. Frizell's cattle range and John Murdock's farm colony.

Lots could be bought for $600 dollars with $10 down and $10 monthly. Homes cost from $5,900 to $18,000 depending upon location. First ones were on Easy Street — so named to attract retired factory workers. Proud buyers of that first home at 102 So. Easy Street — for $5,900 — were Mr. and Mrs. James V. and Kathryn Renshaw, owners of a Punta Gorda printing shop.

Response was so encouraging the Mackles joined in organizing the General Development Corporation to build houses in huge numbers. Under the aggressive salesmanship of GDC, more than 25,000 home lots were sold the first year. By 1958 about 1,000 houses had been built.

Residents anticipated that the development would reach build-out within the decade and make city government desirable. Proponents were encouraged by the incorporation of North Port Charlotte, another GDC development, in Sarasota County in 1959.

Straw Votes

Four informal "straw votes" on incorporation were taken at public meetings in 1960 by the Port Charlotte Civic Association. The final vote tallied 298 for incorporation and 423 against. Another poll in August 1962, using voting machines, yielded 518 yeas and 1,185 nays. Incorporation fever cooled.

However, concern about slow improvements by GDC of roads, ditches, sewers and water prompted the Charlotte County Federation of Civic Associations to launch a determined drive for city status in 1964.

George Stookey was president of the politically active association which assumed the role of "watch dog" over both the county commission and the school board.

State Representative D. Frank Smoak, a resident of Port Charlotte,introduced a bill in the Legislature in the Spring of 1965 authorizing home rule for the community should residents vote for it in public referendum. The proposed charter was 90 pages in length.

Until then, GDC had maintained a "hands off" policy on the matter. However, with city status and self-rule appearing likely, the company came out in strong opposition. Joining the company was the quickly organized Property Owners Protective Association.

428

Biggest concern of critics was the charter section on taxation. It stipulated that property would be taxed at $3 per lot whether it was improved or not. This laid the major share of taxation on GDC which at that time had 50,000 unsold vacant lots.

The charter also provided that utility services would be franchised by the proposed city. Again, this would hit GDC in the pocketbook inasmuch as the firm operated what sewage and water treatment systems were in the core area.

GDC rushed to Tallahassee to try and persuade Rep. Smoak to revise the incorporation bill. Smoak gave the company a weekend to submit written suggestions, but GDC declined. The bill passed the legislature handily. With this, both sides of the issue bombarded citizens with arguments. Debate grew increasingly bitter as the referendum date of Jan. 25, 1966, drew near.

Editorial Prediction

The *Punta Gorda Herald-News* summed up the feelings in an editorial on the eve of voting:

"Certainly there are advantages of incorporation, and the elements are coming more and more into play. To mention one, public safety. Port Charlotte needs street lights throughout the inhabited area. It also needs, or will need, a police force.

"Will there be a cost in these and other municipal advantages? Very probably, at some time or other. Residents will have to decide whether they want this output funnelled through the Courthouse (where the County Commission then met) or be under their own control.

"It is unfair to load Port Charlotte problems on the County Commissioners at an expense to the rest of the taxpayers in Charlotte County. But to get to the point of saying what we believe, this is an inopportune time to create a city.

"The issue of incorporation has torn the community. Friends have become foes. Under these circumstances a city would get off to a shaky, stormy start at a sacrifice of efficient administration.

"There are men and women looking to the future, to the day when General Development Corporation no longer will be on the scene to minister — as the Great White Father — to the needs of the community. As for the charter, it is indeed broad in scope. It has to be in anticipation of the future."

On referendum day, 5,503 Port Charlotte residents were eligible to vote, and 3,837 cast ballots. The result was 2,739 against incorporation, and 1,098 for it. No other organized effort to incorporate has been attempted since the referendum. However, complaints grew about inadequate roads, high taxes, sewage treatment, and lack of community identity. Infrastructure deteriorated.

Then, in 1989, 12,000 customers of General Development filed a class action suit against the corporation. They alleged they had been pressured into paying exorbitant prices for lots and homes — many without adequate utility services.

A grand jury in March the following year indicted the company. Robert F. Ehrling, GDC president; and David F. Brown, board chairman, pled guilty. They paid a $500,000 fine, $100 million in immediate restitution and set up a $12.5 million trust fund to reimburse bilked customers over a 25-year period through mortgage subsidies.

This forced the corporation to file bankruptcy and reorganize as the Atlantic Gulf Communities Corporation and sell its utility department to the county.

As the *Herald* predicted, General Development Corporation no longer was the "Great White Father."

Concerned citizens formed the Tax Watch Committee to monitor the commission, school board and development authority. But there still is dissatisfaction with the way Port Charlotte is governed.

Under a home rule charter, residents would elect council members more sensitive to local concerns. However, state law would require police, fire, health, building inspection, zoning, property assessing, tax collection, public works, parks and other bureaucracy.

Punta Gorda, the county seat, incorporated in 1887 and has prospered by starting small and growing slowly.

Charlotte Harbor Town, Cleveland, and Englewood tried incorporation during the Florida Land Boom of the 1920s. The boom collapsed in 1929 — along with the stock market — and the Great Depression gripped the nation. The newly-charted Charlotte County communities abrogated their charters. There was not enough tax revenue to fund essential services.

Randol predicts that the businesses and residents of Murdock will incorporate "in five years" — perhaps followed by Port Charlotte, Englewood, Charlotte Harbor Town, and Harbour Heights.

Opponents of incorporation point out that any further incorporations would seriously decrease public services throughout the county.

One way or the other, history is being acted out today. Only time will separate the good guys from the villains.

Sign over busy intersection to Toledo Blade Blvd. and Tamiami Trail.

Chapter 100

TOLEDO BLADE BOULEVARD ODDLY NAMED

Ohioans travelling Interstate-75 through Sarasota County are surprised to see a "Toledo Blade" interchange at North Port. Charlotte County folks risking life and limb on Tamiami Trail (U.S. 4l) are puzzled by that unusual name for a prominent street intersection in Murdock.

An elementary school in North Port also bears the name.

Casual motorists often surmise the name refers to the famous steel swords manufactured at Toledo, Spain; but Buckeyes know it for the 158-year-old newspaper of Toledo, Ohio.

431

Everyone who notices the name wonder how it came to be applied so far from either source, and why it pops up in so many places hereabouts.

The answer starts in 1954 with the Yellow Knife Bear Mines, Ltd., a Canadian investment firm. It formed a partnership with Mackle Brothers Construction Co. of Miami and bought 70,000 acres of land along 14 miles of Tamiami Trail from Rancher A.C. Frizzell for $2.3 million.

Mackle began building inexpensive two-bedroom homes on Easy Street, a development and name appealing to northern retirees. After selling 250 homes, Yellow Knife-Mackle merged with the Chemical Research Corporation of Delaware in 1956. They formed the General Development Corporation, since reorganized as Atlantic Gulf Communities following a legal suit against misleading sales practices.

GDC launched an advertising blitz in northern newspapers — including a generous schedule with the *Toledo Blade*. Undoubtedly the *Blade* received favorable consideration inasmuch as Mackle's executive vice-president and a GDC director, Thomas A. Ferris, began his successful career as a reporter there.

Lots in Port Charlotte, Charlotte County, and North Port, Sarasota County, were sold for $10 down and $10 per month. Four model homes starting at $6,090 homes were built on Sunrise Trail, the first street off Elkcam Blvd., Charlotte County. The name is Mackle spelled backward.

In a short time 125,000 lots were sold. Surveyors worked from dawn to dusk laying out new streets. Florida law requires streets to be named, recorded and marked with corner signs so buyers can find their property.

Naming Streets Difficult

Naming streets is not as easy as one might think. Each had to be different from all others in the county for efficient postal service. In addition they had suggest something in which prospective customers would accept. No one would live on Skunk Avenue, for example; and Easy Street was already reserved.

Developers soon run out of relatives and friends to honor with a street name. Flowers, trees, fruits, exotic plants, states, cities, seas, birds, animals — and foreign variations thereof — were soon exhausted. Numbered streets are efficient but lack sales appeal.

If streets are inadvertently duplicated, the postal service will insist on a change for the least populated one — preferably with another starting with the same initial.

Everyone in General Development was encouraged to suggest names for the fastest growing communities in Florida history. Even corporate executives pored over plot plans, checked postal directories, and racked their brains for ideas.

The boulevard that wound through both Port Charlotte and North Port was hard to describe because of its meandering in two counties.

Ex-reporter Ferris spoke up for the *Blade* once more, pointing out that the newspaper had produced a large number of customers for GDC. He also named another street in Port Charlotte after George Jenks, his best friend at the Blade in his younger years.

The *Blade* was founded in 1835 amidst the turmoil of the "Toledo War." Ohio was the first state to be carved from the Midwest Territory in 1803. When Michigan sought statehood in 1835, it disputed Ohio's claim to a little frontier village at the mouth of Maumee River on Lake Erie.

An Ohio surveying party, laying out a line to substantiate the Buckeye claim, was arrested by Michigan militia and carried a few miles north to the village of Tecumseh. The nine men were released the next day, but the Ohio Legislature was incensed. The dispute was taken to Washington, D.C., and a new survey was ordered.

While the survey was being made, militia men from both states took up positions on opposite banks of the Maumee. The day before the survey results were to be announced at Toledo, Ohio judges and clerks stole into the sleeping town at 3 o'clock in the morning, held a meeting in its tavern, recorded the notes, and were toasting the event when a shot or two rang out. The exact number varied among witnesses.

The Ohio delegation vacated the premises without completing the toast, but reveled in victory later that day when the survey proved its claim. The Michiganders fired a few more shots into the air in disgust but returned to Tecumseh without "invading" Ohio. Michigan partisans declared Ohio lost the bloodless Toledo War by having to accept responsibility for a backward town of rustics.

Paper Named For Sword

A *Blade* publisher, Bill Block, Jr., says the paper was named for the legendary "cutting edge" of Toledo, Spain, swords. George B. Way, the paper's first editor, explained the name in his first editorial:

"We hope the *Blade* will always leap from its scabbard whenever the . rights of individuals or of the community shall be infringed upon."

In 1987, *Blade* Editor Mike Bartell was vacationing in Florida and saw the Toledo Blade sign at North Port's interchange with U.S. 75. "I thought, 'Oh heck, since I've worked for the paper 20 years I might as well take a picture of it.'

"I stopped my car and walked back with my camera to the sign. As I was photographing it, a trucker stopped to see if I needed help. Boy, was he steamed when I told him what I was doing. I guess he couldn't believe someone would stop to take a picture of a sign."

A framed photograph of the sign now hangs in the paper's newsroom.

If any developer is stumped for a name of a new street, developers might consider "Sun-Herald."

The "young lions" of PGI, from left, front row: Robert J. Barbee, vice-president; Russell C. Faber, vice-president treasurer; E. Drayton Farr, Jr., corporation counsel; Wilber H. Cole, president; and Alfred M. Johns, board chairman. Top row — John Matarese, vice-president; and Samuel A. Burchers, vice-president.

Chapter 101

PGI CANALS TRANSFORM SAND FLATS

The tragic deaths of Wilber H. "Bud" Cole, a founding partner of Punta Gorda Isles, Inc., and members of his immediate family, narrow the number of "young lions" who came to Punta Gorda after World War II to build a unique neighborhood laced with salt-water canals.

Cole, 63, was piloting his plane when it crashed July 31, 1993, at Great Abaco Island, Bahamas, while attempting to land during a thunderstorm. Killed with him were his wife Maureen, his son John, and the latter's fiance Loretta Bouman. Only the family's pet dog survived.

Among those shocked by the accident is Alfred M. Johns, the other partner. Both men were native Floridians. The two had worked for the Central Intelligence Agency on Tachen Island off the China coast during the Korean War. Their mission was to divert Chinese from going to Korea to join the war against the Americans. Johns, chairman of the board; and

434

Cole, president, launched the publicly owned Punta Gorda Isles Corporation in 1958. They brought in Bob Barbee, Sam Burchers, Tom Messina and others to form a dynamic group of salesmen and managers to turn a vast tidal flat into up-scale home sites.

In 1968, on the company's tenth anniversary, Bud Cole wrote a history of PGI titled "How It All Started." One can get no closer to the facts:

Cole's Account

For myself, Punta Gorda Isles is not a thing, but an experience — the bare beginning of which, I suppose, stretches back to a day in the summer of 1950. It was hot, and I was flying as a passenger in a "gooney bird" that was just setting down on a little island in sight of the China coast.

We taxied to a stop on the dirt runway, and I alighted to be greeted by a cloud of red dust. The center of this red tornado, it soon appeared, was occupied by an extremely disreputable jeep driven by an even more disreputable, mustached, native Chinese pirate.

I piled into the jeep and discovered on the ride to our quarters that under the layers of grime, behind the wild eyes, and past the inscrutable countenance, an ugly American was lurking. His name, it turned out, was Al Johns.

Al and I assisted the Government in various unlikely projects for three years or so before returning to the States. A few months after my arrival in the Far East, Sam Burchers (another ex-CIA agent) appeared on the scene, and the three of us became close friends.

The mid-50's found me, Al, and Bob Barbee, a schoolmate and friend of Al's, in Ft. Lauderdale learning to be "land development businessmen" from, perhaps, the most successful developer of prime waterfront property in the country — James Stone Hunt of Coral Ridge properties.

We experimented with this new knowledge on a small subdivision in Fort Lauderdale and then a larger one in North Miami Beach. By 1957, we were involved in waterfront development of 300 lots on Biscayne Bay in Coral Gables. Sam Burchers had come back from directing a motion picture in Mexico and joined us. We were just four happy bachelors in the big city.

At a conference with James Buchanan, then board chairman of General Development Corporation, the plans for Port Charlotte were unrolled. This was the first mention of the city of Punta Gorda. I had never heard of it, while Al risked the statement that it meant "something big" in Spanish.

What with big things brewing on the west coast of Florida, Bob and Al took a sight-seeing trip by plane and promptly fell in love with the Punta Gorda "point." The idea of the second largest harbor on the entire Gulf of Mexico, a county with more shore line than any other in the state, and a 100-square-mile public hunting preserve was awful strong

435

medicine. The clincher was an unrivaled location — protected, secluded, and yet immediately available to the outside world.

Bud was dragged over by car and shown the view of the point from the bridge. He was told that "you can't exactly get there from here; but it sure is pretty and we better buy it." Bud and Sam agreed. With considerable help and understanding from the owners, Gerald Moody of Greenfuel Gas Company of Fort Myers; and George Sanders, owner of Edison Mall; title of the first 550 acres passed to Punta Gorda Isles, Inc., on the last day of the year 1957.

One local wag, when he heard that the mangrove swamp with its millions of fiddler crabs was to become a beautiful subdivision with canals throughout made a sage observation, "They must be out of their cotton-pickin' heads." Several others thought so as well. Fortunately W.T. Price, of Price Dredging Corporation and also president of Coconut Grove Bank, had faith that the young corporation could make the subdivision go. He backed up his belief with credit in the form of earth moving and road building.

At about this point, unmistakable Italian gentleman came chugging down the pike in a 1934 Plymouth automobile minus two hub caps, from the big, cold city, looking for sunshine and clean air. John Matarese had no previous experience in anything related to the land development business. He knew what he wanted and was not afraid of hard work.

He stated from the first day that he would have a house, boat and family in Punta Gorda Isles one day. Though it seemed unlikely at the time, John made it happen and contributed to the success of the venture in so doing. The first four homes were constructed on the west shore of what is the basin behind the office (now the Isles Yacht Club). These were

Earth from canals raised level of tidal flat four feet.

Scholtz package homes. A temporary sales offices — which is now the maintenance building located on another site — served as company headquarters. In early '58, an office had been built on U.S. 41 in Charlotte Harbor, on the north side of the bridge. Prospective buyers were taken by boat to view, from the water, the future Punta Gorda Isles. the building was soon sold, however, and is now occupied by the Sea Horse Marina. The first three homes to be occupied in Punta Gorda Isles were the Wilder house adjacent to the tennis courts, the Ettenger home and the Cole residence on Donna Court.

About the time we started making the first sales, we needed some professional management for our finances and record keeping. Russ Faber, C.P.A., who was in business in Coral Gables, supplied this commodity. A couple of years later, Russ, tired of running back and forth, was induced to take up residence here permanently.

Meanwhile, back in the subdivision, a few more neighbors moved in — Sam, Bob and Al taking up residence in the model homes. The first Isles baby, John Cole, put in his appearance on Sept. 17, 1960. John was followed not long afterward by Kevin Johns, Sammy Burchers and others.

Sales Slow

Sales were slow those first two years, but by the early 60's the basic "pioneering" was over and the future course set.

The detailing of our basic group would not be complete without our attorneys, the Farrs — Drayton Farr, Jr. doing most of our work. Without him, certainly our company would have taken another form. His knowledge of the local conditions, attitudes, etc., as well as his legal counsel, contributed heavily to our success.

Don Witter's interest and the backing of the First Federal made possible our minor housing boom when out-of-town financial institutions wrinkled their noses. As a matter of fact, the understanding of the local people, in public life and out, made the project possible.

When I think back on those early days, certain scenes seem to characterize the times. There was, of course, no B&B Shopping Center, (now U-Save and Charlotte Shopping Center) much less the Punta Gorda Mall and the two motels. The old Hotel Charlotte Harbor, constructed in 1886, occupied most of what is now the Punta Gorda Mall Shopping Center. The hotel's monstrous pool was located near the Howard Johnson site (built and owned by PGI). The hotel burned to the ground one night in 1959.

The Punta Gorda Federal Savings and Loan — now First Federal Savings and Loan — did business in one small office in the "Mall" in the King Building of East Marion Ave. (now the original Smith Arcade). They had one safe, about the size of a file cabinet. The Post Office occupied the rear end of that "Mall."

437

The First National Bank was located on the southwest corner of U.S. 41 and Marion Avenue. What little business activity there was resided on West Marion. A great number of the stores, however, were boarded up, had broken glass and cobwebs. There were but two restaurants in the area, neither of which had air-conditioning.

The hospital was like a barracks building. The road to the Isles was unpaved. The Isles telephone had seven other parties on it.

Looking back, I get little snatches of memories of different people — Westy Westfall, with a prospective customer and a bit of sage advice for us, invariably sound. Rumsey Thompson paying all cash for a house and lot while wearing a pair of 69-cent Japanese sandals. Pete Bontsema, who single-handedly started the first Civic Association. Bill Crosland's dog jumping into the Ettenger pool. Myself backing up and falling off the seawall while engaged in enthusiastically showing a customer the glories of PGI — Bob Barbee's 22-pound snook.

The building of the Isles has been a stimulating experience shared by many; and, I truly believe, the best is yet to come.

Continued To Grow

Indeed, PGI continued to grow. Its twin, Burnt Store Isles, soon followed. Other subdivisions were Deep Creek and Burnt Store Marina.

Cole resigned as president of Punta Gorda Isles, Inc., in 1977 to pursue other business interests and manage his citrus farm and cattle ranch 10 miles east of Punta Gorda. He had been a pilot for 20 years, and had his own airstrip. He maintained a summer vacation home on Man O'War Cay, Bahamas, but flew home as necessary to attend First Federal directors' meetings. Johns also gave up his chairmanship in 1987 to start his own development company. His present enterprises include the Seminole Lakes home and golf subdivision, Sand Hill Properties shopping centers, and citrus groves.

Johns and Cole managed to develop the Punta Gorda flats where others had failed. A notable attempt to build homes on a canal there was announced in late 1925 by the Ruff Realty Company of Tampa. The development was to be called Pasa Bonita. It featured a canal 300 feet wide and 20 feet deep running through the entire property. The project was a casualty of the Great Land Boom which collapsed in 1929.

Johns and Cole laid out 55 miles of canals 100 feet wide and 17 feet deep. Dredged sand was piled up on the flats to raise the level of land four feet. This provided dry home sites with access to the harbor and gulf. Home owners can keep their boats in their back yards. PGI lots originally sold for $5,000, and homes for $32,000. Earlier this year, an older waterfront home was sold for $495,000 and immediately demolished by the new owner so he could construct a $1.5 million home. Surely Bud Cole was pleased to see his prediction come true, "The best is yet to come."

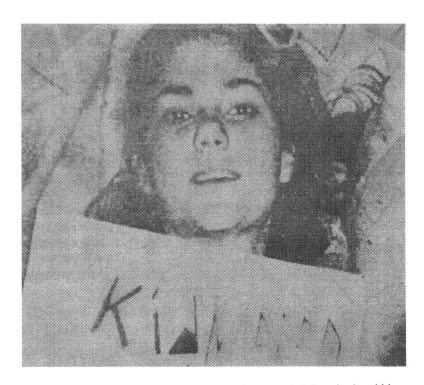

Beverly Mackle forces a "sorry smile" in this photograph taken by her kidnappers to convince her parents she was alive.

Chapter 102

KIDNAPPED AND BURIED ALIVE

"No! No! No! You can't do this! You've got to let me out. Wait! I'll be good." Barbara pleaded with her kidnappers not to bury her alive.

Gary Krist, alias George Deacon, escaped convict from a California prison, snarled, "Don't be such a baby." Methodically he began screwing down the lid of a coffin-like box — ignoring the screams of his 20-year-old victim as she pounded frantically in her tomb.

Barbara Mackle was a student at Emory University, an exclusive girl's school at Decatur, Georgia, a suburb of Atlanta. When she became ill with influenza during the epidemic of 1968, she had to take a room at a nearby motel. The college infirmary was full with other sick girls. Mrs. Jane Mackle drove from Coral Gables, a posh suburb of Miami, to take care of her daughter. Christmas was just eight days away.

Robert Mackle and his two brothers, Frank and Elliot, were wealthy land developers who had launched Port Charlotte and North Port Charlotte — among other planned communities.

Conclusion of the most bizarre kidnapping in U.S. history took place on Hog Island near El Jobean. The principal participants were Special

Deputy Milton Buffington and Major Richard McLeod of the Charlotte County sheriff's department. Milton, now is retired at Punta Gorda. He treasures a scrapbook of news stories about the sensational kidnapping and recalls details vividly.

"Barbara and her mother stayed in a $32-per-night motel room," says Milton. "They were hoping Barbara's fever would abate enough to allow them to go home for a family Christmas celebration. Barbara's boy friend, Stewart Woodward, came by in the evening to keep the two women company. He left about midnight. As he drove away in his white Ford, Stewart noticed two people sitting in a blue Volvo station wagon. He thought nothing of it at the time because of the many guests there.

"At 4 a.m. there was a knock on the door. 'Who is it?' Mrs. Mackle called out. 'The police,' replied a male voice. 'We are investigating an accident. A young man driving a white Ford has been seriously injured.'

"Mrs. Mackle went to open the door. Barbara said 'Don't,' but it was too late. Outside the door was a big man holding a shotgun. With him was a smaller person in a ski mask and holding a pistol. The latter was thought to be a boy but was discovered later to be a young Honduran woman named Ruth Eisemann-Schier.

Do As We Say

"They rushed in and put their weapons to the heads of Mrs. Mackle and Barbara. 'Do as we say, and nobody will be hurt.' Mrs. Mackle was more annoyed than frightened. She thought they were being robbed. 'Just take our money and get out of here!' she demanded.

"The big man pressed a cloth saturated with chloroform over her nose and mouth. In moments Mrs. Mackle was unconscious. The slightly built intruder started to do the same to Barbara, but held back when Barbara said she would 'be good' and not scream or look at her captors.

"Krist and his accomplice placed Barbara face down on the back seat of a blue Buick and drove for about 20 minutes into a wild, uninhabited area. Krist pulled up Barbara's night gown and jabbed her with a hypodermic needle which he said contained a harmless sedative. Then Schier placed a chloroform cloth over Barbara's face briefly.

"Barbara became woozy but remained conscious. Krist ordered her to hold a crude sign KIDNAPPED while he photographed her with a Polaroid camera. He didn't like the picture because she was grim faced. He ordered her to smile so her parents would know she was alive. Then he photographed her again.

"He also took an opal ring from her finger. Then he slid her, feet first, into an open hole which already contained the plywood box.

"There were two ventilating pipes into the box which Krist referred to as a "capsule." Speaking into the tubes, Krist told hysterical Barbara that she had food, water, a blanket, a small light and ventilating fan operated by batteries, and a pump to get rid of water should it rain. A bed-pan was provided for bodily functions.

"The supplies and batteries will last a week if used sparely — two and a half days if wasted' said Krist. In a box of sanitary napkins was a note saying she would be released in a week even if the ransom was not paid.

"Mrs. Mackle, bound hand and foot with Venetian blind cords — mouth taped — regained consciousness an hour or so later. She banged on the wall with her feet but got no response. Struggling to her feet, she hopped to the door. She managed to open it from behind her back. She did the same with her parked car and pressed the horn with her head.

"The blaring horn brought the motel night-clerk in a hurry. 'Cut that out, lady! You're waking all our guests.' Mrs. Mackle stood up, enabling the manager to see her fetters and gag. 'Oh, my God! What's wrong?' Within 10 minutes the police arrived. Road blocks were thrown up. All Atlanta-area patrol cars were ordered on alert. Robert Mackle was called. He rushed to the scene in his private plane commanded by two pilots.

"At 9:30 a.m. the Mackle's unlisted telephone rang. A friend summoned to the house for the purpose, answered. 'Listen carefully, I will say this only one time. I am the kidnapper of your daughter. Look under the rock at the base of a palm tree near your front gate. Follow instructions there faithfully if you want to see your daughter again.'

"Under the rock was a bottle with three sheets of typewritten paper. They explained that Barbara was buried in a box and would be allowed to 'suffocate' if a ransom of $500,000 was not paid, or the police notified. The money was to consist of used $20 bills, not in serial order, and bound in $1,000 packets. The ransom was to be put in a single suit case and readied for further instructions.

Decatur, Ga., motel from which Barbara Mackle was abducted.

"If the terms were accepted, Mackle was to place a classified ad in the Miami Herald under the personal section. The ad was hurriedly placed at a cost of $3: 'LOVED ONE. Please come home. We will pay all expenses and meet you anywhere at anytime. Your family.'

"Mackle's bank spent all that day and night preparing the ransom and listing the serial numbers. There was difficulty finding a suitcase large enough to contain the money. Finally, the wife of the bank vice-president found one in her closet at home.

"On Wednesday the postman delivered a letter containing Barbara's opal ring and the Polaroid photo her. At 4 a.m. Thursday — exactly two days since the kidnapping — Robert Mackle received another call. He was to drive immediately to the foot of Fair Isle Drive at Biscayne Bay. The road and bridge was blocked off every evening at 8 o'clock. He was to leave the ransom on a sandy strip near the bridge and depart.

"Mackle did as instructed. However, shortly afterward a neighbor heard a motor boat coming up the shallow channel between Fair Isle and the mainland. Fearing burglars who often hit waterside homes via boats, he called police. Two officers were sent to investigate.

Abandoned Ransom

"They saw two persons coming out of a small woods near the bridge and ordered them to halt. Instead, the suspects dropped a large, heavy suitcase and bolted safely into the woods. The suitcase was discovered to contain more money than they had ever seen. Not knowing of the ransom payoff, the officers assumed they had interrupted a big burglary. They took the money to the police station. It soon was discovered the money was the Mackle ransom.

"Mackle was devastated when told of the accidentally botched payoff. He feared his daughter would be killed. 'I don't care about the money. We just want our daughter back.'

"A white boat and a blue Volvo were found abandoned at the scene. The boat's registration number indicated the craft belonged to the University of Miami Institute of Marine Sciences.

"In the Volvo, police found a passport for Ruth Eisemann-Schier, two one-way airline tickets to Las Vegas and six Polaroid snapshots. Some of the photographs were of a man, others of a woman. Both were nude or scantily dressed. One photo was of a grim Barbara Mackle. The license plate was traced to a George Deacon who worked for the Marine Institute. Dozens of fingerprints were lifted from various surfaces of the automobile and quickly identified as Gary Krist, fugitive felon. The University identified the woman in the Polaroid prints as a biologist at the Marine Institute," recounts Buffington. During these developments, Barbara was struggling to keep her sanity. Her light and fan had ceased to function. Water was dripping into her box — soaking her nightgown and blanket.

After her ordeal, Barbara wrote a book of her experience. It was suggested by President Elect Richard Nixon, a close friend of the family. The book was titled *83 Hours Till Dawn*.

"After a couple of days I thought about dying. I said to myself, 'This is where I am going to die.' Three or four times I thought this is going to be my casket. When I got morbid I would think of who would find me. Who and when and how. Maybe it would be a farmer. Or someone building something. In ten years? Twenty years?

"I started to count sheep. I pretended to see a little wooden rail fence. I had white sheep jumping, and I counted eight or nine hundred. I thought about decorating our Christmas tree.

"You know how you try to make a bad situation seem better than it is? Well, I kept thinking to myself. It's nice and cozy and warm here. If I were outside, It would be cold. What better place could there be than right here? If were out, why, maybe something would go wrong and the kidnappers would want to shoot me. But here they can't. I'm safe here. I'm glad I'm here.

"I talked to myself this way, but it didn't work for long. I was cold and I was wet, and I ached. I couldn't stretch out. Once I scrunched up and got stuck. I got real panicky thinking I was going to die this way.

Total Darkness

"My tiny light ceased to work very soon. Then I was in total darkness. I thought about being blind. When I was a child I used to close my eyes and pretend I was blind. It was pretty scary. I used to work for the blind, and I wondered what it would be like to be blind. Now I know. You want to see. You are so frustrated. You can't see your hand in front of your face. And I thought, if they can spend their whole life like this, well, I can tolerate it.

"I would turn off the ventilating fan from time to time just to stop the noise. It was getting to me. And then I would deliberately sing happy songs. I have such a bad voice that when I hear myself sing, I laugh. I felt silly singing, but it felt good.

"My mind was just wandering. I was thinking of walking on the Emory campus with Stewart. Ice skating, and I remember he was falling down, and I was laughing, and one time it was cold and we were just running — just running and playing leap frog. Childish things, but it was fun. I thought of all the happy and fun things I could.

"The time came when I started to talk to God. For awhile in my life, I was kind of agnostic, I suppose. I believed in God most of the time. When I was down there in the ground I thought that maybe I should believe more. I just started talking, as if God were there beside me. I said, 'God, `I know you are not going to let me die here. Even if no one knows where I am, You know where I am.' I found this very comforting."

Van and boat used by kidnappers.

Robert Mackle was distraught when he learned the delivery of a half-million-dollar ransom for his daughter was aborted accidentally by an alert police officer in Miami. "My God, they're going to kill my daughter," Mackle declared.

By a twist of fate, a Punta Gorda butcher played a key role in bringing the kidnapper to justice. Milton "Butch" Buffington, at that time in 1968, was the popular meat department manager for U-Save. He also was a special deputy for Charlotte County Sheriff Jack Bent. Milton owned two bloodhound "track dogs," and two German shepherd "attack dogs." He was called on frequently to aid searches for fleeing criminals.

It was in this capacity that Milton became involved in the famous kidnapping of Miss Mackle. He relates the thrilling conclusion:

"Mr. Mackle pleaded with the FBI to do something to save his daughter. It was decided to issue a press release addressed to the kidnappers," said Milton as he opened a scrapbook containing the newspaper statement by Mackle.

"The statement read: 'I had nothing to do with the action Thursday morning of the Miami police who tried to arrest you and recovered the money which I had left for you. I regret that you did not get the money because my only interest is the safety of my daughter. I pray that you have not harmed my daughter. I did everything you told me to do. I had nothing to do with the accidental appearance of the Miami police on the scene. Please contact me again through any channel. I will do anything you ask so my daughter will be freed.'"

Milton Buffington continued: "This statement was featured in all the afternoon newspapers. At 10 p.m. that evening, Mr. Mackle received a telephone call from Krist. Instructions, given only once, were simple — 'Go now to the end of a dirt road off Tamiami Trail nine miles west of

Miami. Leave the suitcase of money. If there was no interference, You will receive another call before noon Friday telling you where to find your daughter.' Mr. Mackle did as directed. A checkup at 3 a.m., disclosed that the money had been picked up.

"Mr. and Mrs. Mackle and the FBI waited tensely at the Coral Gable mansion. By noon, no call had come. The group feared the worst.

"At 3 p.m., the switchboard operator at the Atlanta office of the FBI received a call from a man who said, 'Listen carefully. I'll only give this once so you can't trace me.'

"With this, Krist gave directions in tenths of a mile to Barbara's location. Eight cars of FBI agents raced to the spot. It was an abandoned homesite overgrown with thorny bushes. However, there was so sign of the living grave. Agents were about to give up when one man heard a faint knock, knock, knock. He fell to his hands and knees and crawled into the bushes. There he found freshly turned earth with two, protruding pipes. The agent called, 'Barbara, is that you? This is the FBI. If you can hear me, knock again.' The knocking sound was repeated.

"'Here she is!' shouted the agent. Frantically the men began clawing into the earth with their bare hands and sticks. Twelve minutes later, their hands bleeding, the agents reached the coffin lid. 'Hang on, Barbara! It's the FBI. We'll have you out in a jiffy.'

Agents Cried

"They pried off the lid with a tire iron. There was Barbara, still dressed in her nightgown, weeping with relief and shock. 'How are my parents?' The agents cried as they lifted her out of the box. She was unable to stand so they carried her to the cars and radioed that Barbara had been rescued.

"FBI Director J. Edgar Hoover personally telephoned the Mackles to tell them Barbara was alive and in remarkable good shape considering the ordeal she had suffered through three nights and four days.

"Meanwhile, the police at Miami were closing in on Krist. A car he had rented was discovered in West Palm Beach at a parking lot near the waterfront. A canvas of stores and homes in the area located a marine dealer who had sold a small boat Friday afternoon to a man who gave his name as Arthur Horowitz and paid for it with $20 bills. Among $400 worth of equipment the man bought was a chart for the waterway through Lake Okeechobee to the west coast. Minutes after the purchase, the man who called himself Horowitz sped up the Intracoastal toward St. Lucie and turned into the Okeechobee canal.

"The police learned he had passed through the Okeechobee locks and sped down the Caloosahatchee just an hour earlier. The Coast Guard at St. Petersburg was lofted to patrol the Gulf Coast. The pilots spotted the suspect off Cayo Costa. As the copter dropped low the boat driver looked up and was positively identified.

445

Federal, state and local police used air boats to hunt kidnapper.

"The fleeing boat suddenly swerved through Boca Grande Pass in an apparent effort to elude the chase craft. Ahead was a desolate shore. Krist headed for it and rammed his boat into a sandy strip amid dense mangroves. He leaped from the boat with a small suitcase and struggled into the mud and mangroves.

"The place was Hog Island near El Jobean. Sheriff deputies, state police and FBI agents — in all, 200 armed men — swooped to the area by car, boat and air sleds. Captain John P. Shannon, later a Charlotte County judge, set up a command post at the Lazy R fishing camp in El Jobean.

"In the abandoned boat they found a duffel bag with $480,000 in $20 bills. I was ordered to join the hunt as soon as I could change into my uniform while my two sons loaded the dogs. When I got to the Lazy R, I found the FBI agents with their three-piece suits floundering in the mud. Many had lost their shoes — sucked off by the mud. It was obvious that none of them had ever tangled with a mangrove thicket. We tied yellow ribbons around our hats to identify ourselves. I still have mine. They ferried my dogs over to Hog Island, and we worked the sandy strips. We couldn't do any good because everything was wet and muddy. Scents don't hold in the wet.

"At nightfall, we gave up trying to track the fugitive. I took my dogs home, changed into dry clothes and returned to El Jobean. There I and Deputy Major Richard McLeod were ferried over to Hog Island about 10 p.m. where the search party had gathered around a campfire to wait for

Lulubelle Babcock

Chapter 103

A GENUINE TRICEF

The Charlotte Sun-Herald obituary of M
treatment for good reason — she was one c

* * *

Lulubelle Babcock, bovine celebrity,
years, died Sept. 30, 1991, at the Crescent-
Gorda, Florida.

Born Jan. 17, 1967, to humble be
called, soon stunned the cow world wh
from the middle of her forehead while

Amidst the intense publicity of this
to the quieter pastures of the Bab
Georgia town of Colquitt. There s
heifer into coquettish cowhood.

trademark third horn re
polished on the
d no end of ar
t the bull lot th

daylight. Air boats circled the island continually to keep Krist from wading across to the mainland.

"Mac and I tried to put ourselves in the fugitive's shoes. We figured Krist didn't realize he was on an island and would try to make his way to the lights at El Jobean on the mainland. We decided to wade around in the dark to the landward side of the island and wait for sounds.

"Sure enough, about midnight we heard soft splashing like some one walking along the edge of the mangroves. We eased out into water up to our chests so we wouldn't splash. I held my pistol over my head to keep it dry, and held a flashlight in my left hand aside at arm's length — ready to flick it on, but at a distance so any shots at it wouldn't hit me. Mack held a carbine over his head.

"The splashing would stop for a minute or two, then resume. An air boat came by in the dark, and the splashing stopped. We waited a half-hour or more in silence for the splashing to resume. Finally we heard a rustle in the bushes. Mac whispered to me to move away from him a bit and get ready for his signal to turn on the flash light toward the spot where we had heard the rustling. 'Now!' shouted Mac. I flicked on the light and there on a log sat Krist with a small suitcase. 'Put up your hands,' Mac shouted. 'You're under arrest.'

Captured

"Krist raised his hands; and we waded up to him, guns cocked. 'I'm tired,' he said. 'Can I have a drink?' I walked around behind him and put my hand cuffs on him. Mac fired three shots to call for help. They brought an air boat around, but it was too difficult in waist-deep water to get the handcuffed prisoner aboard. We waded him to camp. When we dragged him ashore he collapsed from fatigue. In his suitcase we found $18,000 of the ransom money. That was the last of the $500,000 he had hoped to get away with.

"When we got to El Jobean, the FBI agents grabbed our prisoner and rushed him to one of their cars. Mac protested that Krist was our prisoner and should be taken to the nearest federalized prison, ours, at the Punta Gorda court house. The agents paid no attention to us. They pushed Krist into one of their cars and raced away to Fort Myers. However, they forgot to take the suitcase of money I was carrying — crucial evidence the FBI needed for a trial. The next day, a couple of FBI agents came back and very nicely asked us to relinquish the evidence.

"Only casualty of the massive search occurred when two state wildlife officers — rushing in their car to get an airboat — slammed into another car on Tamiami Trail. The officers suffered broken bones; but Harry Taylor, a 63-year-old car salesman, was killed.

"Mac and I received citations from Sheriff Bent for our capture, letters of commendation from FBI Director Hoover. The 18,0

447

boat and outboard motor with which Krist fled was given to M
because it was purchased with his money. Mr. Mackle gave i
Bent's office. Then it was ruled the boat belonged to the West
dealer because the purchase money had been confiscated by

"Mr. Mackle re-purchased the boat for Charlotte Coun'
first marine craft for the sheriff's department. Gary Krist
given 20 years. The death-penalty for kidnapping — ins'
kidnapping and murder of Charles A. Lindberg's bat
repealed. Krist served 10 years, and upon release went

"His girl friend, Ruth Eisemann-Schier, gave up th
after they were nearly caught in Miami trying the first '
ransom money. She was caught in Texas where she w
and served two or three years in prison as an accompli'
what finally happened to her," said Buffington.

After the above story was published in the S'
Henderson of Punta Gorda wrote the editor to dis
girl friend: "My husband, W.P. Henderson, M.D
and took a job as director of the Jones Medical S
Central State Hospital in Milledgeville, Ga. S
were serving time at the nearby women's prison
their desire to become rehabilitated upon th'
hospital to learn various skills — medical, se'

"Ruth Eisemann-Schier was highly educ
and was part of my husband's secretarial poc
serious worker. While he was there, she wa'
to be allowed to return to the United Stat

For her entire life she was unable to avoid the incessant curiosity of an
amazed and adoring public. Ranchers from across the United States visited
her to gaze in disbelief.

Her owner, Fred Babcock, thought she might serve as the foundation
stock for a new breed known as the Triceracow. Since ranchers especially
value reproductive ability in their cows, Mr. Babcock created the breed
slogan: "Triceracow, the horniest cow in America."

After raising 18 calves — all two-horns — Miss Lulu retired to her
native range at Punta Gorda where her second career as world renowned
bovine super star really took off. Featured as a regular on the ranch tour,
Babcock Wilderness Adventure, Miss Lulu attained notoriety on national
television and in print. She was the object of a very flattering article in the
glossy French magazine *Nature*, and received rave reviews in the German
newspaper *Die Welt*, and the Paris newspaper *Le Figaro*. All of Miss
Lulu's calves predeceased her. She does have 143 living grandcalves and
298 great-grandcalves.

She was returned to the sandy soils of her youth by a close circle of her
valued cowmen — who then adjourned to a wake in her honor held on the
porch of the old Rouxville Commissary. There they sadly wished her
"happy grazing" as they raised their Old Milwaukee beer in toast.

Miss Lulu's life will be memorialized by an accurately sculptured bust
which will be displayed at the Babcock Wilderness Adventures reception
center.

*   *   *

Actually, not to put a delicate point on the matter, Lulu's forequarters
and unique rack were preserved by a skilled taxidermist and mounted in the
Dutch-door of a small barn where she can be easily photographed by
visitors.

Charlotte County sheriff depu

450

Elks lodge at Eagle Nest in Solana traces roots back 120 years.

Chapter 104

EAGLES NEST HUNTING LODGE A FAVORITE

It is somewhat confusing to adjust one's comprehension of an Eagle's Nest being home of the Elks — but such is the case regarding the historic waterfront lodge at Solana.

Solana, a "suburb" of Punta Gorda, was settled in 1873 by a snowbird named Frederick W. Howard of Kinderhook, N.Y. Census and tax records disclose that he and his wife homesteaded 132 acres and built a five-room cabin on the property. The Howards came to Florida only in the winter. Arrival of the Florida Southern Railway in 1886 increased the value of their property ten-fold. They hired Kelly B. Harvey to survey their land and lay out town lots. The name chosen for the development was a combination of Sol (the sun) and Anna (Howards' wife). The Solana plat was filed at Arcadia in Nov. 1889, and the first lots sold a year later. Encouraged by brisk sales, the Howards moved here permanently in 1890 and built a large two-story frame home still occupied at the corner of Howard Street and Shore Drive.

Among early purchasers of Howards' lots was C.M. Carrier of then DeSoto County. In 1919, he bought all of Block 1 which includes the present lodge building of the Punta Gorda Fraternal Order of Elks. The property was appraised at $50 and a 60-cent tax levied on it.

The following year, Carrier built a small frame house on the site which increased the value to $550. This turned out to be a profitable investment because in 1920 Carrier sold lots 4 and 5 of his block — including the waterfront — to John Morrison of New York state for $1,200.

Morrison also was a winter visitor who came here for the hunting and fishing. He either enlarged the Carrier cottage, or replaced it entirely with the sprawling Elks building in 1921. Morrison named his home Eagles Nest because a pair of these stately birds had a nest in a nearby pine tree.

Mr. and Mrs. Morrison were a wealthy couple who traveled extensively and had prominent friends who sometimes visited them here — Mrs. Thomas A. Edison, for example. They filled their home with exotic hand-carved furniture from around the world, including a fireplace mantle, matching chests — since donated to the historic Freeman House in Punta Gorda — and large "slave" fans imported from the Orient.

During the summer, when Eagles Nest was closed, local men were hired to maintain the grounds which included imported shrubbery. The last caretaker for Morrison was Ulysses S. Whiteaker, grandfather of Historian U.S. Cleveland well known to this book.

Land Boom Speculator

John Morrison also speculated in Solana and Punta Gorda property during the Florida Land Boom of the 1920s. He appears to have done well despite the Great Depression. He sold Eagles Nest in May 1937 for a sum disguised by the legal term of "one dollar and other valuable considerations." Morrison perhaps had grown lonely after the death of his wife. The deed of transfer notes him as "a single man of Charlotte County." He moved out of the area — perhaps back to New York state to be with his family.

New owners of Eagles Nest were Mr. and Mrs. James E. Kelly of Dayton, Ohio. He was a golf professional and proprietor of a sporting goods store. In 1935, Kelly developed a heart condition. The doctor advised him to spend the winter in a warmer climate.

Kelly drove his family to Florida with out any destination in mind. Accompanying him was his wife, Jeannette, and their two little children. Young James was just three. His sister Sheila was a babe in arms. After a weary day of driving, the family reached the village of Punta Gorda.

"I went into the Seminole Pharmacy to inquire about food and lodging," Kelly recounted in later years. "The owner, Wallace Mobley recommended the Princess Hotel across the street. I then asked him where I could go for good hunting and fishing.

"Mobley replied, 'Look no farther. You're in the heart of the best hunting and fishing in all Florida. I'll show you tomorrow.' The next day he and his brother Hugh, the pharmacist, put a sign in the store's door, 'Gone Fishing.'

"We spent the day hauling in fish from the bay. The day after that, Wallace's grandson, Jimmy Mobley, and Paul Rasch took me hunting. I stayed two months.

"The following winter, I took the family to join Dayton friends at the old hotel in El Jobean. Jannette liked to fish and hunt also. By this time I knew all the good hunting and fishing spots and spent most of my time guiding my friends. I figured I might as well get in the resort business myself, so I sold the store in Dayton and moved to Punta Gorda.

"Lou Calder, president of the Union Bag and Paper Co., had built the beautiful Allapatchee Lodge on Alligator Creek where he entertained important customers and his friends. I heard he wanted to lease it. We agreed on terms, and we Kellys moved to Punta Gorda. My wife and I operated the lodge for four years.

Bought The Nest

"When I heard John Morrison's Eagles Nest was for sale, Jeannette and I got enough money together for a down payment. Then we added five cabins for guests and kennels for hunting dogs. We turned the place into a busy hunting and fishing lodge."

Father Jim Kelly placed ownership of the Eagles Nest in Jeannette's name, and the whole family pitched in to make the lodge one of the most popular in the area.

Young Jim grew up at Eagles Nest and naturally took to the outdoors. As an adult, he started a camp for boys and became a rifle instructor in the Army. He remembers with enthusiasm his early years at Solana. "Many important businessmen, sports figures, and military leaders vacationed at Eagles Nest," says Kelly.

"The Calder brothers, Bob and Lou, were guests. Lou Calder enjoyed several stays there. Bob and his wife spent ten weeks there every winter. Bob Calder, Jr., of Campbell Soups, joined his family at the Nest. Frank G. Burke, Jr., of Sweetheart Soap, which later sold to Purex, spent four months at the Nest each winter. He enjoyed the good times he had hunting around Punta Gorda and fishing down at Boca Grande Pass.

"He loved the area so much he requested that upon his death his body be cremated and his ashes scattered at Boca Grande Pass. When he died, his wife and favorite fishing guide followed his wishes.

453

"Mike Holmes, a businessman from Rye, N.Y., also requested upon his death that his ashes be placed in the Peace River from the Eagles Nest dock. His wishes were carried out by his widow, his sister, and his brother-in-law. Mike vacationed at Eagles Nest for 32 winter seasons.

"Vern Den Herter, pro-end with the Miami Dolphins, came to the lodge to hunt quail. Golf's Sam Snead and Dr. Carey Middlecoff — pro-golfer and television personality covering many leading tournaments — enjoyed hunting trips from the Nest.

"Other pleased guests were Freddie Hutchinson, manager of the Cincinnati Reds baseball team; Jimmy Braggan, coach for the Reds; and Dave Bristol, one of baseball's youngest big-league managers,

Gen. Omar Bradley A Guest

"Generals Omar Bradley, Bedel Smith and Cornelius Wickersham were frequent guests. Gen. Bradley was a great man and a sincere gentleman. General Smith, in addition to his military career, was also ambassador to Russia. General Wickersham brings back many wonderful memories of days spent hunting and fishing with this truly great and modest man.

"General Wickersham was General Dwight Eisenhower's legal adviser during the occupation of Europe and a senior partner in one of New York City's largest law firms.

"Admiral Eddie McDonnel, and his brother, General McDonnell, were both good sportsmen. After a couple of highballs, all you had to do was ask them, 'How did the Army-Navy football game come out this year?' then sit back and enjoy the brothers' fireworks!

"The admiral held the Congressional Medal of Honor. Unfortunately he was killed in a plane crash enroute to an Eagles Nest vacation.

"I grew up in the resort business and was guiding parties at the ripe old age of 12. I am still guiding. I was at the Eagles Nest for 40 years.

"When people ask me about the great and important people I have had the privilege to know over those years, I reply that the greatest people I ever knew there were my mother, father, sister, and my wife Shirley. We worked together to make the Nest successful."

The Eagles Nest was purchased by the newly organized Punta Gorda Elks in April, 1980. Extensive renovations and a new dock were recently completed. A gorgeous buffet of drawers left by the Morrisons was also donated at this time to the Freeman House in Punta Gorda.

However, the eagles nest is gone. The old, bare tree harboring the eagles blew down years ago. The eagles set up housekeeping elsewhere, but 120 years of memories live on among the Elks..

Award winners at the first Charlotte County sidewalk art show at Punta Gorda. The artists then organized the Art Guild. A few charter members are identifiable: Della Larkin, in black dress front row, was elected president and served three years. Dora Price, standing above Mrs. Larkin. Burnice Hendrickson is standing to right of post. Lorraine Newton is standing far right, and next to her is Peter Koster.

Chapter 105

ART GUILD STARTED IN PARKING LOT

The Charlotte County Art Guild has come a long way since it showed paintings in parking lots and worked on the vacant fourth floor of the Courthouse.

Back in 1960, Della Larkin, Burnice Hendrickson and Dora Pierce would get together at some picturesque spot to paint and critique each other's work. The crowd that gathered to watch convinced the artists there was a community interest in art.

Della's husband, George, owned and operated the Sunland Printing and Office Supply store in the Charlotte Shopping Center at Punta Gorda. The merchants association there was searching for a promotion to attract customers.

George and Della suggested a "sidewalk art show." Merchants liked the idea. The show was held Tuesday, Feb. 14 in the shopping center parking lot. George built dozens of panels on which to display paintings and printed 1,000 ballots with which visitors could vote for paintings they liked best.

"The day before the showing, Della asked me to make some more display panels and print another 1,000 ballots," says George Larkin. "Response to advance publicity indicated a huge crowd would attend. I worked late into the night to make more easels and print more ballots.

"Show-day was overcast. We worried that the event would be rained out. However, the rain held off until late afternoon. As the storm

455

approached, artists moved their paintings into the various stores. Still, the crowds came."

Approximately 3,000 people attended the show. Understandably the show committee ran out of ballots. Those paintings most popular with spectators were almost the same as those chosen by judges in 15 categories. Merchants were pleased and sponsored a second exhibit two weeks later for "handicrafts." It, too, was a huge success.

County artists had so much fun they began talking about forming an art guild. Consequently Della Larkin invited everyone interested to meet Sept. 26, 1961, at the First Federal Savings and Loan community room to decide whether to do so. A large turnout was enthusiastic. Temporary officers were voted: Della Larkin of Punta Gorda, president; John Hady of Punta Gorda, secretary; Christine Oberst of Port Charlotte, treasurer; and Edward Meltzer of Punta Gorda, custodian.

A number of distinguished artists became charter members. Joe Vrtel designed the 50-star United States Flag. Peter Koster studied art in Europe and was well known for his large Florida scenes. Charles Brethauer also studied in Europe and is remembered for large murals he painted in the American Legion Building at Port Charlotte. Lorraine Newton had been a commercial artist for years. She illustrated children's books, designed U.S. warships, and was proficient in ceramics.

Art Classes Offered

Glada Walker spent a life-time teaching art up North before her retirement. As a result of the art show, she and her committee were invited to conduct an art appreciation course in the Charlotte High School at Punta Gorda.

"At this time, the school did not offer classes in art." recalls Mrs. Larkin. "Bringing art into the schools opened the eyes of the Board of Education, and it finally approved regular art classes.

"After the Guild was crowded out of the Court House, we were allowed to set up a studio in the high school. Exhibits were held at the Library, First National Bank, and Charlotte Shopping Center. Members displayed religious paintings in store windows all over town during the Christmas holidays," says Mrs. Larkin.

"I heard that the building owned by the Baptist Church on the corner of Taylor and Retta Esplanade was sold to Fred Babcock, so I talked with him and sold him on the idea of permitting us to use the building, which he did free of charge.

"In 1965, we presented a membership card to Mr. Babcock designating him the first Patron of Arts for his services to the Guild." Babcock was a major contributor to the County Visual Arts Center.

Guild meetings were held in the Babcock studio building until construction of the Port Charlotte Cultural Center in 1968. At that time, studio space became available there for the guild and its popular art classes. Guild Artist Lula Vrtel, donated $1,000 to the Cultural Center studio as a memorial of her late husband. The Charlotte County Art Guild assisted Arcadia in starting its own Guild. These joined the Sarasota and Fort Myers Guilds to form the Art Council of Southwest Florida.

As the adult education classes at the Port Charlotte Cultural Center grew, so did pressure on the Art Guild to find new quarters. A committee was appointed to find ways and a place to build a permanent studio and display hall.

Punta Gorda city council in 1985 granted the Guild a 30-year renewable lease on 2.5 acres on Maud Street near Fishermens Village. A community-wide fund-raising campaign followed in 1986.

Fred Babcock was named honorary chairman and Henry Lohse general chairman assisted by Pat Burlin. Don Witter was named advanced gifts chairman. Phyllis Smith headed three special gifts division, and Norma Reder served as Guild membership chairwoman.

Following a successful community fund-raising effort, the building committee consisting of 15 members sought matching grants from the state. With the assistance of Rep. Vernon Peeples and other area legislators, the Guild was awarded three grants totaling $325,000.

Why Building Oddly Placed

The Guild Hall is a beautiful building sitting at a skewed angle on its lot. The unusual placement was necessary to fit the structure along an old Atlantic Coast Line railroad right-of-way which curves down Maud Street to the Municipal Dock, now leased to Fishermen's Village. Architect Brian Rommel designed the Art Center, and Builder Wayne Goff constructed it at cost.

The fountain gracing the entrance plaza originally was the center piece of landscaping at the Hotel Punta Gorda built in 1886. It was donated by Old Punta Gorda, Inc.

Under the presidency of Mrs. Reder, the Guild grew to 850 members. On display are outstanding paintings, sculpture and craft works by local and guest artists.

Classes in all the arts and crafts are offered to the public at modest fees. A gift shop has outstanding art items for sale.

There is even a spacious parking lot where the Guild can hold art shows any time its members grow nostalgic.

459

460

461

464

465

466

467

468

469

470

471

478

479

WHEN CHARLOTTE COUNTY WAS A GARDEN OF EDEN
Early Settlers benefited from virgin earth. Rev. Benjamin F. Oswald of
Solana, harvested 176 papayas from a single plant